BRITISH POLITICS AND
THE STAMP ACT CRISIS

BRITISH POLITICS
AND THE
STAMP ACT CRISIS

The first phase of the
American Revolution,
1763–1767

by

P. D. G. THOMAS

CLARENDON PRESS · OXFORD
1975

Oxford University Press, Ely House, London W.1

GLASGOW NEW YORK TORONTO MELBOURNE WELLINGTON
CAPE TOWN IBADAN NAIROBI DAR ES SALAAM LUSAKA ADDIS ABABA
DELHI BOMBAY CALCUTTA MADRAS KARACHI LAHORE DACCA
KUALA LUMPUR SINGAPORE HONG KONG TOKYO

ISBN 0 19 822431 1

© *Oxford University Press 1975*

*Printed in Great Britain
by Billing & Sons Limited, Guildford and London*

Preface

THIS book is a study of British policies and attitudes towards the American colonies during the first four years of the crisis that escalated into the American Revolution. It has developed from teaching a specialist course on the subject which made me aware of what still seemed to be a major gap in its historiography some sixty years after the late Sir Lewis Namier had perceived it.

I owe much to the work of others in the field, and in particular a great debt to Mr. John Brooke and Professor Ian Christie, who both read the whole text in typescript and made many valuable suggestions for its improvement. Dr. John Money and Mr. John Sainty kindly made available results of their unpublished research. I am grateful to the authors of the unpublished theses listed in the bibliography for implicit or explicit permission to consult them, and to their universities for making them available; Dr. Langford's thesis has since appeared as a book. I also wish to thank the editor of the *English Historical Review* for permission to reproduce parts of an article that appeared in that periodical in 1968.

A grant from the Twenty-Seven Foundation was of great assistance in enabling me to examine and obtain copies of a great deal of my source material. The book has also owed much to the generosity of owners of manuscripts, and I am grateful to the following for permission to cite and quote from manuscripts in their possession or in public repositories: the Trustees of the Bedford Settled Estates, the Earl of Dartmouth, Earl Fitzwilliam and his Trustees, the Duke of Grafton, Lord Henley, the Earl of Malmesbury, and Mr. Humphrey FitzRoy Newdegate. The Grenville MSS. formerly in the possession of the late Sir John Murray were currently unavailable for study. Permission to use their manuscript holdings was given by the William L. Clements Library, University of Michigan, and by the Henry E. Huntingdon Library: since I was not able to visit America both readily supplied information and photographic copies. I have also received invaluable help from the staff of the following libraries and institutions in Britain: the History of Parliament Trust; the British Museum; the Public Record Office; Sheffield City Library; the Bedford Estates Office; the Record Offices for Bury St. Edmunds and West Suffolk, Hertfordshire, Kent, Northamptonshire, Staffordshire and Warwickshire; the Institute of Historical Research; and the Library of the University College of Wales.

Contents

1. GEORGE GRENVILLE COMES TO POWER   1

2. THE HUB OF EMPIRE: WHITEHALL AND WESTMINSTER   21

3. AMERICAN PROBLEMS AND POLICIES IN 1763   34

4. THE AMERICAN LEGISLATION OF 1764   51

5. THE BACKGROUND OF THE STAMP ACT   69

6. THE PASSAGE OF THE STAMP ACT   85

7. THE LATER AMERICAN POLICY OF THE GRENVILLE MINISTRY   101

8. THE CHANGE OF MINISTRY IN 1765   115

9. THE AMERICAN CRISIS   131

10. THE DECISION ON POLICY   154

11. THE REPEAL OF THE STAMP ACT: I   185

12. THE REPEAL OF THE STAMP ACT: II   214

13. THE ROCKINGHAM MINISTRY AND THE EMPIRE   253

14. THE CHATHAM MINISTRY AND AMERICA IN 1766   283

15. COLONIAL PROBLEMS AND POLICIES IN 1767   300

16. CHARLES TOWNSHEND AND AMERICAN TAXATION IN 1767   337

17. CONCLUSION: BRITISH POLITICIANS AND AMERICA IN THE 1760s   364

Select Bibliography   372

Index   383

I George Grenville comes to Power

THE appointment of George Grenville as the King's first minister in April 1763 was a great surprise to contemporaries.
Grenville himself was not thought to be a man of sufficient
stature for the post: but this consideration was temporarily
overshadowed in the public mind by the revelation of one of
the best-kept political secrets of the eighteenth century, the
decision of George III's favourite Lord Bute to resign as minister
at the very moment when he had triumphed over his opponents.
The determination of the new young King on his accession in
1760 to make his former tutor the first minister had given
offence to most politicians on constitutional as well as personal
grounds. Everyone agreed that the sovereign had the right to
select his minister: but the choice of Bute meant the substitution of royal favour for the usual criteria of rank, ability,
and experience. This point was made concisely by an anonymous writer in the *Annual Register* for 1763, probably Edmund
Burke. 'The spirit of the constitution required that the Crown
should be directed in the exercise of this public duty by public
motives and not by private liking and friendship.'[1]

Popular opinion did scant justice to George III: but his
initiative had undoubtedly intensified the instability existing
since the death of Henry Pelham in 1754. The crisis of the
Seven Years War, known in North America as the French and
Indian War, had produced 'a shot-gun marriage' between the
Duke of Newcastle, that veteran master of patronage, and the
domineering William Pitt, who had proved the architect of
victory in that war. Newcastle as First Lord of the Treasury
and Pitt as Secretary of State for the South led 'a broad-bottom
administration' comprising all politicians of note. The coalition
included the Duke of Bedford, head of the only close-knit political group independent of Newcastle, and Lord-Lieutenant of
Ireland; and Henry Fox, Pitt's chief rival in the House of
Commons, who had preferred financial profit to a say in policy
and was busy making a fortune as Paymaster-General of the

---

[1] *Annual Register*, 1763, p. 41.

A*

Forces. In 1760 George Grenville, although forty-eight years of age and an M.P. since 1741, was still only in the second rank of politicians. Hitherto overshadowed by his wealthy elder brother Lord Temple and his great brother-in-law William Pitt, Grenville had been thought of by them for Chancellor of the Exchequer in 1754 and 1757: but neither had exerted himself to advance George's career, and he remained a mere Treasurer of the Navy while they were in power. At the beginning of the new reign Grenville seemed destined to end as Speaker of the House of Commons, for he had agreed to take the Chair after the general election of 1761. The change of sovereign altered his career. George III and Bute had a high opinion of Grenville, and even when approving his choice as Speaker, the King told Newcastle that he would 'himself have rather kept him for some employment of greater consequence'. Newcastle thought George III meant the post of Chancellor of the Exchequer, and commented to Lord Hardwicke, his old friend and former colleague as Lord Chancellor, that this was 'an additional reason for his being Speaker'.[1] The Duke already suspected that Grenville might be used against him: and, as events turned out, George III was able to make use of Grenville's political ambition to achieve his aim of putting Lord Bute into power.

The ministry would soon have fallen to pieces at the end of the war without outside pressure, but George III's intervention accelerated the collapse. Bute entered the cabinet at once, and became Secretary of State for the North in March 1761. There followed the impasse of what in the eyes of informed contemporaries was a ministry with three heads, Newcastle, Pitt, and Bute. This was partly resolved in October 1761 by the resignation of Pitt when the cabinet refused to accept his demand for an immediate war on Spain. Lord Temple, also in the cabinet as Lord Privy Seal, resigned with him: and both men were estranged from Grenville when he was persuaded by the King and Lord Bute to abandon the prospect of the Speaker's Chair and become Leader of the Commons. Grenville was nevertheless reluctant to stand comparison with William Pitt, even though Henry Fox had agreed to back him in the Commons. Grenville therefore remained Treasurer of the Navy, declining through modesty or scruple the office of Secretary of State

[1] B.M. Add. MSS. 32917, fos. 203–4.

vacated by Pitt: but he did enter the cabinet, and it was at his suggestion that the Secretaryship was given to his brother-in-law Lord Egremont.

Six months later Grenville played a prominent part in the fall of Newcastle. He led the opposition in the cabinet to the renewal of the subsidy to Britain's ally Prussia, the issue over which the Duke resigned in May 1762. When Lord Bute succeeded Newcastle as First Lord of the Treasury Grenville refused to become his subordinate as Chancellor of the Exchequer, seeking to follow him as Secretary of State for the North. George III thought him unfit for responsible office. 'I dont doubt but if he could he would have some office where he could in his opinion figure more, than as an assistant in a board: he is very far out if he thinks himself capable for a post where either decision or activity are necessary.'[1] Within a year George III was to make Grenville his first minister! In May 1762, despite the King's additional objection that his brother-in-law was already the other Secretary, Grenville became Secretary of State.[2] Responsibility revealed Grenville as a man with a mind of his own. From July he and Egremont led cabinet opposition to the lenient terms of Bute's peace, frequently with success; and Egremont allowed little discretion to the Duke of Bedford, who had been sent to negotiate the treaty in Paris, a matter that was to rankle as a grievance with the Duke the next year. This behaviour, and Grenville's lack of success as Leader of the House of Commons in the previous session, led to his demotion in October. Henry Fox, promised a peerage, agreed to replace him as Leader of the House and carry the peace terms through the Commons; and Grenville was also made to exchange offices with Lord Halifax, the First Lord of the Admiralty. This move was a blow to Grenville's pocket, a drop in salary and perquisites from more than £8,000 a year to little over £2,000;[3] to his public prestige; and seemingly to his political hopes: but Grenville had reason to think that appearances were deceptive. He received private assurances from Bute of 'the high opinion and goodwill the King entertained of me', and Bute also told Grenville that he himself had 'always wished to see me at the

---

[1] *Bute Letters*, pp. 104–5.
[2] *Grenville Papers*, i. 446–50.
[3] B.M. Add. MSS. 32943, fo. 206.

head of the Treasury, that he knew my fitness and talents for that great department': but the King insisted that Bute should retain that post himself.[1]

Political precautions were necessary because a Parliamentary attack on the peace was imminent. William Pitt was certain to criticize the leniency shown towards France, and the Duke of Newcastle was slowly coming round to the idea of making an issue of the provisional terms. This was doubly difficult for the Duke: after having held cabinet office almost continuously since 1724, he found it hard to break old political habits and go into opposition; while the terms themselves were similar to those envisaged during his own ministry. These habits and scruples were overcome; but Newcastle did not yet realize how few of those he had come to think of at the Treasury as his friends and supporters would follow him when out of office, and his political lists during the autumn of 1762 show that he anticipated the support of almost half the House of Commons. The truth was a sad revelation for the Duke, and the opposition fiasco was made complete by Pitt's refusal to co-operate with Newcastle's friends. He left the House without voting after a famous speech on 9 December, and altogether only ninety-six M.P.s voted against the peace terms then and the next day. There is no need to look to the old story of bribery for an explanation of this rout of the opposition. The peace, both in principle and in detail, was popular with the independent members who formed the majority of the House: and few politicians in mid-career or dependent for their livelihood or comfort on official salaries were prepared to sacrifice themselves for an old man, when defiance of a young king and his favourite might mean expulsion into the political wilderness. Even before the general election of 1761 Lord Bute and veteran politician George Bubb Dodington had concurred in a belief that 'the Parliament would be the King's, let who will choose it',[2] and this judgement was to be borne out by the record of the House of Commons elected in that year. Henry Fox told Bute on 11 March 1763 that 'there never was one so well disposed to be governed',[3] and the House gave a majority to five successive

---

[1] *Grenville Papers*, i. 484–5.
[2] *Dodington Journal*, p. 418. This was in a conversation on 6 Feb. 1761.
[3] Fitzmaurice, *Shelburne*, i. 144.

administrations chosen by the King from among the whole spectrum of politicians.

At the end of 1762 Newcastle found that those who had followed him were some men of his own generation, loyal and now lacking ambition, notably Lord Hardwicke; rich young noblemen like the Marquess of Rockingham and the Duke of Grafton; and other young men rich at least in the time they could afford to wait for office. They included George Onslow, the younger Thomas Townshend, and the Cavendish family of the Duke of Devonshire, all eager to oppose but lacking both Parliamentary and administrative experience. This was not promising material from which to construct a successful opposition. Newcastle knew that Parliamentary leadership able to exploit any popular cause was necessary: for mass support from independent members represented the only chance of opposition success against any ministry. Neither leadership nor popular support was forthcoming for the remainder of the session of 1762-3. Pitt had virtually retired from the scene, and Newcastle looked in vain for a man to lead his own band of followers. Henry Legge was the only experienced politician in the Commons eager to oppose. Chancellor of the Exchequer under Newcastle during the war, he had made an enemy of Bute over a Hampshire by-election in 1759 and had been dismissed in 1761. Legge, however, was not anxious to take the lead, and suffered from the ill health which caused his death in 1764. Newcastle had to look elsewhere, and during his years in opposition he never gave up hope of obtaining the assistance of two men reckoned to be among the best Parliamentary debaters of the day, his brilliant but unreliable relative Charles Townshend and Hardwicke's second son Attorney-General Charles Yorke. For the moment, in early 1763, these hopes were disappointed. Yorke stayed on as Attorney-General, and Townshend in February became President of the Board of Trade.

Near the end of the session opposition morale rose, when Chancellor of the Exchequer Sir Francis Dashwood introduced a cider tax in March: for this caused a number of independent M.P.s from the cider counties of south-west England to break the habit of voting with the administration, and afforded hopes for the future embarrassment of ministers on the same subject. There were seven divisions on the tax in the House of Commons, where Pitt opposed the measure and the minority vote twice rose to over a hundred, and even two divisions in the House of Lords.[1] But the opposition flattered itself in thinking that the Parliamentary attacks on the cider tax had played any part in Bute's decision to resign as the King's minister: the tax was not proposed until 11 March, and Bute had already made up his mind to quit at least ten days before.[2]

Bute, despite his assurances to Grenville in the previous autumn, intended to recommend Henry Fox as his successor. George III regarded this prospect with dismay, telling Bute that Fox was 'of all men the one I should be most grieved at seeing in his place'.[3] Fox himself, informed by Bute on 2 March of his decision to retire, sought to persuade him to change his mind in a long memorandum of 11 March urging a reconstruction of the existing ministry. Fox envisaged the appointment of two new Secretaries of State, Bute's young protégé the Earl of Shelburne and Lord Gower, a friend of the Duke of Bedford. Gower was thought to be the only possible Secretary of State for the South who would not quarrel with President of the Board of Trade Charles Townshend, and his appointment would ensure that Bedford did not join the other Dukes in opposition. Fox anticipated little difficulty in managing the House of Commons and, wishing to retire himself, proposed that the lead there should be given to an able Scotsman James Oswald, acting as Bute's acknowledged mouthpiece. Oswald, already a junior Treasury Lord, should become Chancellor of the Exchequer in place of Dashwood, who 'is not fit for the situation he is in'. Fox also picked out another member of the Treasury Board who would be useful in the Commons. 'Lord North is young and interested, and his views of rising in the House of Commons will, I fancy, make him I wont say only tractable, but obsequious.' The plan involved the removal of both Secretaries of State, Halifax and Egremont. 'The first is vain and presumptuous, aiming at the highest degree of power . . . insincere, regardless of his word to a supreme degree, and

---

[1] Harris Diary, 11–30 Mar. 1763; *Commons Journals*, xxxix. 555, 600.

[2] For more detail on the political background to the end of the Bute ministry see Namier, *England in the Age of the American Revolution;* Hardy, M.A. Thesis, pp. 1–99; Wiggin, *Faction of Cousins*, pp. 213–85; and Brooke, *King George III*, pp. 73–103.

[3] *Bute Letters*, pp. 196–7.

regardful only of what may serve his vanity and ambition, which are without bounds.' Lord Egremont 'has been rather an useless, lumpish, sour friend than an enemy'. Nor did Fox rate Grenville highly: here is his comment on the man who was to succeed him as Leader of the House and become first minister within a month.[1]

G. Grenville is, and will be, whether in the Ministry or in the House of Commons, an hindrance, not a help, and sometimes a very great inconvenience to those he is joined with. He is a man of very weak understanding, and I wish I could impute to that alone what is wrong with him. His refusing to go on with the King's measures towards peace your Lordship will call timidity. . . . But, my Lord, a man who can be a mule with his friend and benefactor, has neither good nature, good sense, nor honesty; and, indeed, I think him deficient in all. In the House of Commons he will ever be a tiresome incumbrance, unless the chief persons there have authority enough to set him, like other incumbrances, aside and out of the way.

George III thoroughly disapproved of Fox's scheme, especially 'his aversion to Mr. Grenville': but with Bute adamant about resignation the King agreed with great reluctance that Fox should be offered the Treasury. 'Mr. Grenville has thrown away the game he had two years ago, as to Halifax, I think him the worst man could be in the place except Ch. Townshend.'[2] Fox now astonished George III both by declining the post, on grounds of ill health at his wife's insistence, and by suggesting Grenville as the least bad candidate. In a paper of 17 March submitted at Bute's request Fox suggested alternative proposals for a new ministry: Lord Halifax or another peer could become First Lord of the Treasury, with Oswald as his Chancellor of the Exchequer; or Grenville could take both offices, an arrangement Fox recommended despite many objections to it.

He has lost the esteem of the House of Commons, where on this supposition he ought to be in the highest. He is in disgrace there, from being supposed to have been tried and found insufficient, and from the ill repute his speaking there is in. I waive other objections because not allowed by those who know him better than I do, yet

---

[1] B.M. Add. MSS. 51379, fos. 148–52.   [2] *Bute Letters*, pp. 199–201.

they speak of a great timidity, a sad quality in the minister of the House of Commons. But upon the whole, and especially knowing Lord Bute's good opinion of him, I very reluctantly (I can hardly bring myself to it) give the preference to Mr. Grenville.

Fox suggested that Halifax could then remain as Secretary of State, but Shelburne should replace Egremont. 'If, as I hope, that should drive Charles Townshend from the Board of Trade, let Oswald succeed him, and between Lord Shelburne and Oswald that greatest and most necessary of all schemes, the settlement of America, may be effected.' Lord Gower could succeed Grenville at the Admiralty, and Lord Egremont become Lord President of the Council.[1]

Bute forwarded Fox's paper to the king with his own comments. George III in reply accepted Bute's warning about 'having men not too much allied in the active posts of government that my independency may be preserved'. This would imply the demotion of Egremont if his brother-in-law Grenville obtained the Treasury; but the King thought that Shelburne should not become Secretary of State as an inexperienced stripling of twenty-six, asking Bute 'whether some able personage could not be found out not too young who might be Secretary of State with Halifax: if not I recommend the cajoling Egremont, and Grenville's coming into the Treasury will so hurt Halifax that it will dissolve his union with them'.[2] Bute thought he had persuaded George III to agree to Shelburne's appointment: for, after sounding Grenville about the Treasury on 24 March, he stipulated that Shelburne should replace Egremont when making a formal offer of the post next day.[3] The King would not agree to this arrangement, and told Bute so in a letter of 24 March. 'If I take Grenville, Townshend may go to his place, and Lord Shelburne be the head of the Board of Trade; and then a little while will bring him to be the Secretary of State, without my having the whole House of Lords crying out upon me.'[4] Grenville's reply to Bute on 25 March reflected his acceptance of the fact that the administration he was to lead would be chosen for him. The conditions of secrecy made it impossible for Grenville to consult other politicians, and he

[1] Fitzmaurice, *Shelburne*, i. 146–9.   [2] *Bute Letters*, pp. 203–4.
[3] *Grenville Papers*, ii. 32–3.   [4] *Bute Letters*, pp. 204–5.

gave his opinion only 'upon those parts of the system which have been opened to me'. Even when objecting at length to Shelburne's appointment Grenville did 'not presume to suggest who is the most proper for that high office. I make no objection to any who is, in the public eye and opinion, big enough to fill it if Lord Egremont leaves it.'[1] Bute then proceeded to carry out the suggestions in the King's letter of 24 March, which met with the approval of Halifax and Egremont as the price of retaining their own posts.[2] Grenville himself did not see the King until 5 April, when George III made it quite clear that he was a poor substitute for Bute and owed his post entirely to the favourite's nomination.[3] Grenville was allowed a say only in two minor appointments: he secured one of two vacancies at the Treasury Board for his friend James Harris, and the place Harris left at the Admiralty Board went to Grenville's cousin Thomas Pitt.

The construction of the new ministry did not proceed smoothly. Henry Fox, who was expected to resign his Paymastership of the Forces on receiving his promised peerage, announced that he had no intention of doing so. He even hinted to his friends that he might reconsider the offer of the Treasury, and when Bute took no notice Fox asked for a viscountcy as well as the Pay Office, threatening otherwise to stay on in the Commons and embarrass the new ministry there. He had to be content with a barony and the retention of the Paymastership, and retired from the political stage as Lord Holland.[4] Shelburne had promptly accepted the Board of Trade, and Charles Townshend, after long hesitation, agreed to take the Admiralty on 14 April; but the next day he made a last-minute condition that his friend Peter Burrell should be appointed to the Board with him. Townshend was informed that there were now no vacancies, and, persisting in his demand, found himself without office.[5] The Admiralty was finally given to Lord Sandwich, one of the Duke of Bedford's friends. The Duke himself declined office even though he made no attempt to persuade his relatives and supporters to do so. On 2 April

---

[1] *Grenville Papers*, ii. 32–40; *Bute Letters*, pp. 205–6.
[2] Fitzmaurice, *Shelburne*, i. 175–7; *Grenville Papers*, ii, 41.
[3] *Bute Letters*, pp. 209–10.   [4] Fitzmaurice, *Shelburne*, i. 149–64.
[5] *Bute Letters*, pp. 223–4; Namier and Brooke, *Charles Townshend*, pp. 94–8.

Bute wrote to the Duke, who was still in Paris, offering him the Lord Presidency of the Council. He explained that the King had given the Treasury to Grenville as 'the only person in the House of Commons in whom he can confide so great a trust'. Bute told Bedford that he was confident the new administration would succeed: the ministers would have 'to struggle, not in my opinion with a very formidable opposition, but with titles, and estates, and names like *Pitt* and *Legge*, that impose on an ignorant populace'.[1] Bedford replied on 7 April that he would deserve to be regarded 'as a madman' if he joined the men who had treated him so badly during his embassy. The Duke was also less sanguine about the ministry's prospects, and an additional unexplained motive for his refusal was a strong distrust of the influence of Bute himself.[2]

A belief that the new ministry, deprived of Bute and of Fox in the Commons, would last only a few months was the usual reaction when news of Bute's resignation became public on 6 April.[3] It is found in private opinion as well as public comment. Contemporaries did not think that Grenville could command the Commons. Hardwicke observed to Newcastle, 'how the business of the House of Commons can be carried on without Mr. Pitt I know not'[4]: and Hardwicke's son Attorney-General Charles Yorke had warned Bute at once on 9 April that he 'doubted much how the House of Commons could be put on so narrow a plan. That though I had a respect for Mr. Grenville . . . the Duke of Newcastle's friends were more than ever alienated with him, because they thought him the instrument of what happened the last year.'[5] Scepticism about Grenville's ability to handle the political situation was reinforced by the conviction that he was 'the phantom of a prime minister', Lord Bristol's phrase to Pitt.[6] The Duke of Devonshire made this comment to Newcastle on 9 April. 'Lord Bute undoubtedly means to be the Minister behind the Curtain . . . this is an experiment to see whether he can govern this country in this mode as it was plain he could not long maintain himself at the head of the Treasury. That is the notion that we must endeavour

---

[1] *Bedford Papers*, iii. 224–5.   [2] *Bedford Papers*, iii. 227–30.
[3] For some contemporary comments see Wiggin, *Faction of Cousins*, p. 289.
[4] B.M. Add. MSS. 32948, fos. 54–7.
[5] B.M. Add. MSS. 32948, fos. 92–8.   [6] *Chatham Papers*, ii. 217–18.

to propagate and keep alive.'[1] Grafton and Rockingham, he said, were of the same opinion, and Newcastle accepted this interpretation of what was otherwise to him an inexplicable event. 'People generally think, that my Lord Bute will be minister behind the Curtain, though his Lordship absolutely denies it.'[2]

Bute's intention to retire from politics was in fact quite genuine. He had assured Halifax and Egremont when informing them of his resignation 'that he would take no other place, nor remain at all about the Court to have the imputation of being a Minister behind the Curtain. That his health was very bad; disorders in his bowels, and upon his nerves; chiefly owing to the want of exercise.'[3] Bute also gave health reasons to Charles Yorke at an interview on 9 April, adding 'that he should leave the King's affairs in much abler hands than his own. Lord Halifax, Lord Egremont, Mr. Grenville, whom he had known from 12 years of age, a very worthy and able man, and whose turn lay towards the Revenue, and to that public economy, that was so much wanted.'[4] It was publicly given out 'that the Ministry is Mr. George Grenville, My Lord Egremont and My Lord Halifax, and that everything *important* was to be determined by their *unanimous* opinion'.[5] This was 'the Triumvirate', the popular designation used even by George III himself.[6] They must have felt that they were the King's government only in form. Although Bute had no sinister motives, George III insisted on consulting him before making decisions on public business, at the rate of a letter a day: and when his favourite left on 2 May for a month's cure at Harrogate the King confessed to him the fear 'that many mistakes will be committed by me for want of experience'.[7] In his correspondence George III made clear his personal dislike of his new ministers, and Bute on his return on 1 June considered removing them. An approach was

---

[1] B.M. Add. MSS. 32948, fos. 86–7.

[2] Newcastle to Sir Joseph Yorke, British ambassador at The Hague, 13 Apr. B.M. Add. MSS. 32948, fos. 120–2.

[3] B.M. Add. MSS. 32948, fos. 54–7. For a similar explanation by Bute to a Scottish friend see *Caldwell Papers*, ii (1), 176.

[4] B.M. Add. MSS. 32948, fos. 92–8.

[5] B.M. Add. MSS. 32948, fos. 120–2.

[6] *Bute Letters*, p. 228.

[7] *Bute Letters*, pp. 216–34.

made to Lord Rockingham through Lord Chief Justice Mansfield, the most eminent lawyer of the time: he had opted out of political life but was reputed to have influence with George III. Mansfield told Rockingham that 'Lord Bute was very uneasy. He did not know what to do; that he liked neither part of the administration and would be glad to know whether the opposition, as he called them, would come in, and serve the King?'[1] Nothing came of this move, or of various attempts to persuade Hardwicke and even Newcastle to accept places.[2]

The Triumvirate had ministerial responsibility without the effective power or security of office that would come from royal support. A Bute problem existed, although not the one that the opposition had anticipated: and after the ministers had developed more confidence and solidarity they gave the King an ultimatum. On 2 and 3 August Grenville and the two Secretaries each told George III that he must choose between supporting his present ministry and forming another one. The King asked for ten days to consider the matter, and Grenville persuaded his colleagues to agree.[3] Bute made an approach through Shelburne to Bedford, who insisted on Bute's withdrawal from politics but agreed to take the Treasury if Pitt would join the new ministry. Pitt refused to serve in any administration that included Bedford or any one concerned in making the Peace of Paris.[4] This put an end to the negotiation, and on 21 August George III told Grenville that he intended to continue the existing administration: but on the evening of that day the political crisis was renewed when Lord Egremont died from an apoplectic stroke.[5]

This time a direct approach was made to Pitt himself. After Shelburne had again made the preliminary arrangements, Bute met Pitt on 25 August,[6] and the next day George III told Grenville that he intended to call in 'Mr. Pitt to the management of his affairs'.[7] The announcement was premature, for the terms Pitt presented to the King the following morning

---

[1] B.M. Add. MSS. 32949, fos. 70–5.
[2] B.M. Add. MSS. 32948, fos. 275–7; 32949, fos. 226–9; *Grenville Papers*, ii. 191; Fitzmaurice, *Shelburne*, i. 199.
[3] *Grenville Papers*, ii. 83–8.
[4] Fitzmaurice, *Shelburne*, i. 199–204.
[5] *Grenville Papers*, ii. 193.
[6] B.M. Add. MSS. 35352, fo. 416.   [7] *Grenville Papers*, ii. 195.

were unacceptable. The ministry Pitt then outlined had Lord
Temple as First Lord of the Treasury, Henry Legge as Chancellor of the Exchequer, Charles Townshend and Pitt himself
as Secretaries of State, Hardwicke as President of the Council,
Rockingham as First Lord of the Admiralty, and Newcastle
as Lord Privy Seal. The King asked for time to consider the
proposal, a euphemism for consulting Bute and bargaining with
Grenville; and Pitt was summoned two days later to learn of
its rejection. In the interval George III had obtained a promise
from Grenville that he would serve as first minister, but on
condition that the King would 'arm him with such powers as
were necessary, and suffer no secret influence whatever to prevail against the advice of those to whom he trusted the management of his affairs. The King told Mr. Grenville that Lord
Bute desired to retire absolutely from all business whatsoever.'[1]

From 29 August Grenville was minister in fact as well as in
name. His firmness with the King reflected his new self-confidence, and the strength of his position had been revealed to the
political world by the failure of the attempts to dislodge him.
Bute had created a minister he could neither control nor
remove, and in September retired from London to his Luton
home to implement the King's assurance to Grenville. As early
as 20 September Bute told Shelburne, 'I protest on the word of
a gentleman I know no more of politicks, of the King, or the
Ministers' ideas or measures than I do of the Mogul's Court'.[2]
Bute spent an idle and discontented winter, as he explained to
a Scottish friend in March 1764. 'You will probably find me in
town, not from any business I can have there, but from it
suiting better my age and spirits than a country life, which I
have had now six months of. Luton, for the future, will seldom
see me but for a day or two in a week.'[3] Bute's return to London
was caused by simple boredom, not political ambition.

The cohesion of the ministry was strengthened by the extravagance of Pitt's demands, which lost nothing in repetition. The
politicians in office, and any others associated with the peace,

---

[1] *Grenville Papers*, ii. 197–201. The quotation is from Mrs. Grenville's Diary.
[2] Fitzmaurice, *Shelburne*, i. 209.
[3] *Caldwell Papers*, ii (1), 243. Charles Jenkinson later wrote a memorandum on
Bute's political withdrawal during the Grenville ministry. B.M. Add. MSS.
38338, fos. 274–81: printed, *Jenkinson Papers*, pp. 393–400. He stated that Bute
did not discuss politics with the King or public business with Grenville.

were given to understand that a change of administration
would mean their dismissal or exclusion. The Duke of Bedford
was the man most affected by the events. He had learnt of
Pitt's proscription of him, while Egremont's death and Bute's
loss of power had removed the two great obstacles to his joining
the rest of his connection in office. After Sandwich had visited
the Duke at Woburn, Grenville offered him the Presidency
of the Council, and Bedford accepted early in September.[1]
Halifax moved to the Southern Secretaryship of State and
Sandwich became Northern Secretary, his Parliamentary influence earning Grenville's recommendation. Shelburne, embar-
rassingly involved in the negotiations, resigned as President of
the Board of Trade: now attracted to Pitt's orbit, he had broken
with Bute by the end of the year. Shelburne was succeeded by
Lord Hillsborough, an old friend of both Grenville and Halifax.

Most important of all was the change in the relationship of
George III and George Grenville. They had lost their chief
props respectively in Bute and Egremont. Grenville feared
isolation in his new cabinet, which was composed not of his
own friends but of men chosen to strengthen the King's government, as he reminded George III on 8 September. 'That these
might prove too strong for him, his only reliance was upon his
Majesty's truth and honour, and on that he trusted he might
depend. The King assured him he might; that he would never
fail him, nor forget his services.'[2] George III soon found two
occasions to fulfil this pledge. Bedford, on assuming office, at
once laid claim to a share of patronage for himself and the two
Secretaries of State. The King persuaded Grenville to avoid an
open clash on this point by a private assurance that he would
approve no appointments and make no promises until he knew
Grenville's views. In October the King's support enabled
Grenville to kill an attempt by Sandwich to revive the Triumvirate, with himself replacing Egremont, and George III
assured Grenville that 'he meant to put his Government solely
into his hands'.[3]

---

[1] *Grenville Papers*, ii. 108–12.
[2] *Grenville Papers*, ii. 205. Mrs. Grenville's Diary.
[3] *Grenville Papers*, ii. 207–12. For more detail on the creation and consolidation
of the Grenville ministry see Tomlinson, M.A. Thesis, pp. 17–47. Hardy, M.A.
Thesis, pp. 122–39, has a fuller account of the negotiations of Aug. 1763.

There were two bases of a minister's power in the eighteenth century. Grenville had secured the Court. He now had to establish his mastery of the House of Commons, a task widely regarded as beyond him when he took office in the light of his earlier failure as Leader of the House. But in 1763 circumstances had changed. Grenville himself now possessed the control of patronage that had previously lain with Bute; he had the prestige of being the King's chief minister, always a great advantage in handling the Commons; and he had acquired a self-confidence that was to be reflected in his Parliamentary performance. He was to triumph even though he was immediately tested by a major political crisis, the question of the *North Briton No. 45*. This issue of the weekly political paper, published on 23 April, attacked the King's Speech from the throne at the end of the Parliamentary session, a speech that had commended the Peace of Paris. Here is one passage that offended King and ministers.

This week has given the public the most abandoned instance of ministerial effrontery ever attempted to be imposed on mankind . . . Every friend of his country must lament that a Prince of so many great and amiable qualities . . . can be brought to give the sanction of his name to the most odious measures, and to the most unjustifiable public doctrines, from a throne ever renowned for truth, honour, and unsullied virtue.

The anonymous author of the article was widely known to be John Wilkes, an opposition M.P. for Aylesbury and a man of unsavoury personal reputation. The publication was almost universally condemned, Lord Hardwicke thinking it 'the most unguarded and audacious I have ever seen'.[1] Swift government action followed. On 25 April Secretary of State Halifax asked the law officers for an opinion. Attorney-General Charles Yorke and Solicitor-General Sir Fletcher Norton reported that in their view the paper was a seditious libel, and on 26 April Halifax issued a general warrant for the arrest of 'the authors, printers and publishers'. Proof of Wilkes's authorship came in evidence taken from the first printers apprehended. Yorke and Norton then gave their opinion that Wilkes could be arrested, thinking the libel a breach of the peace and so not covered by

[1] B.M. Add. MSS. 32948, fos. 188–91.

Parliamentary privilege.[1] The two Secretaries Halifax and Egremont proposed the issue of a new warrant naming Wilkes, but Philip Carteret Webb, Solicitor to the Treasury, and Lovell Stanhope, law clerk to the Secretaries of State, both opposed this step. There resulted the all-important decision that Wilkes should be arrested under the original general warrant.[2] The Grenville ministry's alleged attack on the constitution was no more than a technical blunder by politicians badly served by their legal advisers. Wilkes was apprehended on 30 April, and released on 6 May by Chief Justice Charles Pratt in the Court of Common Pleas on the ground of his Parliamentary immunity, a decision contrary to the opinion of most lawyers. When Parliament met later in the year the House of Commons would certainly be called upon to consider the question of whether Wilkes's arrest had been a breach of privilege.

The administration faced a major clash. Newcastle's friends made clear their intention of exploiting the *North Briton* case, despite many personal reservations about the libel and Wilkes's disreputable character. And they would have the valuable assistance of Pitt; for, although never enthusiastic about opposition for its own sake, he regarded the administration's action as an attack on both Parliamentary privilege and the liberty of the press.[3] Grenville therefore made his plans well ahead of the Parliamentary session. The three-part government strategy comprised a resolution to declare *No. 45* a seditious libel; another to declare that Parliamentary privilege did not cover this offence, thus exposing Wilkes to legal action; and finally a motion to expel him. Grenville intended to make the question a matter of Parliamentary confidence in his ministry. Defeat would mean his resignation, for, as he explained to his friend James Harris, 'this would be a test, whether Government could support itself or not'. Grenville did not realize that it would be the subsidiary, procedural, issue of the general warrant that would give rise to the main political battle. He anticipated Parliamentary difficulties on one other subject, but this was the cider tax and not the programme of American legislation currently being drafted

---

[1] *Bute Letters*, pp. 232–3.
[2] Malmesbury MSS. Memo, of 11 Jan. 1764: quoted by Tomlinson, M.A. Thesis, p. 53n.
[3] B.M. Add. MSS. 32950, fo. 73.

by his administration. Grenville intended to oppose repeal of the tax, but was willing to accept reasonable modifications to it.[1]

Contemporary government analyses of the House of Commons suggested that Grenville had little to fear. At an informal private dinner given by James Harris to other members of the Treasury Board on 4 November Thomas Hunter produced a calculation for his colleagues of 349 members for administration and 200 members as opposition or 'doubtful'.[2] At the same time Treasury Secretary Charles Jenkinson was making alterations to a Parliamentary list originally compiled for Bute in 1761.[3] Jenkinson classified 489 members then in the House, 287 as 'pro' administration, 88 as doubtful, 97 as opposition, and 17 as absent. His work on the list was apparently incomplete, for the members unclassified included known supporters: and it is possible to supplement his analysis in the light of the behaviour of members during the coming session, which revealed both changes of allegiance and mistakes in his forecast. Thirty-three of the expected government supporters sided with the opposition, and eight members Jenkinson deemed opposition supported the administration. Altogether, after further adjustments to his lists of absent and doubtful members, there emerges a broad division of 336 members inclined to support the ministry and 173 the opposition, with the remainder absent or too uncertain or too independent to be classified. This was only an indication of attitudes, not of the behaviour of members on popular issues. The contrast between paper majorities and political reality was to be shown by the subject of general warrants.

The Parliamentary session began with a stormy Commons debate on 15 November. The House gave priority to Grenville, with a message from the King about the libel, over Wilkes's

---

[1] Malmesbury MSS. Memo of 29 Oct. 1763: quoted by Tomlinson, M.A. Thesis, pp. 48–9. For further details on the *North Briton* case and political events before Parliament met see Tomlinson, M.A. Thesis, pp. 50–68; and Hardy, M.A. Thesis, pp. 105–21, 138–51.

[2] Malmesbury, MSS. Memo. of 4 Nov. 1763: quoted by Tomlinson, M.A. Thesis, p. 110.

[3] B.M. Add. MSS. 38333, fos. 74–106. Tomlinson made an annotated copy of the list: M.A. Thesis, pp. 657–706. He calculated that of the 586 M.P.s who sat in the House of Commons during the Grenville Ministry 358 were government supporters and 182 in opposition: ibid., pp. 105–10.

claim of a breach of privilege, after a vote of 300 to 111 on this procedural point had shown the administration's strength. Lord North then moved the ministerial resolution that *North Briton No. 45* was 'a false, scandalous and seditious libel . . . and most manifestly tending to alienate the affections of the people from his Majesty, to withdraw them from their obedience to the laws of the realm, and to excite them to traitorous insurrections against His Majesty's Government'. This passed after a vote of 273 to 111 over the word 'traitorous'.[1] The second part of Grenville's programme was completed on 24 November, when a resolution by North 'that privilege of Parliament does not extend to the case of writing, and publishing, seditious libels' was carried by 258 votes to 133.[2] Wilkes, exposed to legal action, fled to France during the Christmas recess; and when it was evident that he would not return, he was expelled from the House on 19 January 1764 after four divisions in which the minority vote dropped from 102 to 57.[3]

The government policy had been carried out with no danger to its Parliamentary position. The threat to the administration's majority was to come when Wilkes's personality and writings no longer distracted and disturbed political opinion: but before the opposition counter-attack came on the issue of general warrants the question of the cider tax was raised in the Commons. On 24 January a Committee of the Whole House on the subject was proposed by William Dowdeswell, M.P. for Worcestershire, an independent who took a prominent part in debates and had usually voted against government since 1761. An administration amendment restricting the power of the Committee to consideration only of alterations and not repeal was carried by 167 votes to 125. On 31 January another motion by Dowdeswell on the tax was defeated by a mere twenty votes, 172 to 152.[4] The ministry feared that this hostility of the west country M.P.s would be carried over to the Wilkes issue, and Grenville offered concessions on 7 February that satisfied most of the 'cider members'.[5] The administration alarm had been exaggerated: on 15 November 1763 diarist Harris noted that

[1] *Commons Journals*, xxix. 667–8; Harris Diary, 15 Nov. 1763.
[2] *Commons Journals*, xxix. 675; *Corr. of George III*, i. 62–3.
[3] *Commons Journals*, xxix. 722–3.
[4] *Commons Journals*, xxix. 737; Harris Diary, 24 and 31 Jan. 1764.
[5] B.M. Add. MSS. 32955, fos. 391–2; Harris Diary, 7 Feb. 1764.

the majority of the members from the cider counties had voted with the ministry, and he recorded that even on 6 February 1764 'most of the cider members were in the majority' in the first Parliamentary clash over general warrants.[1]

That day had seen a development ominous for the ministry. Sir William Meredith, an M.P. who had left administration for opposition over the Wilkes case, moved for the production of the general warrant in the House. Grenville put forward what was to be the standard official argument, that the legality of the warrant was *sub judice*, as the question was still before the law courts: but the evasive device of the previous question, proposed to avoid a direct vote on Meredith's motion, secured a government majority of only 217 to 122.[2] The opposition saw, or thought it saw, the rare opportunity of overthrowing a ministry by defeat in the House of Commons. The arrest of some fifty persons on the authority of a warrant which named no one had caused widespread concern: and this was increased when evidence produced before the House on 14 February showed plenty of precedents but no legal justification for the practice. Many independent members therefore deserted or opposed the ministry on this one issue. When a direct opposition attack came in a motion by Meredith that a general warrant was 'not warranted by law' the administration won a postponement by only ten votes, 207 against 197.[3] George III anticipated the possibility of a ministerial defeat when the debate was resumed on 17 February, for he gave this assurance to Grenville beforehand. 'The Opposition might, for what he knew, carry the question of the warrants on Friday . . . but that would make no change in him in regard to his present Administration, which he meant to support to the utmost.'[4]

Grenville had not been rattled, and it must remain uncertain whether he would have resigned if defeated on general warrants, for his pre-sessional intention to make the *North Briton* case a matter of confidence had concerned a policy already completed. Grenville did not have to face the decision, despite a comprehensive opposition attack. The oratory of William Pitt was

---

[1] Harris Diary, 15 Nov. 1763 and 6 Feb. 1764.

[2] *Commons Journals*, xxix. 792; Harris Diary, 6 Feb. 1764.

[3] *Commons Journals*, xxix. 843; Harris Diary, 14 Feb. 1764. The division tested the opinion of the House on a procedural point.

[4] *Grenville Papers*, ii. 491.

reinforced by that of Charles Townshend and Charles Yorke, who had resigned as Attorney-General before the beginning of the session. There had also been another notable recruit to the opposition in General Henry Seymour Conway, an M.P. since 1741 and a friend of Grafton: he had been abroad on military service during the previous session. This formidable battery of speakers failed to persuade the House to reject an adjournment motion proposed by the new Attorney-General Sir Fletcher Norton, administration winning the day by 232 votes to 218.[1] The crisis was over and the ministry had survived, for scores of independents who had left the administration on general warrants now returned to the government fold. Altogether 247 members had voted with the opposition on 6, 14, and 17 February, but many were rated 'friends' of the ministry.[2] On 26 February, after the excitement was all over, Treasurer of the Navy Lord Barrington described the Parliamentary battle to Grenvillite Lord Buckinghamshire. 'There were in the course of this proceeding several very long days, and near divisions, many persons extremely well disposed to Government and in employment, voting (in what they called a constitutional point) with the opposition. I think they will most or all of them come back to their friends.'[3] Grenville, whom Henry Fox in March 1763 had thought to lack the confidence of the House of Commons, had within a year won one of the most hard-fought Parliamentary battles of the century and emerged in a seemingly impregnable position. The Parliamentary opposition would have been powerless to prevent the passage of the Grenville ministry's American legislation in 1764 and 1765 even if it had shown any serious inclination to do so.

---

[1] *Commons Journals*, xxix. 846; Harris Diary, 17 Feb. 1764.

[2] Charles Jenkinson listed forty-nine such members who were in the minority on 17 Feb. B.M. Add. MSS. 38337, fo. 193. For information on the sources for the opposition voting lists see Namier and Brooke, *The House of Commons 1754–1790*, i. 525; and Namier, *Structure of Politics*, p. 151.

[3] *H.M.C. Lothian*, p. 248.

2   The Hub of Empire: Whitehall and Westminster

B Y the middle of the eighteenth century decision-making in British government had become a complex process. In the period of the Stamp Act Crisis Britain's American policy was influenced in varying degrees by the King, his ministers, lesser politicians in office, permanent officials in government departments, unofficial advisers of ministers, and outside pressure groups. Most important of all was the need to secure the approval of Parliament: if administration policies rarely failed to obtain this, it was often because they had been devised in the light of known Parliamentary opinion. The constitutional balance between Crown and Parliament was none the less real for being implicit.

Only in form was the policy that of the King. George III, having appointed his ministers, accepted whatever they decided, and usually with approval. He often expressed his views to them beforehand in correspondence and in conversations in the royal closet: but they usually ignored this pressure unless it was in accordance with their own opinions. Ministers had effective decision of policy, but their method of operation was complicated by outmoded forms of the constitution. The official duty of advising the sovereign lay with the Privy Council, but this was now being superseded in many respects by the cabinet.

The Privy Council, chaired by the Lord President unless the King himself attended, had a nominal membership of about a hundred.[1] It included all adult male members of the royal family, prominent peers and prelates, and many politicians who held or had held high office under the Crown; for while nomination to the Privy Council accompanied appointment to the chief offices of state and some lesser ones, signifying that the men had become official advisers to the sovereign,

---

[1] Lists of the Privy Council for the years 1763 to 1766 are printed in *Acts P.C.Col.*, v. 733–43. The standard work is still E. R. Turner, *The Privy Council of England 1603–1784*: but it has little on the reign of George III.

dismissal or resignation did not entail the loss of what had become a dignity: for any person to be struck off the Council list was a rare event, and George III's expulsion of the Duke of Devonshire on 3 November 1762 was only the sixth instance of such royal action since 1700.[1] Politicians therefore retained membership of the Council when they lost office and went into opposition; but it would seem that by convention they then attended only on ceremonial occasions and were not summoned for business meetings. The thirty-two members present for important American business on 13 May 1767 were all either ministers or leading supporters of the administration in both Houses of Parliament, with the exception of some bishops and one of the King's brothers.[2] The Council referred a great deal of business to Committees, colonial affairs being delegated to the 'Committee of Council for Plantation Affairs'. This was a Committee of the whole Council, and often the same members attended who would have been present at a Council meeting proper. The twenty-six members present at a Committee on 9 May 1767 included the Lord Chancellor, Lord President, First Lord of the Treasury, both Secretaries of State and other lesser office-holders. Also present were the Speaker, one Lord Chief Justice, and one opposition peer apparently summoned by mistake.[3] For routine business the attendance was minimal: only three members, the two Secretaries of State and the President of the Board of Trade, were present at a Committee meeting on 6 October 1763.[4]

The Privy Council played an important role in the machinery of empire, for the colonies came directly under the Crown. It was the Council that heard appeals from the colonial law courts, and decided on the validity of legislation passed by colonial assemblies. The Council also received and considered memorials concerning the colonies from such government departments as the Treasury, Admiralty, and Board of Trade; referred question to appropriate departments, and to the law officers of the Crown; and gave directions to the Secretaries of State and government departments for the issue of instruc-

[1] Charles Jenkinson on this occasion compiled a list of explusions since 1660. *Jenkinson Papers*, pp. 77–9.
[2] B.M. Add. MSS. 32982, fos. 68–70.
[3] B.M. Add. MSS. 32982, fos. 68, 97–8.
[4] Shortt and Doughty, *Canadian Documents*, p. 159.

tions to colonial governors, naval officers, customs officials, and so on. Orders of the Privy Council were necessary to authorize a wide range of official actions; but it was not the place where real decisions were made.

The Council was endorsing decisions already taken by the cabinet. By 1763 a small 'Effective Cabinet' of less than a dozen members had developed from the earlier and larger 'Nominal Cabinet'. The basis of any cabinet was usually the three great officers of state and four or five departmental ministers. The Lord Chancellor and Lord President of the Council were invariably members, and the Lord Privy Seal nearly always so. Departmental ministers were headed by the First Lord of the Treasury, now the post usually associated with the leadership of each ministry, and included the two Secretaries of State, for the North and the South, and the First Lord of the Admiralty. Otherwise membership was elastic and depended on personality, political expediency or accident: office-holders like the President of the Board of Trade and the Chancellor of the Exchequer were summoned only for appropriate business. The cabinet considered all major issues of policy, and any controversial matters of detail. In times of crisis the cabinet took decisions on its own initiative: but usually departmental ministers proposed items of business, and other members then gave their opinions. Cabinet decisions were the result of weight of argument or even weight of numbers, for there are apparent instances of the cabinet voting on important matters of policy.[1] These policies presented to the cabinet were the product of decisions taken within the appropriate departments, and responsibility for the American measures of the Grenville administration was shared by a number of ministers, Boards, and officials.

The minister formally responsible for the colonies in 1763 was the Secretary of State for the South. Lord Egremont, who held this post during the first months of the Grenville administration, consulted both Henry Ellis, a former governor of Georgia, and his fellow Secretary Lord Halifax; according to

---

[1] For accounts of the cabinet during the Grenville ministry see Tomlinson, M.A. Thesis, pp. 126–41; and Christie, *E.H.R.* 73 (1958), 86–92. Further information may be found in Christie, *Myth and Reality*, pp. 55–108, and Turner, *Cabinet Council*, ii.

Lord Chesterfield it was 'on account of the colonies' that Halifax chose to succeed Egremont in this post on his death in August.[1] The influence of Ellis survived this change, for in October Chief Justice William Allen of Pennsylvania, then in Britain, sent this report home to America. 'It is surprising to find how deficient they are in the knowledge of American affairs . . . Many schemes and plans have been laid before the ministry. Among the rest Ellis, late governor of Georgia, makes them believe that he knows the affairs of the continent better than anybody.'[2] More significant, however, was the influence of the permanent staff of the department, headed in 1763 by Under-Secretary Edward Weston: a distinguished government servant, he had retired through ill health in 1751, but at the request of Lord Bute he returned in 1761 to become Under-Secretary successively to Bute, Grenville, Egremont, and Halifax before his final retirement in 1764.[3] There was a separate Under-Secretary for American Affairs, Edward Sedgwick; and the department also had an Assistant Under-Secretary, Peter Morin, and ten clerks.[4]

The Secretary of State was concerned also with home affairs and foreign policy relating to Southern Europe:[5] both he and the Privy Council usually referred colonial questions at once to the Board of Trade and Plantations, a department solely concerned with the colonies.[6] The Board of Trade, consisting of a President and seven other politicians in office, was an advisory body and had no executive authority. This subordinate role was a situation that various Presidents of the Board had sought to alter. Lord Halifax, President from 1748 to 1761, temporarily won more power for the Board by an order of the Privy Council on 11 March 1752. This vested the patronage of colonial appointments in the Board, and directed that all

---

[1] *Chesterfield Letters*, vi, 371.

[2] 'Allen–Chew Correspondence', *P.M.H.B.* 90 (1966), 214.

[3] Edward Weston (1703–70). Under-Sec. of State 1729–46, 1761–4; Chief Secretary for Ireland 1746–51. On 21 Nov. 1765 Grenville, when recommending his son to Lord Clive for Indian patronage, stated that Weston had 'executed the office of Under-Secretary of State for many years with the highest reputation and ability'. Grenville Letter-Books, vol. 2.

[4] S.P. 44/138, p. 85.

[5] An account of the functions of the Secretary of State's Office drawn up by Charles Jenkinson in 1761 said nothing on the colonies. *Jenkinson Papers*, pp. 3–5.

[6] For more detail see Basye, *The Board of Trade 1748–1782*.

correspondence of the governors and other officials should be sent to the Board, except in wartime or on matters involving foreign states. These qualifications had made the order virtually a dead letter in respect of correspondence, while the Duke of Newcastle, as Secretary or First Lord of the Treasury, had usurped much of the colonial patronage before another order of the Privy Council on 15 May 1761 formally deprived the Board of patronage and restricted it to correspondence. Even this function had lapsed in practice when Halifax left the Board of Trade in March 1761. Charles Townshend vainly tried to resurrect the Board's claim to colonial correspondence during his brief spell as President early in 1763. Shelburne, soon after taking office as President in April, addressed a memorandum to Lord Egremont asking for a restoration to the position concerning correspondence envisaged for the Board of Trade in 1752. The Secretary's reply was evasive, and the Board remained in the inferior status of a consultative body.[1] Symbolic of this was the failure of its President to establish a claim to a place in the cabinet. On 28 March 1763 Lord Shelburne attempted to make his acceptance of the Presidency conditional on having equal access to the King with the Secretaries of State. Bute refused this request the next day. 'How contradictory is this to the plan taken, how impossible for me to bring about, and how sure a nest-egg of ministerial discord at our first setting-out.'[2]

Any literal interpretation of the constitution would undervalue the role of the Board of Trade in the formulation of colonial policy. The President was to be often summoned to the many cabinet meetings that considered American matters during the next few years: and recommendations and suggestions of the Board often formed the basis of ministerial decisions. For the Board possessed the advantages of time and knowledge, and also of a greater permanence of office than was customary for politicians in the middle of the eighteenth century. Among the Lords of Trade who survived many ministerial changes were Soame Jenyns, at the Board from 1755 to 1780, Edward Eliot, who sat there from 1759 to 1776, and George Rice, a member from 1761 to 1770. Such continuity gave Lords of

[1] Fitzmaurice, *Shelburne*, i. 192–5.
[2] Fitzmaurice, *Shelburne*, i. 175–6.

B

Trade the opportunity to acquire experience of colonial matters. A further reason for the Board's importance in American questions was the influence of its permanent Secretary John Pownall. Service at the Board since 1741 had given Pownall knowledge and administrative expertise that enabled him to play a key role in decisions on colonial policy.[1] Benjamin Franklin, after two years in Britain as Pennsylvania agent, thought that Pownall's influence had a harmful effect on Anglo–American relations, for he wrote home this comment on the Board of Trade in December 1766: 'America has rarely, for many years past, had a friend among them. The Standing Secretary seems to have a strong bias against us, and to infect them one after another as they come to it.'[2]

John Pownall was the subminister with most influence on American policy in the 1760s, but others in the tiny civil service also played their part. The role of Under Secretaries Weston and Sedgwick is impossible to assess in the light of surviving evidence, but their interest in American questions is constantly reflected in their personal correspondence.[3] Of the other departments concerned with the colonies, the Treasury was involved in any financial measures: advice and information were obtained from officials within the department and at least two subordinate ones. The Customs Board provided an independent and permanent voice, since its members were debarred from Parliament; and its experienced Secretary William Wood was reckoned a colonial expert. The Stamp Office was responsible for drafting the Grenville ministry's most famous measure, Secretary John Brettell and several Commissioners being personally concerned with the legislation. The influence of such permanent officials was significant if often incalculable. It arose not only from the administrative experience and expertise of men dealing with politicians temporarily in office, but also from personal contacts with ministers in an age when the civil service was part of a small political world.[4]

[1] John Pownall (1720–95). Clerk to the Board of Trade 1741–5, Solicitor 1745–53, Joint Secretary 1753–8, Secretary 1758–76. For Pownall see Wickwire, *W.M.Q.* 20 (1963), 543–54.

[2] *Franklin Papers*, xiii. 522.

[3] Some is printed in *H.M.C. Weston Underwood*.

[4] On this subject see Wickwire, *British Subministers and Colonial America*.

No central machinery for the government of the first British Empire existed, even though the Board of Trade did supply some unofficial cohesion. This position was widely accepted as being unsatisfactory by those interested in America. In 1764 Thomas Pownall, a former governor of Massachusetts and brother of the Secretary to the Board of Trade, produced a scathing account of the lack of any imperial organization in his *Administration of the Colonies*. He described how military commanders reported to the Secretary of State for the South; naval commanders to the Admiralty; colonial governors and other civil administrators to either the Secretary of State or the Board of Trade; and revenue officers to the Customs Board or the Treasury. Yet their colonial functions were not rigidly departmentalized; soldiers were governing wide areas, and naval ships were engaged in the enforcement of trade laws. Decisions relating to the colonies might be made by a department in ignorance of relevant knowledge elsewhere in Whitehall. There was no one body to collect all such information, although *ad hoc* arrangements were to be made at the height of the Stamp Act Crisis.

Government policy, once it had been decided upon, could sometimes be implemented directly by means of the royal prerogative. The Proclamation of 1763 concerned new territories ceded to the Crown, and was issued by the King in Council. Nor was the authority of Parliament required for a wide range of executive and administrative actions by the Grenville ministry involving the enforcement of trade regulations or the deployment of the army and the navy, even though they virtually constituted new policies: such orders could be issued by the Treasury, Admiralty, or Secretary of State. Most government decisions, however, and certainly any concerning changes in the revenue, required the endorsement of Parliament as legislation. By the eighteenth century the House of Commons had developed formal procedures for much of its business. Any proposals involving government expenditure, such as the army estimates, were made in the Committee of Supply. Proposals for raising money were the concern of the Committee of Ways and Means. The appropriate resolutions were then reported back to the House, and subsequently incorporated into legislation. Both Committees were Committees of the Whole House open to any member. The Commons often adopted the same procedure for important questions of policy, resolving itself into a Committee which examined papers, heard witnesses and then passed resolutions. This was to be done for consideration of the Stamp Act Crisis in 1766. All bills had to pass three readings in the House, with a Committee stage for detailed consideration after the second reading.[1] Legislation also had to undergo the same stages in the House of Lords, which comprised some 200 hereditary and ecclesiastical members, presided over by the Lord Chancellor. It was a constitutional convention that the Lords never interfered with financial legislation, and at this time it was usually a body amenable to the wishes of the King's government. America was to prove an exception. Both the Rockingham ministry in 1766 and the Chatham ministry in 1767 faced serious challenges there on colonial policy. The latent political importance of the House of Lords became a reality in the Stamp Act Crisis.

What influence could the American colonies, lacking representation in Parliament, have on decisions made in this way by the British executive and legislature? The official representative of each colony was its agent. Sometimes the same man acted for more than one colony, and sometimes colonies had more than one agent, either as a matter of policy or because the Council and Assembly of a colony wanted separate delegates. The total number rose to eighteen during the Stamp Act Crisis.[2] An agent was usually responsible to the Committee of Correspondence appointed by his colony's Assembly. This situation led to many difficulties. Agents were often handicapped by too rigid instructions or by Assembly representations too inflammatory to lay before Parliament. Sometimes there was the alternative disadvantage of a failure to receive adequate or indeed any instructions in time, and agents might then be reprimanded for acting too much on their own initiative. A further weakness of the system was the reluctance of colonial assemblies to spend enough money on

[1] For the practice and procedure of the Commons see my *House of Commons in the Eighteenth Century*.

[2] For this account of colonial agents I have used Kammen, *Rope of Sand;* Sosin, *Agents and Merchants;* and Namier and Brooke, *The House of Commons 1754–1790*.

their agencies. An agency was therefore a part-time post, with salaries varying from £500 to £50 a year. Only Robert Charles, acting for New York from 1748 to 1770, and receiving £500 a year from 1764, can be considered a career agent. Charles Garth, agent for South Carolina from 1762 to 1775, was paid only £200 and expenses, but was one of the most active agents during the Stamp Act Crisis. Some agents were colonists, either living permanently in London or sent over for a special purpose: two notable colonials who came across the Atlantic in 1764 were Benjamin Franklin from Pennsylvania and New Haven lawyer Jared Ingersoll from Connecticut. Most agents were Englishmen, usually merchants or minor politicians with some interest in the colonies. A few were lawyers, like Joseph Sherwood, who represented New Jersey and Rhode Island; Edward Montagu, agent for Virginia; and Richard Jackson, who acted for Connecticut from 1760 to 1770, Pennsylvania from 1763 to 1769, and also for Massachusetts during 1765 and 1766. He then replaced an aged woollen draper Jasper Mauduit, who had acted for Massachusetts since 1762, assisted by his brother Israel. The agents, whatever their occupation and origin, naturally shared some identification with colonial views: and if several remained discreetly inactive during the Stamp Act Crisis, only one agent, William Knox (Georgia), was actually dismissed for lack of sympathy with the colonial reaction.

The chief function of an agent was to put the views and interests of his colony to the King's government, not to Parliament. Historians have recently formalized the role of the agencies into an institution of the First British Empire, and compared the agents with the High Commissioners of the modern British Commonwealth. This is to exaggerate their dignity, and the importance of their work. Their role in practice was often that of petitioners at the doors of such departments as the Treasury and the Board of Trade. The lobbying of ministers and officials was essential for such objectives as the success of colonial petitions and the passage of desired legislation. Much of this work concerned personal or local matters within the agent's own colony, and sometimes conflicted with the interests of another one: but agents naturally worked together on wider subjects of common interest, and they had learned the habit of co-operation over the reimbursement of colonial war expenses during the recent French and Indian War. In the next few years the collective role of the agents was to become a political factor of considerable significance, as they sought to exert pressure on government and to influence British public opinion. In this activity they often obtained the assistance of merchants, manufacturers, and others interested in the economic welfare of the colonies, especially that of the Committee of North American Merchants; in 1763 this was headed by David Barclay, who was a London banker and agent for Delaware from 1760 to 1765. Such pressure helped to obtain improvements in the conditions of colonial trade by the abolition or relaxation of various restrictions. Successful participation in the decisions of government in this way, by direct pressure on the Treasury, the Board of Trade, or other appropriate department, was normally easier for agents to achieve than influence on the decisions of Parliament itself; but even this was attempted at times, and especially at the height of the Stamp Act Crisis.

At Westminster the colonial lobby was weak.[1] One reason was simply the lack of a sufficient number of voices and votes. The colonial agents should have provided the bond for the construction of an American interest in Parliament; but very few agents sat in the House of Commons, and those that did were not united in political action. James Abercromby, who represented the Virginia Council, spoke and voted for Grenville's policy on America. John Sargent, a special agent for New York, was found a seat by Grenville at West Looe in January 1765, and he remained quietly 'neutral' in the Stamp Act controversy of the next session until he realized that there was a majority for repeal.[2] Two others also had connections with Grenville, Charles Garth, who succeeded his father John as M.P. for Devizes in January 1765, and Richard Jackson, an M.P. from 1762 to 1784. Garth's father had obtained patronage for him from Grenville in 1763, and Jackson held

---

[1] For more detail see Namier, *England in the Age of the American Revolution*, pp. 229–82; and relevant biographies in Namier and Brooke, *The House of Commons 1754–1790*.

[2] *De Berdt Letters*, p. 318. 'So greatly are people imposed on in America', wrote De Berdt on hearing that the New York Assembly had voted Sargent a service of plate.

the sinecure post of secretary to Grenville himself in his office of Chancellor of the Exchequer: but neither man seems to have been inhibited in any activities on behalf of the colonies. The only other agent in the Commons was the younger John Thomlinson, agent jointly with his father for New Hampshire from 1763, and politically attached to the Duke of Newcastle. In July 1766 the two Thomlinsons were joined in this agency by their merchant partner Barlow Trecothick, an active champion of the colonists who by then was chairman of the Committee of North American Merchants.

There was in any case no possibility of any colonial lobby of significant size in the Commons. Only one American, John Huske, sat in the House during the period of the Stamp Act Crisis; and there were at most forty or fifty other members with personal knowledge of or a direct interest in North America. These were navy and army officers, merchants, and West India planters; and their acquaintance with the colonies had not always bred sympathy with American views. Perhaps a dozen army officers and most of the score of naval officers in the House had some experience of America, but the majority did not approve of the behaviour and attitudes of the colonials: from among them only Colonel Isaac Barré, provided with a seat by Lord Shelburne, was to prove a vigorous champion of colonial views. Of the merchants in the House about a dozen had direct American connections. Foremost among them was Sir William Baker, an M.P. for the City of London and respected both there and in Parliament. A man with widespread commercial interests in America, he was one of Newcastle's advisers on the colonies, and a prominent speaker in the Commons on their behalf.

Historians, following contemporary opinion, have often drawn contrasts between this weak American lobby and the supposedly formidable and hostile West Indies interest in Parliament.[1] Such an interpretation does not correspond with the real situation by 1763, and obscures rather than clarifies the nature of the quarrel between Britain and the North American colonies. The size of the West India interest in the House of Commons was always exaggerated by contem-

[1] For an essay on this subject in May 1766 see the *Gentleman's Magazine*, 36. 228–31.

poraries, and probably fewer than twenty members at this time had direct connections with the sugar islands. By the earlier eighteenth century there had developed the classic clash of economic interest within the old empire, that between the British West Indies sugar planters and the settlement colonies of North America. These colonies exchanged their surplus lumber, fish, and farm produce for cheap molasses from foreign West Indian Islands, using this sugar product to make rum for their own consumption and for a triangular slave trade to West Africa. The Molasses Act of 1733 gave the British islands a legal monopoly of their colonial market by fixing a prohibitive import duty of 6*d.* a gallon on foreign molasses: but since they were unable either to supply sufficient quantities of molasses or to purchase all the mainland products in exchange, the Molasses Act had been virtually a dead letter, evaded by smuggling and the connivance of customs officials. Thirty years later this clash of interest was less important, and the West Indies influence much weaker, unable to prevent modification of the Molasses Act by the American Duties Act of 1764 and a further act in 1766. This old quarrel was overshadowed by the new one between Britain and her American colonies, and in this the weight of the West India interest was to be thrown on to the side of the colonists. The two leading West Indian voices came from Jamaica planters, William Beckford, a follower of Pitt, and Rose Fuller, a supporter of Newcastle. Both were to speak frequently on the American side in the next few years.

Such diverse elements formed an unsatisfactory basis for an American interest in Parliament: but the weakness of the American cause in British politics was more than a question of Parliamentary numbers or organization. The strength of the West India interest had come not from a score or so of M.P.s, but from the circumstance that their own economic interests corresponded to the prevailing economic theories of mercantilism. No such favourable climate of opinion existed for the political objections of the American colonies to government policies. There was no fund of goodwill in Britain towards the colonies, and an almost universal belief in Britain's right to exercise full sovereignty over them through Parliament. British public opinion in 1763 remembered that the colonists had traded with the enemy in the French and Indian War, and believed that they had refused to fight until their costs had been underwritten by Britain. Certainly the war had shown the inadequacy of the traditional system of raising money from the colonies by 'requisitions'. The constitutional theory was that the King's government could 'require' each colony to make a contribution towards the cost of defence. Only a few colonies directly menaced by foreign invasion had complied at all satisfactorily with these requests, despite the reimbursement of a significant part of their expenses by Parliament. Elsewhere the assemblies had contributed little, or nothing at all. This experience was to be of particular significance in the coming clash over direct Parliamentary taxation. Colonial suggestions of a return to this system as an alternative method of raising money were brushed aside, as being motivated by reluctance to pay a fair share towards the cost of imperial government.

More fundamental was the strong resentment at any denial of Parliament's authority to be found at all levels of British opinion: in 1767 Benjamin Franklin wrote this reflection on the Stamp Act Crisis as seen by an American in Britain. 'Every man in England seems to consider himself as a piece of sovereign over America, seems to jostle himself into the Throne with the King, and talks of OUR *subjects in the colonies*.'[1] This general lack of sympathy with colonial attitudes was a sentiment shared by most of the independent members who held the balance of power in the Commons between government and opposition. The few politicians who to varying degrees aligned themselves with the colonial reaction were normally unable to influence British policy. The repeal of the Stamp Act in 1766 was to come about because of an unusual combination of circumstances, not through any widespread support for the colonial cause. In the general context of British political attitudes towards America it was a misleading fluke.

[1] *Franklin Papers*, xiv. 65.

B*

3 American Problems and Policies in 1763

W E ought to set about reforming our old colonies before
we settled new ones.'[1] Lord Bute's reputed comment on
America at the beginning of Grenville's ministry put the
colonial situation in proper perspective. There was widespread
concern among contemporaries about the potential difficulty
of governing the vast new territories acquired in North America,
where the entire continent east of the Mississippi river had been
added to the original settlement colonies: typical was this
comment by James Oswald to Bute. 'The settlement of America
must be the first and principal object. It will certainly be the
chief point upon which all future opposition will attempt to
throw its colours and raise its battery. It will prove, in a word,
the chief engine of faction.'[2] This forecast was to prove erroneous. The subject was not to be one that occupied much ministerial time or aroused Parliamentary debate. The immediate
problems arising from the new lands were to be solved by the
end of 1763; and although the Board of Trade continued to
study the Indian question and the difficulties arising from the
presence of a French population in Canada, the Grenville
ministry and its successors paid little attention to the 'western
lands'. American policy was to be primarily concerned with the
older colonies: their defiance of the trade laws was notorious
in Britain, and their growing political maturity had already
become a cause of concern to the politicians who troubled to
inform themselves of colonial matters.

Lord Bute's observation had been made after reading a paper
drafted by William Knox on 'the defects in the constitutions
and modes of government of the North American provinces'.[3]
This had presumably described the political developments in
the colonies during the previous 'century of salutary neglect'.
The assemblies in the colonies had taken the opportunity to

[1] H.M.C. Knox, p. 282.
[2] Quoted in Namier and Brooke, Charles Townshend, p. 96.
[3] H.M.C. Knox, p. 282.

encroach on the authority of the King's government as vested in the governors and their subordinates. By the reign of George III royal government in the old British colonies of North America had been undermined. This development was the consequence and the reflection of a growing spirit of independence in the colonies which was noted by observers and visitors in the middle of the century; and to many it seemed that the situation had already got out of hand or that little time was left to restore British control. Governor Bernard of Massachusetts told Lord Barrington in 1765 that the colonies claimed 'to be perfect states, no otherwise dependent upon Great Britain than by having the same King; which having compleat legislatures within themselves, are no ways subject to that of Great-Britain'.[1]

Some observers in Britain of the American scene thought that the pretensions of the colonial assemblies stemmed from the power of the purse, through their payment of salaries to the governors, officials, and judges, and that an empire was being lost for the sake of a pittance: at a time when Britain's yearly budget amounted to over £8,000,000, the total annual cost of civil government in the American colonies was under £50,000.[2] An obvious solution was for the British government to take over responsibility for the payment of the expenses of colonial administration: this would have to be financed by some sort of Parliamentary tax on the colonies, for the climate of British political opinion would not allow the government simply to transfer even this small burden from the colonies to Britain. This analysis was founded on an inadequate and inaccurate conception of colonial constitutional development:[3] but it occurred naturally to British politicians aware of events in America and of the role of Parliament in their own country's history. Grenville's ministry soon considered the possibility of financing colonial administration by an American revenue payable to the Treasury:[4] in the letter Secretary of State

---

[1] *Barrington–Bernard Corr.*, p. 96. The above is a summary of contemporary opinion on the colonial situation. For a modern interpretation see Bailyn, *Ideological Origins of the American Revolution.*

[2] For this calculation see below, p. 361.

[3] See, for example, Greene, *The Quest for Power.*

[4] This is suggested by Johnson, *W.M.Q.* 16 (1959), 512; and denied by Sosin, *Whitehall and the Wilderness*, p. 79n.

Egremont wrote to the Board of Trade on 5 May 1763 initiating a colonial policy he asked for suggestions about colonial contributions to the cost of 'their civil and military establishments'; but the Board replied that it was not competent to answer this inquiry.[1] Later in the year Henry McCulloh, part-author of the Stamp Act, included the payment of colonial government costs in the scheme for colonial taxation he presented to the Treasury.[2] Surviving evidence does not make it clear how long or how seriously Grenville's ministry considered the idea. Agent Mauduit of Massachusetts was afraid of some such plan as late as 11 February 1764.[3] That ministers were divided on the principle can be seen from this entry in Mrs. Grenville's diary for 6 January 1764. 'Lord Halifax dined with Mr. Grenville. After dinner they talked upon American affairs, and upon the appointment and salaries of the officers appointed for the colonies. Mr. Grenville would not consent to their having salaries from England. Lord Halifax was against this regulation, and was extremely heated and eager.'[4] Whatever this dispute may have been about, Grenville himself evidently opposed the direct payment from Britain of colonial officials, through political caution or financial economy. But though the Treasury rejected the idea, there may have been an interdepartmental dispute on the matter. That there was support for the plan in the Secretary of State's office at the time can be deduced from this comment made by Edward Sedgwick, Halifax's Under-Secretary for America, on the scheme introduced by Charles Townshend in 1767.[5]

I applaud Mr. C. T. for having provided for the expense of the whole civil administration in the colonies, and made the several officers concerned in it independent of the people. This step ought to have been taken, for the want of it has been sufficiently felt, many years ago. Without it, it was absurd ever to think of preventing smuggling or collecting any revenue whether old or new. But now we may hope to see the laws observed and many evils corrected which have hitherto been incorrigible.

[1] Fitzmaurice, *Shelburne*, i. 178, 192.
[2] See below, p. 72.
[3] Johnson, *W.M.Q.* 16 (1959), 512.
B.M. Add. MSS. 42083, fo. 57, printed *Grenville Papers*, ii. 481.
[5] *H.M.C. Weston Underwood*, p. 406.

Grenville's ministry did not make this direct attack on the power of the colonial assemblies: but the issues of political sovereignty and of the role of the assemblies in revenue matters were to be raised by the taxation of the colonies by Parliament for military purposes. For politicians in Britain no such questions arose. Public opinion, with hardly a dissenting voice, had no doubt of Parliament's right in the matter, and this certainty was to be reinforced by the citation of precedents. These precedents were less impressive in reality than they appeared on the statute book. The example most frequently cited as an instance of internal taxation was the American postal service, established in 1711. But taxation had not been the purpose, and the colonial Post Office did not begin to yield a surplus at all until 1764, a change due to the efforts of Benjamin Franklin in his role as Deputy Postmaster-General. This revenue was a mere £494 in that year: it rose to over £3,000 a year by 1774, but this was still a small amount even in the context of American taxation. Other precedents collected by the Grenville ministry included an act of 1672 imposing duties on certain goods passing from one colony to another, and an act of 1729 imposing a levy of 6*d.* per seaman per month for the support of Greenwich Hospital. Customs duties imposed on colonial trade, although intended for the regulation of commerce, were also sometimes cited as examples of taxation.[1] All the evidence implied that Parliament had not yet deliberately and directly taxed the colonies and showed that such revenue as had been raised was a by-product of measures devised for other purposes.[2]

Grenville was to be the minister who taxed America, but the decisions both for new colonial expenditure and for colonial taxation had already been taken by the Bute administration. In a sense no decision to maintain a large army in America was ever formally made; it was a matter already determined by the assumptions, implications, and necessities arising from the military situation in North America, and the only real choice concerned the exact size of the army.[3] The force proposed for

---

[1] Gipson, *British Empire*, x. 247–52.

[2] Knollenberg, *Origin of the American Revolution*, pp. 148–56, argues against both Parliament's right to tax the colonies and the precedents for it.

[3] Shy, *Towards Lexington*, pp. 45–83. Colonial suspicion of political considera-

North America and the West Indies was twenty-one battalions, or about 10,000 men. The cost of this army was at first estimated at £224,904. Since any additional tax burden would be unwelcome news for the House of Commons at the end of an expensive war, the Bute ministry decided that the cost must be borne by the colonies themselves. The earliest evidence of this decision is in a memorandum by Newcastle on 19 February 1763,[1] and in this remark in a letter written on 23 February to the Duke of Bedford in Paris by Richard Rigby, the leader of his friends in the Commons: 'I understand part of the plan of the army is, and which I very much approve of, to make North America pay its own army.'[2]

The Committee of Supply on the American and other army estimates took place on 4 March.[3] Newspapers reported 'the fullest House of Commons that has been since the commencement of the session', probably in anticipation of a major opposition attack on army costs.[4] Newcastle, Rockingham, Henry Legge, and Lord John Cavendish had been working out alternative tactics beforehand. If Pitt attended the debate they would not force a vote on the size of the army, for Pitt was known to support the estimates. If Pitt was absent, however, Legge would attack 'at least the American part', Newcastle told Hardwicke. The debate proved an anticlimax, for Rockingham saw Pitt at noon that day and learnt that he was going to attend.[5] Secretary at War Welbore Ellis explained the disposition of the soldiers in North America in his speech, and assured members that after the first year the colonies themselves would pay for the American army. There was no discussion of the specific issues of an American army or its financial support during the ensuing debate. Pitt supported the plan of the large army on two grounds, the inadequacy of the recent peace and fear of

---

tions was not entirely without foundation. See Barrow, 'A Project for Imperial Reform: Hints Respecting the Settlement for our American Provinces, 1763', *W.M.Q.* 24 (1967), 108–26. The author prints, with comments, a document dated 25 Feb. 1763 and attributed to Knox.

[1] B.M. Add. MSS. 32947, fos. 46–8.

[2] *Bedford Papers*, iii. 210.

[3] Not 25 Feb., as stated by Knollenberg, *Origin of the American Revolution*, p. 35; Shy, *Towards Lexington*, p. 80; and Namier and Brooke, *Charles Townshend*, p. 90.

[4] *London Evening Post*, 5 Mar. 1763; *St. James' Chronicle*, 5 Mar. 1763.

[5] B.M. Add. MSS. 32947, fos. 163–5, 172–3, 180.

unemployment.[1] Nor was the American army mentioned in the brief debate on the report of the army resolutions to the House on 7 March.[2]

Charles Townshend spoke on neither occasion, but it was he who the same month suggested the taxation of the colonies by the reduction of the duty on the import of foreign molasses from the prohibitive level of 6*d.* a gallon imposed by the Mollasses Act of 1733 to the rate of 2*d.* This would be low enough to allow legal importation on a commercial basis, and at the same time it would yield a significant revenue. The date of Townshend's speech is not certain, but it was probably made on 18 March in the Committee of Ways and Means: for the next day a report from the Committee to the House recommended the continuance 'with amendments' of the Molasses Act, which was due to expire the next year.[3] Townshend, at this time President of the Board of Trade, had suggested on his own initiative a policy long under consideration by the ministry: for here is George III's comment on the incident to Lord Bute.[4]

Mr. Jenkinson's account has much hurt me with regard to the part every branch of Government took of being silent on the proposal of Mr. Townshend for the American tax. Not only the Treasury, but Mr. Fox and Mr. Grenville ought to have spoken. This subject was new to none, having been thought of this whole winter. All ought to have declared that next session some tax will be laid before the House, but that it requires much information before a proper one can be stated, and thus have thrown out this insidious proposal.

The Bute ministry had evidently agreed on the principle of an American tax, but not on the method. Now Townshend had produced a simple one that the Commons had adopted.

[1] Five reports by M.P.s of this debate have been found: (a) Harris Diary, sub. 5 Mar. 1763; (b) Newdigate Diary; (c) H. Walpole, *Memoirs*, i. 195; (d) Rigby to Bedford, *Bedford Papers*, iii. 218; (e) Jenkinson to Bute, partly quoted in Namier and Brooke, *Charles Townshend*, p. 91. Ellis's statement about a colonial tax was noted only by Jenkinson.

[2] *Commons Journals*, xxix, 530–1; H. Walpole, *Memoirs*, i. 196; Harris Diary, 7 Mar. 1763.

[3] *Commons Journals*, xxix. 597. Agent Jasper Mauduit's report to Massachusetts, dated 23 Mar., stated that the suggestion had been made 'some days ago'. Namier and Brooke, *Charles Townshend*, pp. 91–2.

[4] *Bute Letters*, pp. 201–2.

Steps were promptly taken to enact Townshend's plan into legislation. After the House had approved the report from the Committee of Ways and Means on 19 March, a Select Committee was appointed to draft the appropriate bills. On 24 March a bill 'to continue and amend' the Molasses Act of 1733 was presented to the Commons. It received a first reading at once and a second reading on 26 March: but the Committee stage, fixed for 28 March, was postponed until 30 March, when the bill was killed by the procedural device of a further postponement for one month, beyond the end of the current session.[1] This decision was taken after a dispute between Grenville and Townshend, with Grenville opposing any reduction of the molasses duty and Townshend arguing for a significant one.[2] George Grenville is known to history as the man who taxed America: but his first speech on the subject was a successful intervention to stop such a tax.

Taxation was to be the most famous part of Grenville's colonial policy, but most of the attention his administration devoted to America in 1763 was not concerned with this subject. It was concentrated on two other matters, the obvious question of the new territories, and the third important aspect of the colonial problem, the breakdown of the economic regulation of the empire. The formal initiation of a post-war policy for America was marked by this official instruction by Secretary of State Egremont to the Board of Trade on 5 May 1763.[3]

North America naturally offers itself as the principal object of your Lordships' consideration upon this occasion, with regard to which I shall first obey His Majesty's commands, in proposing to your Lordships some general questions . . . The questions which relate to North America in general are
1st. What new Governments should be established there? What form should be adopted for such a Government? and where the residence of each Governor should be fixed?
2ndly. What military establishment will be sufficient? What new forts should be erected? and which, if any, may it be expedient to demolish?

[1] *Commons Journals*, xxix. 597, 606, 614, 617, 623.
[2] Harris Diary, 30 Mar. 1763, fully quoted in Namier and Brooke, *Charles Townshend*, p. 92.
[3] The letter is printed in Shortt and Doughty, *Canadian Documents*, pp. 127–30.

3rdly. In what way, least burthensome and palatable to the colonies, can they contribute towards the support of the additional expense which must attend their civil and military establishments upon the arrangement which your Lordships shall propose?

This letter was to result only in the Proclamation of 7 October 1763 establishing new colonies and fixing a westward boundary for the older ones: for the Board postponed consideration of the question about the military establishment,[1] and disclaimed knowledge of the best method of raising a colonial revenue.[2] The basis of the policy behind the Proclamation was to be found in earlier wartime decisions.[3] There had been promises to Indians of no more encroachment on their lands, and in 1761 a Privy Council prohibition of further settlement without permission from the Board of Trade. Arrangements had already been made for military occupation of the western lands, and for the regulation of Indian trade. The Proclamation of 1763 was to sanction all these measures. Its genesis may be found in the activity of the two Secretaries of State Halifax and Egremont at the end of the Bute ministry, in February and March 1763. Lord Mansfield suggested that they should draw up a plan concerning the new American territories before any formal request for advice was made to the Board of Trade, so that it could be submitted privately to the Board at the same time. This idea was adopted, and Egremont had a scheme ready by early March, the paper he enclosed with his letter of 5 May and entitled 'Hints relative to the Division and Government of the conquered and newly acquired countries in America'. The document was probably written by his confidant Henry Ellis, and foreshadowed in most respects the Proclamation of that year. It contained the important proposal to 'fix upon some line for a western boundary to our ancient provinces,

---

[1] Fitzmaurice, *Shelburne*, i. 187. On 31 July Secretary at War Ellis informed Shelburne, President of the Board, that the Commander-in-Chief would decide the matter. Sosin, *Whitehall and the Wilderness*, p. 58.

[2] Shortt and Doughty, *Canadian Documents*, p. 147.

[3] For fuller detail and documentation see Sosin, *Whitehall and the Wilderness*, pp. 39–64, and Humphreys, *E.H.R.* 49 (1934), 241–64. These accounts correct on many points the earlier one by Basye, *Board of Trade*, pp. 128–36. Shy, *Towards Lexington*, pp. 193–5, attributes the Board's attitude to deliberate obstruction by Shelburne with the aim of bringing Pitt into office. This antedates Shelburne's allegiance to Pitt.

beyond which our people should not at present be permitted
to settle'. Canada, whose predominantly French Catholic
population presented special difficulties, should be divided into
two colonies of Upper and Lower Canada, each administered by a governor and council until fit for a representative
assembly.[1]

The Board of Trade was guided by its secretary, John Pownall,
who drafted a 'Sketch of a Report'.[2] Pownall agreed with Ellis
that it would be unwise to permit settlement in the newly
acquired inland areas. Such colonies might develop economic
and political independence, and their creation would alienate
the Indians. He therefore thought the limits of the old colonies
'for the present' should be the mountain watershed before the
Mississippi valley, which 'should be considered as lands belonging to the Indians, the dominion of which to be protected for
them by forts and military establishments in proper places,
and with full liberty to all your Majesty's subjects in general
to trade with the said Indians upon some general plan and
under proper regulation and restrictions'. Quebec should
form a single colony, his only significant disagreement with the
'Hints'; and there should be two new colonies of East and West
Florida. Pownall's recommendations formed the basis of the
official report made by the Board on 8 June.[3]

The report was accepted by the cabinet on 8 July, Lord
Shelburne being present; and the cabinet approved Lord
Egremont's draft of his reply.[4] This answer, despatched on
14 July, proposed to include in Canada the 'old North-West',
the area between the Great Lakes and the Ohio.[5] The Board
of Trade considered the letter the next day, and ordered Pownall to draw up a representation on this point. The reply,
which was approved by the Board on 5 August, emphatically
rejected the suggestion. By this time news of the Pontiac Rising
had come, and the Indian trouble caused the Board to recommend the immediate issue of a Proclamation prohibiting

---

[1] C.O. 323/16, fos. 93–9. It was printed and edited by V. W. Crane, *M.V.H.R.*
8 (1921–2), 367–73. Crane's attribution to Ellis has been generally accepted.

[2] It was printed by Humphreys, *E.H.R.* 49 (1934), 258–64.

[3] The report was printed in Shortt and Doughty, *Canadian Documents*, pp. 131–47.

[4] Tomlinson, *Additional Grenville Papers*, p. 317.

[5] C.O. 323/16, fos. 138–42; printed in Shortt and Doughty, *Canadian Documents*,
pp. 147–50.

settlement in the area reserved to the Indians in order to allay their fears.[1]

This document was not discussed by the cabinet until 16 September, after the ministerial changes of the previous month. It was read out by Lord Halifax, as the new Secretary of State for the South. He had earlier been concerting ideas with Egremont, and the 'western lands' policy remained unchanged despite the death of Egremont and the resignation of Shelburne. The cabinet accepted the Board's opinion about the boundary of Canada, but only after Grenville had criticized the plan of not putting all the new territory under some form of government and objected to the line reserving the lands beyond for the Indians. Grenville was alone in this attitude, and he did not persist in his objections against the opinion of Lord Halifax and the rest of the meeting.[2] The head of the ministry was thus overruled in cabinet on an important matter of policy.

Halifax took charge of the implementation of this decision. He was the friend and patron of the new President of the Board of Trade, Lord Hillsborough; and the remarkably prompt production of the Proclamation reflected the unanimity of official opinion on the subject. Halifax wrote to the Board of Trade on 19 September, directing the preparation of a comprehensive proclamation concerning the new territories in America.[3] The Board made the necessary order when it met on 28 September, and considered a draft on the next three days, referring it to Attorney-General Charles Yorke on 1 October. Yorke made a few technical alterations and returned it on 3 October. After John Pownall had inserted some verbal amendments to emphasize the temporary nature of the restrictions on the westward expansion of the older colonies, the final document was sent to Halifax on 4 October, approved by the Privy Council next day, and formally promulgated by George III on 7 October.[4]

---

[1] *J.C.T.P.* *1759–63*, pp. 374, 380; Shortt and Doughty, *Canadian Documents*, pp. 150–3.

[2] Tomlinson, *Additional Grenville Papers*, pp. 317–18.

[3] S.P. 44/138, pp. 106–10; printed in Shortt and Doughty, *Canadian Documents*, pp. 153–5.

[4] *J.C.T.P.* *1757–63*, pp. 381, 384–5; *Acts P.C. Col.* iv. 573; Shortt and Doughty, *Canadian Documents*, pp. 156–9. The Proclamation has been printed many times.

Consideration of the economic circumstances of the thirteen old colonies had been proceeding simultaneously with the organization of the new territories. The concern of the Treasury Board was to make the economic machinery of the British Empire work in accordance with the Parliamentary legislation of the previous century. In mercantilist thought the purpose of having a colonial empire was to derive economic benefits from it. Accordingly under 'the old colonial system' that had grown up since 1660 various restraints had been imposed on colonial economic enterprise: all trade had to be carried in British or colonial ships; certain colonial products, known as 'the enumerated commodities', could be exported only to Britain; and most foreign goods imported into the colonies had to pass through Britain. Although there were benefits for the colonies in this economic system, such as a monopoly of the British market for some products, many regulations were found irksome and restrictive in America, and frequently they were ignored or evaded. For decades before the accession of George III the Board of Trade and the Customs Commissioners had been acquiring a wealth of evidence on the defects of the trade laws. These included the inefficient, collusive, or corrupt practices of many customs officers; local pressure on colony officials to turn a blind eye to abuses; difficulty in obtaining convictions of smugglers in jury trials; and the simple impossibility of patrolling the vast extent of the North American coastline. The result was that the average annual revenue from the American customs was estimated by the Customs Board in 1763 to be a trifling £1,800.[1] Although the trade laws were regulatory measures not designed to produce revenue, this figure was prima facie evidence of a collapse of the system.

The most famous breach concerned the Molasses Act of 1733: the duty of 6*d*. a gallon had produced a total revenue of £21,652 in a period of nearly thirty years.[2] It was evaded less by clandestine smuggling than by collusion with customs officers, who 'indulged' the import of foreign molasses by imposing duties of about 10 per cent of the legal rate. This

---

It may be conveniently found in Jensen, *American Colonial Documents*, pp. 640–3, and in Shortt and Doughty, *Canadian Documents*, pp. 163–8.

[1] T.1/426, fos. 269–73. For more detail see Barrow, *W.M.Q.* 22 (1965), 93–104.

[2] T.1/430, fos. 318–19.

violation of the Molasses Act was well known in Britain, and regarded as respectable trading practice in the colonies. But the evidence collected by government departments also disclosed illegal commerce with Europe. Most of the information was acquired while the French and Indian War was in progress. Its conclusion in 1763 gave an opportunity to overhaul the economic machinery of the empire. The remedies were obvious: almost every measure to be adopted by the Grenville ministry had long been suggested by men familiar with the colonies.[1]

Enforcement of the existing trade regulations was attempted before any alteration to them. An act already passed in 1763, and perhaps initiated by Grenville when First Lord of the Admiralty, proposed to strengthen the incentive of customs officers in law enforcement by entitling them to at least half of the value of goods lawfully confiscated. It also authorized naval ships to seize smugglers on the same terms. This act was implemented by an Order in Council on 1 June 1763.[2] On 9 July 1763 Secretary of State Lord Egremont wrote to all colonial governors explaining the measure and requesting their assistance in enforcing it; the Board of Trade also sent a circular letter to all governors on 11 October; and forty-four naval ships were stationed in American waters. A report from the Customs Commissioners to the Treasury on 21 July contained other proposals for the better enforcement of existing and any new trade laws, including the recommendation that all absent customs officials should be ordered to their posts on pain of dismissal.[3] This was approved by the Treasury Board next day, and Secretary to the Treasury Charles Jenkinson issued the appropriate order to the Customs Commissioners on 25 July.[4]

A later report by the Customs Board on 16 September included recommendations that would require legislation: heavier penalties for smuggling; the bonding of all ships

---

[1] Barrow, *Trade and Empire*, pp. 134–57.
[2] The order was renewed on 12 Oct. 1764. *Acts P.C. Col.* iv. 560–2. For an account of the act see Barrow, *Trade and Empire*, pp. 176–7.
[3] T.1/430, fos. 346–50.
[4] For the customs enforcement measures see Johnson, *W.M.Q.* 16 (1959), 509–10, and Gipson, *British Empire*, x. 202–3, 206–7. Gipson prints some replies of absentee customs officials. For an exception made, see *Jenkinson Papers*, pp. 188–9.

entering and leaving American ports; and payment of fines
and other penalties in British and not colonial money. On 21
September the Treasury Board instructed the Customs Commissioners to incorporate their proposals in a draft bill, and most
of them were to be included in the American Duties Act of
1764. That measure was also to contain various clauses to
compel or encourage customs officials to enforce the trade laws.
Any customs officer guilty of accepting a bribe was to be liable
to a fine of £500 and to dismissal. All colonial governors were
to take an oath to enforce the trade regulations. Another
clause was to provide that if customs officials had had 'probable
cause' for seizure of suspected smugglers there could be no
award of costs or suit for damages against them. Customs
officers in America had sometimes been fined heavy penalties
for mistaken or wrongful seizures. This had often been injury
added to insult. Many of the seizures had been wrong not on
the face of the evidence but merely in the eyes of juries of
common-law courts. The legal condemnation of obvious
offenders had long been a basic problem in the enforcement
of the trade laws. The Duties Act of 1764 was to contain a
controversial clause dealing with this vital point.[1]

The means was already to hand. Ever since 1696 the Vice-
Admiralty Courts in the colonies had enjoyed equal and concurrent jurisdiction with the common-law courts in trade and
revenue cases. In 1763 there were eleven of these courts in
North America, and others were soon added in the new territories. These courts sat without juries, but the judges, although
named by the colonial governors, were nearly all American
lawyers, and many had proved amenable to local pressures in
smuggling cases. A proposal to remedy this situation was
included in a memorial of the Treasury Board to the Privy
Council on 4 October 1763. This recommended the appointment to the colonial Vice-Admiralty Courts of 'persons qualified
for so important a trust'.[2] The Privy Council approved the
suggestion, and the Duties Act provided for such a step. The
practical implementation of the proposal was left to the Admiralty Board, which submitted a report on 14 March 1764

---

[1] Gipson, *British Empire*, x. 205–6, 227–8; Jensen, *American Colonial Documents*,
pp. 645–8.
[2] *Acts P.C. Col.* iv. 569–72.

recommending that an eminent civilian lawyer should be appointed as 'Judge of the Admiralty for all North America and the Maritime Ports thereof', and that he should receive a salary of £800 to avoid dependence on fees and perquisites. The Treasury approved the plan on 7 April, and on 13 April the Privy Council decided that the new court was not to hear appeals from the existing Vice-Admiralty Courts but to have concurrent jurisdiction.[1] It was therefore created as an alternative to the existing courts, but one that would be free from local pressures: for it was established at the remote garrison town of Halifax in Nova Scotia, and the judge chosen was a British lawyer, Dr. William Spry. He was appointed in May, and opened his court in October. The new court led to colonial protests even before a single case had been referred to Halifax, but its remoteness proved a grievance only in theory. Few customs officers took their cases there, and this solution to the problem of enforcement proved ineffective. The British government was soon obliged to think again.[2]

In the Duties Act of 1764 these measures of enforcement, although important in themselves, were to be overshadowed by numerous alterations in the laws of trade themselves. The most significant of these was the alteration of the 6d. duty on foreign molasses entering the colonies, for this involved a change of policy. The motive was revenue and not regulation of trade. The Grenville ministry had immediately seen in increased receipts from colonial customs duties a potential source of revenue. On 21 May 1763 Secretary to the Treasury Charles Jenkinson asked the Customs Board for an explanation of the low revenue from the American customs and for suggestions as to how it might be increased.[3] In their reply on 21 July the Customs Commissioners accepted the new principle of 'producing a beneficial revenue' as well as the old policy of 'suppressing a pernicious trade with the dominions and ships of foreign powers'. The report stated that the high rate of the molasses duty made smuggling inevitable and that it was impossible to prevent. Many customs officers had suggested 'the expediency of introducing the produce of foreign colonies into North

---

[1] *Acts P.C. Col.* iv, 663–4.
[2] Ubbelohde, *Vice-Admiralty Courts and the American Revolution*, pp. 3–71.
[3] T.11/27, p. 282. Jenkinson sent a reminder on 20 July: ibid., p. 303.

America in exchange for our fish and lumber at lower duties in British ships only as the molasses particularly being necessary to the distilleries in New England will continue to be run'.[1] The report of the Customs Board thus spelt out the logic of the reduction of the prohibitive duty on molasses to a rate that the trade would bear, so producing a revenue. This recommendation was amplified in a subsequent report of 16 September, which pointed out that the consequences of the recent war strengthened the case for not interrupting the trade between North America and the foreign West Indies. The enlarged British mainland colonies would need additional supplies of sugar and molasses; while the French islands, after the loss of Canada by France, were almost entirely dependent on the British colonies for provisions and lumber.[2]

The conversion of the molasses duty from a prohibition to a source of revenue had been the suggestion of Charles Townshend in the House of Commons in March. Grenville himself had then killed the plan, but his Treasury Board now approved the principle, and began to consider what would be the optimum rate of duty. The paper, neither signed nor dated, which appears to have been the basis of the Treasury decision estimated the annual consumption of French molasses in the British colonies at 80,000 hogsheads a year, one hogshead being 100 gallons. A duty of 3d. a gallon would, it was thought, reduce imports to seven-ninths of the existing trade. Even so this would produce a revenue of £77,775, a higher yield than could be expected from any other rate of duty.[3] The Treasury accepted the 3d. duty, with complete indifference to the consequences of the anticipated dislocation of trade.

By the end of 1763 rumours of a proposed change in the molasses duty were current in London. Massachusetts agent Jasper Mauduit believed in December that the Treasury had decided on a 2d. duty. When he heard of the higher rate pro-

---

[1] T.1/430, fos. 346–50; for another copy see T.1/426, fos. 269–73.

[2] T.1/430, fos. 339–43. Sosin, *Agents and Merchants*, pp. 39–40, cites another copy, T1/426, fos. 289–91.

[3] T.1/434, fo. 52. This paper is said by Johnson, *W.M.Q.* 16 (1959), 511, to be in Thomas Whately's hand. The papers of the other Secretary to the Treasury, Charles Jenkinson, contain an alternative computation, that a revenue of £75,000 would be obtained from a 2d. duty on 90,000 hogsheads. B.M. Add. MSS. 38335, fo. 243.

posed, he submitted a memorial to the Treasury Board. He
had persuaded only three other agents to sign it, Joseph
Sherwood of Rhode Island, John Thomlinson of New Hampshire, and Robert Charles of New York. The memorial asked
for a 2*d*. duty, stating that 3*d*. was a 50 per cent *ad valorem* duty;
that it would tempt smugglers and encourage the foreign
distillation of molasses; and that the adverse effect on the New
England distilleries would have ruinous consequences on the
fishing industry and the Africa trade, wrecking the delicate
balance of the whole economy. Acting without instructions
from the colonies, Mauduit and the other agents failed to protest against the principle of taxation. The Treasury Board
dismissed the memorial and approved of the 3*d*. duty on
27 February.[1]

The contemporary evidence therefore suggests that maximum
revenue was the chief factor in the decision for the 3*d*. molasses
duty. This soon proved to be a mistake, as Thomas Whately
was at once warned by his friend John Temple, Surveyor-
General of Customs for the northern district of colonies in
America.[2] Grenville later defended the duty as a political
compromise between the West Indian and North American
interests: in a Commons debate of 30 April 1766 he told M.P.s
that 'the West Indians were for lowering it from 6*d*. to 4*d*.,
the North Americans to 2*d*., that he had proposed the middle
way'.[3] Grenville, however, was then arguing against a proposal
to reduce the duty to 1*d*.; and the Parliamentary debates of
1764 on the subject reflect not mutual satisfaction but West
Indian approval and American criticism of the 3*d*. duty.[4]

This was not the only alteration of the Molasses Act to be
incorporated in the American Duties Bill of 1764, and the
relevant provisions of that measure represent an attempt to
satisfy the respective interests of the West Indies and North
America. The planters were intended to benefit from an increase
in the sugar duty from 5*s*. to 27*s*. a cwt, and from the establishment of an enforceable 3*d*. duty on molasses in place of an

[1] Gipson, *British Empire*, x. 225–6; Johnson, *W.M.Q.* 16 (1959), 511–12.
[2] *Bowdoin–Temple Papers*, p. 24.
[3] Harris Diary, 30 Apr. 1766.
[4] Below, pp. 55–8. Sosin, *Agents and Merchants*, pp. 44–5, accepts the argument of
political compromise, chiefly on the basis of a later pamphlet by Thomas Whately.

unrealistic one of 6*d*. American distillers of rum were to get a monopoly by a prohibition on the import of foreign rum.[1]

These provisions have given the final enacted measure the popular names of the Sugar Act or the Revenue Act, but neither does justice to the scope of a complex bill. Some clauses in the American Duties Bill were designed merely to make possible the more stringent enforcement of the trade laws in the ways suggested by the Customs Board. There were also many detailed alterations of the trade regulations themselves, changes that were not purely in the interests of Britain. Colonial rum distillers, for example, were indirectly favoured by new high duties on Spanish and Portuguese wines. There was an increase in the number of foreign articles on which import duties were levied: and if the aim of some alterations was to safeguard the colonial market for British products, new duties on indigo were intended to assist South Carolina.[2]

The American Duties Bill was drafted by John Tyton, Solicitor to the Customs, and Robert Yeates, one of the clerks in the Treasury. On 29 December 1763 Yeates informed Jenkinson that he would be sending 'a fair copy' of the bill to Whately that evening.[3] In order to prepare the Parliamentary ground for the measure Jenkinson on 9 January 1764 asked William Wood, secretary to the Customs Board, to produce accounts for the enumerated duties since 1710 and for the Molasses Act. Wood sent the accounts next day, but took the opportunity to express, with apologies for his presumption, the opinion that the colonial measures should be postponed a year so that fuller information could be obtained.[4] Wood was a man well informed on the colonies and anxious for their welfare; his unheeded advice can be seen in retrospect as an ominous straw in the wind for Britain's relations with the American colonists.[5]

---

[1] For background information see Sheridan, *Journal of Economic History*, 17 (1957), 62–83.

[2] Gipson, *British Empire*, x. 226–7.

[3] *Jenkinson Papers*, p. 245.

[4] *Jenkinson Papers*, pp. 253–4.

[5] Two other important subjects concerning America under consideration in 1763, the regulation of colonial currency and the preparation of stamp duties, are discussed in subsequent chapters.

4   The American Legislation of 1764

THE Parliamentary session commencing in November 1763 was dominated by the case of John Wilkes's *North Briton No. 45*, and there was at first little mention of America in the House of Commons. The general opening debate on the Address on 16 November included an attack by William Beckford on the Proclamation of the previous month. Beckford, however, was not concerned with the broad principles of that measure, merely with its restriction of land grants to soldiers who had served in North America. 'Why not to all soldiers?' he asked. Beckford was called to order by George Rice of the Board of Trade, who said that Beckford's account of the Proclamation was inaccurate. Later in the same debate Treasury Lord James Harris noted cryptically in his diary that John Huske was 'short, but spoke well upon the American revenue'.[1] Huske was an American who had come to Britain in 1748 at the age of twenty-four: Horace Walpole thought him 'a wild, absurd man, very conversant with America'.[2] Although a supporter of Grenville's administration, Huske was to oppose that minister's American taxes: but that he was not averse to the general principle of American taxation is shown by a suggestion he threw out in a debate of 31 January 1764 on the cider tax for a poll tax to be levied on Scotland, Ireland, and America.[3] The only other discussion that concerned the colonies before the ministerial legislation was introduced took place on 5 December. Charles Townshend put forward two motions, one for accounts of rum and brandy imports and exports for the previous two years, and the other for the customs receipts in the same period. His aim was to assess the value of the use of naval ships against smugglers. After the House had accepted Townshend's proposals, Lord Harry Powlett made a lengthy and complicated motion asking for an account of the naval ships 'employed in the smuggling service'. This was a clumsy

---

[1] Harris Diary, 16 Nov. 1763.
[2] H. Walpole, *Memoirs*, ii. 213.
[3] Harris Diary, 31 Jan. 1764.

attempt to embarrass the administration by focusing attention on the cost of the customs enforcement measures. Grenville replied that the expense of the crews in the cutters should not be taken into consideration, as they came under the naval estimate. The only accountable expense was the purchase and maintenance of the ships themselves, and this should be balanced against the value of the seizures and the increased revenue from the reduction of smuggling. After several members had criticized the complexity of the motion, James Harris noted with amusement from the Treasury Bench that 'his Lordship desired that others would move his motion for him. This made a laugh. He had formed a motion against ministry, which would not do, and then wished them to form one for him against themselves.' The motion was then withdrawn.[1]

There had thus been little attention to America in Parliament before the introduction of the administration measures in March 1764, and by then the opposition in the Commons had collapsed after the failure to defeat Grenville on general warrants in the previous month. William Pitt, tired and unwell, had departed to his home at Hayes,[2] and the organization of any resistance to Grenville's American policy was left to the Duke of Newcastle and his friends. It was not to be challenged directly: the proposals were popular with independent opinion in the House; Parliament's right to tax America was affirmed even by acknowledged friends of the colonies; and the man on whom Newcastle relied for a lead on the subject in the Commons was Charles Townshend, himself an enthusiastic advocate of colonial taxation. That Newcastle himself had no predetermined views on the subject at this time is shown by the letter he wrote to Townshend on 25 February on 'the disposition of North America. The Duke of Devonshire has already talked to you upon it, and you must suggest to us what it may be proper to do there.'[3]

On 7 March Grenville gave notice that he would move his Budget proposals on 9 March, and offered the House 'some general idea of his plan, particularly as to the taxing America'. William Beckford at once raised what would become the central

---

[1] *Commons Journals*, xxix. 692; Harris Diary, 5 Dec. 1763.
[2] H. Walpole, *Letters*, vi. 2–12, 21.
[3] B.M. Add. MSS. 32956, fos. 103–5.

issue of the Stamp Act Crisis, the constitutional role in this respect of 'the American legislatures'. He was answered by Charles Townshend. 'That our plan of expenses being so great, America ought to share—wished everything at that time might be debated with temper.'[1] Townshend, however, despite his strong views on America, was not to be present on Budget Day. The Duke of Newcastle, giving priority over America to the election of the second Lord Hardwicke to succeed his father as High Steward of Cambridge University, dispatched Townshend there to manage his campaign. Newcastle arranged that Sir William Baker should take the opposition lead in the Budget debate, and Townshend bequeathed Baker his notes and advice.[2]

The Committee of Ways and Means on 9 March was chaired by Thomas Whately.[3] George Grenville's first Budget debate was a personal triumph. His opening speech won praise even from Horace Walpole, who conceded that he 'did it with art and ability'; while James Harris noted with satisfaction that 'he was perfectly well heard the whole time, and gained the applause of the *whole* House'. Grenville's success was doubly ensured by the absence of the most formidable opposition debaters: William Pitt and former Chancellor of the Exchequer Henry Legge were ill, and Charles Yorke and Charles Townshend both at Cambridge.

The colonial revenue was the main new proposal being put forward, and Grenville devoted the last part of his speech to this subject. He began by reminding the House that his decision was justified by Britain's expenditure on behalf of the colonies in the recent war. 'We have expended much in America. Let us now avail ourselves of the fruits of that expense.' He then stated the twofold purpose of his proposals. 'The great object is to reconcile the regulation of commerce with an increase of revenue.' His aims included the protection of the

[1] Harris Diary, 7 Mar. 1764, quoted fully in Namier and Brooke, *Charles Townshend*, pp. 114–15.

[2] B.M. Add. MSS. 32956, fos. 248–9. For this episode see Namier and Brooke, *Charles Townshend*, pp. 115–16, and Winstanley, *The University of Cambridge in the Eighteenth Century*, pp. 88–92.

[3] The following account of the debate is based on the *Ryder Diary*, pp. 233–8; Harris Diary, 9 Mar. 1764; H. Walpole, *Memoirs*, i. 309–10; and a letter from Newcastle to C. Townshend, B.M. Add. MSS. 32956, fo. 342. All quotations are from the *Ryder Diary*, unless otherwise indicated.

West Indies trade, and the prevention of colonial trade with foreign ports. On the question of taxation Grenville stated that the total cost of maintaining an army in America was £359,000. The revenue from customs duties, including the new 3*d.* duty on molasses,[1] would be inadequate, partly because of smuggling. Some further tax would be necessary, and at this point Grenville mentioned his proposed stamp duties.[2] He then threw out the challenge that he would at once take the sense of the Committee if any member doubted his assertion of Britain's right to lay an internal tax on the colonies, a challenge that was not met. Grenville concluded by saying that he knew the path was difficult, but that he was determined to proceed in the national interest. Altogether he spoke over two and a half hours, and moved twenty-four different resolutions.

Sir William Baker followed Grenville, speaking to Charles Townshend's brief, or so Newcastle told Townshend. Certainly Townshend would have approved the two main points Baker made among many detailed comments on Grenville's proposals. He thought the molasses duty too high, and he expressed approval of Parliament's right to tax America as being a curtailment of the royal prerogative. 'Agrees perfectly to our right to tax the colonies. Thinks the power of the Crown extends no further over the colonies than it does in England.' Charles Jenkinson rose next to assure members that he could prove the right to tax the colonies by reference to various Acts of Parliament and resolutions of the House of Commons. There followed a long speech from John Huske. Speaking as a man born and bred in America, he informed the Committee that in the colonies no social stigma attached to the merchants engaged in the illicit molasses trade. 'Smugglers of molasses instead of being infamous are called patriots in North America. Nothing but a low duty can prevent it.' He urged a duty of 2*d.* rather than 3*d.* on molasses, stressing the importance of the triangular rum–slaves–molasses trade to Africa and the West Indies as well as to North America; and he also put forward a financial argument for that rate, disputing Grenville's calculation. 'A duty on molasses at 2*d.* a gallon will yield about £58,000;

---

[1] Harris recorded Grenville as calculating a revenue from this source of £90,000, Ryder one of £40,000 to £60,000.

[2] Discussion of the stamp duties is postponed to the next chapter.

at 3*d.* it will not produce £25,000.' During a rambling discourse on Grenville's proposals, however, Huske agreed that 'no doubt can exist, of the right to tax North America in England. We know we are subject to the legislature of this country.'[1] An attack by Huske on the West Indian interest provoked William Beckford into speaking next. He agreed that 'the colonies should be subservient to the mother country, which should be the monopoliser. Said Mr. Grenville's plan was good.' Before the end of the debate West Indian approval of Grenville's proposals was confirmed by Rose Fuller.

Chairman Whately reported the resolutions to the House next day.[2] Two were referred back to the Committee for reconsideration, one raising the duty on foreign sugar imported into the colonies from 5*s.* to 27*s.* a cwt, and one removing duties on foreign wines re-exported to the colonies through Britain. The others were read twice, and the House made an order for a bill to incorporate all of them except the resolution for stamp duties. The only member recorded by diarist Harris as speaking at this stage was merchant Richard Glover, who discussed the resolution for a duty on foreign linens exported to America.[3] The Committee of Ways and Means reconsidered the two resolutions on 12 March. Its report the following day confirmed the proposed increase in the sugar duty, but modified the other resolution so as to retain some of the duties on foreign wines, if imported into Britain by foreigners or in foreign ships. The House ordered both to be included in the bill.[4]

The consequent American Duties Bill was introduced and received a first reading on 14 March. Glover asked to have the resolution about foreign linens put into a separate bill, but he made no formal motion to that effect and there was other-wise no debate.[5] The timetable for the bill announced by the administration was that the second reading would be on 16 March and the Committee stage on 22 March. On that day, so Newcastle was told by his former Treasury Secretary

---

[1] Ryder's report stops at this point, but Harris continued his diary until the end of the debate.

[2] *Commons Journals*, xxix. 934–5; Harris Diary, 10 Mar. 1764.

[3] The proposal was to remove the existing drawback or rebate on exports to America of the British duty on foreign linen and calicos.

[4] *Commons Journals*, xxix, 941, 945–6.

[5] *Commons Journals*, xxix. 949; Harris Diary, 14 Mar. 1764.

James West, it was expected that the merchants concerned would petition to be heard against the duty on foreign linen. At Newcastle's request West informed Charles Townshend of the arrangements for the bill, but he thought that Townshend would not be able to attend the House of Commons because of his father's death on 12 March and the Cambridge University election, which was now fixed for 24 March.[1] Opposition leaders believed that Grenville was taking advantage of the fortuitous absence of their chief spokesmen in the Commons to hurry the bill through the House. William Pitt and Henry Legge were ill, while Charles Yorke and Charles Townshend had suffered the deaths of their respective fathers.[2] Yorke, indeed, wrote to Newcastle on 15 March,

'as to the *American Bill*, I wish to see it, and have lived so much out of the world, as not to know the plan of it. But I think it impossible, that the House can suffer it to come on, in the absence of those who have such a right to be heard upon it, as Mr. Townshend; and the rather, because the *Budget* was opened in the absence of him, and many others.[3]

Newcastle in reply regretted Yorke's absence and told him that 'Mr. Grenville declared to the House yesterday that he intended that the American bill should be committed for Thursday next, the day of our election at Cambridge, and done on purpose to prevent Mr. Townshend's being in the House'.[4] Newcastle had his dates wrong. The postponement of the University election to 24 March would make it possible for M.P.s concerned to attend the first two days of the Committee.[5]

The opposition policy was not to challenge the American Duties Bill outright, but to modify it. Newcastle, indeed, was under pressure from the West Indies interest to prevent any resistance at all to the bill. Rose Fuller wrote to the Duke before the second reading to point out the disadvantages of any delay. An interval between the expiry of the existing law

[1] B.M. Add. MSS. 32957, fo. 47.   [2] B.M. Add. MSS. 32957, fos. 230–4.
[3] B.M. Add. MSS. 32957, fos. 85–6; cited and partly quoted in Namier and Brooke, *Charles Townshend*, p. 116, where it is attributed to Townshend.
[4] B.M. Add. MSS. 32957, fos. 87–8; quoted in Namier and Brooke, *Charles Townshend*, p. 117.
[5] B.M. Add. MSS. 32957, fo. 59. For a detailed account of the University election, see Winstanley, *The University of Cambridge in the Eighteenth Century*, pp. 55–137.

at the end of the session and the enactment of the current bill might lead to North America 'being filled with French produce both of Europe and America'. Fuller's letter reflected West Indies satisfaction with the measure. 'He thinks the American Bill a very beneficial one to this kingdom and most especially to the sugar colonies. That he can see no reason for putting off the commitment of it beyond Thursday, unless it be designed to give opposition to it, which he should be concerned to find, and in which he could not join.'[1] On 16 March there was no debate on the second reading nor any attempt to postpone the Committee. Neither James Harris in his diary nor James West in a letter to Newcastle mention any discussion of the bill that day; West told the Duke only that it had been decided that the objections of merchants to the foreign linen duty would be considered on 23 March.[2]

In the Committee on 22 March brief discussions arose on various clauses of the bill.[3] Sir William Baker attacked the tax on French indigo. Anthony Bacon criticized the bill on the ground that some import duties might drive the colonies into manufacturing; he was a merchant who had lived in Maryland and among other enterprises imported tobacco from the colonies. Sir William Meredith, an opposition M.P. representing the port of Liverpool, supported the bill, and so later did William Beckford, spokesman of the West India interest. John Huske suggested reducing the duty on French wines to the rate on other foreign wines, but this was opposed by Charles Jenkinson. Rose Fuller raised the subject of sugar imports from the French West Indies, and a higher duty was suggested by administration supporter George Amyand, a man with wide banking and commercial interests. Grenville himself rose to say that this was impracticable.

The most important debate of the day began when John Huske proposed a reduction of the molasses duty from 3*d.* to 2*d.* Anthony Bacon replied that 3*d.* was too low. Richard Jackson said that it was too high, arguing that the French would manufacture the molasses into rum themselves instead of exporting it to the British colonies. Sir William Baker urged

---

[1] B.M. Add. MSS. 32957, fo. 116.
[2] Harris Diary, 16 Mar. 1764; B.M. Add. MSS. 32957, fo. 114.
[3] Harris Diary, 22 Mar. 1764.

C

adoption of the lower duty as it would prevent smuggling. Grenville then defended the Treasury decision. He reminded the Committee that this would be the most lucrative of all the duties in the bill, and that the existing duty of 6*d.* had been scandalously compounded by the customs officials in America. The French islands would trade at the 3*d.* duty. 'They want our lumber, as much as North America does their molasses.' Threepence a gallon on 4,000,000 gallons would yield £50,000 a year. Baker made a brief reply, but Beckford added to Grenville's argument about the French dependence on the trade. 'The French must take fish off you. Tis not for religion, but to support their negroes.'[1] Thomas Townshend, back from Cambridge for the debate,[2] spoke against the 3*d.* duty, 'being of the coterie'—the phrase used by diarist James Harris for the group of Newcastle's friends. The Committee then divided, and confirmed the 3*d.* duty by 147 votes to 55. Harris analysed the alignment in this way. 'The taxes of this bill being principally laid on commodities imported from the French sugar islands to North America we had the traders to the last joined with the Coterie against us, but the West Indians with us.'[3] Apart from this attempt of the Newcastle group to embarrass the ministry over the molasses duty, the discussion of the bill had been conducted on non-political lines, and for the most part by members with personal knowledge of or business interests in the colonies.

The opposition had fared badly. Charles Yorke had deliberately absented himself from the House on the bill, thinking 'the questions of expediency and regulation arising out of the Bill now depending too speculative and too nice to be much agitated'. This explanation is from a letter written by Charles Townshend to Newcastle the next day to explain why he himself had not spoken in the Committee. Townshend found further discouragement in the lack of any hope of co-operation on the bill from William Pitt and his followers.[4]

---

[1] For a Treasury opinion that the French planters would pay the duty see B.M. Add. MSS. 38304, fo. 112.

[2] B.M. Add. MSS. 32957, fo. 59.

[3] With a total lack of political realism some colonial agents still hoped even after this debate to persuade Grenville to adopt a lower rate of duty on molasses. Sosin, *Agents and Merchants*, pp. 45–6.

[4] B.M. Add. MSS. 32957, fos. 239–40.

Mr. Pitt I find is against *all* taxation . . . and there seems no possibility of coming to any sort of union or concurrence upon this matter which, unless *systematically* and *unanimously* opposed tends only, by a *partial* opposition and *thin* attendance, to lessen the appearance of individuals, spread an idea of disunion among the chiefs, and strengthen ministry. I propose therefore, as far as relates to me, to attend merely as upon a litigated question; and I took no active part yesterday upon the molasses duty, because I saw the face of the House, the absence of our friends, the opinions imprest on the former Friday too strong to be shaken, and resistance useless, if not imprudent. I divided, in courtesy to Sir William Baker.

On 23 March the Committee met for the pre-arranged consideration of the duty on foreign linen.[1] Richard Glover and merchant Peregrine Cust, as the leading opponents of this provision, called a succession of merchants and ships' masters as witnesses to prove two points: that there existed a great deal of smuggling to the American colonies from Holland and elsewhere, and that there was already some manufacturing of cloth and linen in Philadelphia and other places in America.[2] The purpose of this evidence was simply to provide a foundation for the argument that the higher price of legal cloth imports would accelerate these undesirable developments.[3] When the witnesses had been heard Grenville was called upon to speak first by Chairman Whately. He met some objections by a proposal to substitute *ad valorem* duties for the system of taxing linen by quantity, not quality. This motion was opposed by Cust, Baker, and Huske, but members began to leave and it was approved without a vote being forced.

The linen duty was not a subject of popular concern or political moment; when the House rose George Onslow told Newcastle that 'nothing happened worth his Grace's knowledge'. Of more interest to the Duke than the day's debate was Onslow's report that Charles Townshend intended to speak in the House when the bill was reported from the Committee on 26 March. 'C. Townshend will on the report of this bill on Monday treat

[1] Harris Diary, 23 Mar. 1764.

[2] For the names of twenty-five witnesses ordered to attend see *Commons Journals*, xxix, 968, 979. Harris in his diary mentions only four as giving evidence.

[3] That this was a valid objection with regard to colonial production of linen is shown by the comment on the clause made by Benjamin Franklin to Richard Jackson. *Franklin Papers*, xi. 235.

it and the author of it as they deserve, for having after all the boast of the whole session given up every point so as to reduce the revenue almost to nothing.'[1] Townshend must have had in mind Grenville's postponement of the stamp duties, and perhaps also his insistence on the 3*d.* molasses duty, a rate Townshend believed to be unremunerative. In 1764 Newcastle and his friends were willing to countenance an attack on Grenville for not levying enough American taxation. The Duke, far from discouraging Townshend, spread the news of his intention with delight, for he was concerned about the financial reputation Grenville was acquiring.[2] Townshend, however, failed to perform. Instead he was indignant with Newcastle for having betrayed his confidence, telling the Duke of Devonshire afterwards that the proposed speech had depended on the attendance of Charles Yorke in support, a condition that had not been fulfilled. Newcastle wrote him an abject apology.[3]

The report stage of the bill on 26 March therefore proved an anticlimax. Harris briefly noted 'a thin House, and no opposition, but from Huske, who was *seen*, not *heard* to talk for near an hour'.[4] A last attempt to spur Townshend into action was made by the Marquess of Rockingham the next day. He saw Charles Yorke for a private conversation at the House of Commons, and sent this account to Newcastle. 'The result was that Charles Yorke will see Mr. Charles Townshend and try to show him the difficulties which may hinder his being able to attend in the House of Commons on this point of revenue—and also by that to prevent its having any material influence upon Charles Townshend by any surmizes it might occasion him to have.'[5] But neither Townshend nor any other opposition member rose to speak on the third reading and passage of the American Duties Bill on 30 March. Rose Fuller seconded the motion for passing the bill and 'much commended it', according to diarist Harris.[6] Grenville himself took the bill up to the House of Lords on 2 April. The concurrence of the Lords was

---

[1] B.M. Add. MSS. 32957, fos. 235–6.
[2] Ibid., fos. 230–4.
[3] Ibid., fos. 296–7.
[4] Harris Diary, 26 Mar. 1764.
[5] B.M. Add. MSS. 32957, fos. 278–9.
[6] Harris Diary, 30 Mar. 1764; *Commons Journals*, xxix. 1015.

reported to the Commons on 4 April, and the bill received the royal assent the next day.[1]

There is no foundation for the claim that Parliament had proceeded to pass the bill in face of colonial warnings. No American petitions against it were presented to the House of Commons;[2] and the colonial agents in London, after the failure of the memorial of 27 February, decided as a matter of policy not to resist the measure. Mauduit explained in a letter of 23 March to Massachusetts that by such opposition 'we should lose the only friends who could serve us, and throw ourselves into a Minority, who could do us no good'.[3]

The Parliamentary debates on the American Duties Bill had revealed a unanimity of opinion that the American colonies ought to contribute towards the cost of the army stationed in their continent, and the right of Parliament to raise such taxation had been generally assumed. Although Beckford had tentatively raised the claim of the colonial assemblies on 7 March, nothing more had been heard of this point. Two days later Baker had implied that the only alternative to Parliamentary taxation was action by the Crown, and Grenville's challenge for a vote on the question of Parliament's right had not been taken up. American John Huske, indeed, had assured M.P.s that the colonies themselves did not doubt it, and even Beckford had changed his tune. Newcastle's attempt to organize opposition to the bill arose from concern about Grenville's growing prestige rather than about the measure itself: and he had been prepared to countenance a demand by Charles Townshend for a larger American revenue. To at least some pro-American observers in 1764 Grenville appeared as more moderate than his critics on this key question: here is the comment of Israel Mauduit to Massachusetts on 7 April. 'The only difference of opinion . . . was that Mr. Grenville said he did not expect that America should bear more than a good part of this expense [of the army]; whereas other leading members not of the Ministry said it ought to bear the whole.'[4]

[1] Harris Diary, 2 Apr. 1764; *Commons Journals*, xxix. 1027, 1029.

[2] Cf. Morgan, *Stamp Act Crisis*, p. 49. Knollenberg, *Origin of the American Revolution*, p. 139, states that the Massachusetts petition, apparently the first to come, did not arrive until 17 March.

[3] Gipson, *British Empire*, x. 225.

[4] Gipson, *British Empire*, x. 231.

The end of the session saw legislation on another colonial problem, the status of colonial paper money as legal tender: colonial legislatures issued paper bills of credit for a specified number of years, and they served as local currency.[1] The Currency Act of 1764 applied only to the nine colonies south of New England, for a similar act had been in force there since 1751. The currency of a mere two colonies, Virginia and North Carolina, was suspect: but a general regulation applying to all the colonies from New York southwards was thought by the Board of Trade to be preferable to a discriminatory measure against a few colonies. It was this attempt to avoid any apparent unfairness that provoked eventual widespread discontent. The problem centred on the use of depreciated Virginia currency for the payment of colonial debts to British creditors, for there was little direct trade between Britain and North Carolina. By 1764 the nominal value of Virginian notes in circulation was over £230,000, and the real exchange rate was about £160 for £100 sterling. The problem had a long and complicated history, but as seen through British eyes was relatively simple. It arose not only from the natural indebtedness of an underdeveloped economy needing capital loans but also from the extravagance of the local gentry: Lieutenant-Governor Fauquieur told the British government in November 1762 that 'the most thinking gentlemen of the colony' knew this, but the truth was so disagreeable 'to the generality that they obstinately shut their eyes to it'; the Virginians, he observed, were 'not prudent enough to quit one article of luxury, till smart obliges them'.[2] Virginia was living beyond its means, and the planters were expecting the British merchants to subsidize their standard of living by accepting repayment of debts in depreciated currency that had been declared legal tender by the Virginia Assembly, many of whose members were themselves debtor planters.

The Board of Trade took action at the end of the war; and again the first initiative came during the Bute ministry. On

---

[1] For fuller information on colonial currency problems and British attitudes to them see Evans, *W.M.Q.* 19 (1962), 511–33; Sosin, *P.M.H.B.* 18 (1964), 174–98; Ernst, *W.M.Q.* 22 (1965), 33–74; Gipson, *British Empire*, x. 158–79; and Sosin, *Agents and Merchants*, pp. 22–31.

[2] C.O.5/1330/fos. 339–40.

1 February 1763 the Board heard the views on the subject of British merchants and of the two Virginian agents Edward Montagu and James Abercromby, acting respectively for the Assembly and the Council. Resolutions by the Board the next day adopted the view that the recalcitrant attitude of the Virginia Assembly involved both injustice to British merchants and disrespect to the Crown. The agents were informed that Parliament would act if the Assembly did not mend its ways, and that this would mean the abolition of all the existing legal-tender currency in Virginia.[1]

Virginia did nothing, and towards the end of 1763 the Board of Trade, now under Lord Hillsborough, began to consider the question once more. After hearing evidence from London merchants and from Montagu, the Board on 8 December approved a proposal of the merchants that British debts should be paid in sterling.[2] On 19 January 1764 merchants and colonial agents appeared before the Board to present opinions and information about any extension of the 1751 act to the other colonies. Subsequent petitions from the ports of Glasgow, Bristol, Liverpool, and London, however, showed a divergence of interests between the Scottish and English merchants. The debts owed to Scottish merchants were mainly in colonial currency, because of their practice of using local representatives in America: they therefore wanted to preserve this currency and to enhance its value. Debts due to English merchants were owed in sterling, and their aim was the elimination of legal-tender colonial money as far as possible. On 2 February the Board heard expert witnesses in the persons of former governors of Nova Scotia, Massachusetts, New York, and South Carolina, the governor of New York, a former Lieutenant-Governor of Virginia, and the Proprietor, Chief Justice, and agent of Pennsylvania. There was general agreement on the need for an act to stop both the issue of new legal-tender money and the prolongation of that already in existence: but agent Richard Jackson of Pennsylvania, backed by the Proprietor of the colony, asked for a session's postponement.[3] The

---

[1] *J.C.T.P. 1759–63*, pp. 330–3.
[2] *J.C.T.P. 1759–63*, pp. 393–5, 412, 414, 418–19.
[3] For Jackson's account of the meeting to Benjamin Franklin, see *Franklin Papers*, xi. 175–7.

same request was made the next day by the agents for New York, New Jersey, Virginia, North and South Carolina, and Georgia, on the ground that they needed instructions from their constituents. The Board of Trade pointed out the inconvenience of further delay, and asked the agents whether they would oppose a bill on the subject. They made their reply on 7 February through Robert Charles, agent for New York. 'That it was their unanimous opinion, that a certain quantity of paper currency ought to be allowed of in each colony, to be a legal tender in all contracts and dealings within the colonies, and that time should be allowed for each colony to consider and report what that sum should be.' The Board refused to postpone the matter, and on 9 February Lord Hillsborough sent to the Privy Council a report on prospective legislation that was primarily concerned with the question of colonial paper money. A historical account of the problem was followed by the conclusion that the whole practice of legal-tender paper money was 'in its nature founded in fraud and injustice'. The recommendations formalized the decisions of 2 February: that there should be a ban on all future legal-tender paper money, and that the duration of existing issues should not be extended. Realization that they were asking the impossible came too late to the agents: not until 13 February did two of them, Charles Garth of South Carolina and William Knox of Georgia, put to the Board proposals that would meet the views of both English and Scottish merchants. They suggested that colonial money should not be legal tender for debts owed to persons in Britain, and that no new issues of legal-tender money should be made without royal consent.[1]

By then the matter was already before the Privy Council, which on 10 February had referred the Board of Trade representation to its Committee for Plantation Affairs. The Committee made a report in favour of the Board's suggestions on 7 March, and on 9 March the Council endorsed this approval and ordered the proposals to be laid before Parliament.[2] By this time it was late in the session, and Charles Garth thought that nothing would have been done that year but for the initiative of Anthony Bacon as a private member. Bacon was con-

[1] *J.C.T.P. 1764–7*, pp. 3–21.
[2] *Acts P.C. Col.* iv, 623–31, 641–6.

cerned in trade to North Carolina, and he raised the question of colonial currency in the House on 4 April.[1]

Bacon moved for leave for a bill to prohibit the use of colonial paper money as legal tender.[2] He was seconded by George Rice, one of the Lords of Trade. The presence that day in the gallery of the House of Charles Garth and other agents shows that Bacon's intention must have been known in advance. The motion was opposed by two members who had supported the American Duties Bill, Peregrine Cust and Liverpool M.P. Sir William Meredith. Charles Townshend, too, urged that the colonies should be permitted 'some currency that should be legal tender under proper regulations'. Sir William Baker and Bristol M.P. Robert Nugent were among other members who spoke in a debate summarized with perplexity by James Harris. 'There seemed to be difficulties on all sides. The want of cash made the expedient of paper necessary. The abuse of it, made it a grievance.' Bacon's proposal for an immediate prohibition of legal tender money was a more sweeping step than the Board of Trade had suggested to the Privy Council: and Charles Garth later reported to South Carolina that after the debate had continued for some time the members who were Lords of Trade proposed to 'Sir William Meredith and our friends' that the bill should be confined to a prohibition of new legal-tender currency, 'but not affect or set a period to any at present subsisting: Sir William Meredith came to me in the gallery to acquaint me with the proposition made and as the sense of the House was strong in favour of restraining the provinces of this power, we thought it better to close with the petition'. The compromise of 4 April can be interpreted as a concession to the colonies only in relation to the Parliamentary pressure for a more extreme measure, and it is misleading to portray the incident as 'a remarkable example of colonial quasi-representation in Great Britain'.[3] The agents had now

---

[1] Two reports of the debate survive: Harris Diary, 4 Apr. 1764, and a letter by Charles Garth quoted and summarized by Namier, *E.H.R.* 54 (1939), 640. Garth stated that Bacon had first raised the matter in the Commons on 29 March. The *Journals* record no appropriate business for that day, but he may then have given notice of his motion on 4 April.

[2] There is no direct evidence on Bacon's motion, but only such a proposal would make sense of the ensuing debate. The entry in *Commons Journals*, xxix. 1027, is merely the general resolution for a bill on the subject.

[3] Namier, *E.H.R.* 54 (1939), 641.

C*

agreed to a bill that was to incorporate the hitherto unacceptable proposals made by the Board of Trade on 9 February: it both forbade the issue of new legal-tender paper money and prohibited the extension of any such existing money beyond the dates already fixed for its cancellation.

There was no division on the Currency Bill during its passage, and no record survives of any subsequent debate. The Select Committee appointed to draw up the bill comprised five members who had spoken in the debate of 4 April, Bacon, Charles Townshend, Baker, Meredith, and George Rice, and also Soame Jenyns of the Board of Trade. Rice presented the bill to the House next day, and it passed rapidly through all legislative stages in time to receive the royal assent on 19 April, the last day of the session.[1] The initial reaction in Virginia was a sense of relief, because of earlier fears of the prohibition of existing currency arising from the Board's threat of February 1763, a policy never contemplated by the Board in 1764. The Currency Act had little immediate effect, and sustained criticism did not begin to develop until after the repeal of the Stamp Act had removed a more important colonial grievance.

At the end of the session the Board of Trade sent a circular letter to the governors of the American colonies, enclosing copies of the acts that had been passed relating to the colonies. The list included five other measures as well as the Duties Act and the Currency Act.[2] Some of them contained trade laws similar to those in the Duties Act. The distinction was that they had not been initiated by the administration, but proposed by agents of the colonies or merchants trading to them. Here the American lobby can be seen working for constructive action to help the colonies, and not merely responding defensively to government measures.

All the changes contained in this legislation had been approved in advance by the Board of Trade, for it was the Board and not Parliament that acted as the administration check on such proposals. Any rejected by the Board were not even submitted to the House of Commons, such as a plan to allow the

---

[1] *Commons Journals*, xxix. 1027, 1032, 1039, 1044–6, 1049, 1053, 1056.

[2] *J.C.T.P. 1764–7*, pp. 43–4. The list omitted an act permitting Georgia and South Carolina to export rice direct to Madeira and to foreign colonies in America. For the background to this measure see *J.C.T.P. 1759–63*, pp. 328, 420; *J.C.T.P. 1764–7*, pp. 9, 22, 32.

direct import of foreign salt into the colonies, disallowed because of the adverse effect this would have on the British salt industry.[1] The screening was a thorough process. The act for giving a bounty on exports of colonial hemp and flax was preceded by a memorial of merchants asking for such a provision and submitted to the Board on 13 December 1763. It had been drawn up by Charles Garth, approved by other colonial agents, and signed by 102 firms, 'almost all the merchants trading to America, except those who have seats in Parliament, and who, as being to be judges, could not with propriety or decency make themselves parties by signing it'.[2] The Board obtained information from the Admiralty and the Customs Board; heard agents and merchants as witnesses on 26 January 1764; and finally approved the plan on 9 February after further consideration of it on several occasions.[3] In the same way the act 'to encourage whale fishing in North America' originated from a petition of American and British merchants for the abolition of the duty on whale fins exported from the Gulf of St.Lawrence to New England after the request had been approved by the Board of Trade.[4] By contrast a third act shows 'the old colonial system' of trade regulation working in favour of the mother country. Britain, by the acquisition of Canada, had secured a virtual monopoly of the fur trade: the most important part of this was in beaver skin, used in hat-making. Since foreign hat-makers were able to obtain the skins as cheaply as home manufacturers, a petition of British hat-makers to the Treasury in December 1763 asked for an export duty on the skins. The memorial secured the support of Charles Jenkinson and was referred to the Board of Trade.[5] Evidence considered by the Board showed a fall of about 70 per cent in hat exports since 1736: but there developed a clash of interest between the hat-makers and the fur-traders, notably the Hudson's Bay Company, whose governor and chief spokesman was Sir William Baker.

---

[1] *J.C.T.P.* *1764–7*, p. 9.
[2] Garth to South Carolina, 20 Nov. 1763; quoted and cited by Namier, *England in the Age of the American Revolution*, pp. 251–2. The petition is summarized in *Acts P.C.Col.* iv. 646–8.
[3] *J.C.T.P.* *1759–63*, p. 420; *J.C.T.P.* *1764–7*, pp. 3, 6, 9, 13, 18–20; *Acts P.C. Col.* iv. 648–9.
[4] *J.C.T.P.* *1764–7*, pp. 10, 13, 19–20; *Acts P.C. Col.* iv. 640.
[5] *Jenkinson Papers*, pp. 231–3.

The Company contended that a duty would cause both smuggling and colonial hat manufacture. The compromise solution proposed by the Board of Trade, and incorporated in the subsequent act, was the abolition of the existing import duty on beaver skins entering Britain and the imposition of a small duty on re-exports to foreign countries.[1] The Board of Trade had come to a decision on all matters of proposed legislation by 9 February, and appropriate recommendations were included in the representation sent that day by the Board to the Privy Council that also reported on the question of colonial currency. The Council's approval of the various proposals on 9 March, after the report of its Committee of Plantations two days earlier, was made without reservation and with the order that they should be laid before Parliament.[2] Grenville announced all these proposals in his Budget speech the same day,[3] and the passage of the legislation was a formality.

[1] *J.C.T.P. 1764-7*, pp. 10–11, 13, 14, 18, 19; *Acts P.C. Col.* iv. 636–40, 650–2.
[2] *Acts P.C. Col.* iv. 623.
[3] *Ryder Diary*, p. 234.

5 The Background of the Stamp Act[1]

BRITAIN had had stamp duties since the reign of Charles II, nearly a century before the Stamp Act Crisis. The first act imposing them had come into operation in 1671; and although this had lapsed in 1680, from the reign of William III stamp duties have always been in operation.[2] The annual net income in the period from 1756 to 1763 was about £260,000,[3] a much larger sum even in proportion to population than was to be expected from the American colonies. The extension of the stamp duties to the colonies had been frequently proposed, as in 1722, 1726, 1728, 1742, and on several occasions during the French and Indian War.[4] One persistent advocate of an American stamp tax was Henry McCulloh, a London merchant concerned with land speculation in North Carolina. At the end of 1751 he had put forward the suggestion in an essay addressed to Lord Halifax, then President of the Board of Trade, 'that by Act of Parliament there were to be further funds established by enacting that all writings, deeds, instruments, or other matters relating to the law in the said provinces should be on stamp paper or parchment and that the money arising therefrom should be applied only to the security and advantage of the colonies'.[5] In 1757 McCulloh submitted a scheme for American taxation to the Board of Trade. This was essentially a draft bill that would raise money from interest on Exchequer Bills issued to serve as colonial currency, an idea to be suggested later by

[1] Much information on this subject can be found in Gipson, *British Empire*, x. 246–70, and in the articles by Morgan, *W.M.Q.* 7 (1950), 352–92, and Ritcheson, *W.M.Q.* 10 (1953), 543–59. But Ritcheson had the wrong author of the Stamp Act, as he has himself later admitted, while Morgan, wrongly in my opinion, contends that Grenville at first offered to let the colonies tax themselves and then changed his mind. Morgan's interpretation has been challenged on various points by Sosin, *Agents and Merchants*, pp. 49–54.

[2] Hughes, *E.H.R.* 56 (1941), 234–54.

[3] T.1/430, fos. 78–101.

[4] Gipson, *British Empire*, x. 253–8. For the suggestion made in Jan. 1763 to Lord Bute by Governor Dimwiddie of Virginia see B.M. Add. MSS. 38334, fos. 297–301.

[5] B.M. Add. MSS. 11514, fos. 93–4. For McCulloh see Cannon, *W.M.Q.* 15 (1958), 72–3.

Benjamin Franklin: but it also included the following observations.

'A poll tax of eighteen pence per head, negroes included, would amount to upwards of forty thousand pounds per annum, and a stamp duty on vellum and paper would amount to forty thousand pounds per annum more. These if duly collected would raise upwards of £80,000 per annum, and remain a perpetual resource, for growing services in relief of the mother country.[1]

In 1763 it was McCulloh who put forward the fateful suggestion for a colonial Stamp Act. In July he submitted such a plan to Secretary of the Treasury Charles Jenkinson. McCulloh envisaged a revenue of £60,000 a year from North America alone, and enclosed a draft bill.[2] His letter was passed on to Grenville, and the scheme was evidently approved by the Treasury: for on 8 September Thomas Cruwys, Solicitor to the Stamp Office, was instructed by Jenkinson to consult with McCulloh on 'a plan for a general Stamp Law' for the colonies.[3] Cruwys accordingly saw McCulloh for three hours on 14 September, 'consulting him upon his scheme which was quite different from my own'; and the next day he saw Grenville and Sir James Calder, one of the five Commissioners of the Stamp Office Board.[4] He saw McCulloh again on 30 September to obtain information on legal procedure in the colonies, and it was on this day that the Stamp Office Board issued a formal order for the preparation of a colonial stamp bill.[5] On 10 October Cruwys received a list of proposed stamp duties from McCulloh,[6] and the two men had a conference on 12 October.[7] This was mainly concerned with practical problems

---

[1] B.M. Add. MSS. 32974, fos. 310–13.   [2] *Grenville Papers*, ii. 373n.
[3] B.M. Add. MSS. 35911, fos. 15–36. This document is the statement of Cruwys's bill of expenses for the preparation of the Stamp Bill submitted to the Treasury on 29 Oct. 1765, totalling £631. Unless otherwise stated it is the source of information for his activities connected with the bill. Thomas Augustus Cruwys was Solicitor to the Stamp Office from 1750 to 1770, at a retainer of £100 p.a. The son of Henry and Jane Cruwys, he inherited an estate of £600 a year in Devonshire on the death of his mother in 1765. *London Evening Post*, 26 Oct. 1765.
[4] For a 1763 list of the Stamp Office officials see B. M. Add. MSS. 38335, fos. 58–9.
[5] B.M. Add. MSS. 36226, fos. 353, 357.
[6] B.M. Add. MSS. 35910, fos. 136–9, 159.
[7] For notes of this conference made by Cruwys see B.M. Add. MSS. 36226, fos. 357–60.

arising out of the proposed duties. They discussed the appointment of one Stamp Distributor for each colony, to receive 5 per cent poundage; the appointment of Inspectors, to examine legal records and the accounts of the Distributors; and the enforcement of the duties by the invalidation of all unstamped legal documents and the seizure of the cargoes of ships with unstamped papers. Cruwys went to report afterwards to Sir James Calder, and was instructed to prepare a list of duties 'in general exclusive of Mr. McCulloh's'. His list of duties was therefore a complementary one, and there is little duplication of items on the two lists.[1] Cruwys also drew up a plan for the bill, and obtained the approval of Thomas Whately for it on 14 October. Grenville then ordered McCulloh and Cruwys to settle the form of the bill together, and they spent four hours on 26 October reading over a draft fair copy of the bill, making remarks and alterations, and settling the preamble.

McCulloh, however, then himself went to see Grenville on 29 October, and obtained permission to draw up an alternative bill. The difference of opinion concerned not the items to be taxed or the rates of duty, but the use to which the money was to be put. McCulloh still favoured the issue of Exchequer Bills to serve as a colonial currency, and wanted the proceeds of the stamp duties to be used as a fund to secure them. He had suggested this in a note to his draft list of duties,[2] and mentioned the scheme to Cruwys on 12 October. McCulloh had then also discussed the use he would like to see made of the proposed tax revenue towards the financial requirements of the colonies, which he calculated would cost £500,000. He had suggested to Cruwys that 'in time that additional duties to that amount may be raised so as to save the mother country from so great a charge, but at present is certain such an attempt would meet with the fullest opposition'.[3] His own specific ideas for the use of the anticipated revenue from the stamp duties were set out in the preamble of his draft bill, dated 8 November.[4]

To provide presents for cultivating the friendship of the Indians now or hereafter to be in alliance with his Majesty, to pay Rangers

---

[1] B.M. Add. MSS. 35910, fos. 136–9; 36226, fos. 353–6.
[2] B.M. Add. MSS. 35910, fo. 138.   [3] B.M. Add. MSS. 36226, fo. 358.
[4] B.M. Add. MSS. 35910, fo. 204. The same proposals are set out in the draft appropriation clause, ibid., fo. 205.

for the support and protection of the frontiers and to support and provide for the maintenance of his Majesty's forts and garrisons, to encourage settlers and settlements in the frontier parts of his Majesty's colonies or plantations, and to discharge the salaries of his Majesty's governors and other officers abroad.

This was a wide-ranging proposal, and included the potentially controversial step of financing the civil administration in the colonies from this tax. The Treasury rejected McCulloh's scheme after Cruwys had submitted both draft bills on 19 November. Cruwys continued to work on his bill, and handed the final copy to the Treasury on 24 January 1764. In the expectation that the measure would form part of Grenville's budget proposals on 9 March, Cruwys saw Secretary to the Board of Trade John Pownall on 6 March and Thomas Whately the next day: but he learnt on 10 March that the Stamp Bill had been postponed for a year.[1]

What George Grenville said about the proposed stamp duties in the House of Commons on 9 March 1764 is a matter of historical controversy. E. S. Morgan, the leading authority on the Stamp Act Crisis, has argued that in his Budget speech that day Grenville offered to let the colonies tax themselves as an alternative to the stamp duties that he had just announced, and that this was why the tax was postponed for a year: and that Grenville had changed his mind by the time he met the colonial agents to discuss the matter on 17 May, for he then merely requested colonial assent to and suggestions about the stamp duty. This contention hardens during his development of the theme into an assertion of fact, and Morgan therefore accused Grenville of being guilty of bad faith, insincerity, and stupidity.[2]

The chief contemporary evidence Morgan cited were two

---

[1] B.M. Add. MSS. 35911, fo. 20–22. For another account of this phase of the preparation of the Stamp Bill see Ritcheson, *W.M.Q.* 10 (1953), 549–53. Ritcheson then contended that the draft author was not Cruwys but John Tabor Kempe, Attorney-General of New York. In correspondence arising from the article, however, E. S. Morgan showed that Kempe was in New York throughout the period, and Ritcheson accepted this correction. B. Knollenberg then provided convincing arguments and evidence that Cruwys was the author. *W.M.Q.* 11 (1954), 157–60, 512–13. The heading 'Mr. Cruwys' Scheme for an American Stamp Bill' appears in one document. B.M. Add. MSS. 36226, fos. 353–6.

[2] Morgan, *W.M.Q.* 7 (1950), 353–92.

letters by agents to their colonies, Jasper Mauduit to Massa-chusetts on 13 March, and Edward Montagu to Virginia on 11 April. Such reports of agents back to America are a widely used source of information about Parliamentary debates in this period, but they need to be used with caution. The gallery of the House of Commons was not a convenient place to see or hear debates, and no notes were allowed. Many of the reports by agents, moreover, were written a considerable time after the debates in question, and they often failed to date or even distinguish between different proceedings. The report by Jasper Mauduit, indeed, was written only four days after the debate, but it was his brother Israel who had actually heard what Grenville said. It was certainly believed in Massachusetts that Grenville had made some sort of offer that the colonies could tax themselves to avoid the British stamp duties.[1] But the colony was wrong, misled by its own agent and not by the minister. Mauduit gave this reason for the postponement of the Stamp Act. 'Mr. Grenville being willing to give the pro-vinces their option to raise that or some equivalent tax. Desirous as he expressed himself to consult the ease, the quiet and the good will of the colonies.' The Massachusetts Assembly put an interpretation on this letter that would have been more applicable to the account sent by Montagu to Virginia: he reported Grenville as saying that 'it would be satisfactory to him if the several provinces would among themselves, and in modes best suited to their circumstances raise a sum adequate to the expense of their own defence'.[2]

Grenville made no such offer. An accurate picture of what was said about the stamp tax in the debate of 9 March 1764 can be constructed from two diaries written by M.P.s in the House at the time. Nathaniel Ryder was taking the debate down in shorthand, and notes were also being made by James Harris, sitting within a few feet of the minister, who as a Lord of the Treasury may be presumed to have known what was in Grenville's mind.[3] No better sources could be available before the days of *Hansard*.

[1] Morgan, *W.M.Q.* 7 (1950), 367–9; Gipson, *British Empire*, x. 265; Knollenberg, *Origin of the American Revolution*, pp. 184–5.

[2] Morgan, *W.M.Q.* 7 (1950), 357–8.

[3] *Ryder Diary*, pp. 233–8; Harris Diary, 9 Mar. 1764. For a fuller list of sources for this debate see above, p. 53 n 3.

In his Budget speech Grenville spoke of the stamp duty as one of the measures intended for that year. After he had declared that an inadequate return from the customs duties would make necessary further sources of revenue, his next statement was summarized by Ryder as follows. 'Stamp duties the least exceptionable because it requires few officers and even collects itself. The only danger is forgery.' The fifteenth of the twenty-four resolutions he moved was 'that towards further defraying the said expenses, it may be proper to charge certain Stamp Duties in the said Colonies and Plantations'. This would have been a needless formality for a mere declaration of future intent: indeed, it was contrary to Parliamentary practice to introduce resolutions in the Committee of Ways and Means unless legislation followed as a consequence, and Grenville himself was a leading expert on the law and custom of Parliament. Preparation of the draft bill, moreover, was not stopped until the next day. What happened was that Grenville changed his mind as a result of objections during the debate.

Sir William Baker, leading for the opposition group of Newcastle's friends, approved the proposal: 'stamps, does not dislike that duty in America'. The first attack came from John Huske, who argued that notice ought to be sent to North America, as to Ireland, of any important business relating to the colonies. 'Would have this law read two times, printed, and then sent to America for their opinion about it.'[1] William Beckford, who spoke next, was the only member recorded as being 'against the stamp duty'. Grenville rose to speak again at this point, and expressed the hope that the stamp duty 'might be done with good will: that for the present session it might go no further than a resolution'.[2] Huske's suggestion was adopted in principle. When the resolutions of the Committee were reported to the House next day, the one for the stamp duties was read a second time, but omitted from the list of those ordered to form the basis of legislation.[3] Confirmation of this interpretation of the debate of 9 March may be

---

[1] *Ryder Diary*, pp. 235–7.

[2] Harris Diary, 9 Mar. 1764.

[3] *Commons Journals*, xxix. 935. Other evidence on Huske's role in securing the postponement of the Stamp Act is treated sceptically by Morgan, *W.M.Q.* 7 (1950), 354n.

found in an account sent to South Carolina by Charles Garth on 17 April 1764.[1]

The Chancellor of the Exchequer at first proposed it as a measure to take place this sessions, but Mr. Alderman Beckford and Mr. Huske signifying their wish to have the colonies apprized of the intention of Parliament, Mr. Grenville readily acquiesced, declaring it was far from his inclination to press any measure upon any part of the dominions without giving them time to be heard, should they have objections thereto.

Garth was one agent who had understood Grenville correctly: but since others like Jasper Mauduit and Montagu had formed a different impression of the minister's intention, a desire to clarify the situation was probably the reason for the collective decision of the agents, after a meeting among themselves, to seek an interview with Grenville. They also wished to thank him for postponing the tax, and did so when the meeting took place on 17 May.[2] Grenville then explained to the agents his firm intention of introducing the bill for stamp duties, saying he had chosen such a tax on grounds of equity and economy of collection. Garth reported him as being unequivocally opposed to any taxation of the colonies by themselves. 'The raising it within themselves and appropriating it would have been attended with very many difficulties even if it could be supposed that 26 colonies (including the Continent and West Indian Islands) would all have adopted such a recommendation . . . his intention by this delay was to have the sense of the colonies themselves upon the matter, and if they could point out any system or plan as effectual and more easy to them, he was open to every proposition to be made from the colonies.'[3]

---

[1] Quoted in Namier and Brooke, *House of Commons, 1754–1790*, ii. 660.

[2] Two reports of this meeting are known to have been sent by agents to their colonies; one by Jasper Mauduit (again reporting his brother Israel) on 26 May to Massachusetts, the other by Garth on 5 June to South Carolina. Another account was published in 1765 in a pamphlet by William Knox, agent for Georgia. All three were printed by Morgan, *W.M.Q.* 7 (1950), 359–63. Garth's account was previously printed by Namier, *E.H.R.* 54 (1939), 646–8.

[3] In 1776 Israel Mauduit published his own account of the conference. A draft of this in Jenkinson's papers, B.M. Add. MSS. 38337, fos. 259–60, was printed in the *Jenkinson Papers*, pp. 305–7. It gives this misleading summary of Grenville's statement. 'I am not however sett upon this tax, if the Americans dislike it and prefer any other method of raising the money themselves, I shall be content. Write

Grenville warned the agents that Parliament would not accept any arguments about the alleged inability of the colonies to pay, or any doubts about its power to levy such a tax. When questioned by the agents as to the details of the proposed taxes Grenville stated that they would be along the same lines, although perhaps not at the same rates, as the existing stamp duties in Britain. Grenville ended, Garth reported, by declaring that

'he should be very ready to consult with us before the meeting of Parliament thereon to receive any propositions we might in the mean time be instructed upon by our respective constituents with regard to these points, if our assemblies should, as he could not doubt, upon a due consideration they would, transmit us instructions with their assent to the plan for levying this money in the American Dominions.'

The colonial role envisaged by Grenville was therefore a general consent to the proposed Stamp Act, together with the opportunity to suggest detailed modifications. Charles Garth thought there was something of value in Grenville's offer.

'Whether you shall be of opinion that giving your assenting in form, having in the Assembly considered of the nature of the tax as signified unto you to be proposed in Parliament previous to its being carried into the House may not establish a precedent, of being previously consulted on all occasions that a Revenue Bill may be thought of in which America may be affected, may be a question not altogether unworthy consideration.'

As Garth perceived, the first concession might have evolved into a valuable constitutional precedent, implying the assent or veto of colonial assemblies on taxation: the second could have been of immediate practical benefit in relation to the Stamp Act. If Grenville was seriously envisaging such colonial participation in taxation, however, he is open to criticism for not

---

therefore to your several colonies and if they choose any other mode I shall be satisfied, provided the money be but raised.' This is what Mauduit had understood Grenville to have said in the debate of 9 March, and, indeed, he says the minister repeated at the conference what he had offered in the House of Commons. His recollection is at variance with the other evidence. But it must remain uncertain whether or not Grenville was willing to consider any alternative Parliamentary tax, as Garth seems to have thought.

having made the proposal through the official channel of a circular letter from the Secretary of State for the South to the colonial governors for consideration by the assemblies.[1] Some agents did forward Grenville's statement of his views to the colonies: but it is not known how fully and accurately they did so, or if every colony was informed at all.

Only two of the colonies considered Grenville's offer, although the Assembly of Massachusetts, misled by its agent, discussed the possibility of raising taxes itself instead. The Pennsylvania Assembly debated some unknown alternative, but came to no decision. The Assembly of Connecticut, in an official pamphlet, proposed two taxes that would place little burden on their own colony, one on negro slaves and the other on the fur trade. No suggestion about alternative Parliamentary taxation was made by any colony to the British government: instead protests against the proposed Stamp Act were sent by the assemblies of these three colonies and at least five others, New York, North Carolina, Rhode Island, South Carolina, and Virginia. No colony acknowledged Parliament's right of taxation or author- ized its agent to consent to the Stamp Bill: but only two of the eight, New York and North Carolina, attacked the Duties Act on the ground that it was also a tax, other objections to that measure being for economic reasons.[2]

The surviving evidence is probably incomplete, for 'all' the colonial agents, so Garth reported to South Carolina on 8 February 1765, received instructions to oppose the Stamp Act.[3] The agents held several meetings during January 1765, on the initiative of Garth. They were uncertain whether or how to petition Parliament. It was thought that the Commons would not accept petitions that disputed the right of taxation. William Knox of Georgia and other agents therefore suggested a petition that would avoid this delicate point, and one was drawn up; but the idea was dropped when some agents announced that they did not feel that signing it would be

---

[1] Morgan, *Stamp Act Crisis*, p. 81, makes this same criticism of Grenville with respect to what he imagined was the offer to let the colonies tax themselves.

[2] Gipson, *British Empire*, x. 231–45. Morgan, *Stamp Act Crisis*, pp. 51–8. Morgan, *W.M.Q.* 7 (1950), 365–9. For Pennsylvania's instruction to Jackson see *Franklin Papers*, xi. 348–51.

[3] Namier, *E.H.R.* 54 (1939), 648–9, quoted and cited letters of 26 Dec. 1764 and 8 Feb. 1765 from Garth to South Carolina.

compatible with their instructions. A plan to enlist the support of the British merchants who traded with America also proved unsuccessful, even though many were already alarmed by the threat of a colonial boycott.[1] The agents therefore decided to inform the ministry that most colonies were prepared to contribute through the old method of requisitions, in a final move to avert the Stamp Act: and a deputation of four was appointed to wait on Grenville, Benjamin Franklin and Jared Ingersoll as new arrivals from America being chosen to accompany two agents who were M.P.s, Richard Jackson and Charles Garth.[2]

The meeting took place on 2 February. The agents urged the minister to adopt the system of requisitions, and Jackson forecast the end of the assemblies if the army and the civil governments in the colonies were to be financed by Parliamentary taxation. Grenville denied that there was any such purpose or any danger to the assemblies, and then raised the practical question as to whether the agents could 'agree upon the several proportions each colony should raise'. Their negative answer exposed the hollowness of the whole manoeuvre; the agents were simply playing for time, hoping for a further postponement of the Stamp Act.[3] The move had been doomed to failure. Grenville himself by that date was determined to proceed with an American tax, and he told the agents he knew of no better method than the stamp duties.[4] In any case his freedom of action was limited by the effect of the American protests on political opinion in Britain: the issue had been

[1] Morgan, *Stamp Act Crisis*, p. 88.

[2] Garth had just succeeded his father as M.P. for Devizes at a by-election on 15 Jan. 1765.

[3] The conference is described in a letter from Jared Ingersoll to Governor T. Fitch of Connecticut on 11 Feb. 1765. *Fitch Papers*, ii. 324–5. Morgan, *W.M.Q.* 7 (1950), 372, denounced Grenville's question as 'fatuous', because the total sum required from the colonies was not known: but a proportionate allocation did not depend on prior knowledge of the amount involved, and the agents had gone specifically to ask for adoption of the method of requisitions. The inquiry was therefore fair and logical.

[4] This remark was apparently accompanied by an invitation to the agents to suggest an alternative method, a suggestion taken more seriously by Benjamin Franklin than Grenville perhaps expected. Franklin had already thought of one the previous year, a scheme for colonial paper money that would provide the colonies with a uniform and legal currency, and the British government with an assured income from interest on the bills. Franklin and Thomas Pownall formally submitted this proposal to Grenville on 12 Feb., to no avail. *Franklin Papers*, xii. 47–61.

converted from one of revenue to the question of the sovereignty of Parliament.[1]

The need to obtain fuller information has often been suggested or assumed to have been one or even the main reason for the postponement of the Stamp Act.[2] Grenville himself announced this as one motive for the delay in 1764, and made the following statement when introducing the stamp duty resolutions on 6 February 1765. 'The reason of the delaying the proposal to this year was to gain all possible information and to give Americans an opportunity of conveying information to this House, whose ears are always open to receive knowledge and to act to it. The officers of the revenue have done their duty in giving all possible knowledge of the subject.'[3] Grenville was then speaking not in his historic role as the minister who taxed America, but as the man who had opposed colonial taxation in 1763 and postponed it in 1764. Such statements may have been largely a public excuse to allay the criticism of those who had favoured an earlier tax on the colonies, and events do not suggest that lack of adequate knowledge was a significant reason for postponement of the Stamp Act. Little change was to be made in the bill as a result of the additional information obtained in 1764: and the ministry did not hasten to take advantage of the extra time. On 2 July Charles Jenkinson wrote to prompt Grenville into action.[4]

In the last session of Parliament you assigned as a reason for not going on with the Stamp Act, that you waited only for further information on that subject. This having been said, should not Government appear to take some step for that purpose? I mentioned this to you soon after the Parliament was up. I remember your objections to it; but I think the information may be procured in a manner to obviate those objections, and without it we may perhaps be accused of neglect.

Nothing was done for another month, until on 11 August Secretary of State Halifax issued a circular letter to all governors of colonies in North America and the West Indies. This

[1] See below, pp. 86–7.
[2] Morgan, *Stamp Act Crisis*, p. 75. Ritcheson, *British Politics and the American Revolution*, p. 23. Sosin, *Whitehall and the Wilderness*, p. 84.
[3] *Ryder Diary*, p. 254.   [4] *Grenville Papers*, iii. 373.

officially informed them of the resolution of the House of Commons on colonial stamp duties, and instructed them to send a list of the relevant legal documents. They were to obtain the help of the chief law officers in their colonies for this purpose.[1]

Appropriate lists were sent in reply from at least nine of the thirteen colonies that were to resist the Stamp Act, by the Governors of New Hampshire, Massachusetts, Rhode Island, New Jersey, and Georgia, by the Lieutenant-Governors of New York and Virginia, and by the Deputy Governors of Maryland and Pennsylvania.[2] The elected Governor Hopkins of Rhode Island added the comment that the intended use of his list 'must prove extremely grievous to the colony, deprive it of the rights it hath long enjoyed, and thinks itself justly entitled to'. Some governors mentioned their sources of information: Lieutenant-Governor Fauquier of Virginia had consulted the Secretary to the Colony and the Attorney-General, Governor Bernard of Massachusetts 'the Clerks and Registrars', Governor Wentworth of New Hampshire the Attorney-General and the Deputy Judge of Vice-Admiralty; while the lists from New York and New Jersey were compiled directly by the respective Attorney-Generals of those colonies.[3] All the lists were sent off in October or November except that for Pennsylvania, which is dated 10 December; and most of them should have arrived in time to be used in the final preparation of the Stamp Bill. The information merely stated what legal documents were used in the colonies. It made possible more precise definitions in the Stamp Act of the documents that were to be taxed; but its importance was limited to one part of the measure, and it was hardly a sufficient reason for a whole year's postponement.

Treasury Secretary Thomas Whately, who was responsible for supervising the bill, had meanwhile continued this task.

---

[1] C.O. 5/65/pp. 647–9.

[2] T.1/430, fos. 171–86, 192–3, 208–11, 214–16, 222–7. In some cases the enclosed lists are missing. I have not found any replies from Connecticut, Delaware, or North or South Carolina. Replies also came from the Governor of Quebec and the Attorney-General of Nova Scotia. Ibid., fos. 220–1, 288–9.

[3] A copy of the list compiled by Attorney-General John T. Kempe of New York, which is missing from the Treasury papers, may be found as B.M. Add. MSS. 36226, fos. 361–72.

On 31 July he informed his fellow Secretary Jenkinson that he would be sending him a copy of 'the Stamp act' within a few days, presumably Cruwys's draft bill; and that he was consulting William Blair, who had been Chairman of the Board of Stamps until 1761, and W. Cuthbert, one of the Stamp Commissioners.[1] Whately had already been seeking private advice and information from such friends in America as Jared Ingersoll, before he came over from Connecticut, and Customs Surveyor-General John Temple. Both warned him against the plan: Temple argued that the consequence would be a corresponding fall in the value of British exports to America, and Ingersoll stated that the stamp duties would be evaded, as being levied without the consent of the people.[2] It is doubtful whether Whately acquired much additional information as a result of his own inquiries: but when Ingersoll arrived in Britain he had several discussions with Whately, and afterwards claimed the credit for a general reduction of the proposed rates of duty and for the omission of duties altogether on marriage licences, commissions of the peace, and notes of hand.[3]

On 10 October Whately formally directed Thomas Cruwys to resume work on the bill; and a month later, on 15 and 16 November, he was given a full briefing on the proposed stamp duties by Cruwys, McCulloh, and John Brettrell, the Secretary to the Stamp Office.[4] Whately then explained the whole scheme to the Treasury Board on 6 December. The plan he read out was not the draft bill but an exposition of his thinking on the project. Whately informed the Board that the principle was to impose duties on the same items as in Britain, and that a bill had already been drawn up on these lines; only the rates of duty remained to be settled. His paper was mainly concerned with the variations from the British duties. One important difference would be a duty on the grants of Crown lands frequently made in the colonies but forbidden in Britain: since such duties were 'directly contrary to the first principles

---

[1] B.M. Add. MSS. 38197, fos. 259–60.
[2] For Whately's correspondence with Temple see the *Bowdoin–Temple Papers*, pp. 20, 22–9; for that with Ingersoll see *Ingersoll Papers*, pp. 294–301.
[3] *Fitch Papers*, ii. 325–6.
[4] B.M. Add. MSS. 35911, fo. 22.

of colonization' he suggested what he considered to be very low rates of duty. Duties on legal documents should be lower than in Britain to allow for the greater litigiousness of the American people. Licences for retailing ale, cider, and spirits should also bear a lower duty of 10s., because of the poverty of many of the traders concerned. The duty on newspaper advertisements should be halved to 1s., because they were so numerous that the British duty of 2s. 'would perhaps be thought a great grievance'. There was also to be a wide range of other reductions and many exemptions to allow for the different conditions in the colonies. Bonds, for example, would bear lower rates of duty, because they were given frequently in the colonies instead of notes of hand; and there should be no duty on indentured servants. Some duties might be lowered on the principle of maximum yield or novelty, as from 1s. to 6d. on a pack of playing cards to avoid fraud. Whately's paper shows that the proposed variations of colonial duties from the existing British stamp duties were tailored to meet the different circumstances of colonial life.[1]

Cruwys attended the Treasury Board when Whately presented his paper, and the next day revised the bill that he had drafted the previous session. On 8 December he gave Whately the list of legal documents compiled by Attorney-General Kempe of New York. Despatched on 14 October, it had been received by 28 November.[2] It is the only list sent in reply to Halifax's circular letter that is known to have been consulted, although Cruwys's notes do show that he had other lists at hand. Cruwys visited Whately on at least ten further occasions before the end of January 1765, mainly to draw up the preliminary resolutions necessary in the Committee of Ways and Means to prepare the procedural ground for the bill itself.[3]

Cruwys's labours did not end when the subject came before Parliament. He attended the House of Commons when Grenville moved the preliminary resolutions on 6 February, and was busy for the next two days on 'the enacting clauses'. He went to the House to give Whately the bill and a brief before its

---

[1] B.M. Add. MSS. 35910, fos. 310–23; printed by Hughes, *E.H.R.* 56 (1941), 259–64.
[2] *Cal. Home Office Papers, 1760–65*, p. 466.
[3] B.M. Add. MSS. 35911, fos. 22–8.

first reading on 13 February, and he was present again on 27 February when several alterations were made in the bill after the third reading. Cruwys subsequently drew up the bonds for the Stamp Distributors, and was busy correcting the proofs of the bill from 1 May onwards.[1]

Cruwys therefore played a far more important role in drafting the Stamp Act than the better-known McCulloh. By October 1765 McCulloh in a letter to Rockingham was glad to disclaim responsibility for the measure and criticized the alleged failure to obtain or use relevant information from the colonies. 'I was desired to assist Mr. Cruwys in drawing the Stamp Duty Bill . . . however that affair was taken out of my hands, and the Bill was afterwards drawn upon the plan of business in use here which is very different from what ought to have been observed in America.'[2] Certainly very few of McCulloh's proposals of 1763[3] were incorporated in the final bill. Many of his suggestions for duties had been too crude and sweeping: he envisaged, for example, only one duty for grants of office and for land grants, whereas the bill had two and three duties respectively, scaled according to value. Hardly one of McCulloh's proposed duties survives,[4] and his other suggestions were not adopted: these were a proposal that to stop counterfeiting the stamped paper should bear the name of the appropriate colony, and his scheme that the money should be paid into a general fund to secure Exchequer Bills. Cruwys, by contrast, was the man who drafted the successive versions of the bill, and a number of his original proposals for duties[5] survived throughout. Others were increased, reduced, or put in another form. Both Cruwys and McCulloh, indeed, saw their suggested rates of duties variously raised and lowered. No general pattern of rates higher or lower than either of their lists emerges.[6] Each item was considered on its merits.

[1] B.M. Add. MSS. 35911, fos. 29–34.
[2] Wentworth Woodhouse MSS. R65.
[3] B.M. Add. MSS. 35910, fos. 136–9.
[4] McCulloh's proposal of a 10s. duty on grants of office does correspond to the lower rate in the Stamp Act, on offices up to £20; but his vague wording makes a detailed comparison impossible.
[5] B.M. Add. MSS. 36226, fos. 353–4.
[6] Two examples illustrate this point. On ships' cockets or bills of lading Cruwys suggested 4d. and McCulloh 6d.: the rate in the act was 4d. For university degree certificates Cruwys suggested £4 and McCulloh 10s.: the rate in the act was £2.

The final responsibility for such alterations and detailed decisions cannot be established. If Whately could overrule Cruwys or McCulloh, he was in turn under the supervision of the Treasury Board, and not all of his own recommendations of 6 December were accepted: the advertisement duty was to be 2*s.*, the cost of an ale-house licence 20*s.*, and the duty on a pack of cards 1*s.* All such decisions were taken by the administration before the bill was submitted to Parliament. The only changes to such clauses made during its passage were verbal and not substantive, and the final Stamp Act was to show no alterations of any of the duties or rates of duty from those proposed in the resolutions of the Committee of Ways and Means.[1] Over fifty specific duties were imposed, but many were simply different rates of duty on such items as surveys, conveyances and pamphlets. The highest duty was £10 on licences for solicitors and attorneys. Only nine duties, all non-recurrent, were over £1, and those likely to occur frequently were nearly all of 1*s.* or less, like the 4*d.* duty on bills of lading for ships.[2] Stamped paper would have to be used for newspapers, many classes of legal documents, ships' clearance papers, appointments to public offices, liquor licences, surveys, grants and conveyances of land, assurances, mortgages, cards, dice, pamphlets, advertisements, calendars, and apprentice contracts. The tax would be paid regularly by merchants, lawyers or their clients, and newspaper printers; often by publicans and sinners—or at least gamblers; and at infrequent intervals by virtually every colonist.

[1] The resolutions may be found in the *Commons Journals*, xxx. 98–101; and the corresponding clauses of the Stamp Act in Morgan, *Prologue to Revolution*, pp. 35–43. For a list of the contemporary British duties see B.M. Add. MSS. 35910, fos. 138–59. Whately later calculated that the duties in the Stamp Act averaged between two-thirds and three-quarters of the rates in Britain. *Bowdoin–Temple Papers*, pp. 49–51.

[2] According to Whately this duty was intended to prevent fraud rather than produce revenue. *Bowdoin–Temple Papers*, pp. 49–51.

6   The Passage of the Stamp Act

B Y the beginning of 1765 deaths and desertions had weakened
the Parliamentary opposition. The Duke of Devonshire
died on 2 October 1764, a loss to Newcastle's group of their
most respected leader. In the House of Commons the opposition
had been shorn of much of its debating strength. William Pitt
was never to appear there during 1765. With the death of
Henry Legge on 23 August Newcastle had lost a valuable
spokesman and financial expert. Disillusion with the now barren
prospects of opposition had led others to move towards the
side of administration, including such prominent men in the
Commons as Charles Yorke and Charles Townshend. Yorke
was to oppose the ministry in 1765 only on general warrants.
Townshend had been flirting with government throughout
1764, and usually supported the administration in 1765,
receiving the post of Paymaster-General in May. There was
good reason for the optimism in government circles reflected
in the opinion of Lord Barrington in December 1764 that there
was 'the greatest prospect of success, strength and perhaps
unanimity in Parliament this winter'.[1]

An intention to harass the ministry, however, was evident in
the bellicose attitude of Sir William Baker and such younger
men as Thomas Townshend and George Onslow; and at the
beginning of 1765 the Marquess of Rockingham emerged from
rural semi-retirement to take the initiative in organizing and
leading the opposition, as the old Duke of Newcastle accepted
with some resentment the advice of his friends that he should
withdraw from the front of the political stage. The chief
political issue in 1765 was still that of general warrants; and
on 29 January the opposition pressed the ministry to a majority
of only 35 votes, 224 against 189.[2] This was the highlight of
the session, and the passage of the Stamp Act took place during
a lull in the Parliamentary battle.[3] America, indeed, was not

---

[1] *H.M.C. Lothian*, p. 253.   [2] For the debate see *Ryder Diary*, pp. 239–53.
[3] For the political background of the recess and the beginning of the session see
Hardy, M.A. Thesis, pp. 204–50.

a subject of much interest to the 'formed opposition' at the time. The correspondence of the Duke of Newcastle in February and March makes no mention of the Stamp Bill at all: his concern was with two other matters, the Cambridge University election case, then before the Court of King's Bench, and the issue of the dismissal of army officers on political grounds.[1]

If the Stamp Bill meant little to the opposition in 1765, the administration always regarded it as a matter of the highest importance: but by the time the bill was introduced into Parliament, the motive had changed from revenue to the assertion of sovereignty. This difference can be seen in the attitude of the politician most directly concerned with the measure, Thomas Whately. On 5 November 1764 he explained to John Temple that finance was the motive behind the proposed bill.

I own I do not give entire credit to all the objections that are raised on your side of the water. I doubt they are inclined to object to all taxes, and yet some are absolutely necessary . . . some attention must be had to revenue, and the colonies must contribute their share . . . the stamp act seems the easiest mode of collecting a considerable sum.[2]

Three months later, on 9 February 1765, he was writing to Temple in quite different terms. 'The great measure of the session is the American Stamp Act. I give it the appellation of a great measure on account of the important point it establishes, the right of Parliament to lay an internal tax on the colonies. We wonder here that it was ever doubted. There is not a single Member of Parliament that will dispute it.'[3]

This change of emphasis had taken place during the interval between Whately's two letters. At a meeting with Treasury colleagues on 4 December 1764 Grenville had announced only financial reasons for the priority to be given to the bill in the coming session, as James Harris noted in this memorandum.

Mr. Grenville told us that as soon as the Parliament met and that land and malt were voted, we should vote the army, then immediately bring in the American Stamp Act (which it was computed would raise £100,000 a year and with that on molasses already past,

[1] B.M. Add. MSS. 32965, fos. 324–408; 32966, fos. 1–68.
[2] *Bowdoin–Temple Papers*, p. 37.   [3] *Bowdoin–Temple Papers*, pp. 49–51.

and other taxes, might make out perhaps £150,000, part of £350,000, the charge of our American army).[1]

News of the colonial protests against Parliament's right of taxation soon caused Grenville to take the characteristic step of seeking confirmation of the constitutional position. On 23 December he went to consult the most eminent lawyer in Britain, Lord Chief Justice Mansfield, and the next day he received this reassuring and practical reply.[2] 'Though the question certainly does not want this, or any other authority, yet it will be a striking alteration to ignorant people, and an unanswerable argument *ad homines*; and, therefore, I wish you would employ somebody to look with this view into the origin of their power to tax themselves and raise money at all.'

As news came of the colonial protests official opinion in Whitehall and Westminster hardened on this issue of Parliament's right to tax America. On 11 December 1764 the Board of Trade took into consideration the votes of the Massachusetts House of Representatives on 1, 8, 12, and 13 June and the address of the New York Assembly to their Lieutenant-Governor on 11 September; resolved 'that in the said votes and address, the Acts and resolutions of the British Parliament were treated with indecent disrespect, and principles of a dangerous nature and tendency adopted and avowed'; and decided to refer the papers to the Privy Council.[3] The Council, after the matter had been considered by its Committee of Plantations, resolved on 19 December that it was 'worthy the consideration of Parliament'.[4] The administration afterwards decided to establish the right of taxation by passing the Stamp Bill before referring these American papers to Parliament; the bill, Under-Secretary Edward Sedgwick told Edward Weston on 14 February 1765, would be 'the strongest instance, an internal tax'.[5] This decision, an apparent act of negligence by Secretary of State Halifax, was to expose the Grenville ministry the next year to the charge of having deliberately concealed from Parliament the potential danger of the colonial situation.[6]

---

[1] Malmesbury MSS., quoted by Tomlinson, M.A. Thesis, p. 120.
[2] *Grenville Papers*, ii. 478.   [3] *J.C.T.P. 1764–7*, pp. 122–3.
[4] *Acts P.C. Col.* iv. 692.   [5] *H.M.C. Weston Underwood*, p. 382.
[6] See below, pp. 225–6.

Before the Stamp Bill was introduced further evidence of colonial defiance was known to the administration. On 17 January 1765 the Board of Trade considered the votes of the New York Assembly in October 1764, and decided that they tended 'to excite a combination in the several colonies to oppose particular Acts and resolutions of the Parliament of Great Britain relative to the said colonies'.[1] The matter was referred to the Privy Council, which on 30 January also received official news of the riots the previous summer in Rhode Island and New York.[2] The Grenville ministry did not proceed with the Stamp Act in ignorance of colonial opinion, but thought the measure would be accepted under protest: the official view was reflected in this comment made by Edward Sedgwick to Weston on 28 February. 'None of the colonies have as yet denied the authority of the British Parliament to tax them, on the contrary several have expressly acknowledged it to be their duty to obey.'[3]

There was little mention of America in the House of Commons prior to the introduction of the stamp duty proposals. In the Committee of Supply on the navy on 21 January 1765 Charles Townshend chose to assert 'the supremacy of this country over the colonies: [he] would not have them emancipated'. Later in the same debate even Barré only urged politic restraint. 'America should pay, but would wish to wait. Our sovereignty should be acknowledged, but we should be careful not to destroy industry there, or drive them to a species of industry which might hurt us.'[4] Barré's caution presaged the opposition failure to make any direct challenge to the Stamp Bill, but Townshend's remark was taken up two days later in the Supply debate on the army by William Beckford, who said that it implied the Americans were slaves. Townshend explained that he had meant emancipated from the sovereignty of Great Britain. Beckford thereupon attacked Townshend for his confusing 'diarrhoea of words', a phrase that hurt deeply a man proud of his oratorical powers.[5]

---

[1] *J.C.T.P. 1764–7*, p. 139.
[2] *Acts P.C. Col.* iv. 384–7.
[3] *H.M.C. Weston Underwood*, p. 384.
[4] Harris Diary, 21 Jan. 1765.
[5] Harris Diary, 23 Jan. 1765. H. Walpole, *Memoirs*, ii. 34. Beckford's offensive phrase is quoted by both reporters.

The main debate on the stamp duty proposals took place not on the Stamp Bill itself, but on the preliminary resolutions introduced by Grenville in the Committee of Ways and Means on 6 February.[1] Before the House resolved into the Committee Grenville set the stage by moving that the instructions given to the Committee of Ways and Means on 7 March 1764 concerning an American revenue should be read out, and also the report that had been made from the Committee three days later that included the famous fifteenth resolution for American stamp duties. He then proposed an instruction to the Committee 'that they do consider of proper methods for raising a revenue in the British colonies and Plantations in America, towards further defraying the necessary charges of defending, protecting, and securing the same'.[2]

When the Committee was constituted Grenville began with a personal disclaimer that revealed his awareness of the novelty and significance of the step he was about to take. 'Proposed taxing America from public motive. Private considerations of his own choice would have prevented him if they had been consulted. Wishes those who had gone before him had marked out a path to him which he might more easily follow. His conduct would then have been less liable to misconstruction.' He discussed first the question of Parliament's right to tax the colonies.

Wished now to avoid that question if possible, because he thinks no person can doubt it. The objection of the colonies is from the general right of mankind not to be taxed but by their representatives. This goes to all laws in general. The parliament of Great Britain virtually represents the whole kingdom, not actually [the] great trading towns. The merchants of London and the East India Company are not represented. Not a twentieth part of the people are actually represented. All colonies are subject to the dominion of the mother country.

---

[1] The following account of the debate is based on *Ryder Diary*, pp. 253–61; Harris Diary, 6 Feb. 1765; H. Walpole, *Memoirs*, ii. 49–56; and four letters: (a) J. Ingersoll to T. Fitch. *Fitch Papers*, ii. 317–26. (b) R. Jackson to Fitch. *Fitch Papers*, ii. 316–17. (c) C. Garth to S. Carolina; printed Namier, *E.H.R.* 54 (1939), 649–50. (d) G. Onslow to Newcastle, B.M. Add. MSS. 32965, fos. 346–7. All quotations are from the *Ryder Diary*.

[2] *Commons Journals*, xxx. 90. *Ryder Diary*, p. 253.

D

Grenville had evidently taken the advice of Lord Mansfield, for he dealt in detail with the objections raised by individual colonies, showing that none had been granted exemption, by charter or otherwise, from Parliamentary taxation. He followed this up by citing such precedents for taxation as the Post Office Act of 1711, the 1729 act imposing a levy on seamen, and various customs duties, notably the Molasses Act of 1733 and the American Duties Act of 1764. Grenville ended this first part of his speech by telling members that he had gone into great detail 'to show the right, in consequence of the strange language he has met with in conversation and public writings upon this subject'.

Having prepared his constitutional ground Grenville went on to discuss the propriety and expediency of a colonial tax with regard to both Britain and America. All taxes met objections, like the recent cider tax in the west of England. 'The true way to relieve all is to make all contribute their proper share.' The cost of the navy had risen sharply, and this increase was incurred 'in a great measure for the service of North America'. He next dealt with the size of the army in the colonies. 'The military force in North America is said by many military men to be not sufficient. He never heard anybody say there was more than necessary.' An American tax would only be improper, Grenville declared, if it was unjust or too heavy: and he countered both objections, by rehearsing familiar arguments about the expenditure on colonial defence and by reminding the Committee of the light burden of existing colonial taxes and debts.

The next stage of Grenville's argument was to justify the particular method of taxation by stamp duties. The contention that they would arouse colonial opposition was one that could apply to all taxes.

Therefore if we reject this proposition now, we shall declare that we ought not to tax the colonies. And we need not declare after a year's time that we ought not, for then we cannot. As to taxing themselves, how can so many colonies fix the proportion which they shall pay themselves? Supposing each county was to do this in England . . . While they remain dependent, they must be subject to our legislature . . . they have in many instances encroached and claimed powers and privileges inconsistent with their situation as colonies.

If they are not subject to this burden of tax, they are not entitled to the privilege of Englishmen.

Two advantages of the stamp tax were that the revenue would increase in proportion to the prosperity of the colonies, and that it would require few officials to apply it; the tax would be largely self-enforcing, through the nullity of unstamped documents. Grenville ended by pointing out that the colonies themselves, even when asked, had failed to suggest any alternatives. 'He has enquired from North America whether they objected to this particular species of tax, and has not heard one gentleman propose any other . . . The law is founded on that great maxim, that protection is due from the governor, and support and obedience on the part of the governed.'[1]

Grenville's speech, described by Ingersoll as 'able and candid', opened a debate of twenty-eight speeches by eighteen different members.[2] The discussion was begun by William Beckford. 'Admits right of taxing the imports and exports of the colonies, and says the colonies all admit this principle. He approves of the tax laid last year.' But he then gave this warning. 'The North Americans do not think an internal and external duty the same.' Beckford attacked Grenville's principal arguments.

As to representation, all England is not represented, but it is a written part of our constitution, that it is so . . . No precedent found of foreign taxation but the Post Office, and that this [was] certainly for the convenience of the colonies themselves . . . The North Americans would be glad to be rid of the troops from the government and the expense of supporting them.

Beckford concluded by moving that the Chairman should leave the Chair, a procedural device to prevent any direct vote on the resolutions. This motion was seconded by Barré. 'We are working in the dark and the less we do the better . . . There are gentlemen in the House from the West Indies, but there are very few who know the circumstances of North America. We

---

[1] *Ryder Diary*, pp. 253–6. The Harris Diary confirms Ryder's report of Grenville's speech very closely.

[2] Ryder names seventeen speakers, Harris fourteen, Garth and Ingersoll six each, Horace Walpole only four.

know not yet the effect of the act passed last year. The tax intended is odious to all your colonies and they tremble at it.' After Richard Jackson and Thomas Townshend had spoken on the same side, Lord North reminded the Committee that the tax had already been postponed for a year, and that no colony had complained specifically of the method of taxation by stamp duties. Barré replied that some colonial resolutions were vague and others were not yet known. Liverpool M.P. Sir William Meredith then argued strongly for Beckford's motion.

The safety of this country consists in this with respect that we cannot lay a tax upon others without taxing ourselves. This is not the case in America. We shall tax them in order to ease ourselves . . . If we tax America we shall supersede the necessity of their assembling . . . This proposition agreed to last year that we might have more information given to us. The government do not want it, but private gentlemen do want it, and till he received this information he shall wish to adjourn the question.

Bristol M.P. Robert Nugent thereupon threw out the challenge that no one had objected to the principle of the tax. Barré made this delphic reply: 'he approved this tax as much as any internal tax'. He was generally understood not to have denied Parliament's right to tax the colonies; for John Temple was informed by a London correspondent that 'even that great advocate Col. Barry at the grand debates fell in with the whole House in that respect'.[1] Charles Garth obtained an assurance from Grenville that the colonies could submit petitions after the passage of the resolutions, and Rose Fuller opposed the tax on grounds of prudence. There followed the highlight of the debate in a famous exchange between Charles Townshend and Barré. Townshend began by declaring that he had 'heard with great pleasure the right of taxing America asserted and not disputed'. He could see no reason for delay, since there was no doubt either of Parliament's right to tax the colonies or of their ability to pay the tax; and he ended with remarks on the colonies that brought Barré to his feet. 'Planted with so much tenderness, governed with so much affection, and established with so much care and attention.' Barré,

[1] *Bowdoin–Temple Papers*, p. 46.

speaking for the fourth time that day, declared that he questioned the wisdom of provoking the colonies, not their ability to pay. 'We did not plant the colonies. Most of them fled from oppression. They met with great difficulty and hardship, but as they fled from tyranny here they could not dread danger there. They flourished not by our care but by our neglect. They have increased while we did not attend to them. They shrink under our hand.'[1]

Twelve of the eighteen speakers in the debate opposed the imposition of the stamp duties, but the main argument put forward was simple inexpediency. It was true that Beckford and Jackson had challenged Grenville on the question of the non-representation of the colonies; and that Beckford, Barré, and Fuller had doubted the validity of the colonial Post Office as a precedent for direct taxation. But even Beckford does not appear to have explicitly denied Parliament's right to tax America. Two agents did think he had done so: Jared Ingersoll told Governor Fitch that Beckford 'seemed to deny the authority of Parliament'; and Jackson's report to Fitch also said that Beckford had doubted Parliament's right to levy internal taxation on the colonies. The version of his speech by diarist Nathaniel Ryder suggests that Beckford was putting forward such a denial as the colonists' view rather than his own: certainly both Nugent and Charles Townshend claimed unanimity on the point after Beckford had already spoken. The Committee divided at 8 o'clock, when Beckford's motion was defeated by 245 votes to 49. It took the Committee until after 10 o'clock to go through the formality of voting the fifty-five separate resolutions. The small size of the minority was a disappointment to the opposition. George Onslow informed Newcastle that 'he had nothing particular to tell him' about the debate. 'We had a sad division on adjourning . . . Many of our people with them.' Ingersoll later described the minority as comprising 'West Indian gentlemen and a few others connected with America':[2] and there was an element of wishful thinking in his comment to Fitch. 'The truth is I believe some who inclined rather against the bill voted for it, partly because

[1] This is Ryder's account of the exchange, based on his shorthand notes. Barré's oft-quoted phrase about 'sons of liberty' appears only in Ingersoll's letter.

[2] Quoted Namier, *England in the Age of the American Revolution*, p. 240.

they are loth to break the measures of the ministry, and partly
because they dont undertake to inform themselves in the
fullest manner upon the subject.'

There was no debate when Chairman Hunter reported the
fifty-five resolutions to the House next day, and the Committee
appointed to draw up the bill consisted of the five Lords and
two Secretaries of the Treasury, and the Attorney and Solicitor
Generals.[1] Grenville presented the bill to the House on 13
February, when it received a formal first reading.[2] Opposition
to the measure was resumed two days later at the second
reading, the traditional stage both for petitions and for the
main debate on a bill.[3]

About 250 members were in the House on 15 February
when Rose Fuller presented a petition from Jamaica, declaring
that the inhabitants were not able to pay the tax. George
Grenville at once declared that no petition could be received
against proposed taxes, citing a precedent of 8 March 1733
concerning a Rhode Island petition against the Molasses Bill.
William Dowdeswell produced many contrary precedents
from before 1714: but Gilbert Elliot and procedural expert
Jeremiah Dyson both contended that the new rule had evolved
with the increasing financial business of the House and was
now firmly established; and it had certainly been the custom
since the Hanoverian Succession.[4] Sir William Meredith said
that the postponement of the Stamp Bill had been intended to
give the colonies time to petition. Grenville promptly denied
this claim; the bill had been 'postponed to give time for information not for opposition'. General Conway declared that
petitions did not interfere with Parliament's right to impose
taxation. On the contrary, the act of petitioning was an
implicit admission of the right.[5] This preliminary debate ended
when Rose Fuller withdrew the Jamaica petition; but three

---

[1] Harris Diary, 7 Feb. 1765; *Commons Journals*, xxx. 97–101.

[2] *Commons Journals*, xxx. 131.

[3] The following account of the proceedings on 15 Feb. is based on *Commons Journals*, xxx. 147–8; Harris Diary, 15 Feb. 1765; H. Walpole, *Memoirs*, ii. 56; and two letters: (a) C. Garth to S. Carolina, printed Namier, *E.H.R.* 54 (1939), 650–1. (b) J. Ingersoll to T. Fitch, *Fitch Papers*, ii. 332–5. All quotations are from the Harris Diary.

[4] See my *House of Commons in the Eighteenth Century*, pp. 69–71.

[5] Diarist Harris paid little attention to Conway's speech, but a version of it was later published in the colonies. Morgan, *Prologue to Revolution*, pp. 34–5.

more were produced, this time from North American colonies. Sir William Meredith offered one from Virginia agent Edward Montagu, Richard Jackson tendered one from 'the Governor and Company' of Connecticut, and Charles Garth one from three residents of South Carolina then in London. All asked the House not to pass the Stamp Bill, and those on behalf of Virginia and Connecticut implicitly challenged Parliament's right to tax the colonies. Garth, although he realized after the vote on 6 February that there was no chance of stopping the Stamp Bill, had drafted the South Carolina petition to avoid this mistake of inviting immediate rejection; he hoped to establish a precedent against future attempts to tax America without notice. These three petitions were a puny symbol of the massive protest building up in the colonies, only that from Connecticut having been drafted in America. Some petitions sent over from the colonies questioned Parliament's right of taxation so explicitly that no members were willing to submit them to the House:[1] and some agents were so bound by similarly unacceptable instructions that they were unable to draw up any suitable petitions at all.[2]

The other debate of the day took place on a motion by Meredith, seconded by Garth, for leave to bring up the Virginia petition. Charles Yorke began it with what Horace Walpole described as 'a set speech in favour of the bill'. He expounded the historical and practical justification, both for not receiving petitions against taxation and for Parliament's power over the colonies. They could only tax themselves in one of two ways, 'a federal union—God forbid that', or the allocation of quotas by Britain, a system that would lead to endless complaints of unfair proportions. 'Tis for the wisdom of Parliament, to settle everything here at home, and the petitions should be rejected.' Barré called the Stamp Bill 'inflammatory and dangerous . . . hopes to find a new system of liberty in America'. Richard Jackson, also arguing for reception of the petition, pointed out that the money was for the use of the new colonies and not the older British settlements. Jeremiah Dyson denied that men could be taxed only by the consent of their representatives.

---

[1] *H.M.C. Weston Underwood*, p. 382. The New York petition is printed in Morgan, *Prologue to Revolution*, pp. 8–14.

[2] C. Garth to South Carolina, printed Namier, *E.H.R.* 54 (1939), 650–1.

'The constitutional language is by common consent of Parliament.' He recited the precedents for Parliament's power to
tax and legislate for the colonies; but his argument marked a
shift from Grenville's contention that the colonies were represented. Even Rose Fuller now spoke against receiving the
petition; he was presumably influenced by the implicit challenge
to Parliament, and this point may have swayed the feeling of
members more than the formal arguments against petitions
about taxation. The opposition did not venture to divide the
House over the rejection successively of the three petitions,
Garth's 'decent' petition suffering the same fate as the others.
The Stamp Bill then received an unopposed second reading
without further discussion, and was committed for 18 February.
Thirteen members altogether had spoken on the petitions,
five for the ministry, seven against, and Rose Fuller on both
sides: but on the second reading of a bill with such momentous
consequences nothing of note had occurred. George Onslow
made this brief report to the Duke of Newcastle on the debates
of 15 February. 'I have no news for your Grace.'[1]

The Committee on the Stamp Bill lasted only one day,
18 February. The only information on the proceedings under
Chairman John Paterson is in Charles Garth's account to
South Carolina of his efforts to obtain alterations to the bill.
He failed to secure abolition or reduction of the duties on bills
of lading, assurance policies, and wine licences, but managed
to secure a reduction in the duty on newspaper advertisements
to 1s. By mistake this change was never made, as Benjamin
Franklin later told his printer-partner David Hall. 'The 2s.
for each advertisement was not reduced to 1s. as intended but
slipt in passing the bill.'[2] So many alterations and additions
were reported or made at the report stage of the bill, however,
that it was prolonged over two days, 19 and 21 February, and
Charles Garth vaguely referred to the whole process as 'the
Committee'. Among the extra clauses added to the bill on
21 February Garth claimed credit for that exempting bounty
warrants from stamp duty. He failed to mention two other
exemptions made then, of proclamations and of documents
for the purchase of Indian lands; nor did he refer to the

---

[1] B.M. Add. MSS. 32965, fo. 363.
[2] *Franklin Papers*, xii. 171.

important new clause added that day concerning the Vice-Admiralty Courts.[1]

The Grenville ministry had decided to enforce the Stamp Bill in those courts, despite the advice of Charles Yorke to Grenville against the step. In a letter of 17 February Yorke put forward two practical objections; the courts were 'paltry and corrupt', and the new one at Halifax too far away: and he added this argument of principle. 'The stamp duties have nothing of a maritime or commercial nature. The precedent may, in argument, be extended far, to other future taxes upon the colonies.'[2] The administration ignored this main argument, but decided to take account of the colonial objections to the remoteness of Halifax by the substitution of three courts at Boston, Philadelphia, and Charleston.[3] After the Stamp Act had become law the Treasury Board asked the Board of Trade to work out the details of the scheme,[4] and on 4 July formally submitted the proposals to the Privy Council, which referred the matter next day to its Committee on Plantation Affairs.[5] The plan then became a casualty of the change of ministry. The Rockingham administration never instigated a report from the Committee, and former members of the Grenville ministry took the opportunity to criticize their successors for this negligence. On 24 January 1766 Thomas Whately moved in the Commons for all Treasury papers on the subject since May 1765.[6] Lord Halifax raised the matter in the Lords debate of 11 March, and the opposition Lords Protest of that date against repeal of the Stamp Act criticized the ministry for allowing the plan to 'remain unexecuted in every part of it even to this day'.[7] The complete repeal of that act had the effect of nullifying this attempt to meet one colonial grievance.

The eventual failure to implement this provision was not known in early 1765, and the clause was to become the subject of attack during the final debate on the Stamp Bill. This took

---

[1] *Commons Journals*, xxx. 157, 160–1, 172–3; C. Garth to South Carolina, 22 Feb. 1765, partly printed by Namier, *E.H.R.* 54 (1939), 652. James Harris merely noted on 21 Feb., 'no particular business'.

[2] Quoted Wickwire, *British Subministers and Colonial America*, pp. 190–1.

[3] *Bowdoin–Temple Papers*, p. 56.

[4] *J.C.T.P. 1764–7*, pp. 185–6.   [5] *Acts P.C. Col.* iv. 664.

[6] The papers were submitted to the House on 31 Jan. *Commons Journals*, xxx. 496, 508.

[7] Hull and Temperley, *A.H.R.* 17 (1911–12), 581; *Lords Journals*, xxxi. 303.

D*

place over the third reading on 27 February. Thomas Townshend complained of Soame Jenyns's pamphlet *The Objections
to Taxation of Our American Colonies Considered.* 'Twas treating
the Americans with levity and insult.' He also raised the
subject of the seizure of ships trading with the colonies. Lord
North replied that the ships had been breaking the Navigation
Acts. The debate then centred on the Vice-Admiralty Courts.
William Beckford, Sir William Baker and other members
criticized them as acting without juries. They were defended
by several speakers, including Robert Nugent and George
Grenville, as having been established long ago by Parliament.
Grenville asked why Townshend had mentioned only Jenyns's
pamphlet and ignored the many libels on government: and
he took this last opportunity to deny opposition charges of
undue haste in introducing the bill, and to assert once again
Parliament's right to tax the colonies. Richard Jackson spoke
against the Stamp Bill, but in favour of the Vice-Admiralty
Courts. The bill then received a third reading and passage without a vote.[1] There was no debate on it in the House of Lords,[2]
which informed the Commons on 8 March that the measure
had passed without amendment. The Stamp Bill received the
royal assent by commission on 22 March, George III being ill.[3]

The Stamp Act had passed without a vote against it, after
only fifty members[4] had supported the motion to postpone
the preliminary resolutions on 6 February. That test of
Parliamentary opinion had deterred both 'the formed opposition' and the individual 'friends of America' from indulging
in more than desultory sniping at and detailed criticism of
the bill. Altogether fifteen members had spoken against the
resolutions or the bill, but no one had directly challenged
Parliament's right to tax the colonies. Jared Ingersoll had
good reason for his pessimistic conclusion about British political
attitudes towards the American colonies.[5]

---

[1] Harris Diary, 27 Feb. 1765; *Commons Journals*, xxx. 192–3.

[2] The Lords Protest of 11 Mar. 1766 stated that the Stamp Act had passed that
House 'without one dissentient voice'. *Lords Journals*, xxxi. 303.

[3] *Commons Journals*, xxx. 235, 293.   [4] Including the one teller in Committee.

[5] Ingersoll to Fitch, 6 Mar. 1765; *Ingersoll Papers*, p. 317. Ingersoll told Fitch
that Beckford and Conway had challenged Parliament's right to tax America:
but surviving reports of their respective speeches on 6 and 15 Feb. do not bear out
this interpretation.

Here I feel myself obliged to say that except the gentlemen interested in the West Indies and a few members that happen to be particularly connected with some of the colonies and a few of the heads of the minority who are sure to athwart and oppose the ministry in every measure of what nature or kind soever, I say except these few persons so circumstanced there are scarce any people here, either within doors or without, but what approve the measures now taking which regard America.

If Americans were to accept direct Parliamentary taxation at all, they could not reasonably object to the Stamp Act. The total tax envisaged was small: the method of a wide range of stamp duties had been chosen to provide an equitable distribution of the burden: and the detailed variations from and reductions of the corresponding British duties had been designed to meet the different conditions in the colonies. All this care to satisfy American susceptibilities was to be matched by two decisions concerning the implementation of the measure: that all money raised by the tax, and also that arising from the Duties Act, would stay in the colonies; and that the Act itself was to be administered by leading men resident in the various colonies, not by officials sent from Britain. The first point had been decided before the bill was introduced into Parliament, and Grenville explained the proposed procedure to the House of Commons at the first reading on 13 February.[1] After the passage of the Stamp Act Whately and Jenkinson took the necessary technical steps to prevent the American revenue being remitted to Britain by ordering that it should be handed over to the Deputy Paymasters of the forces in the colonies. There was never any foundation for the contemporary and historical myth that the British taxation would drain money from the colonies. According to Whately's estimate, the legislation covered only one-third of the army costs in America, and Britain would need to send more money there to cover the balance than she had done before the late war.[2]

The British Stamp Office was responsible for the detailed administrative arrangements necessary before the Stamp Act could go into effect on 1 November; and the Stamp Commis-

---

[1] Harris Diary, 13 Feb. 1765.
[2] Sosin, *A.H.R.* 63 (1954–5), 918–23.

sioners consulted various Americans in London, including Benjamin Franklin, on the subject.[1] The colonies were divided into nine districts, each with an inspector answerable to a new American Stamp Office of five Commissioners in London. The key post was that of Stamp Distributor, one being appointed for each colony.[2] The decision to appoint only Americans of standing within their own colony to administer the Stamp Act at this level[3] was implemented as soon as the act had been passed. Since the colonial resistance to the measure was not foreseen by Americans in London at the time, there seems to have been some competition for posts that would provide their incumbents with income, patronage, and prestige. The colonial agents appear to have been the main channel of patronage, although on 24 February 1766 Grenville was to tell the House of Commons that some Stamp Distributors had been appointed 'at the recommendation of the assemblies, as Col. Mercer by that of Virginia'.[4] George Mercer was one of three Americans then in London to obtain this appointment for himself, the others being Jared Ingersoll from Connecticut and George Meserve from New Hampshire.[5] If prominent and well-informed colonists in London, some of them like Franklin and Ingersoll newly arrived from America, could not anticipate the violent resistance to the Stamp Act Grenville's administration cannot be blamed for lack of foresight.

[1] *Franklin Papers*, xii. 99–100.
[2] For administrative details see Wickwire, *British Subministers and Colonial America*, pp. 107–10; and Gipson, *British Empire*, x. 276–8.
[3] *Bowdoin–Temple Papers*, pp. 52–3.
[4] Harris Diary, 24 Feb. 1766.
[5] For the appointment of Stamp Distributors see Gipson, *British Empire*, x. 277–8; and Sosin, *Agents and Merchants*, p. 62.

The Later American Policy
of the Grenville Ministry

THE Stamp Act was not the only colonial legislation of 1765. The session saw the passage of two other important measures, an American Mutiny Act and a Trade Act. The first of these was to be the cause of friction between Britain and the colonies after the repeal of the Stamp Act.

That an army should be maintained in America was not a subject of dispute at Westminster, and no direct challenge in Parliament was ever made on the subject; but the question of the American army was raised in the debate on the annual army estimates in the Committee of Supply on 5 December 1763. Secretary at War Welbore Ellis moved the same establishment as before, 'some trivial changes excepted here and in America. Mentioned the utility of forts there, not only as defences but as places for marts and fairs, where the Indians might bring their furs.' Charles Townshend, then in opposition, raised objections over the problems of supplying the army in America. His attempt to embarrass the ministry over colonial obstruction in the matter proved to be a damp squib. Ellis provided explanations of official policy that apparently satisfied the Committee, and informed members that 'a rotation was intended of these American regiments, that though residing in America, they might still be a British army'.[1]

Nothing was said on the American army in the Supply debate on the army estimates in the next session, on 23 January 1765, although William Beckford did touch on American taxation in a rambling attack on the administration.[2] That same day General Gage, the Commander-in-Chief in America, wrote to Secretary of State Halifax the report from which the American Mutiny Act of 1765 originated.[3] This legislation was precipi-

[1] Harris Diary, 5 Dec. 1763.
[2] Harris Diary, 23 Jan. 1765; H. Walpole. *Memoirs*, ii. 34–6; *Letters*, vi. 176–9. For references to America in this debate see above, p. 88.
[3] *Gage Corr*. i. 49.

tate and perhaps unnecessary. Some difficulties for the army had certainly occurred in America, especially over the quartering of soldiers. New York was the colony most affected by the presence of troops, for it contained the main port of arrival. The last quartering act passed by the colony's Assembly had expired on 1 January 1764, and in November of that year the Assembly refused to order the customary supplies of firewood for the local barracks. Elsewhere there were problems of transport and desertion, but Gage seems to have generalized the situation from a few instances of colonial obstruction and resistance.[1] The Grenville ministry took his report at face value and acted promptly to implement most of his proposals.

Gage's report arrived on 1 March, and Secretary of State Halifax forwarded it the next day to Secretary at War Ellis, asking for his opinion. Ellis replied on 7 March to Halifax's American Under-Secretary Edward Sedgwick, stating that except for some clauses the Mutiny Act did not apply to the colonies. Ellis therefore thought that legislation should be introduced to put the army in America on the same footing as in Britain, and he also made this detailed proposal. 'As the public-houses in America are few, and unable to contain the troops, it will certainly be useful and necessary for the magistrates there to have power given them to quarter the troops upon private houses, where there are no barracks, or where the barracks and public-houses cannot contain them.'[2] On 11 March Halifax directed Ellis to draft and introduce into Parliament a bill to extend the provisions of the Mutiny Act to America, together with such additional clauses as were necessary.[3]

George III displayed more political sagacity than his Secretary of State. When the King was informed of the proposed bill on 9 March he was so concerned about the intention of billeting soldiers on private houses that he at once forwarded the relevant papers to George Grenville for his chief minister's immediate consideration. 'Lord Halifax appears to disregard the noise that may be made here in Parliament by extending

---

[1] For the colonial background see Shy, *Towards Lexington*, pp. 163–84.

[2] *Cal. Home Office Papers, 1760–65*, p. 529. Ellis owed this suggestion to Gage or his subordinate Lieutenant-Colonel James Robertson, *Gage Corr.* ii. 262–6.

[3] *Cal. Home Office Papers, 1760–65*, p. 534.

the quartering soldiers in private houses in America. As I think that at a time like this all measures should be duly weighed before they are undertaken, I send them to you before I return them to the office.' The King's letter was sent at 4.30 p.m.[1] Grenville's reply was written at 11.55 p.m. the same day.

On the short examination which I have hitherto been able to give to the letters which have passed between Lord Halifax and the Secretary of War, it seems to me that the clause which your Majesty mentions for the extending the power of quartering soldiers in the private houses in America, is that which is by far the most likely to create difficulties and uneasiness, and therefore ought certainly to be thoroughly weighed and considered before any step is taken in it, especially as the quartering of soldiers upon the people against their wills is declared by the Petition of Right to be contrary to law.

He then offered a solution. The same problem of an insufficient supply of barracks and public houses existed in Scotland, and the annual Mutiny Act therefore had a clause 'to quarter the soldiers in Scotland in such houses as they might have been quartered in there at the time of the Union; perhaps some general words of the like nature referring to the former usage may be the properest precedent to follow in this instance'.[2] Grenville's advice was followed, and a suitably vague clause was inserted in the draft bill. It stipulated that in the absence of adequate barracks or public houses any two magistrates could 'billet the residue of such troops and forces in such manner as had hitherto been practiced to billet His Majesty's Troops in His Majesty's Dominions in America'.[3]

This wording still left open the possibility of billeting on private houses, and failed to avert the anticipated criticism in Parliament. Welbore Ellis moved the House of Commons for leave to introduce such a bill on 29 March, and together with Thomas Gore, the Commissary-General of musters, was formally instructed to prepare it: but William Beckford and Sir William Baker had at once objected to any quartering of soldiers in private houses, and other speakers urged that

[1] *Grenville Papers*, iii. 11–12.

[2] *Grenville Papers*, iii. 12–14.

[3] P.R.O. 30/8/97, fos. 42–4. This document is a working draft of the bill, and shows alterations made during its progress through the Commons.

adequate barracks should be built or obtained as soon as possible.[1] When Ellis presented the bill to the House on 1 April, and the vague billeting clause was made public, it was attacked by several speakers, including Beckford, Baker, John Huske, and Rose Fuller. Diarist James Harris, sitting on the Treasury Bench, laconically noted that they 'talked of Magna Carta, dragoons, liberty, etc.'. George Onslow reported to the Duke of Newcastle during the debate that at 8.30 p.m. the House was still 'sitting on this *strange Mutiny Bill* for America, which gives power to quarter in private houses. We have had a great deal of good talk, especially by Baker. I fancy we shall soon divide.' There was no division on the first reading, but Onslow himself tested the opinion of the House by a motion that the bill should be printed. This was defeated by 55 votes to 19, Charles Townshend being one of the tellers for the minority; and the House finally adjourned at 11.15 p.m.[2] The next day John Huske proposed that the relevant correspondence of General Gage, or extracts therefrom, should be laid before the House. In the short debate that followed this motion it was opposed as being unfair to Gage, and Ellis offered to show the papers to any members interested. He did so, and Huske withdrew his proposal.[3]

The second reading of the bill had been ordered for 4 April. On that day Charles Garth presented a petition from Virginia agent Edward Montagu, asking that he might be heard by counsel against those parts of the bill that authorized the billeting of soldiers in private houses. Beckford, Baker, and other members spoke in favour of receiving the petition. George Grenville cited the Scottish practice, not an analogy likely to appeal to an eighteenth-century House of Commons. Thomas Townshend spoke warmly against Scottish precedents, and although the House refused to accept Montagu's petition the second reading of the bill was postponed until 19 April, after the Easter recess.[4]

The administration took this step to avoid a Parliamentary

---

[1] Harris Diary, 29 Mar. 1765. *Commons Journals*, xxx. 321.

[2] For the debate see *Commons Journals*, xxx. 329; Harris Diary, 1 Apr. 1765; and Onslow's letter to Newcastle, B.M. Add. MSS. 32966, fo. 136.

[3] Harris Diary, 2 Apr. 1765; *Commons Journals*, xxx. 334-5.

[4] Harris Diary, 4 Apr. 1765; H. Walpole, *Memoirs*, ii. 65; *Commons Journals*, xxx. 339, 343-4.

storm over the bill. There was a danger that the determined resistance of the colonial agents and of the nascent American lobby in the House would be reinforced by the two opposition factions of Newcastle and Pitt. Newcastle's friends had already taken the opportunity to harass the administration over the issue, and the possibility developed that even Pitt might be sufficiently roused to attend the House of Commons. After John Calcraft visited Pitt at Hayes on 14 April he reported to Lord Shelburne the next day that Pitt was 'strong against the American Mutiny Bill, as an oppression they ought not to be subjected to, and in a great measure unnecessary'.[1] The ministry already anticipated trouble in Parliament over a proposed Regency Bill,[2] and administration compliance with pressure over the billeting clause in the American Mutiny Bill was thought by the opposition to be merely one of a number of steps to avoid controversy then on other matters.[3]

Foremost among the colonial agents active in the matter was Charles Garth, who on 5 April wrote to South Carolina an account of the resistance he was organizing to the bill.

I have taken every opportunity of giving it all the opposition in my power . . . It has been twice the subject of four or five hours debate already . . . I have sent to the merchants to acquaint them with the purport of it, leaving it to their discretion what steps they will choose to take but not without a hint what I think their friends in America have a right to expect from them upon this occasion.

Garth was acting in concert with Edward Montagu, and hoped to organize resistance to the measure from 'gentlemen connected with America'. He was invited to meet some of the merchants to explain and comment on the bill, with the result that 'the body of merchants trading to America appointed a Select Committee to meet every evening to consider of the most effectual method to avoid a measure so oppressive in its tendency'. Charles Garth and fellow M.P. Richard Glover were invited to attend this Committee and were appointed by it to see George Grenville on the subject. Garth subsequently reported to South Carolina that 'Mr. Grenville gave us an

---

[1] Fitzmaurice, *Shelburne*, i. 225.
[2] For this bill see below, pp. 116–8.
[3] B.M. Add. MSS. 32966, fo. 215.

audience of two hours and dismissed us with the assurance that he would talk with the Secretary at War upon it, and endeavour that the Bill should be altered to our satisfaction'. Welbore Ellis promptly made an appointment with Garth, who took with him Benjamin Franklin and Jared Ingersoll as representatives of more northerly colonies. Garth afterwards told South Carolina of the happy end to the story. 'Mr. Ellis went through the whole bill with us, and altered those parts we excepted against to our satisfaction. I communicated the alterations to the merchants and the rest of the agents, who approving thereof, the bill was passed agreeably thereunto, without any further opposition.'[1]

Garth's letters and a palpably inaccurate account by Lord Shelburne two years later[2] have caused historians to see this episode as an example of successful pressure upon the British government by the colonial agents and their merchant allies.[3] Some modification to this view is necessary. The potential threat of Parliamentary embarrassment was a more important reason for the ministerial concession than the role of the colonial agents. The decision was not made in the way described by Garth, and the administration had already been taking steps to alter the controversial part of the bill before Ellis met the agents.[4] Early in April Charles Jenkinson consulted Thomas Pownall and Benjamin Franklin on the subject. Pownall claimed success in solving the quartering problem in Massachusetts when governor of that colony from 1757 to 1759, and now suggested the same plan for all the colonies. On 11 April Jenkinson reported progress to Grenville, then out of town.

I have talked with Governor Pownall concerning the clause for billeting soldiers on America. He will furnish me with the printed

---

[1] Garth's letters of 5 Apr. and 25 May 1765 to the Committee of Correspondence in South Carolina were quoted and cited by Namier, *E.H.R.* 54 (1939), 641–2. Franklin's papers contain a draft request to Ellis for an audience from Glover and Barlow Trecothick, representing the Committee of North American Merchants. *Franklin Papers*, xii. 107n.

[2] This is in a letter sent by Shelburne on 14 Feb. 1767 to Pitt, by then Lord Chatham. Fitzmaurice, *Shelburne*, i. 311. Ellis had sent Shelburne information on the subject on 10 Feb. 1767. Gipson, *British Empire*, xi. 42n.

[3] Namier, *E.H.R.* 54 (1939), 641–2; Sosin, *Agents and Merchants*, p. 35.

[4] The date of the meeting is unknown, but it does not appear to have taken place by 18 Apr. *Franklin Papers*, xii. 107, 118–20.

Bill which he passed at Boston for this purpose; and he and Mr. Franklin have been framing a clause on the same plan to be passed here; this he has promised to give me, and I will send them both by the next messenger.[1]

Grenville replied two days later.

I approve extremely of Governor Pownall's meeting with Mr. Franklin in order to form a clause for billeting soldiers in America, for I own I have always thought it very disagreeable to put it upon the footing it was proposed if it can be avoided which I think may be done in some shape or other by making provisions of a less exceptionable nature. I wish to see the clause as soon as may be after it is formed.[2]

This letter crossed with one the same day from Jenkinson. 'I send by this messenger a large packet from Governor Pownall. It relates to the clause for quertering the troops in America. I hope that you will find it of use to you, and that it will strike out some lights which may relieve you from the difficulties of that affair.'[3]

The solution in the final form of the bill was a clause enacting that if there were insufficient barracks or ale-houses for soldiers in any area they could be billeted in 'uninhabited houses, outhouses, barns or other buildings'. This was substituted for the clause authorizing the previous colonial practice, which had itself replaced the original plan for billeting in private houses. Since the soldiers were to be put in these temporary or permanent barracks, and not in billets, a further clause stipulated that they should be provided with 'fire, candles, vinegar and salt, bedding, utensils for dressing their victuals, and some beer or cider . . . without paying anything for the same'. This was to be the controversial part of the bill, but in 1765 colonial opposition to the measure was not anticipated

---

[1] B.M. Add. MSS. 38304, fo. 134; printed *Jenkinson Papers*, pp. 358–9. 'Franklin' appears in the letter as 'Frankland', but the letter is a copy, not the original. Tomlinson has argued convincingly that there was an error of transcription and that Pownall's colleague was not Thomas Frankland, M.P., although he was a Vice-Admiral who had served in American waters and married an American wife. *Additional Grenville Papers*, p. 258.

[2] Grenville to Jenkinson, 13 Apr. 1765, Grenville Letter-Books, Vol. 2: printed Tomlinson, *Additional Grenville Papers*, p. 258.

[3] *Jenkinson Papers*, p. 360.

after these alterations. Grenville, when informing Ellis on 27 April that he had no objection to this provisions clause, mentioned that he had told Richard Glover and London merchant Barlow Trecothick of the proposal. 'I thought they seemed to acquiesce in it and therefore think it right that the clauses should be prepared and proposed in that manner to which I hope there will be no substantial objection.'[1]

The bill received a second reading on 19 April, and was committed for 26 April. The Committee stage, when the changes would actually be made to the bill, was then postponed until 30 April, and was the scene for the last debate on the measure. James Harris noted that the bill, 'tho' totally disarmed of its offensive clause, the quartering soldiers, in marches and in cases of necessity, upon private houses, was yet battled clause by clause by Thomas Townshend, and those two disinterested patriots, Alderman Baker and Huske. . . . There was no division, but the affair was not over till ten o'clock.' The bill, with the amendments, was reported the next day, and passed the Commons on 3 May, receiving the royal assent on 15 May.[2] It was later to be ground for surprise and indignation in Britain that the American Mutiny Act, deliberately altered to meet colonial objections, should nevertheless have become a grievance.

The American Duties Act of 1764 had included not only the well-known sugar and molasses duties but also a variety of other trade regulations concerning both duties and methods of enforcement. It was followed by a similar but less important measure the next year, the American Trade Act of 1765: this was intended, so Whately told John Temple, 'to remove all reasonable objections to the act of last year'.[3] Although it contained further steps against smuggling, other clauses were the result not of official initiative but of suggestions made to the administration for the encouragement of colonial trade.

---

[1] Grenville to Ellis, 27 Apr. 1765; Grenville Letter-Books, Vol. 2: printed Tomlinson, *Additional Grenville Papers*, p. 266. The text of the controversial parts of the American Mutiny Act may be found in Jensen, *American Colonial Documents*, pp. 656–8.

[2] Harris Diary, 30 Apr. 1765; *Commons Journals*, xxx. 350, 383, 391, 395, 401, 421, 426.

[3] *Bowdoin–Temple Papers*, p. 53.

The ministry was prepared to consider such proposals, but not any alteration of the molasses duty imposed for revenue, even though colonial protests were already being made that the 3*d*. duty was as effective a prohibition as the former one of 6*d*. The motive behind these complaints was political rather than economic, for the price of molasses in the colonies showed no significant change as a result of the Duties Act.[1] This information, in so far as it was known in Britain, must have seemed confirmation of the ministerial argument that the French planters would be forced to reduce their molasses prices. When Grenville had said this in debate on 22 March 1764 William Beckford had agreed:[2] and on 12 January 1765 Charles Jenkinson commented to the Boston Controller of Customs Benjamin Hellawell that 'the French who have no other method of disposing of them would be forced to pay the duty and not the people of the colonies who purchase them'.[3] Such an interpretation of the situation was later to be found optimistic. That the stability of molasses prices in North America was due to the continuance of widespread smuggling is shown by the failure of the 3*d*. duty to produce the revenue anticipated. The administration had appropriated £60,000 as the expected income from this source:[4] but the molasses duty yielded only £5,200 in 1764 and £4,090 in 1765.[5]

The Grenville ministry, while adamant on this point and indignant at colonial attacks on Parliament's right of taxation, was nevertheless responsive to suggestions that would improve colonial economy and trade. Benjamin Franklin, for his part, balanced such concessions against the imposition of the Stamp Act: when informing a Philadelphia correspondent of that measure on 14 February he added that 'the Parliament will however ease us in some particulars relating to our commerce'.[6] Here was the concept of an imperial legislature concerned for the welfare of all the royal dominions, although no one doubted

[1] Sosin, *Agents and Merchants*, pp. 48–9. The price in Boston actually fell, because of the excessive purchases made before the Duties Act came into force. *Jenkinson Papers*, p. 347n.
[2] Above, p. 58.
[3] B.M. Add. MSS. 38304, fos. 111–13; printed *Jenkinson Papers*, pp. 345–7. This and other similar opinions are cited by Sosin, *Agents and Merchants*, p. 48.
[4] Clark, *Rise of the British Treasury*, p. 137.
[5] T.1/434, fo. 53; printed Gipson, *British Empire*, x. 242n.
[6] *Franklin Papers*, xii. 68.

that the interests of Britain herself would take priority. The Treasury maintained a general control of policy by the practice of selecting for examination by the Board of Trade only certain papers from among the mass of petitions, proposals and suggestions submitted to it. By February,[1] for example, the Treasury had decided on legislation to assist the import of colonial lumber, and Jenkinson sent the appropriate petition to the Board on 19 March. This memorial of the 'merchants trading to the plantations in America' also mentioned such other matters as inter-colonial trade and the enforcement of customs regulations by the search of ships at sea, but the Board was directed to examine only the request for a bounty on American fur and timber imported into Britain. The Board of Trade considered the matter on 26 March, and heard merchants in support of the change on six later occasions before approving resolutions on 25 April to allow bounties on various wood imports from America.[2] On 2 April the merchants attending the Board produced another memorial, asking for the encouragement of iron imports from America to be paid from a levy of 40s. a ton on Swedish iron imports. The Board heard evidence on this subject then and on three subsequent days. On 22 April memorials were produced in support from iron manufacturers of London, Birmingham, Wolverhampton, Walsall, and Willenhall; but a letter was read from Sheffield announcing opposition to the proposal.[3] This killed the plan. The Board came to no resolution on the subject, and the only clause in the Trade Bill concerning the colonial iron trade was one permitting the extension of imports from London to the whole country. The Board of Trade also refused an application for a modification of the Hat Act of 1732 to allow hats to be taken from one colony to another. It was made by the hat manufacturers in Glasgow, Coventry and other towns: but on 30 April the Board ruled that the matter was too important to be considered so late in the Parliamentary session, and added that in any case the change would be of doubtful benefit to British manufacturers.[4]

---

[1] Minchinton, *V.M.H.B.* 73 (1965), 146.

[2] *J.C.P.T. 1764–7*, pp. 162, 164, 167, 169. The Treasury estimated that the cost would be over £10,000 a year. B.M. Add. MSS. 38337, fos. 1–3.

[3] *J.C.T.P. 1764–7*, pp. 164, 167–8.

[4] *J.C.T.P. 1764–7*, pp. 170–1.

The Trade Bill contained corrections as well as additions to the Duties Act of 1764. One grievance was removed by the exemption of undecked boats of under 20 tons engaged in coastal trade from the need to have cockets. Another restriction in the 1764 act now to be repealed was the prohibition on the direct export of colonial iron and lumber to Ireland. This had been a regulation unpopular both there and in America. It had puzzled Benjamin Franklin, since those goods had been carried as ballast for the conveyance of flax seed to Ireland; and Pennsylvania instructed agent Richard Jackson to seek repeal of the prohibition.[1] The protests from the merchants of Cork and Belfast probably carried more weight at the Board of Trade, for the Board's decision on 25 April to permit the resumption of such commerce came after the presentation of memorials from the two Irish ports.[2]

Charles Jenkinson was responsible for incorporating all these decisions into one bill.[3] On 13 April he reported progress to Grenville. 'I have gone over the American Bill of this year. I do not send it to you, as there must be many amendments made in it before it is worthy of your perusal.' After asking for Grenville's instructions on some matters of detail, Jenkinson concluded with remarks that show that the Board of Trade had the final voice on detailed policy; for his expectations differed from the Board's decisions.

The Board of Trade have promised that I should have their sentiments on the granting a bounty on timber and iron on Monday. I understand that they will propose a small bounty on timbers, and with respect to iron, they will propose a duty on Swedish ore which may answer the charge of a bounty they wish to have given to America.[4]

The Board of Trade was to be late in its decisions, but on 29 April a motion was made in the House of Commons for leave to introduce a bill 'for more effectually securing and encouraging the trade of his Majesty's American dominions'. The passage of the bill was a formality, since the Treasury and Board of

---

[1] *Franklin Papers*, xi. 235, 351.   [2] *J.C.T.P. 1764–7*, pp. 106, 111, 169.
[3] His papers contain an abstract of clauses in the draft bill, with comments. B.M. Add. MSS. 38337, fos. 1–3.
[4] B.M. Add. MSS. 38304, fos. 135–6.

Trade had taken care to eliminate any controversial proposals, and it received the royal assent on 25 May.[1]

It is common for historians to assume or postulate that the colonial measures of Grenville's ministry constituted an 'American programme'. To put forward such a concept is to stamp too modern an image on Georgian politics. Policy for British ministers in the eighteenth century involved the solution of existing problems rather than more positive thinking. That Grenville's administration gave so much attention to North America was due less to his personal initiative than to the problems he inherited in 1763. The successful war had left Britain with vast new territories for which it was necessary to devise policies: and its conclusion provided the opportunity to tackle other long-standing American problems that had hitherto been ignored or shelved in an era of wars and international crises. The most obvious instance concerned the measures taken to combat the frequent and widespread evasion by the older American colonies of the trade laws, for they had long been advocated by officials and informed politicians. Much of what Grenville's administration did with regard to imperial problems would have been done by any ministry in office from 1763.

Nor does the idea of a 'Grenville programme' for America stand up to detailed examination. It implies a coherence about the administration's colonial measures that did not exist. They sprang from diverse antecedents. The Proclamation of 1763 was in substance based on earlier wartime decisions. The policy of maintaining an army in America, and the public commitment to finance it by a colonial tax, were both legacies of the Bute administration. Some such legislation as the Currency Act had also been threatened by that ministry, and the final initiative for the measure itself came from an independent M.P. The Mutiny Act was prompted by the request of the army Commander-in-Chief in North America, and some of the trade laws adopted during these years owed their origin to outside pressures on the ministry.

[1] *Commons Journals*, xxx. 387–8, 392–3, 404, 407, 419–20, 423, 427, 432, 434. The trade resolutions were reprinted by Almon, *Debates*, vii. 34–5. For summaries of the act see Gipson, *British Empire*, x. 280; and Clark, *Rise of the British Treasury*, p. 119.

Even the argument that these measures must at least all have obtained cabinet approval is one of doubtful validity. The discussion of the Proclamation on 16 September 1763 shows that it would be unwise to assume that Grenville's voice was always dominant there:[1] and cabinet sanction was often merely formal approval of policies formulated by politicians of lesser rank, permanent officials, and even unofficial advisers, in such departments as the Board of Trade, the Treasury and the Secretary of State's Office. Yet after all qualifications have been made there can be no doubt that Grenville left his personal mark on American policy. Only an administration directed by a conscientious and industrious minister would have attempted so much in so short a time; there was no pause to assess the effect of early measures before new ones were introduced. A man so concerned with finance and legal right must have been especially shocked at the disorder and defiance of authority revealed in the American scene; the Stamp Act was intended to redress this situation as much as to raise money. Hence the comment attributed to an unknown contemporary official. 'Mr. Grenville lost America because he read the American despatches, which his predecessors had never done.'[2]

Grenville's American measures had aroused no real controversy in Britain. Criticism and resistance had come from the handful of agents, merchants, and politicians who comprised the American interest at Westminster, but American policy had not been a subject of dispute between government and opposition. Pitt had been absent from Parliament, and his hostility to some of the American measures was a matter of repute not confirmed by his own conduct. Little resistance to American taxation had come from the main opposition faction headed by Newcastle, soon to form a ministry under Rockingham. Their behaviour towards the American Duties Bill of 1764, indeed, had embraced a willingness to support the advocacy of more taxation by Charles Townshend. They played little part in the Parliamentary opposition to the Stamp Bill, and their accession to office did not necessarily imply a change in American policy. Only the man who was to become Chancellor of the Exchequer had voiced any uneasiness about

---

[1] Above, p. 43.
[2] *Rockingham Memoirs*, i. 249.

the political consequences of the American taxation: William Dowdeswell, replying to Grenville's Budget speech on 27 March 1765, had 'talked of the danger of provoking the colonies'.[1] It was nevertheless important that at the time of the Stamp Act Crisis there should have come to power an administration not committed in any way to the measures that had provoked the discontent, and prepared to solve the problem by conciliation. A continuation of the Grenville ministry for another year might well have caused the War of American Independence to start nine years earlier.

[1] Harris Diary, 27 Mar. 1765.

8   The Change of Ministry in 1765

THE partnership of George III and George Grenville founded in the autumn of 1763 lasted little more than a year. By the beginning of 1765 the minister had began to notice a lack of cordiality and confidence in the King's attitude towards him.[1] The last weeks of 1764 and the early months of 1765 saw a series of patronage issues in which Grenville's recommendations were refused.[2] This antipathy of George III towards Grenville was to become implacable. It did not arise over policy, although the King later made this complaint about the Grenville ministry. 'Little business done—no foreign system—the colonies and new conquests neglected—a great scene.'[3] In so far as this comment concerned the American situation, it was a criticism that Grenville had not done enough about the colonies, surely a unique ground of attack on that minister's American policy! This was a retrospective attempt to rationalize and justify a personal antipathy. Grenville's offence in the King's eyes was not only that he demanded too much in patronage matters or that he was tedious and verbose in the royal closet. It was his manner of asking, deemed 'insolence' by George III. In the King's own later account of the change of ministry he recalled that 'no office fell vacant in any department that Mr. G. did not declare he could not serve if the man he recommended did not succeed'.[4] The issue at stake was once again the role of Lord Bute, for places demanded by Grenville were being given to persons close to the royal favourite. The King's behaviour appeared to be a breach of the promises he had made to Grenville in 1763: and Grenville regarded it as not only damaging to his position as minister but also as a symptom of unconstitutional influence behind the throne.[5]

---

[1] *Grenville Papers*, ii. 535; iii. 112, 115–16.
[2] For some examples see *Grenville Papers*, ii. 523; iii. 122, 126; *Corr. of George III*, i. 170–1.
[3] B.M. Add. MSS. 35428, fo. 97. The comment was made to Charles Yorke.
[4] *Corr. of George III*, i. 164.
[5] The estrangement between George III and Grenville is more fully discussed in Tomlinson, M.A. Thesis, pp. 156–64; and in Brooke, *King George III*, pp. 106–9.

George III for his part resented the enforced separation
from Bute, particularly during his serious illness of February
and March 1765. This was not the attack of insanity so long
assumed by historians: the King was mentally well and trans-
acted business throughout the period of his confinement.[1]
But the event alarmed both George III and many contemporaries, and the King decided upon an immediate Regency Bill
to provide for his early death. The illness may also have made
him resolve finally to be rid of Grenville: certainly he saw in
the negotiations for the bill the opportunity to initiate a change
of ministry.

The choice of the potential Regent was a decision of some
delicacy. The King's eldest brother Edward, Duke of York,
was now of age; and in any case bad health excluded from
consideration the King's uncle the Duke of Cumberland, then
only forty-five years old. George III feared another clash such
as had occurred over the Regency Bill of 1751, when partisans
of his mother, the Princess Dowager of Wales, and of Cumberland had been ranged on opposite sides. Once again a sovereign
had to choose between the mother of the heir apparent and the
nearest adult male in succession to the throne. From the first
George III intended to nominate the Queen and not the
Duke of York, with whom he had quarrelled over money.
The King, however, was anxious to avoid undue publicity of
this family estrangement, and he refused to inform his ministers
of his decision until the last possible moment. Both administration and opposition therefore suspected that the King's real
motive was to nominate his mother as Regent. Since she was
a close friend of Bute such a decision carried the future threat
of a full restoration of the favourite's influence: and much of
the political heat of the Regency Bill Crisis arose from this
mistaken fear.[2]

On 3 April the King ordered his ministers to draft a Regency
Bill along the lines of the 1751 Regency Act, but reserving
for himself the nomination of the Regent and Council. Grenville disliked this proviso, but the cabinet agreed to carry out

---

[1] Macalpine and Hunter, *B.I.H.R.* 40 (1967), 175-83.
[2] Differing accounts of the Regency Crisis have been written by Tomlinson,
M.A. Thesis, pp. 165-90; by Jarrett, *E.H.R.* 85 (1970), 282-315; and by Brooke,
King George III, pp. 110-13.

the King's wishes. George III followed this step by an interview with Cumberland on 7 April, when he told his uncle of his decision to have a Regency Bill and, either then or later, of his choice of the Queen as Regent. The significance of this meeting was to link the Regency scheme with a proposed change of administration, for Cumberland was to be the key figure in the negotiations. From 1762 he had been regarded by both the King and Newcastle's friends as a leader of the opposition, though his role was one of guidance from above and not active participation in Parliamentary politics.[1] Cumberland felt that he had been supplanted by Bute in his natural position as adviser of the young King. In 1765 he was therefore willing to play the part assigned to him by George III, that of an intermediary to bring the opposition leaders into office in place of the existing ministry. The King's notes written in preparation for this interview show that he intended to discuss a change of administration as well as the regency question.[2] He did not do so;[3] but the idea of a new ministry was the subject of secret negotiations later that month between Cumberland and intermediaries acting for the King. The Duke insisted that he and the King's brothers should all be named in the Regency Council, and George III told Grenville of this change of policy on 18 April. Grenville must have regarded this information as proof of a plot with Cumberland to replace his administration. The reaction of the ministers only alienated the King further. Grenville, with justification but without tact, complained to George III about his behaviour:[4] and the ministers took the initiative over the popular fear that the Princess Dowager was to be nominated as prospective Regent. On 3 May Lord Halifax obtained permission from the King to propose in the House of Lords the insertion in the Regency Bill of a clause that the Regent would be 'the Queen, or one of the descendants of the late King usually resident in Great

---

[1] B.M. Add. MSS. 32950, fos. 68, 361; 32951, fos. 67–8; 32952, fo. 133: *Bute Letters*, p. 143.

[2] *Corr. of George III*, i. 125. This document was identified by Namier, *Additions and Corrections*, pp. 31–2.

[3] Cumberland's own version implies that the King did not do so. *Rockingham Memoirs*, i. 187. But Newcastle's later account of the change of ministry attributed the initiative to this interview. Bateson, *Narrative*, p. 4.

[4] *Grenville Papers*, iii. 127, 136–9.

Britain', a definition that deliberately excluded the Princess Dowager.[1] George III, aware that the point was immaterial, had been surprised into agreeing to a solution suggested to him, and not until afterwards did he realize the public insult to his mother. Two days later he insisted on her inclusion, and the ministry therefore arranged for the appropriate amendment to be moved in the Commons on 9 May.[2]

The need for the co-operation of his cabinet caused George III to suspend negotiations for a change of administration until the Regency Bill had gone safely through Parliament by 13 May. The discussions were then resumed with Cumberland's help, an approach being made to Pitt; and on 16 May the King admitted to his ministers that he meant to dismiss them.[3] The announcement was premature, for Pitt refused office and Newcastle's friends declined to form a ministry without him. A further blow to the King was the sudden reconciliation between Grenville and Lord Temple, who had been estranged from his brother since Pitt's resignation in 1761.[4] As Pitt always made it a condition of his own return to office that Temple should be invited to accompany him, this decision of his brother-in-law seemed to postpone indefinitely the prospect of any change of administration.[5] George III had to surrender to his ministers. Their terms for continuing in office included the exclusion now of Cumberland as well as Bute from politics; the replacement of Bute's friend Northumberland as Lord-Lieutenant of Ireland by Bedfordite Lord Weymouth; the removal at last of Lord Holland from the Pay Office, which went to Charles Townshend; and the dismissal of Bute's brother Stuart Mackenzie from his place as Lord Privy Seal of Scotland, with the consequent loss of much Scottish patronage. The last was a condition much resented by the King, for he had promised Mackenzie the office for life.[6]

The episode seemed a repetition of those of August 1763,

[1] *Grenville Papers*, iii. 148–9; *Corr. of George III*, i. 73, 78–82.

[2] *Grenville Papers*, iii. 152, 157–9.

[3] *Bedford Papers*, iii. 278–81; *Grenville Papers*, iii. 166, 170–1.

[4] *Grenville Papers*, iii. 39–43, 173–5; *Corr. of George III*, i. 108.

[5] Pitt's desire to have Temple in office with him arose from his own bad state of health. *H.M.C. Stopford-Sackville*, p. 21.

[6] *Grenville Papers*, iii. 41–4, 183–8; *Corr. of George III*, i. 113–15.

a comparison made by Grenville himself. He thought that yet another failure to remove the administration had again left it in a stronger position than before.[1] The ministers now had even forced the King to give them public preference over the Bute connection: and the widespread support at Westminster commanded by the administration was shown by the large attendance of independent members at Grenville's levee on 21 May. Four days later James Harris complacently noted in his diary that there was 'a general satisfaction at the turn things had taken, and an astonishment at the absurd behaviour of Lord Bute in demolishing one administration before he had prepared another'.[2] The ministers felt secure, or professed to do so. Lord Sandwich said publicly that the King had thought 'proper to re-establish his old servants in the management of his affairs'.[3]

All this was an illusion. Whereas after August 1763 George III gave genuine personal support to Grenville, the effect of the Regency Bill Crisis and its aftermath had been to alienate the King finally from his ministers. It had also paved the way for Newcastle and his friends to return to office. 'The Duke of Cumberland has certainly removed all the prejudices to the Whigs, and that is a great point gained', reflected Newcastle to Rockingham on 1 June.[4] George III even expressed a preference for the Newcastle group when Cumberland on 12 June hinted at an offer to Pitt.[5]

I shall rather be surprised if Mr. Pitt can be persuaded to accept office on terms not entirely to my dishonour and to that of those worthy men, Lord Rockingham, the Dukes of Grafton, Newcastle and others; for they are men who have principles and therefore cannot approve of seeing the Crown dictated to by low men; if Mr. Pitt should again decline, I hope the Parliament being prorogued they and their friends will join amicably the few persons that have zealously stood by me.

---

[1] Grenville to Lord Strange, 23 May 1765; Grenville Letter Books, vol. 2.
[2] Harris Diary, 21 and 25 May 1765. The comment reflects the erroneous Grenvillite obsession that Bute was responsible for all the plots to overthrow the ministry. George III had, in fact, stopped consulting Bute in March. B.M. Add. MSS. 51379, fo. 175.
[3] *Chesterfield Letters*, vi. 2657.
[4] B.M. Add. MSS. 32967, fos. 3–5.
[5] *Corr. of George III*, i. 117–18.

Newcastle's friends, however, requested another approach to Pitt, believing that his inclusion was necessary for the success of any new administration; and on 17 June Grafton was sent to ask Pitt to form a ministry.[1] Pitt insisted on seeing the King himself, but, contrary to George III's fears, raised no difficulties about persons: he was willing to keep in the cabinet such royal watchdogs as Lord Chancellor Northington and First Lord of the Admiralty Lord Egmont, and even to restore Mackenzie to his office. Hopes of a Pitt ministry were high after his two interviews with the King on 19 and 22 June.[2] Negotiations broke down when Temple, whom Pitt wanted at the Treasury, refused that office on 25 June. He did not wish to be a party to any royal revenge on his brother, and disliked the role of figurehead assigned to him.[3] The next day Pitt formally declined to take part in a new ministry:[4] but he was now satisfied that any idea of Bute's influence 'behind the curtain' was a myth, and in that sense the negotiations of 1765 helped to prepare the ground for his return to office the next year.

By the end of June Newcastle, Rockingham and their friends were therefore faced with the question of whether they should and could form a ministry without Pitt.[5] Newcastle himself now professed to be without ambition for high office, but favoured the attempt both from a sense of duty, 'the King must have an administration', and because of the opportunity to restore his friends and adherents to the offices and places lost in 1762.[6] On 29 June he was formally told by the Duke of Cumberland's confidant Lord Albemarle that the King 'calls upon your Grace etc to serve him, and deliver him from the hands of oppression and tyranny'.[7] The next day Newcastle, Rockingham and Henry Seymour Conway went to see Cumberland at Windsor. There it was provisionally agreed that Rockingham should become First Lord of the Treasury, with the Duke of Grafton as one Secretary of State and either Conway or Charles

---

[1] B.M. Add. MSS. 32967, fos. 48, 71–2; *Grafton Autobiography*, p. 52.

[2] B.M. Add. MSS. 32967, fo. 79; *Chatham Papers*, ii. 311–13; *Corr. of George III*, i. 123–5; *Grenville Papers*, iii. 60–1.

[3] *Grenville Papers*, iii. 63–4, 199, 200–1.　　　　[4] *Jenkinson Papers*, pp. 376–7.

[5] For more detail on the making of the Rockingham ministry see Hardy, M.A. Thesis, pp. 307–64.

[6] B.M. Add. MSS. 32967, fos. 142–4.

[7] B.M. Add. MSS. 32967, fo. 155.

Townshend as the other: Cumberland himself chose Rockingham for the Treasury, even though the only post previously
held by the Marquess was that of a mere Lord of the
Bedchamber. The three men returned to London to hold a
meeting of their friends the same evening. This sounding of
opinion almost put an end to the plan, for six of the eighteen
peers and M.P.s present opposed the idea of forming a ministry
without Pitt; and it was with difficulty that Newcastle persuaded
Cumberland to continue the negotiation.[1] The construction of
the ministry then nearly foundered on two problems, the widely
held belief that Bute was still influencing George III behind the
scenes, and contemporary doubts as to the ability of such a
ministry to survive without Pitt.

Suspicion of Bute had been manifest at the evening meeting
of 30 June, which had approved a resolution by the Duke of
Portland that Mackenzie should not be restored to his Scottish
post and that some of Bute's friends should be removed from
office. The aim was to show to the political world that the new
ministry was not a Bute creation. George III was astonished
at the demand for any such gesture, but agreed to make
concessions.[2] At a meeting of nine leading members of the
proposed administration called by Cumberland on 5 July
the Duke announced that

His Majesty had given him the strongest assurances that my Lord
Bute should not be suffered to interfere in the least degree in any
public business whatever; and that, if those of his friends who might
remain in office did not vote with, and, by speaking, support the
present administration, His Majesty promised to remove them the
next day.[3]

The message explains why only one of Bute's friends was
dismissed at this time: but it was known only to the administration, and rumours of Bute's influence continued to circulate
in the absence of any public demonstration to the contrary.
George III took one immediate step to implement his promise,

---

[1] Bateson, *Narrative*, pp. 25–8; *Rockingham Memoirs*, i. 218–20.
[2] B.M. Add. MSS. 32967, fo. 193.
[3] Bateson, *Narrative*, pp. 30–1. This was Newcastle's recollection of what Cumberland said, 'I think at that meeting or I am sure very soon after'.

E

a letter to Lord Egmont on 8 July asking him to instruct
Gilbert Elliot and James Oswald to support the new ministry:[1]
but the King's failure to carry out his undertaking during the
American crisis of the next year was to be a ministerial
grievance.

The other problem was of more immediate moment. Many
difficulties in the construction of the ministry were caused by
the reluctance of individual politicians to commit themselves
to an administration that might not last, and by the consequent desire of the new ministers to win the public approbation
of Pitt. One early dilemma was resolved by a decision to keep
Northington as Lord Chancellor. This avoided the necessity
of choosing between Charles Yorke and Pitt's protégé Charles
Pratt. Instead, it was hoped that a peerage for Pratt would
satisfy Pitt, while the Yorke family was to be appeased by the
restoration of Charles Yorke to his old office of Attorney-
General and by the offer of the Presidency of the Board of
Trade and a cabinet place to his brother Lord Hardwicke.
The Yorkes were not to be won so easily. Charles Yorke was
seen by both Rockingham and Cumberland on 1 July, and
raised many objections and complaints about the proposed
arrangements. He refused to make any decision on the offer to
himself, but agreed to mention the Board of Trade to his
brother.[2] Hardwicke declined the post, and when later considering the offer 'made me in July 1765 when the Duke of Cumberland was settling a ministry for the King' noted three reasons
for his refusal; his own desire for a quiet life, fear of the consequences of the Stamp Act, and the general weakness of the
ministry.[3] George III was very anxious for Yorke's support
in the Commons, as he told Cumberland on 8 July: 'If Messrs
Grenville, Townshend and Ld George Sackville should oppose
in the House of Commons Administration would not go on
there pleasantly unless Mr. Yorke was hearty in their cause.'[4]
The new ministers were less worried than the King. They were
confident of Yorke's eventual adherence even after his discontent was increased by the peerage given to Pratt as Baron

---

[1] *Corr. of George III*, i. 146.
[2] B.M. Add. MSS. 32967, fos. 193–4; 35428, fos. 22–3, 76–80.
[3] B.M. Add. MSS. 35428, fo. 22.
[4] *Corr. of George III*, i. 145.

Camden: for his refusal would mean loss of precedence in his profession, the creation of another Attorney-General over his head.[1] It was as late as 9 August when Yorke finally accepted the post at an audience with George III: before doing so he obtained a promise from the King that he would become Lord Chancellor in 1766, and announced that in any case he would 'not undertake as a sub minister in the House of Commons'.[2]

Others expected to take cabinet office made difficulties or refused altogether. The Duke of Grafton had neither seen Cumberland on 30 June nor attended the evening conclave that day, but had been named as a Secretary of State. He did accept the post of Northern Secretary, but only on condition that Pitt could join the administration as its head whenever he chose.[3] Charles Townshend, also unconsulted on 30 June, refused the post of Chancellor of the Exchequer: but for the first week of July Rockingham and Newcastle were confident that he would become Secretary of State, and assumed that Conway would then be Chancellor of the Exchequer. Townshend declined to do so even at an interview with George III himself on 10 July. Grafton and Rockingham had already told Cumberland that the delay in announcing the new ministry was giving rise to damaging rumours, and the formal change of administration took place the same day despite Townshend's refusal. Townshend was left at the Pay Office, Conway became Secretary of State for the South and Leader of the House of Commons, and the Exchequer went to William Dowdeswell: this was a surprise appointment, for Dowdeswell was an independent squire whose link with the Newcastle group derived only from his opposition to the cider tax.[4]

The new ministry was widely regarded as being unequal to the task of government, both in Parliament and in administrative ability. At the end of July, before Conway's appointment

---

[1] *Grenville Papers*, iii. 219; *H.M.C. Stopford-Sackville*, p. 21.

[2] B.M. Add. MSS. 35428, fos. 22–3, 103–4.

[3] *Grafton Autobiography*, p. 54. Before taking office Grafton told Lord Gower 'that, like a girl who is going to be married, he felt himself much pleased with the general idea, but much frightened as the hour drew nigh'. *H.M.C. Weston Underwood*, p. 390.

[4] *Corr. of George III*, i. 150, 155–6; *Grenville Papers*, iii. 217; Namier and Brooke, *Charles Townshend*, pp. 134–7.

as Leader of the House was known,[1] Lord George Sackville reflected the general bewilderment. 'I wonder what the plan of government is for the House of Commons.'[2] Conway, as Secretary of State the obvious choice, was felt to lack the necessary qualities, as Lord Chesterfield observed. 'Charles Townshend will play booty; and whom else have they? Nobody but Conway; who has only good sense, but not the necessary talents nor experience.'[3] Since Parliament would not meet until the end of the year the ministry's failure to recruit adequate debating strength was not yet a major problem. The other disadvantage was immediate and permanent. All three executive ministers, Rockingham and the two Secretaries, were totally inexperienced in administration. Nor could or would they call on their colleagues for assistance. Newcastle alone had extensive governmental experience: but by now he wanted influence without responsibility, and professed to be indifferent about the post of Lord Privy Seal which he accepted on 15 July.[4] Rockingham, Grafton, and Conway were determined that he should control neither policy nor patronage, and avoided consultation with him as far as possible. They could not look to Lord Chancellor Northington and First Lord of the Admiralty Egmont, for both were men whose loyalty was to the King and not to their new colleagues: while the choice of old Lord Winchelsea as Lord President would have been inexplicable to contemporaries if he had not been Rockingham's uncle.

Youth and inexperience characterized the administration at all levels. The change produced many more alterations of personnel than was usual in the eighteenth century. The new ministers had the motives of revenge and patronage; and they found that loyalty to their predecessors cost them the support of men they would have liked to retain. So a competent Treasury was replaced by men totally lacking administrative expertise. James Harris, Thomas Hunter, Sir John Turner, and Secretary Thomas Whately were dismissed with Grenville,

---

[1] The choice of Conway as Leader of the House was not a formal appointment and was not made or did not become known until late in the year. *H.M.C. Weston Underwood*, p. 398.

[2] *H.M.C. Stopford-Sackville*, p. 21.

[3] *Chesterfield Letters*, vi. 2665.

[4] B.M. Add. MSS. 32967, fos. 389–91.

and Lord North resigned, as did the other Secretary Charles Jenkinson. The three junior Lords chosen to assist Rockingham and Dowdeswell were George Onslow, Thomas Townshend, and Lord John Cavendish, who had all hitherto shown an aptitude only for opposition speeches in Parliament. Lord Egmont found himself with a new Board of Admiralty after the resignation of Thomas Pitt had followed earlier dismissals: it included two Admirals, Keppel and Saunders, named by William Pitt, and of the others only Sir William Meredith promised to be a useful acquisition. Least change occurred at the Board of Trade, where four of the seven junior Lords remained. On 11 July Rockingham offered the Presidency to Shelburne: his refusal had been correctly anticipated, for the post had already been given to Lord Dartmouth, nephew of Henry Legge.[1] Apart from hopes of retaining men like Lord North by not dismissing them, the new ministers seem to have paid little attention to considerations of competence and expertise. Even when men experienced in minor office were available no attempt was made to find them appropriate posts. Thomas Pelham, who had served on the Boards of Trade and Admiralty for eight years, was given only a Court office; so was Lord Villiers, also with experience at the Admiralty Board. Most marked of all was the refusal of Rockingham to employ James West at the Treasury, where he had been a Secretary for fifteen years. Rockingham presumably feared that his close friendship with Newcastle would give the Duke influence within his own department; but when Newcastle wrote to console West he hinted at a more general reason for the behaviour of the new ministers. 'Young men think they dont want the advice of us old ones, and often dont like to have us amongst them, or at their Boards, least we should appear to know more of their business than they do themselves.'[2]

Changes among politicians were accompanied by alterations in the staff of various government departments. Even here there was a clearance of friends of the previous ministers. Halifax's American Under-Secretary Edward Sedgwick told

[1] Fitzmaurice, *Shelburne*, i. 231; *Rockingham Memoirs*, i. 234–5; *H.M.C. Dartmouth*, i. 331.
[2] B.M. Add. MSS. 32967, fos. 371–2.

his former colleague Edward Weston that 'it is thought improper and disagreeable to give the entire confidence which
Under-Secretaries must enjoy, to men who are known to be
strongly attached or greatly obliged to other great Personages'.
Sedgwick himself did not intend to continue: and Conway
brought in an outsider, the aspiring politician William Burke,
to be his chief Under-Secretary.[1] The lack of any clear line
between politics and administration was shown by the arrangements Rockingham made at the Treasury. The two Secretaries
he appointed to replace Whately and Jenkinson were civil
servants, and neither was an M.P. Charles Lowndes was a
permanent official in the department, and Joseph Mellish a
former Receiver-General of Customs. In September Mellish
returned to his old post, and to fill the vacancy Rockingham
approached Grey Cooper, a lawyer who had written two
pamphlets in defence of the new ministry. Cooper was reluctant
to take a precarious appointment and give up the £1,000 a
year he was earning in legal practice: but he accepted the post
in October on being given an annuity of £500, and was found
a seat in the Commons before the end of the year.[2] For his
own private secretary Rockingham made a fortunate choice:
on the recommendation of Lord John Cavendish he took an
able free-lance Irishman, Edmund Burke, whose oratory was
to prove an immediate weapon for administration after he
entered the Commons in December.[3]

The new administration had signally failed to obtain any
public acknowledgement of Pitt's private goodwill. Shelburne
was not the only follower of Pitt to refuse office. Others who
did so were James Grenville, Isaac Barré, and Thomas
Walpole.[4] The ministers had tried hard enough: apart from
these unsuccessful offers there had been the peerage for Pratt,
the acceptance of Grafton's condition of office, the appointment of Saunders and Keppel to the Admiralty Board, and

---

[1] Grafton failed to persuade Weston to become his chief Under-Secretary, and
his next choice Lovell Stanhope resigned after four days. For further details see
H.M.C. Weston Underwood, pp. 391–3.

[2] *Jenkinson Papers*, pp. 381–2, 387; *H.M.C. Stopford-Sackville*, p. 21; Wickwire,
British Subministers and Colonial America, pp. 39–40.

[3] *Burke Corr.*, i. 207, 210–11.

[4] B.M. Add. MSS. 32968, fo. 142; *Grenville Papers*, iii. 71–2; H. Walpole,
Memoirs, ii. 140.

the willingness to keep the great man's nephew Thomas Pitt in office. But the courtship had been one-sided, and the administration was left without any reward for effort. 'The present ministers perched for some time upon Mr. Pitt's shoulders, but he thought the weight troublesome and he has brushed them off', wrote Lord George Sackville on 29 July, 'and he desires those who are immediately attached to him to declare that he has not the smallest share in the advising or the directing of measures.'[1] This seemed to pose an immediate question-mark over the future of the new ministry, the view of the political world being put elegantly and succintly by Lord Chesterfield.

Here is a new political arch almost built, but of materials of so different a nature, and without a keystone, that it does not, in my opinion, indicate either strength or duration. It will certainly require repairs, and a keystone, next winter; and that keystone will, and must necessarily be Mr. Pitt.[2]

If the public neutrality of Pitt was damaging, the hostility of Grenville and his friends was menacing. A bitter Parliamentary session would have followed even without an American crisis to add fuel to the flames, and it was foreshadowed by a vigorous political controversy in the press during the autumn of 1765.[3] The anger of the new opposition arose not merely from the fact and manner of the change of ministry, but also from a genuine conviction that the replacement of Grenville by his successors was a national disaster, especially as the magnitude of the colonial problem became apparent: this opinion was put forcibly by Lord Buckinghamshire to Robert Nugent in October.[4]

I have lately received a letter from Mr. Grenville. Reflection but the more convinces me of the calamity England has sustained by his being compelled to quit an office which he is not only the best but the only man in these times duly qualified to fill. The candid and informed must lament his retreat, which can only please the interested and the ignorant, or those wretched merchants who living upon expedients make a lottery of trade, and would adopt the same miserable plan for the Public, which in the end must prove equally ruinous to the General as to individuals.

---

[1] *H.M.C. Stopford-Sackville*, p. 21.   [2] *Chesterfield Letters*, vi. 2658.
[3] *Chesterfield Letters*, vi. 2661–5.   [4] *H.M.C. Lothian*, p. 258.

The inexperience and anticipated incompetence of the new ministers and their supporters; the damaging effect on public opinion of Bute's reputed influence and Pitt's open indifference; the certainty of a determined and able opposition onslaught in both Houses of Parliament: all these considerations gave contemporaries ample reason to forecast for the Rockingham administration a short and troubled life. The ministers themselves did not share this view, and it is easy to see why. They had a convincing paper majority in Parliament, and the undoubted, albeit unenthusiastic, support of the Crown. The Parliamentary lists compiled by or on behalf of Rockingham during the late summer of 1765 portrayed an overwhelming command of the House of Commons. The last one, corrected until the end of September, named 294 M.P.s as 'Pro', 127 as 'Doubtful', and only 113 as 'Con': seventeen members were abroad or regarded as otherwise absent, two had not taken their seats, and three seats were vacant.[1] No mark at all appeared against the names of those two most unpredictable of men, Charles Townshend and William Pitt. Uncertainty about Pitt's attitude was reflected in the classification of such members as Barré and Shelburne's brother Thomas Fitzmaurice as 'Doubtful', although Beckford was altered from 'Doubtful' to 'most probably Pro'. Some obvious errors must soon have come to light, such as the classification of Charles Jenkinson as 'Pro' and Richard Jackson as 'Con': but until the American crisis loomed large the Parliamentary situation reflected the happy position customary for almost any ministry appointed by the sovereign during the eighteenth century. The general sense of loyalty to the throne was reinforced by the usual factor of patronage, as Lord Chesterfield pointed out to his son on 25 October. 'The late ministers threaten the present ones; but the latter do not seem in the least afraid of the former, and for a very good reason, which is, that they have the distribution of the loaves and fishes.'[2]

The ministers were confident that George III would support

---

[1] 'List of the Members of the House of Commons': Fitzwilliam (Milton) MSS. Box 1076.

[2] *Chesterfield Letters*, vi. 2672. Doubts as to whether all the King's friends would in fact support them led ministers to consider a general election during the autumn, but Cumberland vetoed the proposal. Langford, *Rockingham Administration*, pp. 94–7.

them, if only because his personal detestation of Grenville and Pitt's unwillingness to serve left him with no alternative choice of administration. They soon came to realize, however, that their demands concerning Bute's influence and friends had annoyed the King. In order to strengthen their position at Court the ministers invited Cumberland himself to take a place in the cabinet. He did so, and acted as virtual head of the administration until his death on 31 October.

In the varied and prolonged negotiations before the formation of the new ministry, places and persons had been discussed often, policy seldom. The terms proposed by Pitt in May did include several matters that came under that heading: a bill or declaration to settle the question of general warrants; amendment of the Cider Act; the restoration of army officers and others dismissed for political opposition; and a new foreign policy that would involve an alliance with Prussia.[1] America was not mentioned: but before the negotiations of June the first portents of colonial resistance to the Stamp Act had arrived.[2] Grenville heard from Lord Chancellor Northington and Lord Lyttelton that in addition to stipulating a Prussian treaty, repeal of the cider tax and condemnation of general warrants, Pitt had then also 'blamed the taxation of the Colonies, the unfunded debt, and the measures taken against smuggling in America'.[3] The American question was still only a small cloud on the political horizon, and at the time it was Pitt's insistence on 'a northern system of alliances' that concerned the King and contemporaries more than any other matter of policy.[4] After Pitt's final refusal the Duke of Newcastle, as part of the preparations for coming into office, drew up a list of 'measures' to be adopted. This programme, compiled with an eye on Pitt's approval, included a plan for a Prussian alliance; the restitution of dismissed army officers; and a declaration that general warrants were illegal.[5] Newcastle made no reference to the colonies: but Grenville, perhaps

---

[1] *Rockingham Memoirs*, i. 193; *Grenville Papers*, iii. 226. These two accounts of Pitt's terms, both second-hand, differ in detail.
[2] *St. James' Chronicle*, 6 June 1765.
[3] *Grenville Papers*, iii. 201, 203.
[4] *Corr. of George III*, i. 124–5. B.M. Add. MSS. 32967, fos. 79, 103.
[5] B.M. Add. MSS. 32967, fos. 120, 124.

E*

because he thought the new ministry would follow what he knew to be Pitt's views on America, already feared some abandonment of his colonial policy; and his wife's diary shows that he spoke to the King on the subject when leaving office on 10 July.[1]

Mr. Grenville told him he understood that the plan of his new Administration was a total subversion of every act of the former; that nothing having been undertaken as a measure without his Majesty's approbation, he knew not how he would let himself be persuaded to see it in so different a light, and most particularly on the regulations concerning the colonies; that he besought His Majesty, as he valued his own safety, not to suffer any one to advise him to separate or draw the line between his British and American dominions; that his colonies was the richest jewel of his Crown; that for his own part he must uniformly maintain his former opinions both in Parliament and out of it; that whatever was proposed in Parliament must abide the sentence passed upon it there, but that if any men ventured to defeat the regulations laid down for the colonies, by a slackness in the execution, he should look upon him as a criminal and the betrayer of his country.

[1] *Grenville Papers*, iii. 215–16.

9 The American Crisis

THE development of the colonial resistance to the Stamp Act was gradual and erratic, or so it appeared in Britain; and the magnitude of the problem only became clear at the end of 1765.[1] The time taken for the arrival of news from America varied considerably, according to the distance of a colony, the speed of individual ships, and the zeal of officials. Governors reported events to the Board of Trade, to the Secretary of State for the South, to both, or to nobody at all. Other officials in the colonies sent reports to ministers, to various government departments, and to personal friends, and so did individuals involved in particular incidents.[2] There was a natural delay

[1] My concern is not to discuss the colonial reaction to the Stamp Act but to show what was known of the American situation in Britain at the time the ministry made its various decisions on colonial policy. Events in the colonies have been described many times, notably by Gipson, British Empire, x. 282–366; E. S. and H. M. Morgan, Stamp Act Crisis, pp. 120–262; E. S. Morgan, W.M.Q. 5 (1948), 311–41. Morgan prints and discusses many relevant documents in Prologue to Revolution, pp. 46–118.

There is a difference of opinion as to the nature of the colonial objection to Parliament's right of taxation. The traditional interpretation, recently championed by Gipson, is that during the Stamp Act Crisis the colonists objected only to internal taxes, such as the Stamp Act, and not to external taxes, revenue deliberately raised from customs duties. Morgan argues that the colonies objected from the first to all taxation, and therefore did not change their ground when Charles Townshend in 1767 levied 'external taxation'. Selections can be made from the volume and variety of evidence to support both views, but the colonial reaction must surely be seen in the context of the Stamp Act. The colonists only specifically denied the right of Parliament to levy internal taxes, defending the claim of their assemblies in this respect: but Morgan has established that the colonists made no positive acknowledgement of Parliament's right to levy external taxes, to raise money at all from the colonies; hence the refusal of the Stamp Act Congress to admit Parliament's right to regulate trade, after experience of the 1764 Duties Act which had aimed at revenue as well as trade regulation. As will be seen, this modern academic controversy reflects the political argument in Britain at the time of the Stamp Act Crisis. The advocates of repeal contended that the colonies were objecting only to internal taxes; their opponents asserted that the colonies completely denied Parliament's right to tax them.

[2] For copies of virtually all these papers (and some replies) see B. M. Stowe MSS. 264–5. Most of them are listed in the Commons Journals, xxx. 448–51, 499. These lists are only of the papers laid before Parliament. Some of the papers were later printed in Almon, Debates, vii. 79–100; Debrett, Parl. Reg. iv. 301–19; and Cobbett, Parl. Hist. xvi. 112–33. Extracts from many documents may be

before the information from such disparate sources could be brought together for ministers. They may sometimes have first learned the news from the press or political gossip in London, for the colonial situation was always a matter of public knowledge. From August onwards London newspapers were carrying reports of riots, resolutions, and other forms of resistance, and the subsequent resignations of Stamp-Distributors. These accounts of colonial defiance were given no special prominence, and appeared as paragraphs in the news columns among others concerned with European, colonial, and home news: but the potential gravity of the situation must have been clear to thoughtful observers by the autumn of 1765, for practical grievances, constitutional objections, and threats of violence were all being reported. A notable example was a letter date-lined from Boston as early as 5 August and published in London in mid-September. 'As to the imposition of the Stamp Act . . . it will, I believe, be of short continuance, for it is universally esteemed here as arbitrary and unconstitutional, and as a breach of charter and contract between K- and subject; and I think we have a right to refuse submission to it.' After a forecast that the stamp officials would not dare to act, and a reminder that the population of the colonies was now 2,000,000, the writer ended with this challenge: 'It is too late in the day to be dragooned out of our rights.'[1]

The first American reaction to the Stamp Act occurred early, the so-called Virginia Resolves being voted by that colony's House of Burgesses at the end of May. Four were finally adopted, asserting that the colonists had always had the right to be taxed by 'persons chosen by themselves to represent them'; but the frequent publication in the colonial press of six or all seven of the resolutions that had been drafted by Patrick Henry and his friends resulted in a widespread and mistaken impression that violent resistance to the Stamp Act was contem-

---

found in a compilation apparently made for the use of ministers and headed 'American Correspondence Relative to the Disturbances Abstracted'. B.M. Add. MSS. 32971, fos. 99-122. These sources often give the date of receipt of many of the papers from America.

[1] *London Evening Post*, 14 Sept. 1765. Charles Townshend was among the first to appreciate the gravity of the American situation, writing on 24 Aug. that 'no Parliament ever met in such a critical minute nor did ever ministers stand upon so bold a precipice'. Charles Townshend Letters, pp. 149-51.

plated there. The Rockingham ministry never suffered from this misconception, for Lieutenant-Governor Fauquier sent an accurate description of what had happened in a letter of 5 June to the Board of Trade: but he ended with this misleading comment. 'I hope I am authorised in saying, there is cause at least to doubt, whether this would have been the sense of the colony, if more of their representatives had done their duty by attending to the end of the session.'[1] When the subject was discussed at a cabinet meeting on 30 August, the ministers therefore acted in the belief that the Resolves were the work of a small minority, and that they would be rescinded at a fuller meeting of the House of Burgesses. The only instruction to Fauquier decided upon was that 'he should support by all prudent measures the authority of the British Parliament in that country'.[2] Conway's letter to Fauquier, containing this optimistic assessment and vague order, was sent on 14 September.[3] The administration did not as yet anticipate any more serious problem than some local difficulties in enforcing the Stamp Act. The Treasury Board on 13 September merely decided on an instruction to the colonial governors directing them to assist the stamp officers, Secretary to the Treasury Lowndes sending off the appropriate circular letter next day.[4] This action was too late to have any effect on the colonial situation.[5]

The only other early news of colonial reactions to the Stamp Act came from Massachusetts. The Assembly there considered the matter in June: the final Address proved to be moderate; more significant was the decision of the Assembly to circulate

[1] C.O. 5/1331, pp. 69–76. Correct versions of the events in Virginia appeared in the London press in October. *London Evening Post*, 17 Oct. 1765. *St. James' Chronicle*, 19 Oct. 1765.

[2] B.M. Add. MSS. 32969, fos. 221, 255–7. In this incident the cabinet superseded the official government machinery. The Board of Trade had read Fauquier's letter on 20 Aug., and referred the matter to the Privy Council on 22 Aug. When the Council considered it on 6 Sept, the cabinet had already done so, and the Council merely referred the subject as a matter of form to its Committee for Plantation Affairs. *J.C.T.P. 1746–7*, pp. 191–2. *Acts. P.C. Col.* iv. 732.

[3] Grafton MSS., no. 788; Cobbett, *Parl. Hist.* xvi. 112–13.

[4] B.M. Add. MSS. 32971, fos. 109–10; T.29/37, p. 123.

[5] Governor Fitch of Connecticut, for example, did not receive this letter until 18 Dec. Fitch replied on 24 Dec., stating that there was no Stamp-Distributor in his colony, but this answer did not arrive until 14 Mar. 1766. *Fitch Papers*, ii. 356–7, 381–2.

the other colonies with a proposal for a meeting of delegates at New York in October; and there was also a proposal to stop payment of the governor's salary. This last suggestion had been made on the ground that as Parliament had now taxed the colonies it ought to provide for the expenses of colonial government; and although it was not implemented in 1765, the Assembly announced an intention of adopting the plan next year if there had been no redress of grievances. This was a move that gave the British government a favourable opportunity to undermine the Assembly's power by removing its chief weapon against the executive: and the Board of Trade at once grasped this point when Governor Francis Bernard reported these events in a letter of 8 July. The Board considered the Massachusetts papers on 24 September, and three days later sent the Privy Council a separate representation on the subject of the governor's salary, proposing a fixed and permanent salary sufficient for his support without reliance on a grant from the Massachusetts Assembly. The Rockingham ministry failed to take this chance of striking at the Assembly's power: the Board's letter was referred to the Committee on Plantation Affairs; and several months later, on 15 February 1766, the Committee formally postponed consideration of the subject. Meanwhile, on 1 October, the Board of Trade had sent a general report on the Assembly's behaviour to the Privy Council, which referred the matter to its Committee the next day.[1] The Committee considered the proceedings of the two assemblies of Virginia and Massachusetts on 3 October, and reported its opinion to the Privy Council on 18 October. This declared that the matter should be laid before Parliament, and described the Virginia Resolves as 'containing an absolute disavowal of the right of the Parliament of Great Britain to impose taxes upon the colonies, and a daring attack upon the constitution of this country'.[2]

Constitutional challenges could be leisurely referred to the future consideration of the legislature, but news of violence led to direct administrative action. The first Boston riots took place on 14 August, when the Massachusetts Stamp-Distributor

[1] *J.C.T.P. 1764–7*, pp. 205–6, 209–10; *Acts. P.C. Col.* iv. 732, 739; Cobbett, *Parl. Hist.* xvi. 121–2.

[2] *Acts. P.C. Col.* iv. 732–3.

Andrew Oliver was forced to resign after being hung in effigy and having his house wrecked. A situation report was made by Governor Bernard to the Board of Trade in letters of 15 and 22 August. He warned that it would be impossible to enforce the Stamp Act: the militia was useless, and there were no soldiers within 200 miles. 'In my present defenceless state, I consider myself only as a prisoner at large, wholly in the power of the people.' The Board of Trade considered Bernard's letters and enclosed papers on 8 October, and sent a letter with copies of the documents to the Privy Council on 10 October.[1] A second Boston riot took place on 26 August, the sack of the house of Thomas Hutchinson, Lieutenant-Governor and Chief Justice of the colony. It was reported to the Board by Bernard in a seventeen-page letter of 31 August. He said that opinion against the Stamp Act was unanimous, even though some men of property condemned the violence; and that his elected Council had refused to allow him to send for help to General Gage or Admiral Lord Colville, the respective army and navy commanders-in-chief in America. This letter and other papers sent by Bernard were considered by the Board of Trade on 17 October, and the same day the Board sent copies and a representation to the Privy Council.[2]

The letters from Fauquier and Bernard were the only reports of resistance that had been received from colonial governors by mid-October. The elected Governor Ward of Rhode Island failed to send any account of the riots at Newport in his colony at the end of August, when there were attacks on property and other disturbances: but news of these events came from other sources. Reports of the Newport riots were sent to Britain by two of the victims, Stamp-Distributor Augustus Johnston and Customs Collector John Robinson, who informed the Stamp Office and the Customs Board respectively;[3] the commander of the frigate *Cygnet* in the harbour sent accounts to the Admiralty, which forwarded them to Secretary Conway on 15 October;[4] and two leading citizens of Newport, lawyer Martin Howard and physician Thomas

[1] *J.C.T.P. 1764–7*, pp. 211–12; *Acts. P.C. Col.* vi. 408–10.

[2] *J.C.T.P. 1764–7*, p. 214; *Acts. P.C. Col.* vi. 410–12.

[3] T.1/439, fos. 96–9; T.1/442, fos. 241–2. Robinson also sent a letter to Halifax on 28 Aug. that arrived on 21 Oct.

[4] *Cal. Home Office Papers 1760–5*, pp. 609–11.

Moffatt, who had their houses wrecked for defending the Stamp Act, fled to Britain and arrived in Bristol by 9 October, and were soon to tell their tale to official ears. By early October, too, news had come of trouble in New York, resulting in the resignation of Stamp-Distributor James McEvers: for on 11 October the Treasury Board already had under consideration a private letter from McEvers informing Barlow Trecothick of this circumstance.[1]

From the beginning the administration was well informed about the colonial crisis; but the evidence on ministerial views and discussions on America during the autumn of 1765 is extremely thin. There may not have been much formal consultation between ministers on the subject, although Newcastle's papers do contain two memoranda for private talks on it with Rockingham;[2] but in October there was at least one cabinet meeting solely concerned with the colonial crisis,[3] and the matter was doubtless discussed at others. Newcastle's personal bewilderment is shown by a letter he wrote to Rockingham on 12 October. 'I am very much at a loss in my own opinion what to do upon these American disputes. . . . I see great inconveniences on both sides of the question, and very little effect by enforcing the execution of . . . the Stamp Duty, . . . for I very much fear you will scarcely be able to get much from it.'[4] Newcastle, soon to be a strong advocate of repeal, had not yet come round to that opinion. A memorandum he noted down on 13 October before meeting Cumberland the next day shows that his ideas then were 'to execute [the Stamp Act] by fair means not by military force', and to give the colonies 'some relief' after they had submitted to Parliament's authority.[5] Four days later, on 17 October, Thomas Whately reported to Grenville that 'the language of the ministry is I am told resolute . . . but I believe they are undetermined about the measures to be taken, and the mode of proceeding if the tumult continues'.[6] The administration was certainly then on

---

[1] T.29/37, p. 165. For the letter see T.1/439, fos. 65–6.

[2] B.M. Add. MSS. 32969, fos. 343–4; 32970, fos. 238–9. Newcastle found an analogy in the Irish storm over Wood's Halfpence in the 1720s.

[3] President of the Board of Trade Dartmouth was not invited, a point on which Newcastle criticized Rockingham. B.M. Add. MSS. 32970, fos. 379–81.

[4] Wentworth Woodhouse MSS. R.1–504.

[5] B.M. Add. MSS. 32970, fos. 312–13.   [6] *Grenville Papers*, iii. 100.

the point of taking executive action to uphold Britain's authority in America. On 23 October Newcastle sent Conway an assurance about Bernard's reliability from two friends of the governor, John Roberts of the Board of Trade and the Bishop of Lincoln.[1] This may have been a final precautionary check on the source of the most important evidence before a decision made by the Privy Council that day. On 18 October the Council had referred the whole colonial problem to its Committee on Plantation Affairs. The Committee reported on 22 October, and in accordance with this report the Privy Council came to this resolution on 23 October.[2]

That it may be advisable for Your Majesty to direct one of your Principal Secretaries of State immediately to write letters to the several governors of your Majesty's colonies in North America, signifying your Majesty's royal will and pleasure, that they do, in their respective provinces, provide by all prudent and popular methods for the support of the honour and safety of government, and use all legal means to preserve peace and good order by a full exertion of the civil power, and in case by the exigency of affairs in any of the said provinces, it should be necessary to procure the aid of the military in support of the civil power, that, for that purpose, the governor of the province where that may happen, do apply to the commanders of your Majesty's land and sea forces in America, or either of them, as the occasion may require to whom it is humbly submitted your Majesty should give the necessary orders for their concurrence and assistance.

The appropriate orders, issued by Conway, were officially dated 24 October; they had probably been drawn up in advance of the Council meeting, for Conway told Newcastle on 23 October that 'the circulars to the American governors are gone to the Admiralty, and the sloop ready to sail'.[3] Conway's letters were later to incur criticism for their alleged lack of

---

[1] 'They were both at school with him, and have kept up their correspondence. They both say, that he is a very ingenious, and a very honest man; was a lawyer of reputation, established at Lincoln; and went to America, to support a numerous family; and was recommended to my Lord Halifax, by Mr. Pownall, Secretary to the Board of Trade, who knew him at Lincoln.' B.M. Add. MSS. 32971, fos. 69–70.

[2] *Acts. P.C. Col.* iv. 733; vi. 412.

[3] B.M. Add. MSS. 32971, fos. 77–8. The draft of a similar letter, unsigned and directed to the Admiralty, is dated 15 Oct. *Cal. Home Office Papers 1760–5*, p. 608.

firmness.[1] Although Gage was told to use force if all else failed, the qualifications inserted by Conway were felt by many to have weakened the strength of this instruction. Conway advised Gage to observe 'the utmost exertion of your prudence' if he was applied to by any governor for assistance, 'so as justly to temper your conduct between that caution and coolness, which the delicacy of such a situation may demand, on one hand; and the vigour necessary to suppress outrage and violence on the other'. This general instruction was repeated to all the governors, but they were told to apply to Gage and Colville

if a timely exertion of force is necessary . . . For, however unwillingly his Majesty may consent to the exertion of such powers, as may endanger the safety of a single subject, yet he can not permit his own dignity, and the authority of the British legislature, to be trampled on by force and violence, and in avowed contempt of all order, duty, and decorum.[2]

These instructions were intended only to preserve order and the authority of Crown and Parliament. They did not embody any decision on colonial policy, for none had been made. Although their implication was the enforcement of the Stamp Act, this was not explicitly stated to be their purpose. The orders, indeed, were not intended to be put into force, and no governor took action as a result of them.[3] Any administration faced with the colonial crisis would have had to issue some such instructions, and their recipients knew how to interpret them. Ministers were in any case aware that the long delay before the orders could arrive and the inadequate state of the military establishment in North America would prevent any effective action in support of the Stamp Act. The instructions were a piece of face-saving, promulgated to avoid any subsequent charge of negligence.[4]

[1] Below, p. 198. This was not the view in the colonies at the time. Joseph Chew, a Connecticut office-holder and later Loyalist, told Franklin that the circular letters were 'couched in the strongest terms you can conceive'. *Franklin Papers*, xiii. 59.

[2] For copies of Conway's letters of 24 Oct. see B.M. Add. MSS. 32971, fos. 91–8, and Cobbett, *Parl. Hist.* xvi. 113–18. That to Gage is printed in *Gage Corr.* ii. 27–9.

[3] *Gage Corr.* ii. 334–5.

[4] For a contrary interpretation see Langford, *Rockingham Administration*, pp. 80–2. On 15 Dec. Conway urged Gage to suppress 'any riotous or rebellious resistance', while at the same time commending him for not having fired on the New York rioters the previous month. *Gage Corr.* ii. 29–31.

Before ministers again considered the American crisis, two letters written in New York on 23 September arrived on 28 October. Lieutenant-Governor Colden officially reported the resignation of the colony's Stamp-Distributor on the mere threat of violence against his property; and General Gage sent a wide-ranging survey of events in the colonies. He described the Virginia Resolves as 'the signal for a general outcry over the continent', and reported that there was a concerted plan to force all stamp officers to resign and to destroy the stamps on their arrival. After mentioning the riots in Rhode Island and Massachusetts Gage warned that 'the neighbouring provinces seem inclined to follow their examples, but were prevented by the almost general resignation of the stamp officers'. The picture painted by Gage was not entirely black. He reported a reaction against violence among men of property, while there had been 'no riots to the southward except in Maryland'. This oblique reference was probably the first news of the Annapolis riot of 2 September: Stamp-Distributor Zachariah Hood had fled to New York after having his house destroyed and being himself burnt in effigy. Gage concluded by reporting that 'everything is quiet at present, and a calm seems to have succeeded the storm': but he warned that the real test would come on 1 November when the Stamp Act was due to go into force.[1]

The day after these letters arrived ministers decided to hold a cabinet meeting on the American crisis at the Duke of Cumberland's house on 31 October.[2] It did not take place, because the Duke suddenly collapsed and died that day. This event may well have had a decisive effect on the administration's American policy. There had hitherto been no idea of concession, and some ministers certainly favoured a strong line. Lord Chancellor Northington had intended to urge at the meeting that 'the Stamp Act ought to be carried into execution in support of the sovereignty of the British Parliament over the colonies'; that the governors should be immediately ordered to enforce it and 'furnished with the assistance of a military force for this purpose'; that there should be 'the most diligent inquiry to detect the persons concerned in this rebellion'; and that if

---

[1] B.M. Add. MSS. 32971, fos. 99–108. C.O. 5/83, pp. 723–30; printed *Gage Corr.* i. 67–8.

[2] B.M. Add. MSS. 32971, fos. 177–8, 187–8; *Grenville Papers*, iii. 105.

these measures proved insufficient Parliament should pass further punitive legislation.[1] Such a policy might have had the influential support of Cumberland himself. In an exchange of views with Newcastle in 1763 he had emphasized the need to keep the colonies dependent on Britain;[2] and although there is no direct evidence about Cumberland's views on the Stamp Act Crisis, Richard Jackson was to express the opinion in 1766 that if Cumberland had not died the government would have sent soldiers to America instead of repealing the Stamp Act.[3] Such a possibility must remain mere conjecture: but the Duke's death was certainly followed by the postponement of any decision on American policy, and it also revived speculation as to the possibility of Pitt joining the ministry.

The public expectation, as reflected in the press, was that Pitt would now be invited to join the administration.[4] There was, indeed, an immediate decision by Rockingham, Grafton and Conway, approved by George III and by Newcastle, to approach the great man;[5] but the ministers were embarrassed as to how to make the application, the King refused to authorize any invitation from himself, and the plan had been abandoned before the end of the month.[6] Newcastle regretted this outcome, and warned Rockingham on 1 December that when he and Pitt had been ministers together Pitt had told him, 'I must be in the first *concoction* of things'.[7] The practical difficulty was perhaps an excuse by ministers who on reflection felt that they now had little need of Pitt and had come to believe in the stability of the administration. Newcastle told Sir Matthew Fetherstonehaugh on 30 November that 'our young ministers were in very high spirits. They think (and I believe in that they are well founded) that they are in full possession of the credit, and favour of the Closet; and they

---

[1] Northington MSS: memorandum endorsed 'my opinion intended to be delivered at the meeting summoned on America at Cumberland House, the evening the Duke of Cumberland died'; partly quoted Mahoney, *Burke Newsletter*, 7 (1966–7), 505.

[2] B.M. Add. MSS. 32950, fo. 82.

[3] Kammen, *Rope of Sand*, p. 123.

[4] *London Evening Post*, 2 Nov. 1765; *Lloyd's Evening Post*, 4 Nov. 1765; *London Chronicle*, 5 Nov. 1765.

[5] B.M. Add. MSS. 32971, fos. 248–9; 32973, fo. 55.

[6] B.M. Add. MSS. 32971, fos. 368–9; 32972, fos. 60–1; *Bute Letters*, pp. 242–3.

[7] B.M. Add. MSS. 32972, fos. 95–9.

depend, in consequence of it, upon their success in Parliament.'[1] This confidence was maintained in the face of the continued failure of attempts to improve the government's debating strength in the House of Commons. In early November there was even an unfounded rumour that Conway intended to return to the army, and that Rockingham would appoint Charles Townshend in his post as Secretary of State.[2] Townshend was again offered a place in the cabinet, but declined it; and Lord North refused the lucrative post of Joint Vice-Treasurer of Ireland.[3] Newcastle, that politician of vast experience, was unhappy both about these setbacks and about the news that Lord George Sackville had accepted one of the Irish Vice-Treasurerships. The Duke correctly feared that this favour to the man whose notorious conduct at the battle of Minden in 1759 had made that victory incomplete would offend not only Pitt but other potential supporters.[4]

The significance of Cumberland's death for American policy can be seen in retrospect as ending the possibility that the administration might seek to apply the Stamp Act by force. Rockingham and his colleagues were now able to avail themselves of more information and more time for consideration before making any decision. On 9 and 10 November news came from the governors of Maryland, New Jersey, and New Hampshire of the resignation of the Stamp-Distributors for their colonies. A few days later, on 15 November, reports of the Stamp Act Congress in New York came in letters from Lieutenant-Governor Colden and General Gage. After stating that the Assemblies of Maryland, Pennsylvania, and Rhode Island had passed Addresses similar to those of Virginia, Gage made this comment on the Stamp Act Congress: 'The question is not of the inexpediency of the Stamp Act, or of the inability of the colonies to pay the tax, but that it is unconstitutional, and contrary to their rights.' Gage ended with an extraordinary deduction from his reports of months of widespread defiance and disorder.

---

[1] B.M. Add. MSS. 32972, fos. 78–9.

[2] B.M. Add. MSS. 32971, fo. 318.

[3] B.M. Add. MSS. 32971, fos. 390–1; 32972, fos. 93–4. The two Irish posts were reckoned at this time to be worth over £2000 each. *London Evening Post*, 2 Nov. 1765.

[4] B.M. Add. MSS. 32972, fos. 95–101.

It is impossible to say, whether the execution of the Stamp Act will meet with further opposition; but from present appearances, there is reason to judge, that it may be introduced without much difficulty, in several of the colonies, and if it is began in some, that it will soon spread over the rest.[1]

This assessment probably caused the ministry to postpone any decision about the Stamp Act until after news came of its reception on 1 November. Gage's optimism was matched by that of the administration. The official view, expressed in Conway's circular letters of 24 October, was that the resistance came only from 'the lower and more ignorant of the people; the better and wiser part of the colonies will know, that decency and submission may prevail not only to redress grievances, but to obtain grace and favour'.[2] Ministers also thought that news of the change of administration would help to allay colonial discontent, an opinion widely held in London and not entirely unfounded.[3] The hope that the American crisis would somehow resolve itself was, of course, a delusion; but it served to deter the ministry from any hasty decision about the Stamp Act.

During the interval of waiting for news the ministry came under pressure for suspension or repeal of the Stamp Act from agents, merchants, and other friends of the colonies. No evidence has been found of any collective action by the colonial agents in the closing months of 1765, but individual agents were extremely busy.[4] Foremost among them was Benjamin Franklin. From at least November onwards Franklin made a point of seeing as many individual M.P.s as possible to inform and instruct them on the colonial crisis:[5] and he had earlier thrown himself into the public debate on the principle and expediency of colonial taxation that was argued in the press by pseudonymous correspondents. Between August 1765 and February 1766 Franklin was responsible for news items that appeared in the *London Chronicle* and *Lloyd's Evening Post,* and he answered attacks on the colonists in these papers and also

---

[1] C.O. 5/83, pp. 767–9; printed *Gage Corr.* i. 69–70.
[2] B.M. Add. MSS. 32971, fos. 91–8.
[3] B.M. Add. MSS. 32971, fos. 77–8; *London Evening Post,* 19 Oct. 1765.
[4] For some details on the activities of individual agents at this time see Sosin, *Agents and Merchants,* pp. 71–3; and Kammen, *Rope of Sand,* pp. 118–24.
[5] Kammen, *Rope of Sand,* pp. 119–20; *Franklin Papers,* xiii. 165.

in the *Gazetteer* and the *Public Advertiser* by letters published over at least seven different pseudonyms. In January 1766 alone Franklin published nine such letters, and about the end of that month produced his famous Stamp Act cartoon *Magna Britannia: Her Colonies Reduced*.[1]

Franklin devoted much time and effort to this private lobbying of M.P.s and public propaganda, but he was well aware that the attitude of the administration would be the key factor in the American crisis. Right at the beginning of the Rockingham ministry Franklin had seen in the political change the hope of repeal, writing to his son Governor William Franklin on 26 July. 'We have . . . so many friends among the *ins*, that we think of endeavouring, if they continue, to get a repeal of the Stamp Act. No endeavour of mine shall be wanting, but I have not much hopes, such things once done are seldom given up.'[2] Even if complete repeal could not be obtained, the ministry might be persuaded to make some lesser concession: and as the news of colonial resistance came from across the Atlantic Franklin made it his business to see personally the men who would make the final decision. On 6 November he had a long audience with President of the Board of Trade Lord Dartmouth, and warned him that the execution of the Stamp Act would cause 'more mischief than it was worth, by totally alienating the affections of the Americans from this country, and thereby lessening its commerce'. The policy Franklin urged upon Dartmouth was a suspension of the Stamp Act for a number of years, until it could be dropped on some pretext without any decision on the question of the right of taxation: money should be raised instead by a return to the former system of requisitions. Alternatively, if the Address of the Stamp Act Congress was such as to make this course of action impossible, a Royal Commission should be sent to America to inquire into colonial grievances.[3] Franklin con-

---

[1] *Franklin Papers*, xii. 183–8, 207, 243–6, 253–5, 278–80, 406–7, 410–16; xiii. 4–8, 18–22, 26–8, 38–9, 44–9, 52–8, 63–72, 118–20, 162–3.

[2] *Franklin Papers*, xii. 222.

[3] Thomas Pownall was advocating the same idea in Jan. 1766. Dowdeswell warned Rockingham on 16 Jan. to expect a visit from him. 'He is very fond of sending some person of *great rank* assisted by a Council to inquire into and settle the complaints of the Americans upon the spot.' Pownall had in mind the King's brother, the Duke of York, and had mentioned the plan to him. Wentworth Woodhouse MSS. R.1–326.

cluded from this interview that 'the present ministry are truly perplexed how to act on the occasion; as if they relax, their predecessors will reproach them with giving up the honour, dignity, and power of this nation. And yet even they, I am told, think they have carried things too far.' A meeting with Rockingham himself on 10 November doubtless confirmed Franklin's impression of the ministry's goodwill towards the colonies:[1] and it was probably the occasion when he handed over or arranged to send a collection of extracts he had made from letters he had received describing the disturbed conditions in several colonies. These included several accounts from Pennsylvania Stamp-Distributor John Hughes of his troubles in Philadelphia; a report from the Maryland Stamp-Distributor Zachariah Hood of his flight to New York; and the opinion of James Parker of Burlington that 'one half of the Americans will die rather than submit to it'.[2]

Two days after seeing Franklin Rockingham had his first meeting with London merchant Barlow Trecothick, who was to play a vital role during the next few months. Newcastle had from the first seen the value of co-operation with the mercantile interest. In early September he urged Conway to consult with 'some honest North American merchants':[3] and later the same month he unsuccessfully tried to persuade Trecothick to stand at a by-election for Shoreham, saying the ministry would be glad to have such an expert on America in the House of Commons.[4] A few weeks later Trecothick himself took the initiative, writing to Rockingham on 7 November to express concern about the effect of the Stamp Act on trade with the colonies. Since American ships with unstamped papers were liable to seizure in any ports in Britain or other colonies, he foresaw an immediate end of colonial exports and a chain of consequent disasters.

Our sugar islands will be deprived of their usual supplies of provisions lumber etc. and perhaps be disabled from sending home their produce or even subsisting their slaves. The British merchants will

---

[1] *Franklin Papers*, xii. 361–5.

[2] Franklin substituted 'submit to it' for the word 'yield' in Parker's letter. The extracts may be found in the Treasury papers, T.1/442, fos. 349–52: and are printed in *Franklin Papers*, xii. 263–6, 269–70, 276–8.

[3] B.M. Add. MSS. 32969, fo. 221.   [4] B.M. Add. MSS. 32970, fos. 54–5.

have little or no chance of remittances . . . these accumulated disappointments must prove fatal to many of the British merchants trading to America . . . a total stop must be put to all purchase of manufactures for a country whence no returns can be expected: from this state it naturally and unavoidably follows, that an exceedingly great number of manufacturers are soon to be without employ and of course without bread!

Trecothick's purpose was to persuade Rockingham to obtain a Parliamentary decision on America before the Christmas recess: otherwise March would be 'the soonest any repeal or suspension of the act can reach America . . . so long a stop to circulation must be fatal to all or most branches of American commerce'.[1] Rockingham asked him to dinner on 12 November, and in his reply explained the ministry's attitude and the reasons why he could not comply with Trecothick's request.[2]

The difficulties are great: the importance of the obedience in the colonies . . . [to the] British legislature is no slight matter and yet perhaps it may be beyond doubt that the occasion which gave rise to all this confusion was ill-judged here. The particular and great inconveniences which you mention were perhaps *intentionally to be so*, in order to force the compliance. When you consider the present circumstances you will not find that an earlier meeting of Parliament than intended can be of the utility you would hope. The persons who were the planners etc of the act will be the chief persons sitting in the House, and the time necessary for re-elections must still be given before you could expect any moderating measures.[3] Even as yet we have not all the evidence, which a few days or weeks will give us of the disposition of America and upon so nice a point it is both necessary and wise to wait for good grounds to proceed upon.

Trecothick's approach to Rockingham reflected the genuine, spontaneous and widespread concern of British merchants about the collapse of colonial trade. The Society of Merchant

---

[1] Wentworth Woodhouse MSS. R.24–43a. No British merchant ever seems to have complained that British ships using American ports would be liable to stamp duties on clearance papers, a fact Professor I. R. Christie pointed out to me.

[2] Wentworth Woodhouse MSS. R.81–181.

[3] Any M.P.s obtaining office had to vacate their seats: those who were now ministers and their chief supporters would therefore be absent from the Commons at the December meeting of Parliament.

Venturers in Bristol had sent a petition to the Treasury as early as 29 October.[1] That port was particularly vulnerable to a recession in American trade, and Trecothick was to tell the House of Commons on 11 February 1766 that the initiative for the national wave of petitions to Parliament early in 1766 came indirectly from Bristol merchants, for it was they who had urged their colleagues in London to take action.[2] Trecothick himself was soon organizing the protest of British merchants and manufacturers about the catastrophic fall in American trade: and on 12 December he led a delegation of merchants who presented the two Secretaries of State Grafton and Conway with a pile of cancelled American orders for British goods.[3] Already Trecothick had instigated the more important step of a national campaign. On 4 December he took the chair at a general meeting of London merchants trading to America, convened by public advertisement. The meeting elected a Committee of twenty-eight members, chosen to represent the commercial interests of the various colonies, and instructed it 'to consider of the best method of application for procuring the relief and encouragement of the North American trade and to apply to the outports and to the manufacturing cities and towns for their concurrence and assistance'.[4] The Committee met two days later, when Trecothick was authorized to send a minute of the meeting of 4 December and the following circular letter to the 'chief magistrate' of the main trading and manufacturing towns.[5]

Sir, the present state of the British trade to North America, and the prospect of increasing embarrassments which threaten the loss of our depending property there, and even to annihilate the trade itself have occasioned a general meeting to be called of the merchants in this city concerned in that branch of business.

As the gentlemen of your city and almost every other maritime and manufacturing part of these Kingdoms must be affected by the distresses of North American commerce we have thought it our duty

[1] Minchinton, *Politics and the Port of Bristol*, pp. 102–3.
[2] B.M. Add. MSS. 33030, fo. 101.
[3] *Lloyd's Evening Post*, 13 Dec. 1765.
[4] B.M. Add. MSS. 38339, fo. 166.
[5] B.M. Add. MSS. 22358, fo. 52. Various copies of this circular letter survive. That cited here was sent to Norwich. For the one to Leeds see Wentworth Woodhouse MSS. R.1–537.

to acquaint you (as we now do by the copy enclosed) with our proceedings, as well as to ask your concurrence and assistance in support of a regular application to Parliament or otherwise by a petition from your body and by all the interest you can make with your own Members and with the Members in your neighbourhood, who with all other land owners we think greatly interested in the prosperity of trade and manufactures from which so great an additional value is derived to their property.

We desire to unite with you in a measure so essential to the best interests of Great Britain, wishing to have your sentiments on the subject, through the course of which we mean to take for our guide the interest of these kingdoms, it being our opinion that conclusive arguments for granting every ease or advantage the North Americans can with propriety desire may be fairly deduced from that principle only.

This circular letter was sent to thirty towns, and twenty-six petitions were to be submitted to the House of Commons early in 1766. No detailed correlation can be established. Some petitions came from towns so small that it is unlikely they were circularized by Trecothick, while several of the large towns that petitioned would probably have done so without any prompting from London. Little evidence has been found either on the reception of Trecothick's letter or on the background of the petitions. Only six towns are definitely known to have received this letter, Birmingham, Bristol, Leeds, Liverpool, Manchester, and Norwich: all except Norwich sent petitions to the Commons. In Birmingham the local *Gazette* was printing news of American riots and trade boycotts from October, but it is probable that Birmingham would not have petitioned without the stimulus of Trecothick's letter.[1] Iron manufacturer Samuel Garbett, a pioneer in industrial lobbying,[2] then took charge of the campaign. A promise of support was sent to Trecothick on 21 December, signed by Garbett and nineteen others. This reply reported the financial embarrassment of merchants who could not recover American debts and had lost their colonial market, and forecast that thousands

---

[1] This is the conclusion of Dr. John Money from his study of the available evidence. I am indebted to Dr. Money for supplying me with information from his forthcoming study of political opinion in the West Midlands during the reign of George III.

[2] Norris, *Econ. Hist. Rev.*, 2nd Series, 10 (1957–8), 450–60.

would soon be out of work. The same day Garbett sent copies
of both letters to Lord Dartmouth, announcing that there would
soon be a meeting of Birmingham merchants to discuss the subject and ask for repeal of the Stamp Act. Dartmouth was doubly
concerned in the matter, as President of the Board of Trade
and as a man with personal investments in the West Midlands
iron industry; and Garbett kept him informed of subsequent
developments in the Birmingham campaign. The Birmingham
meeting took place on 24 December, and nominated a Committee to draft both a petition to the House of Commons and
a circular letter to all peers likely to be sympathetic. The
petition, forecasting dire consequences from sudden large-
scale unemployment, was completed by 4 January 1766.[1]
In Liverpool Trecothick's letter was concealed from the
merchants until Sir William Meredith, one of the port's M.P.s,
told them about it: they then held a meeting and 'resolved to
answer him in the manner that became them'.[2] By the end of
the year a Committee of American merchants in the port had
drawn up a petition and sent copies to other towns so that 'we
may be as uniform as possible in our application'. In Bristol
this suggestion was unnecessary. Here the opposition to the
Stamp Act was organized by the Society of Merchant Venturers, which sent numerous letters to other towns, including
an offer to draft a petition for Birmingham. The Society's
petition, drawn up on on 6 January, closely followed a scheme
suggested by Trecothick in a letter of 2 January: and on the
evening of the same day other Bristol merchants who were not
members of the Society drew up their own separate petition.[3]

The opposition in Parliament was to assert that the petitioning campaign was an artificial creation of the ministers and
their supporters, and cited the role of Meredith in organizing
the petition from Manchester.[4] Trecothick in his evidence to
the House of Commons on 11 February 1766 was to deny this

[1] *H.M.C. Dartmouth*, ii. 28, 32.

[2] Wentworth Woodhouse MSS.: Burke Papers, i. fo. 44; Meredith to Burke,
1 Jan. 1776.

[3] For a brief account of the Bristol background see Minchinton, *V.M.H.B.*
73 (1965), 152–3.

[4] For this point see Wentworth Woodhouse MSS.: Burke Papers, i. fo. 39;
Meredith to Burke, 11 Dec. 1765: and the evidence of Robert Hamilton of Manchester to the House of Commons on 13 Feb. 1766. B.M. Add. MSS. 33030,
fos. 157–8.

charge. He claimed that there would have been petitions without his circular letter, and stated that it had been the policy of his London Committee to refuse to supply draft petitions even on request: 'we thought it too indecent and desired them to speak from their own feelings and that none should complain but what was aggrieved'.[1] This was not the whole truth. The economic distress that led to many of the protests was to some extent the result of deliberate pressure by merchants upon manufacturers: Bristol merchant Henry Cruger related afterwards that 'not one American Merchant gave out a *single order* for goods, on purpose to compel all manufacturers to engage with us in petitioning Parliament for a repeal of the Stamp Act, by which thousands were out of employ and in a starving condition'.[2] The opposition complaint, however, was not about the unfairness of this tactic; and interference by Parliamentary politicians in apparently spontaneous local protests was common practice. Opposition leaders also had influence in several areas. There is reason to think that the need to obtain the support of Lord Gower for canal projects in the West Midlands was an important factor in damping down complaints against the Stamp Act there: and Lord Buckinghamshire's intervention may have been decisive in preventing any petition from Norwich. He was apparently shown the Trecothick circular letter sent to the town, and the mayor's reply to it on 14 December merely promised support for 'whatever is recommended by your Committee consistent with the honour and real interest of Great Britain, and the true and lasting interest of North America'. The London answer, sent on 27 December, announced that the Committee intended to petition Parliament 'on the subject of the present declension and the prospect of a total failure of that trade', and expressed the hope that there would be a supporting petition from Norwich; but none was sent.[3]

This campaign by the merchants provided the first sign that the administration, or at least Rockingham himself, had decided on a policy of conciliation towards the colonies. For Trecothick's circular letter was approved by Rockingham,

[1] B.M. Add. MSS. 33030, fos. 101, 106.
[2] *Commerce of Rhode Island*, i. 145.
[3] Copies of this correspondence survive in Lord Buckinghamshire's papers. B.M. Add. MSS. 22358, fos. 32–3.

and perhaps drafted in concert with him.[1] The Marquess evidently foresaw that a substantial volume of protest about the adverse economic consequences of the Stamp Act on British trade and manufactures would give him room to manoeuvre in any attempt to persuade Parliament to make concessions over the Stamp Act: and he maintained interest in the progress of the campaign, for he told Newcastle on 2 January 1766 that 'Trecothick and the merchants and trading and manufacturing towns, etc, go on well'.[2] Rockingham was able to embark upon a round of consultations in the knowledge that this weapon would be available as one means of pushing Parliament towards conciliation.

The American news in December brought the crisis to a head. Already confirmation of the collapse of British authority in Massachusetts had been arriving in regular reports from Governor Bernard. He still directed most of his correspondence to the Board of Trade, where his friend John Pownall was the Secretary. On 17 December the Board considered, and promptly referred to the Privy Council, a mass of evidence sent by Bernard, including six letters addressed to the Board or to Pownall himself that portrayed the deliberate destruction of royal government by force. Here is Bernard's wry concluding remark on 8 November: 'There is such an appearance of tranquility that I may remain here a cypher some time longer.'[3] This sorry tale was not unexpected, but the information from New York was disheartening to those who had hoped to hear of the peaceful acceptance of the Stamp Act on 1 November. Instead a mob in the town burned the expensive coach of Lieutenant-Governor Colden, with his effigy on top, and sacked the private house of Major Thomas James, commander

---

[1] A delegation from the London Committee visited him; *The Gentleman's Magazine*, 1765, p. 588: and a draft of the circular in the Rockingham papers, which has some verbal differences from the one finally issued, has the following endorsement. 'N.B. This letter concerted between the Marquess of R. and Mr. Trecothick the principal instrument in the happy repeal of the Stamp Act, which without giving up the British authority quieted the Empire.' Wentworth Woodhouse MSS. R.1–335; printed *Rockingham Memoirs*, i. 319. This endorsement is noted on the MS. as having been made by Edmund Burke, but Dr. D. H. Watson believes the writing to be that of Lady Rockingham.

[2] B.M. Add. MSS. 32973, fo. 13.

[3] *J.C.T.P. 1764–7*, p. 235; *Acts. P.C. Col.* vi. 412–15.

of Fort George. Major James himself arrived in Britain on 9 December, and saw Secretary of State Conway the next day.[1] Ministerial reaction was reflected in the comment of George Onslow to Newcastle on 11 December. 'Here is dreadful news from America. Nothing less than a rebellion at New York.'[2] More ominous news even than the riots was that of the colonial boycott intended to force a change of government policy. The resolutions of the New York merchants on 31 October, that orders for British goods should be conditional on repeal of the Stamp Act, were publicly known in London by the middle of December;[3] and by the end of the month news had come of the similar boycott resolutions passed by Philadelphia merchants on 7 November.[4] The recent events had caused even General Gage to change his mind about the prospects of enforcing the Stamp Act: and his revised opinion must have carried the more weight with the ministry in its contrast with his earlier optimism. His letter of 4 November warned that 'unless the act will from its own nature at length enforce it, nothing but a very considerable military force can do it': and another letter four days later explained the colonial strategy.[5]

Their first plan of clamor, in terrifying the stamp officers, and even threats of rebellion to prevent the stamps, being issued, has been completed throughout. And in order to gain the merchants in Great Britain to their interest, the American merchants have wrote that no dry goods may be sent out to them, unless the Stamp Act is repealed, and some go as far as to say they will not pay their debts but upon that condition; and they flatter themselves, from all these circumstances that the Parliament will be prevailed upon to repeal the act.

The news from America had brought home to the administration not merely the gravity of the colonial situation but also the inefficiency of its own arrangements for collecting information; and a decision to streamline this procedure preceded any

[1] B.M. Add. MSS. 33030, fo. 84. For the New York riots see Engleman, *W.M.Q.* 10 (1953), 560–78.
[2] B.M. Add. MSS. 32972, fos. 202–3.
[3] *London Evening Post*, 12 Dec. 1765.
[4] *London Evening Post*, 26 Dec. 1765.
[5] *Gage Corr.* i. 71, 73.

final considerations of policy. The Commander-in-Chief and most colonial governors were now writing directly to Secretary of State Conway: but reports from various officials were also sent to the Board of Trade, the Privy Council, and such other departments as the Stamp Office, the Board of Customs, and the Treasury. This state of affairs was not conducive to the prompt consideration of colonial news, especially as there is reason to think that the Board of Trade was dilatory in its conduct of business. A letter of 5 October from Governor Wentworth of New Hampshire describing opposition to the Stamp Act in his colony arrived on 9 November, but the Board did not read it until 6 December.[1] The Board had to clear a backlog of American business on 20 December, the day after it received requests from the two Secretaries of State for papers to be laid before Parliament: the Lords of Trade then read a letter of 26 September from Bernard, which had arrived on 4 November; a letter of 10 October from Governor William Franklin of New Jersey, and one of 2 October from Lieutenant-Governor Fauquier of Virginia.[2] Such administrative delays obviously constituted an unsatisfactory state of affairs as the time came for a decision on colonial policy, and an attempt to speed the flow of information was made on 25 December. Conway then wrote to the Board of Trade and the Privy Council requesting that all future reports from America should be sent at once to him.[3]

The ministry now had to make up its mind what to do about the Stamp Act. There was no longer any basis for the earlier hopes that the colonial resistance would prove to have been only the reaction of lower-class mobs, and that the act would come into operation after the disturbances had ceased. The practical choice lay between military enforcement of the act and some form of concession: this might be modification or alteration of the act, suspension, or complete repeal. All these possibilities were canvassed in the public debate on America conducted in the press during the closing months of 1765. Even among the commentators who favoured conciliation,

---

[1] *J.C.T.P. 1764–7*, p. 232.

[2] *J.C.T.P. 1764–7*, pp. 236–8.

[3] *J.C.T.P. 1764–7*, p. 240; *Acts. P.C. Col.* vi. 415. Similar letters may have been sent to other departments.

however, there was a general realization that simple repeal would both be and appear as a surrender of Parliament's sovereignty to mob violence. The most popular and realistic suggestion to contemporaries was the face-saving device of suspension, either permanently or at least until there was an opportunity for Parliament to hear petitions from the colonies: in mid-December the aim of the colonial agents was believed to be no more than one year's suspension of the Stamp Act.[1] But the ministry was to devise a more complex and permanent solution than mere suspension to the dilemma of simultaneously pacifying America and allaying the concern of British public opinion about the maintenance of sovereignty over the colonies.

[1] *London Evening Post*, 17 Dec. 1765.

F

PARLIAMENT met on 17 December even though the administration had come to no decision on American policy. The reason was the technicality of the constitution mentioned by Rockingham to Trecothick the previous month. It was essential for the future conduct of business that writs should be issued before Christmas for the re-election of all members who had vacated their seats by accepting office under Rockingham; and such writs could only be ordered by the House of Commons itself. These members included Conway, Dowdeswell, and other prospective administration spokesmen in the Commons, none of whom could be present at the opening of the session. Their absence would prove inconvenient, for a stormy start to Parliamentary business was anticipated. The unpredictable Pitt was for the moment immured at Bath by ill health;[1] but the administration knew that Grenville and Bedford were mobilizing their friends for an immediate attack over the colonial situation.[2] In November there took place at Bath what Lord Chesterfield described as 'a congress of the ex-ministers', attended by Grenville, Bedford, Sandwich, Weymouth, and Gower, but not Halifax.[3] From the first news of colonial resistance to the Stamp Act Grenville and his friends had decided to raise the matter in Parliament; and a determination to press the ministry for strong measures resulted from the fuller knowledge of the American situation that came towards the end of the year.[4] George Onslow told Newcastle on 11 December, 'the old ministers I hear are violent. That will do no good on either side':[5] and Newcastle reported to his old

---

[1] B.M. Add. MSS. 32971, fos. 129–30; 32972, fos. 100–1. Pitt's illness was genuine and not political, as some contemporaries suspected: Chatham Papers, ii. 330, 335–6; Chesterfield Letters, vi. 2672, 2685.

[2] B.M. Add. MSS. 32971, fos. 368–9; 32972, fos. 100–1, 126–33.

[3] Chesterfield Letters, vi. 2678, 2685–6. Bedford took the opportunity of paying a social visit to Pitt, who told his wife that they had had 'fitting discourse for such emeriti'. Chatham Papers, ii. 335.

[4] Grenville Papers, iii. 78, 100–1, 108; Bedford Papers, iii. 323; Jenkinson Papers, p. 393; Gipson, British Empire, x. 371–2.

[5] B.M. Add. MSS. 32972, fos. 202–3.

friend John White on 15 December that 'the Duke of Bedford, Geo. Grenville, Lord Temple, with some stragglers of my Lord Bute's and Lord Holland's are to make the opposition'.[1]

In the absence of either a policy or spokesmen, the ministry adopted the tactic of preparing only a short and formal King's Speech, hoping to avoid a major debate on the colonial crisis. The original intention was to omit any reference to America whatsoever! Rockingham sent Newcastle draft copies of the Speech and the Commons, Address of Thanks in reply on 9 December, saying that he hoped for the Duke's help in framing the Lords' Address. Newcastle returned the drafts next day with his approval.[2] But then came the news of the New York riots of 1 November, and Rockingham regretfully observed to Newcastle that 'the news from North America of great disturbances at New York . . . will oblige us to mention North America by name in the Speech'.[3] The Address prepared for the House of Commons was also altered at the last minute, so Rockingham told the King, 'in order to accommodate it more to some persons in his Majesty's service': but the cabinet decided to make no change in the wording of the Lords' Address.[4]

Even before he knew what the Speech would say Grenville had decided to propose an amendment to the Address 'in support of the legislative authority over the colonies'.[5] The Speech was not finally completed until 15 December, and Jenkinson informed Grenville the same evening of the vague wording of both Speech and Address.[6] He thought that Grenville's best tactic would be to attack the Address without suggesting any formal amendment. Sir Fletcher Norton informed Grenville that he would not support the amendment, and this caution was to be displayed by many who finally

---

[1] Ibid., fos. 249–50.

[2] Ibid., fos. 176–7, 193–4.

[3] Ibid., fos. 214–15.

[4] *Corr. of George III*, i. 199–200. The alteration of the Commons' Address came after criticism from Gilbert Elliot and Charles Townshend. Elliot, *Border Elliots*, pp. 396–7. The Lords' Address already promised 'a resolution to do everything which the exigency of the case may require'. The Speech and Addresses may be found in the *Journals* of the respective Houses for 17 Dec. 1765, and in Cobbett, *Parl. Hist.* xvi. 83–90.

[5] *Jenkinson Papers*, p. 401.

[6] *Grenville Papers*, iii. 110–11.

came down in support of Grenville. But Grenville refused to heed advice, and overplayed his hand in this short December meeting of Parliament.[1]

The debate in the Commons on 17 December was the anticlimax that the ministers had planned.[2] The King's Speech merely stated that 'matters of importance have lately occurred in some of my colonies in America'; and the Address promised 'diligence and attention to these important occurrences in America' after the Christmas recess. Grenville at once rose to attack this 'weak' description of what he called 'an open rebellion', comparable to the Jacobite Rising of 1745. Speaking in a manner described as *en prince* by Pittite George Cooke, he proposed a long amendment to express indignation at events in America and to promise support for the enforcement of obedience to King and Parliament. After Whately had seconded him there followed a debate of several hours in which nineteen members spoke. George Cooke and William Beckford described the resistance as being a series of mob riots rather than a rebellion; and Beckford now questioned Parliament's right to levy internal taxation in the colonies.[3] Most speakers opposed Grenville's amendment by the simple argument that further information was needed before any opinions were voiced or decisions made. They included Charles Townshend, in a speech which confused and amused contemporaries; and also several members who were later to oppose repeal of the Stamp Act, Gilbert Elliot, Alexander Wedderburn, Sir Fletcher Norton, and Lord George Sackville. Altogether thirteen members spoke for the Address; Grenville, seeing that he had pressed the subject too far too soon, withdrew his amendment for the sake of unanimity, and the Address was voted *nem. con.* at 6 o'clock.

The administration had also been apprehensive of the debate in the House of Lords, for there Grenville and Bedford had a

---

[1] *Jenkinson Papers*, pp. 401–2.

[2] The following account of the debate is based on the *Commons Journals*, xxx. 437–8; Harris Diary, 17 Dec. 1765; H. Walpole, *Memoirs*, ii. 350–3; Elliot, *Border Elliots*, p. 397; and two letters (a) G. Cooke to W. Pitt, *Chatham Papers*, ii. 350–3. (b) H. S. Conway to George III, *Corr. of George III*, i. 201–2. Quotations are from the Harris Diary.

[3] Diarist Harris summarized Beckford as follows: 'doubts our power of laying an internal tax, yet says we are omnipotent'.

following formidable alike in debating strength and numbers, and on the question of America they also expected the support of Lord Bute and his friends.[1] The anxiety of ministers was reflected in the care taken to compile a list of the sixty-one peers present at the eve-of-session reading of the King's Speech, a list sent by Rockingham to George III;[2] and the next day saw the first known debate on America in the House of Lords, after the Address had been moved by Hardwicke and seconded by the Duke of Manchester.[3] An amendment similar to that proposed by Grenville in the Commons was put by his follower Suffolk, and supported by Sandwich, Gower, Halifax, Temple, Lyttelton, Buckinghamshire, and the Duke of Bedford. Mansfield made an equivocal speech, attempting to persuade the administration to accept the amendment, and then withdrew before the vote he had tried to prevent. Of Pitt's followers Camden left without speaking or voting, but Shelburne opposed the amendment. For the ministry only the Duke of Grafton, Dartmouth, and Northington spoke against the amendment. No speeches were made by Newcastle, offended because Rockingham had not asked for his debating assistance, or by Rockingham himself, too shy to speak. Shelburne thought the administration had fared badly in the debate. 'The opposition, consisting of the late ministers, showed a great deal of factious ability; which, as it was not much pulled to pieces by any one, appeared to me to pass for real. The administration seemed to have formed a resolution to avoid debate on that day, and therefore interfered but little.' He also told Pitt that 'the prejudice against the Americans on the whole seemed very great, and no very decided opinion in favour of the ministry; yet, such is the power of even a changeable court influence, that the administration divided eighty to twenty-four', a triumph attributed by Horace Walpole to the behaviour of Lord Bute, who with his chief supporters voted for the ministry.

[1] H. Walpole, *Memoirs*, ii. 167.

[2] *Corr. of George III*, i. 200–1.

[3] For this debate see *Lords Journals*, xxxi. 227–30; Harris Diary, 17 Dec. 1765; H. Walpole, *Memoirs*, ii. 167; Cobbett, *Parl. Hist.* xvi. 84–7; and two letters (a) Rockingham to George III, *Corr. of George III*, I. 203–4. (b) Shelburne to Pitt, *Chatham Papers*, ii. 253–6. For a list of the opposition minority, see B.M. Add. MSS. 33035, fos. 206–8.

Bedford then gave notice that on 19 December he would move for papers concerning the American crisis. Grafton thereupon informed the House that he had already been directed by the King to lay such papers before it. He had been given no such personal authority; but the King's Speech had already promised that Parliament would have full information on the subject, and the Duke explained to George III afterwards that he had acted 'to save that day's discussion, and thinking it would have a better appearance'.[1] The King assured Grafton that his answer had been 'perfectly right', and his comment reflected his continuing animosity to the Grenville ministry.

I desire the papers may be made out fully for the Houses, and think that they should see what great care the last administration took by the wise regulations they made for putting the Stamp Act in execution, or else they wont have the whole before them; and then I think the Duke of Bedford and his friends will wish no papers had been called for.[2]

On the next day, 18 December, Grafton sent letters requesting American papers for the House of Lords to the Lord President of the Council, the Treasury, the Board of Trade, and his fellow Secretary Conway.[3]

In the House of Commons that day Grenville, on the report of the Address, again objected to the mild phrase 'important occurrences'. He and his friends gave a verbal negative to the motion, but did not force a vote.[4] Richard Rigby then proposed the motion that Bedford had threatened in the Lords, an Address to the King for copies of all papers received from, or sent to, North America. This was seconded by Grenville, and promptly opposed by Beckford and Sir William Baker, who reminded members that papers had already been promised

---

[1] *Corr. to George III*, i. 203. H. Walpole ascribed the incident itself to 19 Dec. *Memoirs*, ii. 167–8. Morgan, *Stamp Act Crisis*, p. 333, misleadingly states that the House adjourned without agreeing to Bedford's request.

[2] Grafton MSS., no. 482.

[3] *Cal. Home Office Papers 1760–5*, p. 640; *Acts. P.C. Col.* vi. 415; *J.C.T.P. 1764–7*, p. 236.

[4] For the debates of this day see *Commons Journals*, xxx. 441; Harris Diary, 18 Dec. 1765; H. Walpole, *Memoirs*, ii. 167–8; and two letters: (a) G. Onslow to Newcastle, B.M. Add. MSS. 32972, fos. 281–2; (b) Conway to George III, *Corr. of George III*, i. 205.

in the King's Speech. Procedural expert Jeremiah Dyson therefore moved the previous question, a device to avoid a direct vote on the motion. This was carried by 70 votes to 35 after sixteen members had spoken in a brief debate, including James Oswald and Rose Fuller for administration, and Alexander Wedderburn and Lord North for opposition. Lists of the minority show that a number of independent members voted with Grenville, but George Onslow ignored this omen in his jubilant note to Newcastle. 'We have just had a glorious division . . . the Tories and Lord Bute's people with them.'[1]

Diarist James Harris was puzzled by the ministry's determination to reject the motion, since the papers had already been promised in the King's Speech and conceded in the Lords. The Commons could not be denied them; and the next day Conway followed Grafton's example by sending letters asking for papers for the House of Commons to the Lord President, the Treasury, and the Board of Trade.[2] But the motion in the Commons had annoyed ministers as a gratuitous insult to their good faith, and reports of the debate sent to the King were couched in terms of vehement indignation.[3] George III reciprocated these sentiments, thanking Conway for 'the account of the very ungentlemanlike conduct of Mr. Grenville on this day, for others of the opposition, undoubtedly, act in the House of Commons by his advice. I hope people will be on their guard tomorrow, if he should again try to give some pain.'[4] Grenville did make one more attempt to harass ministers, on 20 December putting forward an amendment to substitute 7 January for the adjournment then proposed to 14 January. This was defeated by 77 votes to 35 after a brief skirmish with Beckford, who blamed him as 'the author of all the troubles in America'. Grenville, so Horace Walpole understood, 'threw the blame from himself on the Parliament'.[5]

[1] It is possible to name twenty-six out of the thirty-seven members, including two tellers, in the minority. Six spoke in the debate; Conway named ten others to the King; Harris confirmed six, and named nine more; and one more can be added as a teller.

[2] *Cal. Home Office Papers 1760–5*, p. 641; *Acts. P.C. Col.* vi. 415; *J.C.T.P. 1764–7*, p. 237.

[3] *Corr. of George III*, i. 204–5.

[4] *Rockingham Memoirs*, i. 259. Namier, *Additions and Corrections*, p. 42.

[5] *Commons Journals*, xxx. 445; H. Walpole, *Memoirs*, ii. 168.

Grenville's eager and immediate opposition at this brief meeting of Parliament had been ill judged. When Horace Walpole heard the Parliamentary news in Paris, he thought the outcome favourable to the administration. 'The thinness of both Houses indicates how many were waiting the event; and they, good folks, will hardly resort into a beaten camp.'[1] Grenville's genuine indignation at the administration's failure to produce an American policy had distorted his political judgement: he had ignored the customary absence before Christmas of many independent members, and his attack on the ministry had been thought premature even by some of his friends. Grenville himself had forfeited much of the personal standing in the Commons he had acquired as the King's minister; such at least was the uncharitable opinion of Edmund Burke, not yet himself an M.P.[2]

He was kind to show his personal insufficiency and his party weakness at the very opening of the campaign; his uncandid and ungentlemanly opposition, contrary to his public declarations to men who were not present to answer him has done infinite service. He shows I think no talents of a leader; he wanted the stage of administration to give him figure. He is eager, petulant, inaccurate, without dignity, and quite the reverse of that character, which might be expected from a man just descended from such great situations.

In December the administration made a first positive move towards the formulation of American policy. Rockingham's tactics had always been to obtain as wide and informal a sounding of opinion as possible; and during the last two months of 1765 he and his colleagues received a great deal of advice and information on the colonial problem, much of it unsolicited. The consensus of opinion was in favour of repeal, a course of action urged not only by the merchants trading with America but also by such conservatives as John Wentworth of New Hampshire and former Massachusetts agent William Bollan.[3] The one man whose advice was for modification only was Henry McCulloh, who failed to realize that the colonial

---

[1] H. Walpole, *Letters*, vi. 386. [2] *Burke Corr*. i. 224.

[3] For a full description see D. H. Watson's M.A. Thesis. Much of the evidence is to be found among the papers of Rockingham and Dartmouth.

objection was to the principle of taxation and not to the details of the Stamp Act.[1] By the end of November Rockingham was relying on a small unofficial group of advisers rather than the cabinet, as Newcastle complained to John White on 3 December: he told his friend that he did not intend much longer to attend formal cabinet meetings to be consulted, like Egmont and Northington, on matters that had already been settled beforehand. 'These gentlemen are setting out upon a new plan; and are afraid of being thought to be influenced, or advised, by *any of their predecessors*.' Newcastle blamed this state of affairs on 'my old ungrateful, *conceited* friend Sir William Baker, who thinks he can entirely govern these young men'.[2]

Rockingham then added a second constitutional irregularity to the first. Early in December the cabinet met several times for informal discussions on America, a practice Lord Chancellor Northington regarded as improper and unprecedented. At a meeting on 11 December, after some American papers had been read, he therefore asked whether it was the intention to inform the King of the cabinet's opinion on America. He considered the cabinet to be 'a regular Council for Advice' and had told George III about the meeting. The others disagreed, and Northington privately reported to the King next day 'that their politics seemed to be fixed unanimously to yield to the insurrections and clamors and not to support the Stamp Act, in which I differed and declared my opinion, as thinking it full time to have formed some fixed opinion on so national a subject'.[3]

Rockingham and his confidants meanwhile continued to seek information and opinions in unofficial gatherings. He himself invited Grafton, Conway, Dowdeswell, Hardwicke, and Charles Yorke to his house on 8 December;[4] Dowdeswell was

[1] McCulloh merely wanted to alter some features of the Stamp Act particularly objectionable to the colonists, such as the proposed enforcement of the act by the Vice-Admiralty Courts, and the provision concerning ecclesiastical courts that did not exist. Greene, *H.L.Q.* 26 (1962–3), 253–62.

[2] B.M. Add. MSS. 32972, fos. 126–33.

[3] *Corr. of George III*, i. 428–9; corrected by Namier, *Additions and Corrections*, p. 68. Dartmouth was still not being summoned to cabinet on American matters, for Newcastle told Rockingham on 10 Dec. that Dartmouth ought to be present at any cabinet meetings on the colonies, as his predecessors Halifax and Hillsborough has been. B.M. Add. MSS. 32972, fos. 193–4.

[4] B.M. Add. MSS. 35430, fos. 22–3.

F*

the host to 'a great dinner . . . of Americans' on 13 December;[1] Massachusetts agent Dennys De Berdt and Boston merchant John Smith dined with Lord Dartmouth on 26 December;[2] and no doubt there were other soundings of British and colonial views. Newcastle was deliberately excluded from policy discussions. He had only one private meeting with Rockingham that month, on 26 December,[3] and was not summoned to two important gatherings held by the Marquess immediately afterwards. On 27 December Egmont, Conway, Dartmouth, Charles Yorke, Sir William Baker, and Dowdeswell dined with Rockingham. The meeting revealed a wide divergence of opinion within the administration. Yorke took the initiative and proposed resolutions for both Houses and a Declaratory Act to assert the legislative power of Parliament over the colonies. The others agreed that some such measures were essential, but evidently rejected or shelved Yorke's suggestion that the Declaratory Act should make it treason to deny Parliamentary sovereignty by word or writing, and also his proposal that the colonial assemblies should be made to expunge any such resolutions to the contrary; both ideas were later to be put forward by the Parliamentary opposition. Two tactical suggestions by Yorke, however, were later to form the basis of the ministerial strategy: these were that the declaratory resolutions should precede any conciliatory step, and that any 'relief' offered to the colonies should be ostensibly on economic grounds. Yorke envisaged modification and not repeal of the Stamp Act, and suggested only minor changes in it. These alterations would have been partly administrative, to make the duties payable in colonial currency instead of in sterling, and to remove the trial of offenders from the Vice-Admiralty Courts: and the only changes in duties proposed were the abolition of those on bills of lading and clearance papers for ships. Such meagre concessions would have had no significant effect on colonial opinion. Nothing is known of the discussion, but

---

[1] B.M. Add. MSS. 32972, fos. 202–3.

[2] *De Berdt Letters*, pp. 308–9.

[3] The Duke's memorandum drawn up for the meeting shows that in his mind the policy decision was whether the Stamp Act was to be repealed or merely modified. B.M. Add. MSS. 32972, fos. 333–5; 32973, fo. 3–4. Since Newcastle approved of conciliation, his exclusion was presumably due to personal jealousy of the veteran politician.

the absent Newcastle heard that Egmont and Conway were the chief champions of the colonists at this meeting.[1] Rockingham subsequently assured the aggrieved Duke that nothing significant had happened. 'I considered that meeting merely as taking an opportunity of bringing persons together to talk over their ideas and preparatory for coming to some fixed plan. I am sure the variety of opinions of what is right to be done, is no very easy matter to reconcile and I for one shall heartily rejoice when a real concerted plan can be determined on.'[2] On 31 December Rockingham held another dinner party 'on American topics' that included Baker, Dowdeswell, Trecothick, Dartmouth and the merchant M.P. George Aufrère, while Conway joined the gathering later. Rockingham told Newcastle on 2 January that 'much passed in general conversation on the subject of the trade and the facilities which might be given to it and the alterations of some late regulations'; and then made this general reflection:[3]

Upon the whole that has yet passed, either at the former or at the latter dinner, I think one thing seems to be the general opinion. That is, that the legislative right of this country over the colonies, should be declared, and upon the plan of Act the 6th George 1 relative to Ireland. I think it also seemed the general opinion, that in the King's Speech and in all the Parliamentary proceedings, the intention of giving the colonies every possible relief in trade and commerce should go hand in hand with declarations of authority or censure of the riots and tumults.

---

[1] Two accounts of the meeting survive. Both are second-hand. (a) One is in the letter of reproach about his exclusion written by Newcastle to Rockingham on 1 Jan. B.M. Add. MSS. 32973, fos. 3–4. Rockingham's reply did not correct what Newcastle said. Ibid., fos. 11–12. (b) A generation later the historian John Adolphus put together an account drawn up 'from private information and minutes of the conference'. Adolphus, *History*, i. 189–90; it is summarized in *Chatham Papers*, ii. 362 n., and in Gipson, *British Empire*, x. 375–6. The sources used by Adolphus may have included Yorke's notes of what he said. B.M. Add. MSS. 35881, fos. 275–8. There also exists a draft memorandum by Rockingham. Wentworth Woodhouse MSS. R.49–2.

[2] B.M. Add. MSS. 32973, fos. 11–12. Edmund Burke confided to his friend Charles O'Hara on 31 Dec., 'Administration has not yet conclusively (I imagine) fixed upon their plan in this respect, as every day's information from abroad may necessitate some alteration.' Burke was only Rockingham's private secretary and not involved in the decision at ministerial level, but he had already made up his own mind in favour of repeal. *Burke Corr.* i. 229.

[3] B.M. Add. MSS. 32973, fos. 12–13.

The main matter in which as yet I cannot see exactly where and how the different opinions can be brought to agree, is what must finally be done upon the Stamp Act. *All* would agree to various amendments and curtailings of the Act, *some as yet* not very many to a suspension and *very few* to a repeal. Your Grace knows that among *even ourselves* there are differences of opinions, and I am sure your Grace knows that we must but have one opinion and stick to it steadily when the matter comes into Parliament.

Newcastle replied that

the idea of authority and relief going hand in hand, both in the Speech, and in the Parliamentary proceedings, will be found very difficult; and for one, I shall incline rather to be deficient in that, which is only a declaration in words, then in the other, on which depends the most material interests of this country, viz.—the recovery, or enjoyment of our trade and commerce.[1]

Rockingham had to weigh this view against those of his two foremost lawyers. His comment to Newcastle about the Lord Chancellor, 'I hope he will become more moderate. I think Mr. Yorke does', shows that Northington was still opposed to conciliation. In this predicament Rockingham refused to yield to Newcastle's pressure for an immediate decision.[2]

Rockingham and his colleagues had always been aware that they had to devise a policy that was not only agreed upon by themselves but also acceptable to the King, Lords, and Commons. When Massachusetts agent De Berdt had reported back to his colony on 14 December that the ministers favoured conciliation he warned that they expected 'a warm opposition from the old ministry and what they call the Country Party'.[3] Trecothick's petitioning campaign and Grenville's debating blunders now promised to make this problem of Parliamentary opposition somewhat less formidable than it had at first appeared: but there remained two great imponderables, the attitudes of Lord Bute and of William Pitt; while the opinion of George III on the American crisis was unknown and probably as yet unformulated. On 5 December he had made this neutral

[1] B.M. Add. MSS. 32973, fos. 25–6.
[2] B.M. Add. MSS. 32972, fos. 382–3; 32973, fos. 3–4, 13.
[3] *De Berdt Letters*, pp. 307–8.

comment to Conway. 'I am more and more grieved at the accounts of America. Where this spirit will end is not to be said. It is, undoubtedly, the most serious matter that ever came before Parliament; it requires more deliberation, candour, and temper than I fear it will meet with.'[1] The King as usual left the formulation of policy to his administration, and merely pressed for some decision: in a letter of 11 January 1766 to Lord Egmont he made this comment on the other ministers: 'All I desire is that they will act firmly till the arduous business of the American Colonies is over.'[2] This easy relationship soon came to an end. George III was to be unhappy about the final decision for complete repeal of the Stamp Act; while his ministers were to seek positive help from the King when confronted with what seemed to be the perennial problem of Lord Bute.

In December the Parliamentary opposition had been disappointed in their expectation of Bute's support against conciliation of America. Events soon suggested that this would be forthcoming when Parliament reassembled in January. As early as 18 December Grenvillite James Harris made this optimistic note in his diary: 'Tis said Lord Bute begins now to appear more openly at the head of his friends, which in both Houses are 50 or 60 persons.'[3] During the recess Lord Bute held several meetings of his followers, with the evident intention of aligning with the opposition on the colonial issue.[4] Contemporaries assumed that George III could prevent this coalition if he chose, but he did nothing. Lord Hardwicke sent this report to his brother Charles Yorke on 3 January 1766. 'The King's family and household are divided. I wish his Majesty himself is not *neuter*; and this I collect from what Lord Rockingham told me, that the King professes to know nothing of what Lord Bute is doing, and yet will not speak to his servants, nor send to Lord Bute.'[5] This put an unfair construction on the King's behaviour. George III had not talked politics with Bute since Rockingham took office, and he deliberately refrained from seeing him at this time to avoid political speculation

[1] *Rockingham Memoirs*, i. 256–7.
[2] *Corr. of George III*, i. 220.
[3] Harris Diary, 18 Dec. 1765.
[4] H. Walpole, *Memoirs*, ii. 182–3.
[5] *Rockingham Memoirs*, i. 262.

damaging to the ministry. On 10 January the King informed Bute by letter that he intended to support his administration: but he also gave this opinion on how Bute and his friends should act.[1]

I own I should think I had good reason to complain if those of my friends that are still in office tried to overturn those I employ . . . as to my friends differing from ministers where they think their honour and conscience requires it, that I not only think right, but am of the opinion it is their duty to act so; nay I think that it is also incumbent on my Dear Friend to act entirely so.

This hasty and unguarded promise that Bute and his friends could vote as they liked on America was to involve the King in considerable embarrassment and his ministers in Parliamentary difficulties. It did not arise from any underhand motive of preventing the repeal of the Stamp Act, for the administration had not yet decided on that course of action. The seeming contradiction in the letter may be explained by George III's apparent failure to anticipate that the administration might be defeated over American policy: for he continued to give genuine support to his ministers. When Rockingham again sent him a list of the sixty-three peers who attended the eve-of-session reading of the King's Speech on 13 January George III copied out the list in his own hand and made the comment, 'I am glad to see names among them that I thought doubtfully of before'. Bute was not one of them.[2]

The knowledge that Bute and his followers would almost certainly oppose any American policy of conciliation had already caused the ministers to make another approach to William Pitt.[3] The administration had ample grounds for their assumption that Pitt would support conciliation of the colonies. Although he had not personally opposed Grenville's taxation in Parliament, his hostility to the measures had been known to them when in opposition at the time.[4] Any fears that

[1] *Bute Letters*, pp. 242–6.
[2] *Corr. of George III*, i. 222–3.
[3] H. Walpole, *Memoirs*, ii. 183.
[4] B.M. Add. MSS. 32957, fos. 239–40; 32966, fos. 69–70. Pitt was to claim in the Commons on 14 Jan. 1766 that only ill health had prevented him from opposing the Stamp Act.

his close connection with Lord Temple might bave caused him to change his mind must have been dispelled by the recent debates in Parliament. Temple's speeches had left no doubt of his break with Pitt, while those of Pitt's adherents who had spoken, George Cooke and William Beckford in the Commons and Shelburne in the Lords, had attacked the opposition motions calling for strong measures against the colonies. All three had spoken with prior knowledge of Pitt's ideas on America. Beckford had even been sounded by administration on the subject before Parliament met, George Onslow making this report to Newcastle on 15 December: 'I found Beckford all I could wish. The thing Mr. Pitt doubts about is nothing material. In the American matter he does *not* doubt indeed.'[1] Cooke certainly knew Pitt's views, for on 10 December he informed Pitt that Newcastle 'thought of the American affairs, with respect to the Stamp duty, in the same light that you considered them, when I had the honour of some conversation with you at Burton Pynsent on that subject'.[2] Shelburne had seen Pitt at Bath on his way to London, and assured him on 21 December that in his speech he had acted 'upon those principles which made part of the conversation you honoured me with at Bath'. His assumption that Pitt favoured repeal can be seen from a later part of the same letter: 'Though it is my private opinion, it would be well for this country to be back where it was a year ago, I even despair of a repeal effecting that, if it is not accompanied with some circumstances of a firm conduct, and some system immediately following such a concession.'[3] Pitt replied that he was

under the strongest conviction that, allowing full force to all the striking topics for upholding, in the present instance, the legislative and executive authority over America, the ruinous side of the dilemma to which we are brought is, the making good by force there, preposterous and infatuated errors in policy here; and I shall unalterably sustain that opinion.[4]

[1] B.M. Add. MSS. 32972, fos. 251–2.
[2] *Chatham Papers*, ii. 344. Burton Pynsent was Pitt's house in Somerset.
[3] *Chatham Papers*, ii. 353–8.
[4] *Chatham Papers*, ii. 358–9. This unsigned draft is probably the basis of the letter of 26 Dec. acknowledged by Shelburne in his reply on 30 Dec. Shelburne himself claimed 'a very decided disapprobation of long standing' of the Stamp Act. 'I was apprehensive of the effects I now see it has had.' P.R.O. 30/8/56, fos. 48–9.

The decision to contact Pitt was taken by the end of the year, after the reluctance of Rockingham had been overcome by Grafton and Conway.[1] When seeing the King on routine business on 1 January 1766 the three ministers successfully pressed on an unwilling George III the desirability of ascertaining Pitt's opinion on America. Their aim was doubtless to find out whether he was going to attend Parliament as well as to confirm what were believed to be his views. Grafton asked Thomas Townshend to act as messenger that evening, and Townshend set out for Bath the next morning. Rockingham therefore called a cabinet meeting for 5 January, expecting to know Pitt's reply by then.[2] In effect, Townshend was commissioned to ask Pitt to decide what measure of conciliation the administration should adopt: for opposition by Pitt to official policy would both divide the ministry and destroy any chance of Parliamentary success.

Townshend's mission was not only to ascertain Pitt's opinion on the American crisis but also, if circumstances seemed favourable, to convey an invitation from Rockingham, Grafton and Conway to join the administration: this offer was not authorized by the King.[3] Pitt's answers were respectively unhelpful and embarrassing. He refused 'to give any opinion, to anybody but to the King, or the Parliament, about America'. This was in accordance with sound constitutional doctrine, and at least it implied his attendance at Westminster. His reply to the offer of ministerial office was that while he was ready to act with the three men who had sent the invitation he refused to do so with Newcastle, since 'there could not be two Ministers'.[4] The embarrassed Rockingham only hinted at this condition at the cabinet meeting on 5 January, but Newcastle learnt the full details from Townshend himself the next morning, and at once sent John White to offer Rockingham his resigna-

---

[1] *Bute Letters*, p. 243.

[2] B.M. Add. MSS 32973, fo. 13.

[3] *Bute Letters*, p. 243.

[4] This stipulation shows how ignorant Pitt was about the Rockingham administration: in a letter of 7 Dec. 1765 to George Cooke he referred to 'his Grace's ministry'. *Chatham Papers*, ii. 342–3. For similar remarks see *ibid.*, pp. 345, 360. For Newcastle it was adding insult to injury. The Duke remarked to Frederick Montagu on 10 Jan. 1766, 'it is a little hard, that I who all the world sees, am no Minister; have declared publicly, and often to the King, that I will be no Minister, should have this mark of indignity put upon me'. B.M. Add. MSS. 32973, fo. 84.

tion. Rockingham visited Newcastle the following day, 7 January, and told the Duke that he and the King both regarded Pitt's terms as a demand for 'a total change of administration'. He himself had ground for annoyance, since Pitt had again insisted on the power to offer Temple the Treasury. Rockingham told Newcastle that he would resign himself before agreeing to Pitt's terms, but that Grafton and Conway were for accepting them on the assumption that Pitt would lift his veto on Newcastle.[1]

There followed a brief ministerial crisis. Grafton was foremost in urging George III to invite Pitt to form a ministry. 'He thought no other person (not so much from his superior abilities as from his popular name) able to carry on the national affairs', so the King reported to his Lord Chancellor, adding this comment. 'My own opinion I confess is if possible to keep this administration on foot; if others thought as I do of both the Secretaries of State in point of abilities there would not be many long faces on their retiring.'[2] George III failed to appreciate that Conway was the ministry's only acceptable Leader of the Commons, a role underlined by George Onslow's comment to Newcastle on 10 January. 'If Conway will but stand it, we may certainly weather this. But without him I have no notion of it. I know his consequence, and I know how our people look up to him, and how ill they would hear Charles Townshend.'[3] Conway came round to the view of Rockingham and the King that Pitt's terms were unacceptable, and it gradually became clear that neither Secretary of State would force the issue by resignation. On 11 January King and ministers finally decided that no further approach would be made to Pitt.[4]

The administration therefore met Parliament again on 14 January 1766 before any final decision on policy had been taken. This had been the intention before the approach to Pitt: for on 30 December Charles Yorke sent Rockingham a

[1] B.M. Add. MSS. 32973, fos. 90–1. Rockingham's reaction can be seen in a memorandum prepared for George III. Wentworth Woodhouse MSS. R.1–557.
[2] *Corr. of George III*, i. 212–14.
[3] B.M. Add. MSS. 32973, fos. 90–1.
[4] B.M. Add. MSS. 32973, fos. 68–71, 84, 90–1, 100–1, 104–5; *Bute Papers*, pp. 243–4.

draft of the part of the King's Speech to Parliament that would refer to America, with this comment.[1]

When you have read it *twice* with *care*, you will find, that the King *cannot say less*, and I think it unnecessary and improper for him to say more. You will likewise observe, that the plan of it consists with my idea of the subsequent proceeding in the House of Commons; and whatever may be done in Parliament, the King's Speech will certainly correspond with every man's idea . . . For God's sake, let the Addresses be prepared for both Houses, as well as the speech. The rest will follow, when the Houses are met.

When Yorke saw Rockingham the next day he found that Dowdeswell had also prepared a draft, and seemingly withdrew his own: for he told Rockingham that Dowdeswell's version needed 'amending and polishing. But this you will not repeat. If Dyson is well disposed, I would settle it with him in two or three hours, as conversant in the forms of Parliament, and wording questions for the House.'[2] Rockingham thanked Yorke for the advice,[3] and reported progress to Newcastle on 2 January. 'I have got some heads for the King's Speech upon the plan of authority and relief.'[4] Rockingham intended to send George III a copy of the Speech after the cabinet meeting on 5 January, but consideration of it was postponed until the cabinet met again on 7 January, and not until 9 January did the King see and approve the Speech and also the Lords' Address.[5] The Speech left open a wide possible range of action, within the broad criteria of 'attention to the just rights and authority of the British legislature' and 'affection and concern for the welfare and prosperity of all my people'.[6] The vague wording confirmed some observers in their belief that the ministry had come to a compromise decision, one in favour not of repeal but of some lesser 'palliative measure'. Charles Garth anticipated suspension of the Stamp Act:[7] and Richard

[1] Wentworth Woodhouse MSS. R.1–544.
[2] B.M. Add. MSS. 35430, fos. 25–6.
[3] B.M. Add. MSS. 35430, fo. 27.
[4] B.M. Add. MSS. 32973, fos. 11–13.
[5] *Corr. of George III*, i. 206, 211–12; B.M. Add. MSS. 32973, fos. 45, 52.
[6] *Commons Journals*, xxx. 446.
[7] *S.C.H.G.M.* 26 (1925), 71. Gilbert Elliot also thought the Speech marked a decision not to repeal. Elliot, *Border Elliots*, p. 397.

Jackson had told Governor Fitch of Connecticut that his hopes of repeal had faded.[1]

I am informed by the best intelligence I can procure that the Stamp Act will not be repealed; every other relief may be, I think, expected, and even this law will probably be reduced to nothing more, than a proof of the power of Parliament to impose taxes as well as make other laws for America. Something to assert this power is judged necessary by leading men in both Houses. I wish that some other means of attaining the same end may be thought of rather than this, but I fear no other will.

In the Commons the Address was moved by Lord Villiers and seconded by Thomas Townshend.[2] Henry Seymour rose first to urge the enforcement of the Stamp Act, a policy he chose to read into the Address. Bamber Gascoyne and Robert Nugent spoke to the same effect. George Cooke then declared that the Stamp Act was illegal, and questioned Parliament's right to tax the colonies. He was answered by Hans Stanley, who emphasized the need of an American revenue, however small, as a token of Parliament's sovereignty. William Pitt entered the House while Stanley was speaking, and rose himself next. There followed a famous verbal duel between Pitt and Grenville, diarist Harris noting that 'for some hours the debate lay between these two great masters, and the

---

[1] *Fitch Papers*, ii. 383–4.

[2] This account of the debate is based on *Commons Journals*, xxx. 445–7; Harris Diary, 14 Jan 1766; H. Walpole, *Memoirs*, ii. 184–90; a memorandum by G. Elliot, Elliot, *Border Elliots*, pp. 397–8; and the following letters: (a) Conway to George III, *Corr. of George III*, i. 224–6; (b) J. West to Newcastle (two letters), B.M. Add. MSS. 32973, fos. 133–5; (c) E. Burke to C. O'Hara, *Burke Corr.* i. 231–2; (d) Lord George Sackville to General Irwin, *H.M.C. Stopford-Sackville*, pp. 21–2; (e) B. Franklin to Strachan, *Franklin Papers*, xiii. 41–4; (f) C. Garth to South Carolina, *S.C.H.G.M.* 26 (1925), 69–70.

During 1766 a report of the debate later attributed to Sir Robert Deane, assisted by Lord Charlemont, was printed in three pamphlets: (a) *The Celebrated Speech of a Celebrated Commoner;* (b) *Political Debates;* (c) *The Speech of Mr. P and several others . . . in a late important debate.* The first two are identical, the third has verbal discrepancies. The report is the basis of the accounts of Almon, *Debates*, vii. 61–77; Debrett, *Debates*, iv. 288–99; Cobbett, *Parl. Hist.* xvi. 95–110; and *Chatham Papers*, ii. 364–73, where the attribution of authorship is made. An Irish M.P., Deane would have been permitted to hear the debate. The pamphlet report was summarized in April by the *Gent. Mag.* 1766, 155–9: see *Franklin Papers*, xiii. 40. Most historians have relied solely on this printed account of the debate in one form or another.

ministry stood by, like the rabble at a boxing match'.[1] Pitt began by saying that it was the most important day for Parliament since the Glorious Revolution of 1688, and urged the need to maintain the dignity and authority of Parliament. 'So far, so good', noted Harris at this point, and Franklin remembered that 'Mr. Pitt spoke some time before one could divine on which side of the question relating to America he would be'. The House was listening to a master at dramatic effect. Having riveted the attention of his audience, Pitt embarked on a denunciation of the attempt to tax America. Here is the summary by James West:

That the act ought to be totally and absolutely repealed as an erroneous policy, that no Treasury had ever thought of taxing America in the most necessitous times, that the Parliament had no power to enact an internal taxation in America, that it was not represented here either virtually or otherwise.[2]

Grenville maintained that Parliament had the right to tax the colonies, denying Pitt's argument of non-representation, and denounced the American behaviour as rebellion. Conway welcomed Pitt's declaration in language widely regarded as too obsequious, and with what was generally understood to be an acceptance of repeal. Dowdeswell announced that the Committee of Supply would reveal a deficit in the yield of American taxation anticipated the previous year by Grenville. The debate ended without a division after attacks on the Stamp Act by Beckford, Cooke, and Huske. The Address was reported the next day, when James Harris criticized it for 'too much delicacy and tenderness . . . considering they were now in actual rebellion'. He was the only member to speak.[3]

---

[1] It is impossible to reconstruct an accurate account of this exchange. Both men spoke several times, and some reports do not distinguish between what was said in each speech, while those that do are often contradictory.

[2] Burke, Franklin, Garth, Sackville, and Walpole also all report Pitt as denying Parliament's right to levy *internal* taxation. The weight of evidence makes it essential to correct the contention of Morgan, *Stamp Act Crisis*, pp. 342–4, that Pitt did not distinguish between internal and external taxation. Morgan used only the printed version of the debate. The evidence on the attitude of the Chatham ministry to colonial taxation (for which see below, Chapters 14 and 16) also suggests that Morgan's interpretation is mistaken. By 1774, indeed, Chatham was denying that in 1766 he had questioned Parliament's right to tax America. *Hutchinson Diary and Letters*, i. 191, 202–3.

[3] Harris Diary, 15 Jan. 1766. *Commons Journals*, xxx. 455–6.

The administration had played an ignominious role in the debate of 14 January, but the ministers now had their cue. Pitt's declaration had made a decision on policy possible, and the nature of that decision inevitable. Three days later Lord George Sackville wrote that 'the appearance of Mr. Pitt and the avowed part he took with America has given a new turn to the minds of many, and as Mr. Conway at once adopted his sentiments I conclude the ministers intend to direct their future proceedings by what he then declared'.[1] It was the common judgement of contemporaries that Pitt's pronouncement decided the administration's policy, but this was not the whole truth. The ministry had privately determined on conciliation already, and there had been some support for repeal. The significance of Pitt's declaration was twofold: his advocacy of repeal had an incalculable but undoubted impact on Parliamentary opinion; and it enabled Rockingham to convince reluctant colleagues like Yorke that repeal was both the inevitable course of action for the ministry and a practical policy if accompanied by a Declaratory Act. Pitt's pronouncement in favour of repeal had been accompanied by an insistence on the need to assert Parliament's rights over the colonies, and this accorded with the decision already taken by the administration to pass a Declaratory Act: where Pitt differed from ministers was in his exclusion of taxation from this claim. This point of discord lay some weeks ahead, and Pitt had struck a keynote of conciliation that was henceforth openly official policy. Scorning the conventional image of a child, he had appealed to the House to treat America as a wife by quoting from the poet Matthew Prior.[2]

> Be to her virtues very kind.
> Be to her Faults a little blind,
> Let all her ways be unconfined,
> And clap your padlock on her mind.

Supporters of the Stamp Act had greeted Pitt's declaration with dismay: George Grenville described the debate next day as 'the most extraordinary and most unfortunate day in my

---

[1] *H.M.C. Stopford-Sackville*, pp. 21–2.
[2] These are the closing lines of 'An English Padlock', written in 1704. The lines are incorrectly given by West and Walpole.

opinion for this country which we ever saw'.[1] But those who
favoured repeal had got more than they had bargained for.
All earlier evidence had pointed to Pitt's support of such a
policy, but he had exceeded expectations and adopted what he
believed to be the colonial position, in his denial of Parliament's
right to lay internal taxes on the colonies.[2] This threatened to
provoke a reaction. Many who were willing to repeal the
Stamp Act on grounds of expediency might be reluctant to do
so if such a principle could be thought the reason. The effect
of Pitt's views on the opinion of independent members was noted
by Charles Garth. 'The doctrine has not been very pleasing
to the Country Gentlemen in the House.'[3] It was, moreover,
the reason for Bute's decision finally to oppose repeal. When
Bute commented to Lord Shaftesbury two days later on

Pitt's behaviour in the House of Commons on the 14th when he
(Pitt) gave up the Commons' right of taxing America, he expressed
the greatest concern and astonishment at what *that wild man* (so
Lord B. called him) had been doing. That, as matters stood before,
there might have been some hopes of accommodating them, but
that now for the first time he despaired for the public, and could
not tell, where these disturbances would end. That he himself was
independent of ministers and would so show himself.[4]

Why had Pitt denied Parliament's right to tax the colonies?
The cynical explanation of a spontaneous whim would accord
with one contemporary view of his character: Horace Walpole,
speculating in 1762 on Pitt's attitude to the Peace of Paris,
wrote that Pitt would not 'know what he will do till he is [in]
the middle of his first speech'; and Bute's brother Stuart
Mackenzie, talking about the incident in 1774, still believed
that 'when Mr. Pitt came from home to attend the House of
Commons, he had not determined which side to take: that he is

---

[1] Grenville to Augustus Hervey, 15 Jan. 1766, Grenville Letter-Books, vol. 2.

[2] On 21 Dec. 1765 John Dickinson of Pennsylvania wrote a now famous letter
to Pitt on the colonial crisis. P.R.O. 30/8/97, fos. 32–41. The draft or copy of this
letter in the Dickinson papers has been published by Morgan, *Prologue to Revolution*,
pp. 118–22. It is improbable that the letter reached Pitt by 14 Jan. 1766.

[3] *S.C.H.G.M.* 26 (1925), 71.

[4] This is the summary by James Harris of what Lord Shaftesbury told him on
18 Jan. Malmesbury MSS., Memo. of 18 Jan. 1766. Bute's opposition to repeal
was based on principle and not on any desire to change the ministry. B.M. Add.
MSS. 41354, fo. 97.

sure he had not mentioned his intention to any person; that Lord Temple and Lord Camden came unusually forward upon the floor of the House of Commons, and discovered an eagerness to know what part he would take: that when he found it would be a popular stroke, which might appear from the many petitions for the repeal, then he determined, and at the same time gratified his revenge upon his brother, George Grenville who he hated'.[1] This interpretation ignores the fact that Pitt's doctrine had been anticipated in speeches of his followers, by William Beckford on 17 December 1765 and by George Cooke on 14 January before Pitt's entry into the House. The graver charge of opportunism was also made by James Harris, who thought that Pitt's statement was 'well suited to raise his own popularity'. Certainly one characteristic of Pitt's political behaviour had always been a desire to win favour both in the City of London and in America, but that was not his chief motive on 14 January: he scorned the imputation at the time, and must have known how unacceptable his doctrine was to the vast majority of M.P.s and to the wider political world outside Westminster. The simple explanation is that Pitt had a genuine belief in the principle of representative government that underlay his attitude to the American problem and to the issue of political reform in Britain. In this very debate he linked the two, and threw out incidental remarks about the defects of the British electoral system. Here is James West's note of what he said on that subject: 'That the best representation was that of counties, and that of great cities, but as for the lesser boroughs he was confident their right to send representatives would in less than a century be amputated.'[2]

The immediate result of Pitt's performance in the House was not the final evolution of American policy but another approach to him by the ministry. The next day Rockingham offered George III this advice.

That your Majesty's present administration will be shook to the greatest degree, if no further attempt is made to get Mr. Pitt to take a cordial part, is much too apparent to be disguised . . . the events

---

[1] H. Walpole, *Letters*, v. 248. *Hutchinson Diary and Letters*, i. 288.
[2] B.M. Add. MSS. 32973, fos. 133-4.

of yesterday in the House of Commons have shown the amazing power and influence which Mr. Pitt has, whenever he takes part in debate.[1]

The King accordingly authorized Rockingham and Grafton to see Pitt. The interview, on 18 January, lasted two hours, and Pitt's behaviour convinced even Grafton that any arrangement was impossible. He continued to insist on forming a new ministry, and raised such new obstacles as the office given to Lord George Sackville and the alleged influence of Lord Mansfield. Pitt himself finally said 'that he was afraid nothing was to be done; that he should stay the American affair out, and then return to his retirement'. Rockingham and Grafton reported back to George III, and it was agreed that Grafton should write to Pitt saying that the King did not think any offer to him practicable, and that one to Lord Temple would be improper since 'his Lordship differed so much in measures with his Majesty's present ministers'.[2] In the end Rockingham conveyed this message to Pitt personally on 21 January,[3] and later assured Newcastle that the failure of the negotiation would not affect Pitt's views on policy. 'As to the affair of America, Mr. Pitt declared strongly for the repeal of the Stamp Act; but, as to the other parts of the question, the asserting the right of the Parliament, Mr. Pitt did not seem so strong, as he was, the other day, in his speech.'[4]

George III had at the same time opened another negotiation on his own initiative, interpreting his ministers' action as an admission of their inability to continue in office by themselves. Since he had already informed them that 'if they thought themselves unable to do that, I should not permit them to form me a ministry but should do that myself',[5] he felt free to make arrangements for a new administration and told Grafton so before the visit to Pitt. His aim was to construct a ministry that did not include Pitt, Rockingham, or Grenville, to free himself from dependence on such politicians. In the proposed

---

[1] *Rockingham Memoirs*, i. 270.

[2] B.M. Add. MSS. 32973, fos. 158–9, 174–5, 180–1, 194–6; *Grafton Autobiography*, pp. 63–8. These and other accounts of the negotiation are contradictory in detail.

[3] *Corr. of George III*, i. 243–4.

[4] B.M. Add. MSS. 32973, fos. 237–40.

[5] *Bute Letters*, p. 244.

administration Northington was to be First Lord of the Treasury, Lord Egmont and Charles Townshend the Secretaries of State.[1] Their refusal rendered the negotiation brief and unsuccessful, but the move is of interest as a last attempt to secure an administration that would not repeal the Stamp Act. That may not have been George III's intention, but it was seen as such by some of his supporters: for a memorandum in Charles Jenkinsons's papers apparently drawn up for the King's guidance at this time after a meeting of his political associates contained this observation on the colonial crisis.[2]

The management of the American affairs is certainly full of difficulties but the House is so divided on that subject that whatever sentiments are adopted, they will certainly find support from one side or the other, and whenever the Crown casts its influence there will be success and the measure is of that kind that administration will have only to execute what the Parliament shall determine; and the lawyers who must decide [the] question are almost all on the side of the Crown.

The failure of these negotiations left the final decision on American policy in the hands of an unchanged Rockingham administration; but the ministry had first to extricate itself from what Burke called a Parliamentary 'scrape'. After the Address had been carried in the Commons on 14 January, many supporters of the administration were among the members who left the House while Conway was presenting the American papers promised before the Christmas recess. The House decided to consider them in Committee on 28 January, but Richard Rigby then moved to have sufficient copies printed for the members of the House. Conway objected to this as being unfair to the correspondents: but Nugent supported Rigby's motion and when Pitt did the same the administration gave up the point. John Huske warned that such a step would deter the sending of future information, and Attorney-General Charles Yorke therefore suggested that the House should follow the precedent of the inquiry into the loss of Minorca in

---

[1] For details of this negotiation see *Grafton Autobiography*, pp. 64–6; *Corr. of George III*, i. 215–16, 232–5, 350; Namier, *Additions and Corrections*, pp. 45–6, 48.

[2] *Jenkinson Papers*, pp. 404–8. Internal evidence shows that this undated paper was drawn up during the week after 14 Jan.

1756, when the names were omitted: but the motion was passed for printing the complete papers.[1]

Growing realization that this step could produce undesirable consequences for government officials and other informants in America led to a further discussion the next day. Uneasiness at printing the names of correspondents was voiced by both Sir George Savile, who had been absent on 14 January, and the Speaker, Sir John Cust. Dowdeswell therefore proposed that the Speaker should examine the papers and leave out any parts that might expose the writers to danger in the colonies. This idea was adopted after James Harris had declared that it would not work in practice.[2] That proved to be the case. On the next day the Speaker saw Dowdeswell, who reported to Rockingham that Cust 'saw great difficulties in putting the papers into any proper shape for printing'. He himself therefore would move to discharge the order for printing altogether.[3]

Dowdeswell did so on 17 January, explaining that the Speaker believed that no adequate precaution could preserve their sense, and there began a debate on America that lasted until ten o'clock and in which at least twenty-nine members took part.[4] Charles Townshend declared that the questions of the repeal of the Stamp Act and of trade restrictions should be kept distinct from the right to tax the colonies. Solicitor-General William De Grey now doubted the propriety of the Stamp Act, even though it was a measure that he had perused and approved the previous year when holding the same post under Grenville. Conway made a speech that won the admiration of his friends and the respect of his opponents. Grenville's only counter to the motion was a suggestion that Conway himself should scrutinize the papers, and although thirteen members spoke against it the opposition did not divide the House as 'their numbers were so small'. Newcastle was told

---

[1] *Commons Journals*, xxx. 447–51; Harris Diary, 14 Jan. 1766; H. Walpole, *Memoirs*, ii. 190–1; *Burke Corr*. i. 232. Burke blamed the 'thin House' for the administration setback, but Harris thought Pitt's intervention decisive.

[2] Harris Diary, 15 Jan. 1766; H. Walpole, *Memoirs*, ii. 191; *Burke Corr*. i. 232. No such motion or order is recorded in the *Commons Journals*, xxx. 451–6, for this day.

[3] Wentworth Woodhouse MSS. R.1–326.

[4] For this debate see Harris Diary, 17 Jan. 1766; H. Walpole, *Memoirs*, ii. 206–7 (*sub* 17 Feb.); a letter from G. Onslow to Newcastle, B.M. Add. MSS. 32973, fo. 166; and an unsigned list of speakers in *Corr. of George III*, i. 236.

this by George Onslow, who thought the occasion 'a most honourable debate for us, and most ignominious for them'. Certainly the administration had shown that it did not depend in debate on Pitt, who was absent; and only three speakers had echoed his denial of Parliament's right to tax America, Cooke and Beckford once again and James Hewitt.

Debates in the House of Lords had centred on the question of printing the papers. On 14 January only Suffolk and Sandwich criticized the Address after it had been moved by Dartmouth in what one observer thought 'a very ill delivered formal speech'.[1] Grafton laid the American papers before the House and, like the Commons, the Lords decided to have a Committee of the Whole House on them on 28 January.[2] The Duke of Bedford then moved that all the papers should be printed, and there followed a debate in which thirteen peers made twenty speeches. Those opposing the motion included Grafton, Mansfield, Newcastle, Northington, and Egmont. It was supported by Suffolk, and Temple, Sandwich, and Lyttelton also gave qualified support in the form of attempts to save it by alterations. All such efforts failed, and Bedford withdrew the motion, announcing that he would make another for a Select Committee to choose such papers as were proper to print.[3] He did so two days later, on 16 January, being supported by Gower, Sandwich, Temple, and Lyttelton. The administration speakers were Dartmouth, Grafton, Botetourt, Egmont, and Newcastle, and the motion was defeated by 40 votes to 25.[4] A third attempt to embarrass administration over the papers was made on 20 January, when Weymouth pointed out that the papers sent by the Treasury were incomplete, since the time of arrival was not marked. Rockingham himself, as First Lord of the Treasury, felt obliged to reply, and told

[1] W. Rouet to Baron Mure, *Caldwell Papers*, ii (2), 59–60.
[2] *Lords Journals*, xxxi. 235–9. Grafton presented further papers on 22, 27, 28, and 31 Jan. and 6 Feb. *Ibid.* 246, 249–50, 253, 258.
[3] *Lords Journals*, xxxi. 232–40. Cobbett, *Parl. Hist.* xvi. 93–4. *Corr. of George III*, i. 226–8. The reply of George III to Rockingham is given, under the date of 19 Dec. 1765, in *Rockingham Memoirs*, i. 259.
[4] *Lords Journals*, xxxi. 243; *Corr. of George III*, i. 233. Temple had heard his brother-in-law in the Commons on 14 Jan. with barely suppressed fury. He sent Grenville £1,000 the next day as reward for his defence of the Stamp Act, and thereafter identified himself with his brother's views in his own speeches in the Lords. *Grenville Papers*, iii. 227. *H.M.C. Stopford-Sackville*, p. 22.

the House that it was Treasury practice to record when correspondence was read at the Board, and not the date of receipt. He was attacked by Sandwich, Suffolk, Halifax, and Temple, and ruefully told the King, 'Lord Rockingham never wished more for the power of any degree of oratory than then, though indeed the House in general were rather irritated at the manner of the proceedings'. Lord Chancellor Northington and even Lyttelton had come to his defence, and George III himself made this reply: 'I am much pleased that opposition has forced you to hear your own voice, which I hope will encourage you to stand forth in other debates.'[1]

These early debates on America in the two Houses of Parliament had involved merely some tentative sounding of opinion and manoeuvring for support. Neither government nor opposition had yet sought a vote directly on the Stamp Act. That the question would now be one of complete repeal had been made inevitable by Pitt's declaration on 14 January, but how either House would vote on this issue was as yet uncertain. Pitt had made the expected pronouncement in favour of conciliation, but his denial of Parliament's right of taxation might well prove counter-productive in its effect on independent opinion. Lord Bute, too, had not yet shown his hand, and if the weight of his influence was thrown against the ministry's policy it might be decisive unless the King himself took steps to counter it. This doubt concerning Parliamentary opinion on America rendered more complex a decision already made difficult by internal discord within the administration.

The ministry came to a final decision on American policy immediately after the breakdown of the negotiation with Pitt. Rockingham saw Charles Yorke on the morning of 19 January, and Conway, Grafton, Dowdeswell, and Charles Townshend that evening. Afterwards he reported to Yorke, 'The ideas we joined in are nearly what I talked of to you this morning. That is, A *Declaratory Act* in general terms, afterwards to proceed to *considerations of trade*, and final determination on *the Stamp Act*, a repeal of which its own demerits and inconveniences *felt here* will justify.' Rockingham invited all five, together

[1] *Corr. of George III*, i. 239–40, 244.

with Lord Egmont, Lord Dartmouth, and lawyer Richard Hussey, to dine with him on 21 January, to begin the implementation of these decisions by the drafting of resolutions to put before Parliament.[1] This was to be the administration policy: a Declaratory Act that would not specifically assert Parliament's right of taxation over the colonies, to be followed by the complete repeal of the Stamp Act on the alleged grounds of its inherent faults and the detrimental effect it had had on the British economy.

The continued exclusion of Newcastle from these policy discussions was evidently deliberate. Rockingham did not mention the meeting of 19 January in a letter to the Duke the following day.[2] That evening, however, Newcastle heard that there was to be a meeting at Rockingham's house the next day 'to settle the Parliamentary proceedings upon the American affairs'.[3] To mollify the Duke Rockingham asked his wife to write. Lady Rockingham did so at the very time that the second meeting was in progress, saying that her husband 'has seen tonight, a pretty mixed set of company and bids me say that the conversation he has had with them, promises to be productive of events going on well; and his Lordship seems in admirable spirits'.[4] Rockingham then saw Newcastle on 23 January, and both men became heated after the Duke had complained of not being consulted on America. Lord Grantham was present, and intervened to persuade Newcastle that Rockingham had come to tell him what had happened so 'that he might know the sense of those that were there, in order, *finally* to determine what should be done'. Newcastle allowed himself to be pacified, but he was not deceived. He realized that 'no material alterations' would be made to the resolutions already drafted even though Rockingham sent a copy asking for his opinion that evening.[5]

[1] B.M. Add. MSS. 35430, fo. 31. Rockingham dated this letter 'Sunday 19 Jan.', but Yorke docketed it '17 January', and some historians have adopted this wrong date: Morgan, *Stamp Act Crisis*, p. 336; Kammen, *Rope of Sand*, p. 120; Sosin, *Agents and Merchants*, p. 77; Winstanley, *Personal and Party Government*, p. 262. The correct date is given in Namier and Brooke, *Charles Townshend*, p. 139. That American policy was settled at this meeting is confirmed by a letter from Newcastle to the Archbishop of Canterbury on 2 Feb. B.M. Add. MSS. 32973, fos. 342–4.

[2] B.M. Add. MSS. 32973, fos. 194–7.

[3] Ibid., fos. 202–3.   [4] Ibid., fos. 224–5.

[5] Ibid., fos. 241–5.

Five resolutions were envisaged for the Commons. The first two purported to be statements of fact, that dangerous tumults and insurrections had occurred in North America in defiance of the government and in violation of law, and that these had been encouraged by resolutions of colonial assemblies. The third and fourth were for Addresses to the King, asking him respectively to give directions for the punishment of those responsible, and to order his governors to recommend to the assemblies compensation for victims of the riots. The fifth resolution was declaratory, asserting 'that the Parliament of Great Britain had, hath, and of right ought to have full power and authority to make laws and statutes of sufficient force and validity to bind the colonies and people of America in all cases whatsoever'.[1] Newcastle's reply the next day expressed complete disapproval.

The repeal, your Lordship knows, is the great point with me; that is the only thing that can set things right; and I am afraid, that such a number of resolutions, and some of them in such strong terms, will prevent even the repeal from having its effect; and leave the colonies in the same state of confusion and destruction, as it is at present. I thought, it had been determined at my Lord Chancellor's to lay aside these resolutions, which were produced there by General Conway.[2]

If Newcastle thought the resolutions too strong to be acceptable to the colonies, the Yorke family thought them too weak to be acceptable to Parliament. Charles Yorke went to see Newcastle on the evening of 24 January, 'very warm', the Duke told Rockingham: 'and said, my notions about the American affairs were *insanity*: I think he talked more like a madman than I did'.[3] Yorke also saw Conway that day or the next, and made alterations to strengthen the proposed resolutions: the most significant of them was to add to the declaratory resolution the phrase 'as well in cases of taxation, as in all other cases whatsoever'. Rockingham refused to accept these changes when Conway forwarded them on 25 January,

---

[1] Ibid., fos. 246–7.

[2] Ibid., fos. 260–1. Newcastle's reference is presumably to a cabinet meeting, for they were usually held at the Lord Chancellor's house.

[3] Ibid., fos. 275–6.

warning Yorke that 'the resolutions in general exceed in spirit what the generality of our friends wish, but, in expectation that coming into them will pave the way for the *actual repeal of the Stamp Act*, I think they will be agreed to'. He was also anxious not to goad Pitt, and particularly objected to the deliberate mention of taxation.[1] Yorke in reply expressed uneasiness on this point, thinking 'the words about *taxation*' tactically essential. 'Your Lordship will be pleased to remember what I said of the construction which must be put on rejecting them in the House, supposing they should be offered. . . . To maintain the authority with dignity will assist the repeal.'[2] The next day he submitted another resolution, which Conway and Rockingham adopted, 'being mild' Rockingham told Newcastle. It was 'to assure his Majesty that this House will, upon all occasions, support the lawful authority of his Crown and the rights of Parliament'.[3] Yorke's resolution must have been later dropped, for it was never proposed to the Commons.

Yorke's brother Lord Hardwicke was equally concerned to strengthen the resolutions intended for the House of Lords, where the administration was even less certain to carry whatever it proposed. He consulted the Archbishop of Canterbury, who suggested an extensive recasting and rewording of all the resolutions, and urged Hardwicke to persuade Rockingham

that the administration had much better secure to itself the proposal of resolutions, than let the opposition have the credit of it; and much better move for resolutions that they can maintain as sufficient, than let them be overturned, as feeble and ineffectual, to make place for others, which may be extravagant and mischievous.[4]

Some of the Archbishop's suggestions were to be incorporated in the final Lords' resolutions; but among those that were not was the key substitution of the word 'required' for 'recommend' in the resolution about compensation.

All this concern of the ministers and their friends over the drafting of the resolutions to lay before Parliament as the basis of the proposed legislation reflected a frank appreciation

[1] B.M. Add. MSS. 35430, fos. 37–8: partly printed in *Rockingham Memoirs*, i. 285–8.
[2] Wentworth Woodhouse MSS. R.1–560; partly printed in *Rockingham Memoirs*, i. 288.
[3] B.M. Add. MSS. 32973, fo. 289. [4] B.M. Add. MSS. 35607, fos. 232–6.

of the fact that the passage of repeal would be a political operation of considerable difficulty and delicacy. The formal declaration of Parliament's sovereignty over the colonies was in part an expression of political faith by Rockingham and his advisers, and this belief in Parliamentary supremacy was to be an integral part of Rockinghamite attitudes to the American question in the future: but there were also motives of tactical expediency. One was to secure the unwilling support for repeal of colleagues like Yorke and Northington, and Hardwicke had some basis for this later claim.

It was principally owing to my brother that the dignity and authority of the legislature were kept up by the bill for asserting the dependency of the colonies. I must do Lord Rockingham the justice to say that as far as theory went he declared for asserting the sovereignty of the mother country though he was averse to the exercise of it in point of taxation.[1]

But more important than the motive of ministerial unity was realization that the King, Lords, and Commons would be reluctant to accept a surrender to colonial defiance, despite all attempts by the administration to portray repeal as undertaken in the interests of Britain herself. How one minister professed to see the Parliamentary situation at the time was reported to Massachusetts by agent De Berdt:

Mr. Conway told me there were 3 parties in the House; one was severe method, the other for repeal but for previous resolves to assert the right and power of Parliament, the third which includes the ministry for a repeal without any previous resolutions at all but in order to secure the repeal they were obliged to agree to the resolves in order to secure a majority for a repeal which by that means he apprehended they should be secure in the great question, in which light he hoped the Americans would take their resolutions.[2]

In the conduct of the Parliamentary business necessary to implement the decisions on policy care was always taken that the declaratory resolutions and bill preceded those for repeal. The sugar came before the pill.

[1] B.M. Add. MSS. 35428, fo. 26.
[2] *De Berdt Letters*, p. 312. The meeting between Conway and De Berdt was probably in late January. Conway's picture of a ministry united on unalloyed repeal was mendacious, and his analysis was crude and optimistic.

THE administration's policy was not the only one to be put
before Parliament. Grenville still hoped to prevent repeal
of the Stamp Act,[1] and by the end of January he had planned
a series of resolutions which were to form the basis of the
opposition campaign in both Houses of Parliament. Grenville
assumed that the ministry would begin with a motion asserting
Parliament's right of taxation, and he prepared six resolutions
for his friends and himself to propose afterwards. Three of
them were similar to three drafted by the administration, 'a
censure on the American mobs, a censure on the resolutions
of their assemblies . . . and a reparation to those, who had been
sufferers in the American riots'. Grenville also envisaged 'an
indemnity to those, who had unwillingly transgressed by
neglecting the proper use of stamps'; he intended to move an
Address offering the King support in the execution of the
Stamp Act; and he hoped to conclude with a motion of censure
on the ministry for not summoning Parliament earlier to consider the crisis. This programme was in two ways more moderate than that of the ministry, the absence of any proposals for
punishment and the suggestion, however qualified, of an indemnity. Grenville, when informing James Harris of his plans on
26 January, confided that 'he apprehended the measures of
government on the American affairs would be worse than
Mr. Pitt's; that it would be better (with him) to give up our
right, than first vainly assert it, and then repeal the tax'.[2]

Grenville was to take this line openly in debate, and thus
added to the embarrassment of ministers at the other criticism
of their American policy, Pitt's repeated denials of Parliament's
right to tax the colonies. This view was put deliberately by Pitt
and his friends in a concerted campaign: the similarity between
the speeches made on 3 February by Camden in the Lords and

---

[1] *Grenville Papers*, iii. 356.
[2] Malmesbury MSS. Memo. of 26 Jan. 1766. For a list of resolutions to be
proposed in the Lords, drawn up by Suffolk on 29 Jan. after a meeting of opposition
leaders, see Bedford Office MSS., H.M.C., No. 8, vol. 53, fo. 24.

by Pitt in the Commons was so close that they were thought to have been prepared together beforehand.[1]

As well as this direct and double challenge in Parliament the administration faced a continuous intrigue by the opponents of repeal at Court. Their aim was to persuade George III to announce his open hostility to repeal in order to influence Parliamentary opinion against it, or even to prevent repeal by changing his ministry. This campaign began as soon as the administration's decision was known. On 30 January Lord Harcourt told George III that his ministers had

> little weight and ability . . . the King heard him patiently, and when he mentioned the Stamp Act, the King said he was strenuously for supporting and asserting the right of Great Britain to impose the tax, was against the repeal of the bill, but thought it could perhaps be modified . . . Lord Harcourt suggested at a distance that his Majesty might make these his sentiments known, which might prevent the repeal of the act, if his ministers should push that measure. The King seemed averse to that, said he would never influence people in their parliamentary opinions, and that he had promised to support his ministers.

George III also gave a cool response to Harcourt's suggestion of a change of ministry which would bring back Grenville. Grenville himself, who noted that Bute had expressed the same opinion on the Stamp Act two days earlier to Lord Lyttelton, thought the episode a devious manoeuvre by Bute to change the administration.[2] Thereafter the opposition lived in hopes of an offer to form a ministry; but despite various intrigues and hints to the King no such invitation ever came.

George III's sense of constitutional propriety meant that the decision on his ministry's American policy would be taken in Parliament. The administration behaved with equal propriety by keeping Parliament fully and promptly informed of the colonial situation. Reports from America were presented to the House of Commons as soon as possible after they arrived, by Conway as Secretary of State on 22, 27, 28, and 31 January,

---

[1] *Cust Records*, iii. 95.

[2] An account of this interview was given by Lord Hyde to Grenville. The quotation is from the diary of Mrs. Grenville. B.M. Add. MSS. 42083, fos. 220–1; printed *Grenville Papers*, iii. 353–5.

and 5, 10, 17, and 21 February; and by Dowdeswell as Chancellor of the Exchequer on 3, 10, 19, and 21 February.[1] On 7 February, just before an important debate, Conway even gave the House a verbal account of some papers which had so recently come from America that the clerks in his office had not yet had time to make copies.[2] The ministry may have acted in this way simply to avoid the charge of concealing information; but they may also have hoped that the more that was known about the gravity of the American situation the more amenable Parliamentary opinion would become towards conciliation. If that was the aim, it proved to be a miscalculation: Charles Garth reported to South Carolina on 9 February that the evidence from the papers had been 'received by the Committee with an impression far from favourable to the great object in view'.[3]

A more obvious attempt to influence Parliamentary opinion was the campaign of petitions organized by Trecothick with ministerial approval and assistance. The result had been seen when Parliament reassembled after the Christmas recess. In the second half of January twenty-four petitions from trading and manufacturing towns were presented to the House of Commons.[4] Ten were submitted on 17 January; most of them came from the north of England, but pride of place was given to the one from 'the Merchants of London, trading to North America'. Seven more were presented on 20 January, mainly from the industrial areas of the English Midlands; and the other seven followed in a trickle until 29 January. Altogether complaints came from nearly all the major ports and industrial towns, from Birmingham, Bristol, Coventry, Glasgow, Lancaster, Leeds, Leicester, Liverpool, Manchester, Nottingham, and Wolverhampton. Particularly notable was the protest from the textile industries: petitions had come from Frome, Minehead, and Taunton in Somerset, Bradford, Chippenham, and Melksham in Wiltshire, the silk town of

[1] *Commons Journals*, xxx. 484, 499, 502–3, 508, 513, 516, 524–6, 586, 593, 597–8. For the dates when papers were presented to the Lords, see above, p. 179 and n.
[2] *Ryder Diary*, p. 282.
[3] *S.C.H.G.M.* 26 (1925), 76.
[4] *Commons Journals*, xxx. 462–3, 465, 478–9, 484, 489, 499, 501, 503. Two further petitions, from Worcester and Sheffield, were presented on 24 and 27 Feb., too late to influence the House in its decision. *Ibid.* 601, 611.

Macclesfield and the blanket weavers of Witney. The petitions all asked merely for relief, without presuming to suggest any policy, and were referred to the Committee of the Whole House on the American papers due to commence on 28 January.[1]

The only debate known to have taken place over these petitions occurred on 17 January when Edmund Burke presented the Manchester petition at the request of Sir William Meredith, making his maiden speech on the spur of the moment. Burke subsequently described the experience to his friend Charles O'Hara. 'I know not what struck me, but I took a sudden resolution to say something about it, though I had got it but that moment, and had scarcely time to read it, short as it was; I did say something; what it was, I know not upon my honour; I felt like a man drunk.' There followed a brief discussion before the House proceeded to other business.[2]

The Commons also received petitions from the colonies themselves against the Stamp Act, for it was not contrary to the rules of the House to accept petitions against existing taxes.[3] On 21 January a petition from Virginia agent Edward Montagu reminded the House that the one of the previous year had been rejected, and asked for repeal: the issue of Parliament's right to tax the colonies was omitted from the petition at the request of the ministry.[4] The same day Garth presented a petition from Georgia agent William Knox: it asked specifically for repeal, according to Knox's instructions. After a brief debate on the Virginia petition these petitions were also referred to the American Committee.[5] The administration was anxious to avoid as far as possible any discussion of the issue of Parliament's right of colonial taxation: and after Garth received the South Carolina petition on 4 February he was persuaded by Conway the next day not to present it as

---

[1] Only the petition from London is printed in the *Commons Journals*, xxx. 462. There is also a copy in Newcastle's papers, B.M. Add. MSS. 32973, fos. 421–2; and a draft in Rockingham's papers, Wentworth Woodhouse MSS. R.57–1. For the text of the petition from the Society of Merchant Venturers in Bristol see Minchinton, *Politics and the Port of Bristol in the Eighteenth Century*, pp. 103–4.

[2] *Burke Corr.* i. 232–3.

[3] See my *House of Commons in the Eighteenth Century*, pp. 69–70.

[4] *S.C.H.G.M.* 26 (1925), 86–7.

[5] *Commons Journals*, xxx. 479. For the debate see Garth's report, *S.C.H.G.M.* 26 (1925), 73.

it questioned this right.[1] But by then ministers had failed to prevent a debate on the petition of the Stamp Act Congress.

The administration had tried to stop the presentation of this petition to the Commons for two reasons: the Congress was widely regarded as an illegal assembly, and the petition itself denied Parliament's right of taxation. De Berdt, who had charge of the petition, entrusted it to George Cooke, explaining to Massachusetts that Cooke was 'a man of considerable influence in the House . . . who was so well pleased with the petition that he undertook to present it to the House'.[2] Conway thought that he had persuaded Cooke not to produce it: but on 27 January Cooke unexpectedly did so in evident collusion with Pitt, who made one of his rare appearances to support it; in the words of his old rival Lord Holland, 'Mr. Pitt, with all his insolence about him, went down to order it to be received'. This step put the ministry in a dilemma, for their own followers were divided on the question.[3] The motion to bring up the petition was supported not only by Pitt, Barré, and Huske, but also to varying degrees by Thomas Townshend, Edmund Burke, George Onslow, and Lord Howe, all men holding office under Rockingham: and Conway found himself under strong pressure not to differ from Pitt for fear of forfeiting his future goodwill. Such a course of action, however, would have led to a vote in extremely disadvantageous circumstances. The motion had been opposed immediately by Charles Jenkinson and Welbore Ellis, by the independent member Eliab Harvey, and later by Jeremiah Dyson of the Board of Trade. Nor had Pitt helped his side by an imprudent speech. After saying that the Stamp Act Congress was no more illegal than political

[1] *S.C.H.G.M.* 26 (1925), 86–7.

[2] De Berdt gave the Stamp Act Congress petition to the King to Conway as Secretary of State, and that for the Lords to Dartmouth: 'but the House would not receive it because it was a *memorial* which that House never accepts'. *De Berdt Letters*, pp. 311–12.

[3] The following account of the debate is based on the *Commons Journals*, xxx. 499–500; H. Walpole, *Memoirs*, ii. 191–3; Conway's report to George III and the King's reply. *Corr. of George III*, i. 246–8; and four other letters: (a) Lord G. Sackville to General Irwin, *H.M.C. Stopford-Sackville*, p. 22; (b) W. Rouet to Baron Mure, *Caldwell Papers*, ii. (2), 64–5; (c) Lord Holland to J. Campbell, B.M. Add. MSS. 51406, fos. 128–9; (d) C. Garth to Maryland. This is reprinted in Morgan, *Prologue to Revolution*, pp. 147–8, from *Maryland Hist. Mag.* 6 (1911), 283–6, and is almost identical to the report sent by Garth to South Carolina. *S.C.H.G.M.* 26 (1925), 74–6.

clubs in Britain or the political gatherings that sometimes
occurred at Newmarket race meetings, he reasserted his contention that the power of taxation depended upon representation, and offended many members by declaring that Britain
had broken 'the original compact' with the colonies. An angry
Sir Fletcher Norton declared that Pitt ought to be called
before the Bar of the House for such a statement. Norton was
supported almost unanimously by shouts of 'Hear! Hear!',
and completed Pitt's humiliation by successfully insisting that
any reply would be against the rules of debate.[1] Conway,
as he later explained to George III, 'thought the temper of the
House was much against the petition and that it would have
been a bad question to have our first division on'. He was
afraid that to hold the first important vote on America in such
circumstances might jeopardize the potential majority for
repeal which the administration was endeavouring to construct.
The opposition naturally sought to seize the opportunity of a
tactical victory, and Grenville headed a battery of speakers
attacking the petition. Conway and Dowdeswell therefore
announced that they also opposed receiving it, and expressed
the hope that Cooke would withdraw it. He did not do so,
but refrained from opposing the Order of the Day moved by
Lord John Cavendish and supported by that known friend to
the colonies, Sir William Baker: this was a procedural device
for avoiding a decision on the original motion, and it was
carried without a vote. A technical excuse had been found for
not receiving the petition: it was not signed in person by the
petitioners, as required by a resolution of 1689. De Berdt
reported to Massachusetts that 'the House objected to the
Congress and therefore after two hours' debate it was dropped
without either being accepted or rejected. But General Conway
desired me to assure my friends in America that it was not
from any disrespect to them but purely from the form.'[2] This
was not the whole truth: but the ministry had escaped from
the debate without disaster or even the loss of Pitt's goodwill.[3]

---

[1] M.P.s could speak only once in a debate in the House, but as often as they
liked in Committee.

[2] *De Berdt Letters*, p. 312.

[3] It was perhaps fortunate for Pitt's relationship with the administration that
Charles Yorke had not been present to attack him. His brother Lord Hardwicke
wrote to him the next day. 'I am very sorry you was not at the House yesterday.

At the end of the debate of 27 January, Conway announced to the House the proposed method of proceeding in the Committee of the Whole House, due to begin the next day. The first two days would be taken up with reading through the papers, and, at Pitt's request, consideration of resolutions would begin as early as Friday, 31 January.[1] When Newcastle heard of this decision, he suggested to Rockingham that the House of Lords, also due to start reading the American papers in Committee on 28 January, should postpone consideration of any resolutions until Monday, 3 February, since on the previous Friday all the peers would go to hear the debate in the Commons. 'By this means, the Commons will go first; as I think, it is much to be wished, that they should; for I hope, they will come *soon* to the repeal; or, believe me, my dear Lord, you will see great confusion amongst your own friends.'[2] Newcastle's belief that prior consideration of repeal by the Commons would assist its passage through the Lords was to be justified by events, but the Commons Committee, chaired by Rose Fuller, repeatedly fell behind any timetable. On 30 January George Onslow wrote to tell Pitt, who had gone out of town, that no debate would take place the next day after all. The papers had not been finished on the first two days, 28 and 29 January, and 'it will be as much as we can do, if we get through the rest of the papers and the *viva voce* evidence tomorrow. The House is so fatigued with these long sittings, and attention to useless uninforming papers, that I doubt whether they will be prevailed on to sit on Saturday.'[3] On 31 January the Committee completed reading the papers and began the examination of witnesses.[4] They were four refugees

---

The Great Commoner never laid himself so open, never asserted such absurd and pernicious doctrines, and richly deserved to have been called to the bar, or sent to the Tower. The petition was from an illegal congress, calling the right of Parliament in question.' *Rockingham Memoirs*, i. 290–1.

[1] *Corr. of George III*, i. 246–7. B.M. Add. MSS. 32973, fo. 301. Parliament never sat on 30 Jan., the anniversary of Charles I's execution.

[2] B.M. Add. MSS. 32973, fo. 305.

[3] *Chatham Papers*, ii. 374–5.

[4] The copy of the official transcript of the evidence on 31 Jan. and 11, 12, 13, and 17 Feb. used in this study, including all quotations, is the one in Newcastle's papers. B.M. Add. MSS. 33030, fos. 74–203. Another, not quite identical, one for the evidence on the first four days is in Rockingham's papers. Wentworth Woodhouse MSS. R.27, pp. 1–136, R.27 (A), pp. 1–70. This has been transcribed

from America, Doctor Thomas Moffatt and lawyer Martin Howard from Rhode Island, Major Thomas James from New York, and Colonel George Mercer, the Virginia Stamp-Distributor. This verbal evidence provided first-hand information on colonial defiance and rioting as a final background for the resolutions condemning such events and asserting Britain's authority: but statements by the witnesses revealed an alarming situation in America. Moffatt said that there had been no military force in Rhode Island to stop the riots of 27 and 28 August: he was then asked whether he thought the colony to be in a state of rebellion, but a successful objection was made to this question. Major James described how in New York his force of 151 men had faced a mob of nearly 4,000, and stated that in his opinion resistance in that colony would have become widespread if military force had been used to execute the Stamp Act, with 20,000 men being raised in two days. Colonel Mercer said that an army would also be needed in Virginia, but professed ignorance of the potential manpower of the colony.[1] Much of this evidence about colonial resistance was the result of opposition questioning, for George Onslow wrote to inform Pitt at midnight 'that we just now *finished* all the papers and evidence, which has been lengthened out to this time, I wont say by a *useless*, but by a worse than useless, by the most artful, premeditated string of questions, calculated for a particular purpose, which I trust in God will be defeated'.[2] This fear that Parliamentary opinion would become so incensed about the colonial defiance that concessions

and edited (apart from the evidence of two witnesses already printed, George Mercer and Benjamin Franklin) by B. R. Smith in his M.A. Thesis. Trecothick was critical of the transcript when returning to Newcastle on 3 Mar. 1766 'the copies of the examination in the House of Commons, which, to me, are for the most part, quite unintelligible—owing, I suppose, to the clerks not hearing distinctly, or to his being obliged to keep pace with the Speakers'. B.M. Add. MSS. 32974, fo. 133. Unofficial but lengthy reports of the evidence were also taken down by two M.P.s (a) Sir Roger Newdigate, Newdegate MSS. B. 2545; (b) Nathaniel Ryder, *Ryder Diary*, pp. 291–302.

[1] The evidence for this day is recorded in B.M. Add. MSS. 33030, fos. 78–87; and in Wentworth Woodhouse MSS. R.27, pp. 1–21. It would seem that the witnesses were coached, for Major James, on his return to New York, told Lieutenant-Governor Colden that 'he had a paper of directions how to answer in his examination before the House of Commons'. *Grenville Papers*, iv. 387.

[2] *Chatham Papers*, ii. 378–80. This letter was written on 31 Jan., but has the date of 14 Feb. ascribed to it.

would be politically impossible was one widely shared by the advocates of repeal.

Onslow also told Pitt of an incident that provided an alarming foretaste of the strong opposition that would be made to repeal. Earlier that day in the House of Commons the administration had carried a procedural point on a petition about a Scottish election by only eleven votes, 148 to 137: 'according to parliamentary divination it had all the aspect of an overthrow', Horace Walpole later commented. The minority had been a coalition of Grenville's group with such supporters of Bute as Gilbert Elliot and James Oswald, and had included some army officers and office-holders who normally supported administration, among them Jeremiah Dyson, Lord Strange, and Lord George Sackville. The episode was regarded as ominous by the administration in the light of earlier rumours that Bute's hostility would shatter the cohesion of the customary 'court party' in Parliament, a point made by Conway next day in his report to the King. 'Had there been no previous appearance of any sort of design or separation from your Majesty's service less notice would have been taken of this; but the buzz there has been for some time of such a plan, made it matter of great observation.'[1] The portent was to prove accurate; the members who had deserted administration in this vote were to do the same over repeal: but in his reply George III denied that the event had political significance. 'By what Lord Rockingham dropped to me of both the persons being good men, I did not know that Administration meant to take an active part as such on this occasion.'[2]

Newcastle had taken the alarm as soon as he heard of the Commons vote: and on 31 January, after consulting Lords Albemarle, Bessborough, and Grantham, he wrote to urge Rockingham to

lay the present state of the question before the King: and humbly represent to His Majesty, that, if His Majesty shall be graciously

[1] *Corr. of George III*, i. 249–50. For other accounts of the incident see Harris Diary, 31 Jan. 1766; H. Walpole, *Memoirs*, ii. 196; and G. Onslow's letter to Newcastle, B.M. Add. MSS. 32973, fo. 321.

[2] *Corr. of George III*, i. 221–2: also printed in *Rockingham Memoirs*, i. 295. Conway forwarded this reply to Rockingham with the query, 'does the enclosed answer give you any light or opinion'. Wentworth Woodhouse MSS. R.1–566, 567; printed, *Rockingham Memoirs*, i. 294–5.

G*

pleased, to signify to his Lords of the Bed Chamber, and his servants, at the time of his dressing, or after his levee, that His Majesty wishes the repeal; and thinks it for his service, that it should be done, it will certainly be carried without difficulty . . . I myself, or any of these Lords, have not the least doubt of His Majesty's own inclinations: but there is, at present, so much industry, in propagating everything, that makes against us, that His Majesty's own inclinations, upon such a critical occasion, cannot be too well known.[1]

By the next day Newcastle had realized that Bute's hostility was of more immediate significance for the House of Lords than for the Commons; and he wrote again to remind Rockingham of 'the notion, which now prevails, that Lord B and all his friends (and they are very numerous in the House of Lords) will be all against us'.[2] The Lords, in its Committee of the Whole House 'on the late tumults in America', chaired by Lord Botetourt, had mirrored the Commons in reading American papers on 28 and 29 January and in examining the same four witnesses on 31 January: and was also due to consider resolutions in the Committee on 3 February.[3]

As a result of this pressure from Newcastle and other friends, Rockingham wrote to George III on 1 February asking for an audience. The King, although unwell, arranged to see him at 7 o'clock.[4] Rockingham got little satisfaction from this meeting. George III gave a general assurance that he would support the ministry's American policy, but refused to allow this to be made public or to dismiss any office-holders for voting against the administration on 31 January.[5] Northington informed the King next day of the critical situation in the Lords, and George III then saw Rockingham again, afterwards reporting to his Lord Chancellor.

I gave him every light I could as to the difficulties they will have to struggle with; he called upon my promise at all times of not giving up Administration while they thought they could act; by this you are fully apprised of the part they will take this day, which I believe will prove a fatal day to them; this hour is perhaps one of the most critical ever known in this country.[6]

---

[1] B.M. Add. MSS. 32973, fo. 319; printed, *Rockingham Memoirs*, i. 292–3.

[2] B.M. Add. MSS. 32973, fo. 330; printed, *Rockingham Memoirs*, i. 293.

[3] *Lords Journals*, xxxi. 246–7, 250, 252–4.   [4] *Corr. of George III*, i. 250–1.

[5] B.M. Add. MSS. 32973, fos. 338–41; *Corr. of George III*, i. 251.

[6] *Corr. of George III*, i. 251–2.

Rockingham had no intention of resigning after a defeat in the Lords, and he had already made this clear to Newcastle. 'I think it will be a most strange day in the House of Lords. Every intelligence confirms it . . . After tomorrow we must have a meeting of some of the most considerable friends for whether we carry the day or lose it, our situation in fact will not be much different.'[1] The expected crisis did not occur on 3 February after all. The administration made a late tactical change, and for both Houses put the resolution asserting Parliament's right first instead of last.[2] The two debates that day therefore centred on a question over which there was broad agreement between the ministers and their principal opponents.

In the Lords Grafton began by reading out the five ministerial resolutions, and then moved the one asserting Parliament's supremacy over the colonies 'in all cases whatsoever'.[3] He said that America was as liable to Parliamentary taxation as Britain, and offered the resolution because the right had been challenged both here and in the colonies; but he ended with an advocacy of lenient measures. Lord Poulett opposed the motion, suggesting that Parliament's right did not cover internal taxation. Lord Shelburne deplored the needless discussion of constitutional points. The question was simply whether the Stamp Act should be repealed or enforced. Austria, he told the Committee, did not tax her Netherlands provinces. Lord Lyttelton replied that it was the colonies who had raised the constitutional issue. Sovereignty was indivisible, and the denial of the power of taxation could apply to all legislation. The argument of non-

---

[1] B.M. Add. MSS. 32973, fos. 338–9.

[2] The change was apparently made on 2 Feb., after pressure from the Archbishop of Canterbury and Lord Marchmont. B.M. Add. MSS. 32973, fos. 332–5. Wentworth Woodhouse MSS. R.1–569.

[3] The following account of the Lords debate of 3 Feb. is based on the reports sent to George III by Rockingham and Grafton, *Corr. of George III*, i. 253–4; Mrs. Grenville's diary, *Grenville Papers*, iii. 357; notes by Sir Roger Newdigate, Newdegate MSS. B 2546/17; notes made by or for Grafton, Grafton MSS. 1022 b; a report from C. Garth to South Carolina, *S.C.H.G.M.* 26 (1925), 85–6; a letter from W. Rouet to Baron Mure, *Caldwell Papers*, ii (2), 68; and a report said to be taken from Lord Hardwicke's papers and printed in Cobbett, *Parl. Hist.* xvi. 163–77. This report is there ascribed to 10 Feb., but for the following reasons I believe 3 Feb. to be the correct date. (a) Camden, portrayed as making a maiden speech, spoke on 3 Feb. (b) Mansfield is reported as mentioning that the debate saw the first denial in the Lords of Parliament's right to tax America: such denials were made on 3 Feb. (c) All the speakers named spoke on 3 Feb. in the order given. (d) There is no contemporary reference to any Lords debate on 10 Feb.

representation, if admitted, might also be used by many tax-payers in Britain. He told the House that the colonies made no distinction of internal and external taxation, citing James Otis, and declared that the only issue was whether they were under the Crown. Lord Camden, making his maiden speech in the Lords, put forward the argument that taxation was based on consent, and therefore on representation. Lord Chancellor Northington denounced these doctrines as new and unconstitutional. Lord Mansfield said that political theory, the practice of other states and the question of repeal were all irrelevant. He advanced two propositions, that the British legislature had the power to make laws for all British subjects, and that these included the colonists. With a masterly deployment of constitutional precedents and arguments he demolished the doctrine that representation had been or was a necessary condition of taxation by Parliament. After a debate noted by contemporaries for its high quality the Committee divided at 9 o'clock, the resolution being carried by 125 votes to 5.[1] Newcastle was pleased with the debate, but vaguely apprehensive about Bedford's insistence that the Lords should meet again the next day.[2]

The House of Commons saw a very long debate, one which Charles Garth later commended to the colonies. 'A fuller House I don't recollect to have seen, and it is to the honour of Parliament I must add, that I believe there never was a debate so temperate, serious, solemn and Parliamentary.'[3] When the Committee began, Conway, like Grafton, read out the five ministerial resolutions and then proposed the one asserting

[1] The minority comprised Camden, Cornwallis, Poulett, Shelburne, and Torrington. This and later resolutions passed by the Lords may be found in a memorandum by George III that gives the date when each was agreed by the Committee. *Corr. of George III*, i. 262–4. They were afterwards printed in the *Lords Journals*, xxxi. 262, and in Cobbett, *Parl. Hist.* xvi. 164–5.

[2] B.M. Add. MSS. 32973, fo. 353.

[3] The following account of the debate is based on the *Ryder Diary*, pp. 261–76; H. Walpole, *Memoirs*, ii. 197–200; notes by Sir Roger Newdigate, Newdegate MSS. B 2546/13–15; notes by Grey Cooper, *A.H.R.* 17 (1911–12), 565–74; and three letters: (a) Conway to George III, *Corr. of George III*, i. 354–5; (b) C. Garth to Maryland, Morgan, *Prologue to Revolution*, pp. 148–54: this is virtually identical with Garth's report to South Carolina, *S.C.H.G.M.* 26 (1925), 76–85; (c) Rev. W. Palmer (Speaker's Chaplain) to Rev. R. Cust, *Cust Memoirs*, iii. 95. All quotations are from the *Ryder Diary*. For another account of this debate see Gipson, *P.M.B.H.* 86 (1962), 14–21.

Parliament's right to legislate for the colonies 'in all cases whatsoever'.[1] He blamed Grenville's legislation for the economic depression of the colonies; asserted Parliament's right to levy internal taxation on America, although he thought it could never be expedient to exercise it; and ended by claiming that his circular letters of 24 October had authorized any action short of executing the Stamp Act by military force. After Dowdeswell had seconded, Hans Stanley denounced the resolution as a 'specious preliminary to the surrender of all our rights in America'; said that the colonists had not made the futile distinction between internal and external taxation; and forecast that they would next deny Parliament's right of legislation if repeal was carried. Charles Yorke then made a long and learned speech, quoting a mass of historical precedents in support of Parliament's right of taxation. He denied that the motion was 'merely as a palliative to the repeal and renouncing the authority in fact while we assert it in words': and, in a phrase noted by several reporters, declared that he 'would not repeal wantonly because asked or timidly because it is resisted'. William Beckford made his by now usual denial of Parliament's right of taxation, and Nugent countered by suggesting, but not moving, an amendment to affirm it. The distinguished constitutional lawyer William Blackstone, deploying a wealth of precedents, denied that representation was necessary for taxation, or that there was any distinction either between internal and external taxation or between taxation and legislation. The Speaker's Chaplain thought that 'he seemed to speak fuller and cleverer to the point than Mr. Yorke, though in a manner much like that of reading a lecture in College'.[2] Thomas Pitt said that it would be better to drop the right of taxation than to assert it without enforcement; and he claimed that the alleged inexpediency of the Stamp Act was simply the colonial resistance to it. After Richard Hussey had declared that there was no precedent for taxing a country that had its own assembly, Alexander Wedderburn demonstrated the unrepresentative nature of the colonial assemblies. Serjeant James Hewitt made another denial of Parliament's right of taxation in a speech barely heard and badly reported.

[1] For the full text of the resolution see *Corr. of George III*, i. 262.
[2] Blackstone was Professor of English Law at Oxford University.

Edmund Burke drew an analogy between it and such dormant parts of the constitution as the royal veto on legislation, which had lapsed since Queen Anne's reign. Lord Frederick Campbell replied that taxation of the colonies by Parliament was preferable to the old method of requisitions by the Crown, for that was a relic of prerogative.

It was now after 10 o'clock, and news must have come of the vote in the Lords. Barré therefore moved an amendment to omit the words 'in all cases whatsoever' on the ground that Parliament had no right to lay an internal tax on America. The Stamp Act could be enforced only by the sword, and any coercive action would alienate the colonists. Barré ended with this prophetic warning. 'All colonies have their date of independence. The wisdom or folly of our conduct may make it the sooner or later. If we act injudiciously, this point may be reached in the life of many of the members of this House.' Dowdeswell opposed the amendment, and answered Thomas Pitt's charge by asserting that the reason for repeal was not the colonial resistance but the complaints of British merchants. Grenville spoke next, and devoted much of his speech to an attack on the administration for instigating the petitions, which he portrayed as a cheap political device. He condemned Conway for undue leniency, and said the orders of 24 October were deliberately misleading, since Gage and Colville were known to lack sufficient men and resources to take effective action. Grenville preferred Barré's opinion to the policy of the ministry, who proposed this resolution with the intention of later repealing the Stamp Act. 'This conduct is so mean and so distasteful.' Grenville's speech, timed at fifty minutes by Newdigate, brought this comment from Chaplain Palmer. 'One could not help seeing in him too much of the spirit of opposition.' It was after midnight when Pitt rose to make what Palmer thought 'the best speech I have yet heard from him': but its quality is not conveyed by the scanty surviving reports.[1] Sir Fletcher Norton expressed surprise and scorn that Pitt should still link taxation and representation. 'I thought that argument had been beat out of the House.' Certainly every lawyer in the debate had demolished both that contention and the distinction between internal and external taxation in a

[1] Ryder had by now stopped taking notes.

unanimous and impressive legal demonstration of Parliament's right of taxation over the colonies.

Barré's amendment was negatived at 2.45 a.m. without a vote, Conway telling George III that the words objected to 'would not have had four voices against them as its imagined if the Committee had been divided'.[1] He commented that there had been 'scarce anything that could properly be called a debate', for only Pitt and his friends had seriously challenged the resolution. Pitt himself ruefully wrote to his wife next day, 'we (number three) debated strenuously the rights of America. The resolution passed, for England's right to do what the Treasury pleases with three millions of free men.'[2] The full discussion can have left no one in any doubt that the deliberately vague phrase 'in all cases whatsoever' had been interpreted to include taxation, and the clarification of this point was the most important result of the debate.

After this late night the Commons had adjourned to 5 February, and only the Lords met on 4 February. The resumed Committee passed the second and third ministerial resolutions apparently without debate: these declared that there had been disorders in the colonies, and that they had been encouraged by several of the assemblies. The half-anticipated administration defeat came on the fourth resolution, which was for an Address asking the King to instruct the colonial governors to recommend to their assemblies compensation for those who had suffered in the riots. The opposition had selected this as the weakest point in the resolutions to attack, and Lord Suffolk proposed an amendment to substitute for 'recommend' the stronger word 'require'. In a lively debate this alteration was supported by Sandwich, Bedford, Temple, Lyttelton, and Mansfield. Speeches for administration by Dartmouth, Grafton, Newcastle, Camden, and Marchmont failed to avert a narrow opposition victory, by 63 votes to 60. The majority included Northington, Mansfield, the Duke of York, and most of Bute's friends. Mansfield then intervened to prevent the introduction of the resolution proposing the punishment of the rioters:

---

[1] Garth reported to Maryland, 'I believe from the sound there were not more than ten dissenting voices', amongst whom he himself had been one.

[2] This undated letter is printed in the *Chatham Papers*, iii. 363–70, and there ascribed to 15 Jan.; it was written on 4 Feb.

and this resolution, although in the ministerial list, was dropped. After these setbacks the administration wanted to put an end to the Committee and report the resolutions already voted: but the opposition refused to agree to this step, Sandwich and Bedford insisting that the Committee should meet on 6 February to consider resolutions moved by the opposition.[1]

The next morning the ministers held a meeting to discuss the situation. Those present on 5 February included all the cabinet except Northington, and also such influential supporters as Portland, Albemarle, and Bessborough. Grafton urged immediate resignation of the ministry, but Newcastle persuaded the gathering to await a Parliamentary decision on the main question of repeal.[2] Grafton and Rockingham saw the King afterwards and doubtless told him that defeat over repeal would mean the end of the administration.[3] Newcastle then went to see George III, and was given permission to put three questions to the King. The Duke ascertained that George III had no intention of changing his administration and would support the existing ministry. The crucial third question was whether the King was for repeal. 'I am,' replied George III. 'I was always against enforcing it. I have thought some middle way might be taken, but I am now convinced that nothing but the repeal will do.'[4] The King, however, was unwilling to allow the ministry to use the full weight of his opinion to influence voting in Parliament: he told Newcastle 'that he would *speak*, but did not imagine that he should be able to do much'.[5] The interview nevertheless marked a significant change in the King's attitude which the administration was soon to exploit to the utmost. Only six days earlier the King

---

[1] This account of the Lords' debates is based on the reports sent to George III by Rockingham and Grafton. *Corr. of George III,*, i. 255–6; on a letter from W. Rouet to Baron Mure, *Caldwell Papers*, ii (2), 68–9; and on Mrs. Grenville's diary, *Grenville Papers*, iii. 357–8. Grafton in his later *Autobiography*, p. 69, stated erroneously that Lord Bute himself moved the fatal amendment. For the Lords' resolutions passed this day see *Corr. of George III*, i. 262–3.

[2] Bateson, *Narrative*, pp. 47–8.

[3] Bateson, *Narrative*, pp. 48–9.

[4] This is the wording in Lord Dartmouth's note book. Dartmouth MSS. D 1778/V/221 B. Dartmouth saw Newcastle as the Duke came out of the royal Closet. Newcastle's own later account of George III's reply is less full. 'Yes, I am now. I was not for it at first, but now I am convinced or think *that* is necessary.' Bateson, *Narrative*, p. 49.

[5] Bateson, *Narrative*, p. 50.

had told Lord Harcourt that he was against repeal, although he might agree to modification. George III was then apparently, or at least officially, unaware that his ministers had decided on repeal, for the subject had been discussed in hypothetical terms:[1] and his change of mind was due to his realization that the middle policy he would have preferred was not a practical one in the light of the political situation at Westminster. In a memorandum written a few days later the King recorded that his personal opinion of 'the best mode of restoring order and obedience in the American colonies' had always been for modification of the Stamp Act. Retention of a part was necessary to demonstrate the right of taxation, while alterations would show the government's desire to redress any justifiable grievances.

But if the unhappy factions that divide the country would not permit this in my opinion equitable plan to be followed I thought repealing infinitely more eligible than enforcing, which could only tend to widen the breach between this country and America; my language to all ever continued pointing out my wish for modification.[2]

Before the ministers could take action, more shocks followed in the Commons on 5 February.[3] When the American Committee resumed Conway began by moving the second resolution, the simple statement that there had been riots and defiance in several colonies. He anticipated unanimous approval as in the Lords, but Jeremiah Dyson moved an amendment to add 'whereby the execution of an act of the past session of Parliament in such colonies hath been hitherto defeated'. Pitt expressed approval of the original resolution and of the ministers generally:

[1] Above, p. 186.

[2] *Corr. of George III*, i. 268–9. The King's memorandum is undated, but evidently written after 12 Feb. In the interpretation of this and other papers relating to the King's views on repeal I have relied on the clarification by Namier, *Additions and Corrections*, pp. 50–2.

[3] For the events of this day in the Commons see the *Ryder Diary*, pp. 276–82; H. Walpole, *Memoirs*, ii. 201–2; notes by Sir Roger Newdigate, Newdegate MSS. B 2546/16; and the following letters: (a) G. Cooper to Rockingham, Wentworth Woodhouse MSS. R.1–573; printed *Rockingham Memoirs*, i. 309–10, where it is attributed to 24 Feb; (b) G. Onslow to Newcastle, B.M. Add. MSS. 32973, fo. 359; (c) J. West to Newcastle (2 letters); B.M. Add. MSS. 32973, fos. 361–3; (d) C. Garth to South Carolina, *S.C.H.G.M.* 26 (1925), 86. The resolutions agreed this day can be found in *Corr. of George III*, i. 262–4. For another account of the proceedings see Gipson, *P.M.H.B.* 86 (1962), 22–5.

and George Onslow slipped out of the debate to tell Newcastle that Pitt had said 'that it was happy for this country that they were about the King's person, happier if their principles were rivetted in his heart'. Pitt urged Dyson to drop the amendment. Dyson thereupon stated that his motive was opposition to repeal, since the impossibility of enforcing the Stamp Act was the strongest argument used in favour of that policy. Sir William Meredith denied this, saying that the value of the colonies was economic and that coercion would not produce trade. Bedfordite Rigby then seconded Dyson's amendment. It was opposed by Barré as immaterial, Burke as undesirable, and Charles Yorke as unnecessary. Gilbert Elliot supported the amendment in a speech urging modification rather than repeal of the Stamp Act: but Dyson and Rigby agreed to withdraw it when Grenville expressed a desire for unanimity.

In his speech Grenville said that he was willing to agree to the repeal of any parts of the Stamp Act that might be found erroneous, an admission that was promptly seized upon by Edmund Burke and William Pitt. If it was consistent with the dignity of the House to repeal part of the act under duress, Pitt declared, it was equally so to repeal the whole. Grenville mildly replied that he would value Pitt's good opinion, because he was acting on his principles; and then reminded the Committee that before introducing the Stamp Act he had vainly asked the colonial agents to suggest other methods of taxation. This exchange between Pitt and Grenville lasted half an hour before the original resolution was agreed at 6 o'clock without a division. Treasury Secretary Grey Cooper, writing then to Rockingham, regarded this first debate of the day as a good omen. 'I never was in better spirits. If this might be well managed every thing yet may be more solid than it was before the mine of yesterday was sprung. Mr. Pitt has taken the alarm.' Certainly the supporters of the Stamp Act had failed to persuade the Committee to accept a form of words implying that the motion for repeal was surrender to colonial violence: and the debate had shown that the behaviour of Bute's faction in the Lords the previous day had caused Pitt to realize that the policy of repeal was in jeopardy.[1]

[1] *Chatham Papers*, ii. 375–6.

Later events in the Committee that day were less satisfactory for administration. The third resolution proposed by Conway, that the disorders had been encouraged by the votes of some assemblies, was approved without any debate. The fourth, concerning punishment of the rioters, had been the one withdrawn in the Lords the previous day at the behest of Lord Mansfield, and Conway said he was willing to do the same. It was dropped after Pitt, Gilbert Elliot, and Grenville had all concurred in the step. The fifth resolution, on compensation to victims of the riots, was the one over which the ministry had been defeated in the Lords the day before: and the same amendment, to substitute the words 'require of' for 'recommend to' in the instructions from the governors to the assemblies, was proposed by Robert Nugent as soon as Conway had moved the resolution. Another important debate began. Lord George Sackville and Attorney-General Charles Yorke argued that 'recommend' was the customary usage, but Solicitor-General William De Grey disagreed. Speakers for the amendment outnumbered those for the ministerial resolution, and included Mr. Speaker himself, Sir John Cust. The debate was turned by the Master of the Rolls Sir Thomas Sewell, who declared that the whole resolution was contrary to precedent. Pitt took up the same argument, but said he was in favour of compensation. Grenville thereupon stated that although he favoured the amendment he was willing to suggest an alternative resolution, and 'drew out of his pocket a general resolution that compensation ought to be made to the sufferers by the riots from the colonies where the riots were committed'. James West reported this to Newcastle just after Pitt had accepted Grenville's resolution with a promise that he would support legislation to enforce compensation if the colonial assemblies took no action; and West added the comment. 'There appears to me as if there had been some understanding between them.' His suspicion was unjustified. Pitt thought he had outmanoeuvred Grenville, for he told his wife the next day, 'we overturned and beat . . . the triumphant factions, and brought them to agree, in words and substance, to somewhat more moderate even than the ministry themselves meant'.[1]

---

[1] This letter, printed in *Chatham Papers*, ii. 375–7, is there dated 11 Feb., but was written on 6 Feb.

Comparison of the various motions confirms Pitt's claim, but his action had the consequence that the administration had now lost control of the proceedings.[1] Grenville carried not only this resolution but two subsequent ones. The first of these had not been one he had told Harris about on 26 January: declaring that all colonists who had supported any act of Parliament were loyal subjects and entitled to protection, it was carried without debate. The other was part of his original plan, and proposed an indemnity for those who had not taken out stamps, but only after payment of the relevant duties. Conway attempted to remove the teeth from the resolution by suggesting that this condition should be omitted, and the third debate of the day began. James West told Newcastle of the ministry's predicament in a letter written the next morning. 'Pitt spoke faintly on the subject and then left the House. Mr. Grenville then redoubled his argument and was supported by his friends with a good deal of noise not to withdraw the motion.' But Lord Strange and Gilbert Elliot suggested a compromise, the alternative wording of 'under proper restrictions': and Grenville, although his supporters still pressed for a division, thought it more prudent not to offend Lord Bute's friends before the main question of the repeal was considered.[2] Grenville none the less only agreed to the alteration on condition that the resolution would be incorporated in a bill: and he ended with a declaration summarized by James West. 'That he did not know a clause in the Stamp Act that ought to be repealed and that the act would cost many, many days before it could possibly be repealed.' Grenville had captured the initiative, for he announced his intention of moving an Address to the King as a consequence of the resolutions already voted, and obtained the agreement of the administration that he could do so when the Committee next met, on 7 February.[3]

Rockingham was disturbed to hear what had happened in the Commons, and his concern was increased by events in the House of Lords on the following day, 6 February. When the American Committee was resumed, Lord Weymouth moved

---

[1] Chaplain Palmer thought that Grenville had been greatly assisted by 'the mysterious conduct of Mr. Pitt'. *Cust Memoirs*, iii. 96.

[2] *Grenville Papers*, iii. 358.

[3] G. Grenville to H. Stanley, 6 Feb. 1766. Grenville Letter-Books, vol. 2.

Grenville's new resolution asserting that colonists willing to obey Parliamentary legislation were loyal subjects and entitled to protection.[1] This had been carried in the Commons Committee without debate, but Lord Temple now proposed a controversial amendment specifically mentioning the Stamp Act; and this was supported in the debate by Lord Bute himself. According to Lord George Sackville,[2]

his Lordship spoke with propriety and firmness, declaring that it was not time then to give his opinion upon the Stamp Act, but that in general he would declare that he would not be satisfied with supporting the legislative authority of Great Britain by resolutions only, and that if the ministers of the Crown acted upon other principles he was resolved, notwithstanding his duty and affection for the King, strenuously to oppose them.

Sackville realized that Bute's behaviour was the significant point of this and the previous debate. 'The great event was that Lord Bute voted with the Opposition in both questions, and drew after him very many Lords in employment.' The ministry was defeated by 59 votes to 54, the majority including Bute's friends, Northington, Mansfield, and two of the King's brothers, the Dukes of York and Gloucester. In his report to George III Rockingham tactfully omitted any details of the debate, saying that 'it was so confused that scarce any one knew on what they divided': but he asked the King for an immediate interview because of the recent developments in the two Houses of Parliament.[3]

This crucial meeting took place on 7 February. Rockingham, no doubt informed by Newcastle of what the King had said two days earlier, told George III that the practical choice was between repeal and enforcement. The King at once declared himself for repeal and made the vital concession Rockingham wanted. He freely gave his minister permission to make his

---

[1] For reports of this debate see Mrs. Grenville's diary, *Grenville Papers*, iii. 358–9, and two letters: (a) Lord G. Sackville to General Irwin, *H.M.C. Stopford-Sackville*, p. 22; (b) W. Rouet to Baron Mure, *Caldwell Papers*, ii (2), 70–1.

[2] Rouet's account of Bute's speech is similar. Horace Walpole's later brief account of the administration's difficulties in the Lords included the statement that 'Lord Bute himself, almost acting patriotism, said nothing should oblige him to be for the King's wish if he did not approve the measures of the King's Ministers'. *Memoirs*, ii. 200.

[3] *Corr. of George III*, i. 261.

opinion public.[1] This was done before the important debate in the Commons that same day.[2]

Grenville moved the Address he had always planned, containing an assurance of support for the enforcement of 'all the laws of this Kingdom'.[3] His speech made it clear that he was calling for the execution of the Stamp Act. Grenville had been encouraged by the events of 5 February,[4] and believed his motion had a genuine chance of success: for he told Stanley on 6 February, 'the degree of resistance it is likely to meet with in the present unsettled state of men and things, I scarce know how to form a guess'.[5] But by this motion Grenville overplayed his hand, with disastrous consequences for his hopes of averting repeal.

After Seymour had seconded Grenville, Charles Townshend made his only important speech of the session. He said that he was as much concerned about America as Grenville, and some of his remarks foreshadowed what was to be his own solution of the next year, the plan of paying the salaries of colonial officials and judges out of Parliamentary taxation levied on the colonies. 'He thinks if some proper plan is not formed for governing as well as quieting them at present and for the future, it will be extremely dangerous. The magistrates at present in many colonies elective, the judges dependent on the assemblies for their salaries.'[6] But Townshend opposed Grenville's Address

[1] *Corr. of George III*, i. 268–9.

[2] According to Horace Walpole, Lord Strange told George III on 10 Feb. that the ministry's 'great majority had been entirely owing to their having made use of his Majesty's name'. *Memoirs*, ii. 205.

[3] No two reports agree exactly on the wording. The sources used for the following account of the debate are *Ryder Diary*, pp. 282–91; Harris Diary, 7 Feb. 1766; notes by Sir Roger Newdigate, Newdegate MSS. B2546/18; H. Walpole, *Memoirs*, ii. 202–4; and the following letters: (a) J. West (three letters) to Newcastle, B.M. Add. MSS. 32973, fos. 373–7; (b) Revd. R. Palmer to Revd. R. Cust, *Cust Memoirs*, iii. 96; (c) Conway to George III, *Corr. of George III*, i. 266–7; (d) C. Garth to South Carolina, *S.C.H.G.M.* 26 (1925), 88–9; (e) H. Cruger to H. Cruger, sen., *Commerce of Rhode Island*, pp. 141–2; (f) Lord George Sackville to General Irwin, *H.M.C. Stopford-Sackville*, pp. 22–3. All quotations, unless otherwise stated, are from the *Ryder Diary*. For another summary of this debate see Gipson, *P.M.H.B.* 86 (1962), 25–31.

[4] *Cust Memoirs*, iii. 66.

[5] G. Grenville to H. Stanley, 6 Feb. 1766. Grenville Letter-Books, vol. 2.

[6] This is Ryder's summary. Of the other reporters only Newdigate noted this point. 'Unless the plan of government in North America be altered—the governors —judges for their salaries.' For more extensive quotation of reports of Townshend's speech see Namier and Brooke, *Charles Townshend*, pp. 140–1.

as premature and prejudging the main issue of the Stamp Act itself: moreover, enforcement of the act at this time would be both impractical and provocative. Independent member Thomas Molyneux then made a savage attack on 'ungrateful America . . . Shall we stay till some Oliver rises up amongst them? Four sorts of people appear among them; hypocrites, agitators, preachers and levellers.' Edmund Burke urged that full consideration of the whole question should precede any decision. 'Before we do determine, we must have our preparatory grounds before us. Our merchants object to it as having brought them to the brink of ruin. Let us hear them.' Charles Jenkinson agreed that the British economy needed to be taken into consideration, but denied that the motion involved any final decision. Charles Yorke said he was in favour of some Address, but this one was unsuitable. After Sir Fletcher Norton had replied, Pitt rose to speak. He declared that although the Address was not in form a decision to maintain the Stamp Act, public opinion would assume that it was; and he forecast its heavy defeat. Passage of the motion might mean the immediate dispatch of instructions to America, with consequent bloodshed—and all for nothing if repeal followed. Pitt's speech was one of his best performances. Chaplain Palmer wrote next day, 'For my own part, I never heard him speak with so much reason and eloquence united before. He kept close to the point in debate; a merit which he has not always': but, as Palmer sadly reported, he partly spoilt the effect 'and lessened the regard which was due to him, by walking out of the House in a contemptuous manner as soon as ever Mr. Grenville rose to reply'.[1] Grenville made a spirited retort, reminding members that Pitt himself had been virtually unsupported in his denial of Parliament's right of colonial taxation, and asking whether it was decent for any man to say, 'I am against it, the question is over'. While laws existed they

---

[1] Pitt had begun his speech by saying that his health would oblige him to leave early, but his behaviour was generally regarded as a gesture of scorn. Lord George Sackville thought he had treated Grenville 'not very respectfully'; Newdigate noted that 'Mr. Pitt walked round the table and would not hear a word'; while Harris recorded that 'he stalked out, like Ajax in the shades, without attending to what Mr. Grenville had to offer by way of reply'. The next day Pitt wrote a letter of apology to Grenville, who made what his wife called 'a cold answer'. *Grenville Papers*, iii. 231–2, 359.

should be applied. Conway rejoined that the Stamp Act could not be enforced without civil war, and Britain's European enemies would then intervene. He deplored the argument that 'no man is a friend to his country who is not an enemy to America'. Nugent countered by attacking 'those who call law option'. The debate continued until 10 o'clock, the closing highlight being a personal altercation between the past and present Attorney-Generals, Sir Fletcher Norton and Charles Yorke, seen by Onslow as a contest for the future Lord Chancellorship. Henry Cruger, an American by birth but now a Bristol merchant, who watched the debate from the gallery, thought a late speech by the old soldier General George Howard had been of great significance: Howard had announced his refusal to execute the Stamp Act 'in the blood of his country-men who were contending for *English* liberty'. Altogether thirty-one members spoke during the debate before the Committee divided on a motion by Charles Yorke for the Chairman to leave the Chair, the only procedural device possible in Committee to avoid a direct vote on the Address: here is Lord George Sackville's account of what happened.

We could not well give a direct negative to a proposition which taken abstractedly every body must approve of. We divided there-fore upon that question, and to my great astonishment the ayes on the right were 274, noes on the left 134, majority 140. The most sanguine on our side did not expect to carry it by above seventy, because on that division all the Bute following declared itself . . . This event has staggered all the politicians. The stocks which fell three or four per cent on Wednesday, Thursday and Friday rose as quick on Saturday, and the conversation is that the ministry may now stand their ground.

Grenville's tactical blunder in proposing a motion whose passage, in Sackville's opinion, 'would have amounted to an immediate declaration of war'; the King's declaration that morning in favour of repeal; the course of the debate itself, as determined by Pitt's speech and also those of Charles Townshend and Charles Yorke, men known to have an authori-tarian attitude towards the colonies and not yet publicly committed to repeal, as both had reminded the Committee: this combination of circumstances had enabled the ministry to obtain a shattering majority in the first important vote on the Stamp Act.

The significance of the vote was at once realized by many on both sides. Charles Garth reported to South Carolina two days later that 'the division raised our spirits, which I own had been a little drooping from some late appearances'. James West wrote after the debate to Newcastle,

I have scarce ever seen a minority more apparently dejected. Every one of your friends seems to think, this is the very moment to form a strong complete Whig administration. You have beat Lord Bute, the Duke of Bedford, the Cocoa Tree and Lord Temple united. Trecothick, Hanbury and a great number of merchants with the agents full of thanks in the Lobby.[1]

A similar analysis was later made by Horace Walpole.

Lord Bute's friends and all the Scotch and the Tories, and Lord Granby, and near a dozen of the King's own servants, voted in the minority. It was a matter of ridicule, that in the lists given out by Lord Sandwich, *their* faction had been estimated at 130; and Lord Bute's tools had vaunted that he could command fourscore or ninety votes. The astonishment and mortification of Grenville and the Bedfords were unequalled.[2]

George III commented on Conway's report that the majority must have been much larger than expected, and observed to Rockingham that 'the great majority must be reckoned a very favourable appearance for the repeal of the Stamp Act in that House'.[3] This letter, written early on Saturday, 8 February, was promptly and publicly displayed by Rockingham as documentary proof of the King's support of repeal.[4] On the Monday, 10 February, however, George III saw on business his Chancellor of the Duchy of Lancaster Lord Strange, an open opponent of repeal: and, having heard the report that he was said to be for repeal 'in all cases', the King explained

---

[1] B.M. Add. MSS. 32973, fo. 377. The Cocoa Tree was the coffee house that formed the traditional meeting-place for 'Tories'.

[2] H. Walpole, *Memoirs*, ii. 204.

[3] *Corr. of George III*, i. 266–8.

[4] *Corr. of George III*, i. 270. Mrs. Grenville noted in her diary for 9 Feb. that the ministers 'plead the King's name for the repeal of the Stamp Act'. *Grenville Papers*, iii. 361.

to Lord Strange that he himself would have preferred modification, but that he favoured repeal rather than enforcement of the whole act. Lord Strange was authorized to publicize this royal opinion, and lost no time in doing so.[1] The version in circulation by the same evening was that George III did not want repeal of the Stamp Act, only its modification; and Rockingham found himself accused of having misrepresented the King's opinion.[2] He therefore saw George III on the next day; and on the following day, 12 February, after the King had seen Lord Strange again, Rockingham obtained papers endorsed by George III as a true statement of his views.[3] Rockingham had taken along as a draft this sentence, 'That Lord Rockingham was on Friday, allowed by His Majesty to say, that his Majesty was for the repeal'. The King, however, insisted on adding this clarification, 'The conversation having only been concerning that, or enforcing'.[4] George III also gave Rockingham two other papers in his own hand. One was merely an alternative version: 'Lord Rockingham's question was, whether he was for enforcing the Stamp Act, or for the repeal. The King was clear that repeal was preferable to enforcing, and permitted Lord Rockingham to declare that as his opinion.' The second was intended to salve Lord Strange's feelings: 'Lord Rockingham, I desire you would tell Lord Strange, that I am now, and have been heretofore, for modification; but that when many were for enforcing, I was then for a repeal of the Stamp Act.'[5]

---

[1] For this interview see the King's memorandum, *Corr. of George III*, i. 269–70; Mrs. Grenville's diary, *Grenville Papers*, iii. 362; and H. Walpole's later account, *Memoirs*, ii. 205.

[2] *Rockingham Memoirs*, i. 300–1; *Corr. of George III*, i. 269.

[3] *Corr. of George III*, i. 269–70; *Grenville Papers*, iii. 364–5; B.M. Add. MSS. 47584, fo. 40 (diary of Lord Villiers); Dartmouth MSS. D 1778/V/221/B; H. Walpole, *Memoirs*, ii. 205. Walpole wrongly states that George III saw Lord Rockingham and Lord Strange together.

[4] This paper is printed in *Corr. of George III*, i. 266, and in the *Rockingham Memoirs*, i. 301, where it is said to be in the King's hand. That George III added the second sentence is stated by Newcastle, B.M. Add. MSS. 32974, fo. 5, and Bateson, *Narrative*, p. 52; by Lord Villiers, B.M. Add. MSS. 47584, fo. 40; by H. Walpole, *Memoirs*, ii. 205; by Lord Dartmouth, Dartmouth MSS. D 1778/V/ 221/B; and by Mrs. Grenville, *Grenville Papers*, iii. 365.

[5] *Rockingham Memoirs*, i. 301–2. Both are said to be in the King's hand. George III thought these papers 'entirely must exculpate my conduct in this unpleasant affair'. *Corr. of George III*, i. 270. Horace Walpole portrayed the whole episode as an example of the King's treachery to his ministers. *Memoirs*, ii. 204–6.

This was George III's final position on the American question. That the King's personal preference was now publicly known to be for modification rather than repeal was not an entirely satisfactory outcome for his ministers, who feared that members of the customary 'Court Party' would vote on repeal according to their own opinion without fear of dismissal. The administration continued to stress the popularity of repeal and its prospects of success to hold George III to his promise, and even sought to win his more whole-hearted support for that policy, but in vain: and the ministers had to be content with the King's reluctant acquiescence in the policy of repeal as the lesser of two evils.

Both Houses of Parliament had meanwhile met again after the week-end. In the Commons on 10 February the Committee on American affairs spent the whole time reading further papers.[1] In the Lords the American resolutions were reported that day from the Committee.[2] There was no debate or division,[3] for the administration had decided not to challenge the word 'require' in the fourth resolution, even though the ministers could now have made use of proxy votes for absent peers: this procedural device, which usually gave an advantage to the King's government, was not permitted in Committee. The ministerial tactics can be deduced from this letter the next day from Newcastle to Rockingham. 'I firmly believe the House of Commons will go on well, but we must not discourage them by losing any more questions in the House of Lords, and therefore, we must pick up all we can get.'[4] While attempts were made to rally support in the Lords, the administration decided not to raise the American question there: the Committee on the American papers was allowed to lapse, further papers presented on 10 February being ordered to lie on the Table.[5] For the rest of the month political interest centred on the Commons.

The first stage of the campaign for repeal was over. The ministers could now rely on the minimum royal support

[1] *H.M.C. Stopford-Sackville*, p. 23.

[2] *Lords Journals*, xxxi. 262–3.

[3] For the correct date of the debate ascribed to this day in Cobbett, *Parl. Hist.* xvi. 163–177, see above, p. 195 n 3.

[4] *Rockingham Memoirs*, i. 302.

[5] *Lords Journals*, xxxi. 263.

necessary for Parliamentary success, after a period of crisis
when defeats in the Lords and difficulties in the Commons had
led them to contemplate resignation, or so it was widely
believed. American Henry Cruger afterwards told his father
that

at one time the present ministry were bent on resigning, on finding
the Duke of York and Duke of Gloucester were against them, also
all the King's *immediate* servants, such as the Lords of the Bedchamber, and nine Bishops. They were for carrying fire and sword
to America, with this argument, that since you snarl and begin to
show your teeth, they ought to be knocked out before you are able
to bite.[1]

Instead of throwing in their hand the ministers had persuaded
George III to provide a public declaration in support of
repeal.

After the Commons debate of 7 February, the issue was no
longer the choice between repeal and enforcement of the
Stamp Act. The opposition thereafter abandoned any attempt
to insist on complete retention of the act and resorted to other
tactics. One was delay; by 12 February Grenville had urged
the postponement of any action for six weeks, arguing that the
colonial boycott would soon collapse and that Americans
would tire of being in a state of lawlessness:[2] but the chief
opposition strategy was to support the policy of amendment
now known to be preferred by George III himself. This course
of action was difficult: whereas the ministerial objective of
complete repeal had the advantage of simplicity, an alternative
policy that conceded the need for some amendment was likely
to produce a variety of opinions among its supporters. How
far any such proposals were ever formulated in detail by
opposition leaders is uncertain. The only information comes

---

[1] *Commerce of Rhode Island*, p. 141. The date, and, indeed, the certainty of any
ministerial intention to resign cannot be established with confidence. Grafton
later attributed the reaction to the first defeat in the Lords on 4 Feb. *Autobiography*, p. 69. He had himself urged resignation then. Above, p. 200. A letter
from Dartmouth urging Rockingham not to resign is dated 'Sunday evening',
but 12 Feb. has been added: since 12 Feb. was not a Sunday, a catalogue date of
9 Feb., which was, has been assigned to the MS. letter. Wentworth Woodhouse
MSS. R.1–574, printed *Rockingham Memoirs*, i. 303.

[2] *Commerce of Rhode Island*, pp. 140–1.

from Benjamin Franklin. In a letter of 24 February Franklin told Joseph Fox of Pennsylvania that for many who supported amendment the policy meant 'a Stamp on cards and dice only, and that merely to keep up the claim of right'; and in his later notes on his examination before the Commons on 13 February he stated that 'there had been a considerable party in the House for saving the honour and right of Parliament by retaining the act, and yet making it tolerable to America, by reducing it to a stamp on Commissions for profitable offices and on cards and dice'.[1] The problem now facing ministers was to persuade Parliament to reject any attractive alternatives and to accept the less palatable choice of complete repeal. To contemporaries their success by no means appeared certain. Charles Garth reported the volatility of Parliamentary opinion on 9 February, 'country gentlemen many of them wavering in opinions and others easily inflamed';[2] and Edmund Burke's brother Richard wrote on 11 February that 'the affair is not yet decided, nor is it very certain how it will be decided'.[3] The administration had won the first battle, but the fight was not yet over.

---

[1] *Franklin* Papers, xiii. 132n, 168. Franklin did not name anyone associated with this idea, which Conway was to attack in the debate of 21 Feb. Below, p. 230.

[2] *S.C.H.G.M.* 26 (1925), 87.

[3] *Burke Corr.* i. 238.

THE political strategy of the ministry to persuade Parliament to agree to repeal was as simple as its objective. The ground for repeal was to be the disastrous economic consequences for Britain of the Stamp Act Crisis, abundant evidence of which would be produced before the House of Commons. The inability of the colonies both to pay the taxation demanded and to buy the same quantity of British goods as before was the ostensible reason for this state of affairs. It was, of course, misleading. Although the earlier legislation and regulations of the Grenville ministry might be held by now to have had adverse effects on the colonial economy, their repeal or alteration was not the point at issue. The Stamp Act itself could not have had such consequences: it had not been due to go into operation until 1 November 1765, and then the taxes were not paid. The Rockingham ministry, aware of the deliberate boycott by American merchants of British goods until repeal of the Stamp Act was conceded, acted on the premiss that the reason for the economic recession in Britain was political. The administration therefore assumed that repeal, by restoring the American trade, would not only conciliate the colonies but also end the economic recession in Britain. This analysis was wrong. After an immediate post-war boom there was a general depression of trade and industry in both Britain and America from 1764 onwards, and the political solution of repeal failed to alleviate the economic situation. Britain's trade to America, which in any case amounted only to about one-eighth of her total exports, did not begin to recover its former level until some years afterwards. Indeed, although individual American orders were cancelled earlier, the formal boycotts in colonial ports did not begin until 31 October 1765, and could have had little if any direct impact on the British economy by the beginning of 1766. The similar pressure of the British merchants themselves on the manufacturers who supplied them may have been of more immediate significance: but the evidence that was to be presented to the House of Commons in February

1766 depicted an industrial decline that had lasted for at least several months and begun before the colonial mercantile reactions to the Stamp Act.[1]

The administration misunderstood the situation, but in any case the attempt to establish an economic causal connection between the Stamp Act and the recession in Britain was a deliberate sham. This emphasis on Britain's own economic distress was the chief tactic of the administration in securing the consent of the House of Commons to repeal: but for good measure the attention of M.P.s was also directed to other reasons, notably the substantial debts owed by colonists to British merchants that would be jeopardized by any failure to produce a satisfactory solution, and the practical difficulties of enforcing the Stamp Act or any part of it. This last point was one of particular delicacy for the administration to establish, since Parliament would never accept repeal for such a reason: but both witnesses and debaters repeatedly made allusive and direct references to the military aspects of the colonial situation.[2]

The ministry also chose to misrepresent the American situation, accurate knowledge of which might arouse the indignation and resentment of the independent members whose support was vital. The deliberate violence and the constitutional claims of the colonists were both played down, being portrayed respectively as mere mob riots and as a challenge to Parliament only over internal taxation. The wide-ranging nature of the Commons investigation into the crisis made this a tactic of peculiar difficulty. There was no attempt to withhold or conceal relevant papers from the two Houses, while the witnesses before the Commons were freely questioned by opposition members as well as by supporters of repeal. But if the papers were not suppressed or mutilated, the witnesses could be and were selected. Most of their evidence was nothing more than a gigantic red herring. It was concerned with the British economic situation rather than with the state of the colonies; and their function was to convince the House of

---

[1] Langford, *Rockingham Administration*, pp. 184–9, discusses some of these considerations. For the American boycott resolutions see Gipson, *British Empire*, x. 362–3.

[2] The witnesses on 31 Jan. had already done so, and some speakers on 7 Feb.

Commons that Britain's trade with her American colonies was of such importance and so badly interrupted by the crisis that repeal was the only possible solution. In this second stage of the inquiry, all the government witnesses, with the exception of George Mercer and Benjamin Franklin, were merchants and manufacturers concerned with British trade to North America. There is reason to think that a connection with the ministry explained the choice of many of them, and some were consulted and rehearsed beforehand to ensure that their testimony would be consistent. Even under what amounted to cross-examination from opposition members none admitted that a mere modification of the Stamp Act would be an adequate solution, and they professed an ignorance about inconvenient facts that was quite remarkable. Opposition M.P. James Harris had good cause to make this indignant comment about the examination of the witnesses on the first two days. 'All primed (except Col. Mercer) to say every thing against the Stamp Act, and neither to answer nor to know any thing on the other side.'[1]

By early 1766 a large number of merchants and manufacturers had come to London from the other towns and ports of Britain, to give evidence to Parliament and otherwise to help the cause of repeal; John Glassford and other Glasgow merchants, for example, had arrived by 10 January.[2] Many doubtless made themselves as busy as Henry Cruger, who after returning to Bristol wrote to his father on 14 February: 'I was three weeks in London, and every day with some one Member of Parliament, talking as it were for my own life. It is surprising how ignorant some of them are of *trade* and *America*.' The choice of witnesses to appear before the House of Commons represented a process of selection, explained by Cruger to his father. 'The House at last came to a resolution to examine only *one* person from each place that brought petitions. Mr. William Reeve being the *senior* of us who went from Bristol was put in the Votes.'[3] The total was swollen by the counter-tactic of opposition members in summoning a score of witnesses, including ten colonial agents on the initiative

---

[1] Harris Diary, 12 Feb. 1766. For detailed evidence on the rehearsal of witnesses see Langford, *Rockingham Administration*, p. 178.

[2] *Caldwell Papers*, ii (2), 58–9.

[3] *Commerce of Rhode Island*, p. 139. William Reeve was summoned as a witness on 7 Feb. *Commons Journals*, xxx. 521.

of Robert Nugent. Orders for fifty-five witnesses appear in the *Journals* of the House,[1] but the names of eleven witnesses who gave evidence are not recorded there. If at least sixty-six witnesses were summoned to attend, only twenty-six actually gave evidence during the five days from 11 February to 18 February when the Committee examined witnesses. The first three days, 11 to 13 February, were devoted to ministerial witnesses, the last two days, 17 and 18 February, being reserved for witnesses selected by the opposition.

On 11 February the House first heard a Jamaica petition against the Stamp Act from Stephen Fuller, agent for the colony, and brother of Rose Fuller.[2] When the Committee began Sir William Meredith proposed that the witnesses should be examined only as to the consequences of the Stamp Act. This suggestion was opposed by Charles Townshend, who declared that he would not agree to repeal merely because there had been violent resistance to the act, but only, if at all, for reasons of its impracticability or inexpediency or the inability of the colonies to pay the tax. He insisted that the witnesses should be examined 'as to the whole state of America', and the ensuing inquiry may have been wider in scope than the administration had intended.[3] Townshend's behaviour on this day and the next, when he supported Grenville against Conway's objection to one of his questions, led to speculation that he was against repeal.[4]

Barlow Trecothick was the first witness, and the most important to be heard by the Committee.[5] He was examined for about four hours, and James West told Newcastle that he 'gave a full, clear and satisfactory account of the distress at home and abroad and stated everything as he did to Your Grace this morning', a clear indication that his evidence had been rehearsed. Trecothick had been busy collecting information, and told the Committee that he estimated the value of Britain's export

[1] *Commons Journals*, xxx. 455, 504, 513, 521, 531, 538, 546, 582, 587.
[2] *Commons Journals*, xxx. 532.
[3] B.M. Add. MSS. 32973, fo. 411.
[4] Harris Diary, 11 and 12 Feb. 1766.
[5] For the evidence of this day see B.M. Add. MSS. 33030, fos. 88–113 (Trecothick's evidence is partly printed in Jensen, *American Colonial Documents*, pp. 686–8); Wentworth Woodhouse MSS. R.27, pp. 21–72; Newdegate MSS. B 2545/20 (*sub* 10 Feb.); *Ryder Diary*, pp. 291–4; and a letter from James West to Newcastle, B.M. Add. MSS. 32973, fo. 411.

H

trade to her American colonies to be between £2,500,000 and
£3,000,000: it was of particular importance, he said, because
Britain's trade everywhere else was declining. The American
trade had now almost ceased, for nearly all the orders were
cancelled or made conditional on repeal. He repeatedly said
that he himself would not export again to the colonies unless
the Stamp Act was repealed, because of the disorder there and
the difficulty of recovering debts. Only repeal would restore
peace to America. Military force would be needed to execute
the Stamp Act, and no modification would satisfy the colonists.
He then described how Boston was already taxed by a heavy
duty on trade profits. Under hostile questioning Trecothick
said that the colonies objected to the stamp duties both in
themselves and as an internal tax. 'From their writings I collect
they think the right of imposing taxes is confined to the Assemblies.' When next asked 'Has not that objection been made to
external taxes?' he made this politic reply: 'Only to the weight
of taxes; none to the authority laying them.'

Trecothick also drew attention to a colonial grievance not
appreciated in Britain. Although care had been taken to ensure
that money would not leave America as a result of the Stamp
Act, the colonies without any army units in them would be
drained of specie to pay for the subsistence of soldiers elsewhere;
the 'old fishing colonies' of New England would suffer in this
way, whereas New York and Pennsylvania would get their
money back: this was in fact a more serious cause of complaint
than Trecothick said, for the distribution of army units meant
that most of the military expenditure would take place in
Canada and the Floridas. The other main point to emerge
from Trecothick's evidence was his computation of the colonial
debts currently due to British merchants. Those in London
were owed £2,900,000; Bristol, £800,000; Glasgow, £500,000;
Liverpool, £150,000; and Manchester, £100,000. When the
sums owed to Whitehaven, Lancaster, Leeds, Birmingham,
Sheffield, and elsewhere were taken into account, the whole
debt amounted to £4,450,000. He forecast that if the Stamp
Act was not repealed much of this would be forfeited and that
many bankruptcies would result. His figures were challenged
on the ground that they included 'old book debts' for many
years back, an assertion Trecothick denied. Henry Cruger was

doubtless thinking of this evidence when he told his father three days later, 'We have proved the debt from the continent of America to England is *five millions* sterling. This Grenville attempted to disprove, and it is what makes the examinations at the Bar so tedious.'[1]

Trecothick's contention that the colonial trade would only be resumed on repeal was confirmed by the other two witnesses that day, Capel Hanbury, who traded to Maryland and Virginia, and Daniel Mildred, who exported to Philadelphia and New York. Both were members of his London Committee. Mildred said that whereas his exports to America were usually worth between £70,000 and £80,000, he had 'none this year, but a few trifles to New York'.

The Committee began the next day, 12 February, by examining three Americans.[2] Virginia merchant James Balfour estimated that the Stamp Act would cost the colony £25,000, falling mainly on the lower class of people, and said the cost of Virginia's own government was very high: yet the grievance was the principle and not the amount of taxation, and only repeal would be a satisfactory solution. He would not resume business until the Stamp Act was repealed. 'The continuance of trade will depend on the act, for the madness of the people is such that it will be imprudent to hazard any goods till the act is repealed.' Since Balfour had left Virginia as late as 22 June 1765 he was asked to explain that colony's attitude to the Stamp Act, and made this answer. 'They make the distinction between internal and external taxes and think now the money is taken out of their pockets.' To the question, 'do not the Virginia Resolutions go to the whole?', he replied, 'I think they never meant it': and gave other evasive answers to further opposition questions. 'Will in your opinion the Virginians resist the Stamp Act? Declines answering . . . Do they prefer an internal prohibition to an internal imposition? They know their own interest best . . . Will any sense of distress bring the Virginians to submit to the Stamp Act? I believe it will make them united.'

[1] *Commerce of Rhode Island*, p. 140. Trecothick was also questioned about the petitions: above, pp. 148–9.

[2] For the evidence on this day see B.M. Add. MSS. 33030, fos. 113–45; Wentworth Woodhouse MSS. R.27, pp. 72–136; Newdegate MSS. B 2455/22 (sub. 11 Feb.); and the *Ryder Diary*, pp. 294–300.

Colonel George Mercer then made a second appearance before the Committee. He said that Virginia's militia numbered 52,000, the same figure given previously by Capel Hanbury and James Balfour. The Stamp Act was believed to raise £35,000 there, but he admitted under opposition questioning that his own calculation was £12,000. Several of his answers were more frank than those of other witnesses.

If the act should be repealed under the present tumult wont it be an encouragement to the people to oppose any other revenue act? I must repeat that this is the only act I should object to. I can't pretend to say but hope it would not lead them to object . . . If the Stamp Act was to be repealed would not the Americans think their riots and tumults and stop to the trade had been the occasion of it? That might be . . . but I should scarce think they would imagine themselves able to frighten the people of Great Britain.

These replies must have given more weight to his insistence that the colonies would not accept any mere modification of the Stamp Act or any similar new tax. 'The grand objection was to any internal tax and this is the only instance in which the legislature has been aspersed.' He concluded by saying that if he had been able to act as Stamp-Distributor of Virginia he would have needed twenty-five under-distributors, and that he had left the colony because the governor would not allow him to resign and the people would not let him execute his office.

The third witness was William Kelly, a leading New York merchant, who had sailed from that port on 26 February 1765. When asked, 'from what have the dissensions been owing?', he replied, 'from an opinion that the internal tax is unconstitutional without representation and the tax too heavy': and he warned that a shift in the colonial economy from agriculture to manufacture would mean a permanent loss of trade if the Stamp Act lasted two or three years. Much of his evidence foreshadowed the future complaints of New York after the Stamp Act had been repealed. He said that discontent would remain because of the earlier legislation and restrictions on trade, and that the British West Indies could not supply one-eighth of the molasses needed in North America. The 3*d.* duty of 1764 had therefore had a disastrous effect. Foreigners now undersold American rum in the African trade. A dozen slave ships a year used to leave New York, but he thought none would do so while the duty remained: and the fall in demand for molasses meant that the price there had risen only 1*d*. or 2*d*. a gallon after imposition of the duty. Kelly admitted that foreign manufactures had been imported from Holland and Hamburg: but he said that none had come from the foreign West Indies, and blamed the great price difference between British and foreign goods for the smuggling.

The later witnesses that day were six English manufacturers, who painted a uniformly black picture of economic depression. The first three were hosiers: Thomas Morris of Nottingham stated that he had dismissed 100 men in six months and expected further redundancies; Robert Crafton of London said that any orders from America were conditional on repeal, and that his trade had fallen by two-thirds; so did Joseph Bunney of Leicester, who had discharged 1,000 men. Obadiah Dawson, a Leeds woollen manufacturer, said that half his goods usually went to America; but he had not received a single order since last August, and thought there would be none until repeal. He had dismissed nearly 1,000 of his 1,200 men and had stocks to last several months. Emanuel Elam, also of Leeds, who had visited America twice since 1760, thought that the colonies could develop a cloth industry competitive in price and quality with that in Britain. Finally Benjamin Farrar, who lived between Bradford and Halifax, reported that 30 per cent of the workers for over 10 miles around had been discharged by ballot. Henry Cruger, who stayed to hear the witnesses on the first two days, told his father that he thought this evidence of particular significance.[1]

A manufacturer from Leeds was ordered to the Bar, who said, since the stagnation of the American trade he had been constrained to turn off 300 families out of 600 he constantly employed. This fact will have great weight when added to many more evidences of the like kind. The Country Members are somewhat alarmed at so many people losing employ. If anything repeals the act, it must be this. The present ministry see and have declared the *expediency* of repealing on *this ground* . . . When I left London the 12th inst. it was about three to one the act *would* be *repealed*.

---

[1] *Commerce of Rhode Island*, pp. 140, 142.

The tale of economic woe was continued the next day, 13 February.[1] After the Liverpool petition had been read, Liverpool merchant William Haliday described the American trade of his port as employing ninety ships averaging 200 tons and as being worth £240,000 a year. Now all orders had been cancelled and £250,000 was owing in colonial debts. London goldsmith George Masterman described the adverse effects of the crisis on bullion imports.[2] William Reeve, Master of the Society of Merchant Venturers of Bristol, said that Bristol's trade to America, now 'totally stagnated', was usually worth £500,000 a year. He could produce 500 letters making orders conditional on repeal, and £500,000 was currently owed by Americans. When asked, 'is not the opposition to the Stamp Act the cause of the stagnation?' he replied, 'I submit to the judgement of this House. I know the Stamp Act is the grievance.' Robert Hamilton of Manchester said that one-quarter of Manchester's trade and one-third of his own goods went to America, but this trade had now stopped, orders being conditional on repeal. He had dismissed 400 weavers and had about £10,000 worth of goods in stock that would normally have gone to America. Glasgow tobacco merchant John Glassford stated that £500,000 was owed to his port, £50,000 to him personally, and could not be recovered while the Virginia courts were shut: tobacco imports and exports were both worth £150,000 a year. At the end of the day London shoemaker John Hose said that because of the decline in American

---

[1] For the general examination of witnesses on 13 Feb. see B.M. Add. MSS. 33030, fos. 146–81 (the evidence of Reeve and Glassford is printed in Jensen, *American Colonial Documents*, pp. 688–91); Wentworth Woodhouse MSS. R.27(A), pp. 1–70; and Newdigate MSS. B 2545/16. Both James Harris and Nathaniel Ryder noted only some of Franklin's evidence: Harris Diary, 13 Feb. 1766; *Ryder Diary*, pp. 300–2, also printed in *Franklin Papers*, xiii. 159–62. A full account of Franklin's evidence was published in Philadelphia in Sept. 1766, soon afterwards elsewhere in the colonies, and by John Almon in London the next year. A summary of Almon's pamphlet appeared in the *London Chronicle* for 7 and 9 July 1767, and the same month in the *Gentleman's Magazine*, 1767, pp. 368–72. *Franklin Papers*, xiii. 126–7. The full account was later reprinted by Almon in his *Debates*, vii. 106–40, and in Cobbett, *Parl. Hist.* xvi. 137–60. It has now been superbly edited in the *Franklin Papers*, xiii. 129–59, where Franklin's own notes are used to identify most of his interrogators.

[2] Grey Cooper later advised Rockingham not to call Masterman to give the same evidence to the Lords. 'I think the tendency of it is not so favourable as was at first imagined.' Wentworth Woodhouse MSS. R.34–5d. It implied a higher level of bullion imports since 1763.

trade he had reduced the number of his workmen from 300 to forty-five. He blamed the Stamp Act, but his ignorance of that subject was exposed by questioning. 'What is the Stamp Act? The paying a duty on anything as I am told. Do you think there is a stamp on shoes? Yes.' His evidence had been preceded by the four-hour examination of Benjamin Franklin, the highlight of the whole investigation.

Franklin, then just sixty years of age, was a man of so many parts that this politician, agent and postmaster was noted by Newdigate as being a 'physician' and by Harris as 'the celebrated electric philosopher'. Although some questions had been prearranged with supporters of the ministry and such other friends of America as John Huske, at least eighty-nine of the 174 questions he answered came from opposition members, and a notable feature of the examination was the skill with which he evaded or turned to advantage hostile interrogation. The broad run of his answers served to underpin the ministerial policy. Like so many previous witnesses, he denied that any modification of the Stamp Act would suffice: but he said that the colonies would be satisfied with repeal, even if accompanied by a declaration of Parliament's right, on the assumption that this would no more be exercised than the similar dormant claim with respect to Ireland. The colonies were not trying to avoid taxation, but believed in the old system of requisitions from the Crown, and Franklin thought that they would provide money as well as supplies if asked in this way. Failure to repeal would mean alienation of affection and loss of trade. The colonies, he claimed, would soon be able to produce everything they required, even, he said in the face of sceptical questioning, enough woollen cloth within three years. He denied the opposition contention that the colonists would think that the repeal had been forced on Parliament by their violent resistance. In an early answer to John Huske Franklin estimated that there were 300,000 white men of military age in the colonies, but subsequent questions about their potential military strength met with successful objections: and later he discreetly gave a different reason when explaining why the Stamp Act could not be executed by the army: 'Suppose a military force sent into America, they will find nobody in arms; what are they then to do? They cannot force a man to take stamps who chooses to do without them. They will not find a rebellion; they may indeed make one.'

Franklin was frequently interrogated about the precise nature of the colonial objection to the Stamp Act. In answer to an early prearranged question he stated that the only challenge to Parliament was over its right to levy internal taxes, and elaborated this point under repeated cross-examination. The colonies denied this right because they were not represented in Parliament, and Franklin explained the lack of precedents for the colonial case by saying that not until now had they had any reason to make such objections. He later gave another reason for the distinction of internal and external taxation. All indirect taxes were voluntary, being dependent on the purchase of goods and services. When Grenville contended that the colonial Post Office charges were a tax, Franklin replied that they were not only optional but also a payment for service. He explained that by 'taxes' the Pennsylvania Assembly resolutions meant only internal taxation, and denied that those from Massachusetts explicitly mentioned external taxes. Earlier he had made this devastating reply to an opposition question whether the objections to internal taxes could not apply also to external taxes. 'Many arguments have been lately used here to show them that there is no difference, and that if you have no right to tax them internally, you have none to tax them externally, or make any other law to bind them. At present they do not reason so, but in time they may possibly be convinced by these arguments.'

Franklin was no tame ministerial witness. He cannot have helped the cause of repeal by completely denying, in answer to questions from Charles Townshend, Nugent and Grenville, that Britain's recent wars had been fought on behalf of the American colonies. This was the only part of his testimony recorded by James Harris, who noted that Franklin

appeared a most complete American, a perfect anti-Briton, denying not only the authority of our legislature, but that our last two wars were undertaken on American motives. The captures by the Spaniards, which occasioned the first, were, he said, captures of goods belonging to British merchants. The disputes about limits, and the forts erected on the back of the settlements by the French had nothing it seems to do with the Americans; the ground where those forts stood were no American property; it was the ungranted land of the Crown. This last answer was rather weak, in others he was sufficiently acute.

This part of Franklin's evidence caused Robert Nugent next day, to make a violent attack on American ingratitude as even worse than that of Austria and Portugal.[1]

All the administration witnesses had now been heard. The tactic of demonstrating that only repeal of the Stamp Act would end the economic recession in Britain had been very successful, and opposition attempts to establish the reason for this state of affairs had been frustrated by overt evasion and professed ignorance. But Grenville and his allies now had the opportunity to redress the balance by presenting their own evidence. The plan of business was to examine the opposition witnesses on Friday, 14 February, and then to debate the repeal on Monday, 17 February. Once again the programme was upset, this time by a long debate on the army estimates in the Committee of Supply on 14 February.[2] The discussion soon centred on America, after Grenville had ascertained from Secretary at War Lord Barrington that there had not been the usual rotation of regiments abroad that year. The official reason was the state of Ireland, but Grenville denounced the move as a deliberate plan to keep an inadequate force in America. Conway counter-attacked by accusing the Grenville ministry of having deliberately concealed important information from the House before the passage of the Stamp Act. This concerned the failure of his predecessor Halifax to lay before Parliament the resolutions passed by American assemblies in 1764, even though the Privy Council had made an order in November of that year that this should be done. The charge was that Parliament had been misled about the probable American reaction to the tax. George Onslow said that many who supported the measure would otherwise have opposed it, and threw out the wild suggestion of impeachment. A point had been made that could provide members now favouring repeal with a defence against the accusation of inconsistency:

[1] The only record of Nugent's speech is in a note by Franklin himself. *Franklin Papers*, xiii. 159n.
[2] *Commons Journals*, xxx. 574. Harris Diary, 14 Feb. 1766: and a letter from J. West to Newcastle. B.M. Add. MSS. 32973, fo. 430.

H*

and General George Howard and other speakers announced
that with this fuller information they would have opposed the
passage of the Stamp Act. The whole debate lasted until late
evening, and the American Committee was postponed until
17 February.

When the Committee met that day the partiality of Chairman Rose Fuller ensured that the first witnesses heard were not
opposition witnesses at all, but two in support of the Jamaica
petition against the Stamp Act submitted on 11 February
by his brother Stephen Fuller.[1] Jamaica merchant James Carr
described how a Stamp Act in that island, in force from 1760
to 1763, had been inconvenient and inequitable, involving
costly and slow legal procedures and a disproportionate burden
on the poor. Jamaica planter James Irwin confirmed this, and
forecast that the effect of Grenville's Stamp Act would be
even worse. The case for repeal was even inadvertently strengthened by the evidence of the first opposition witness, Beeston
Long, Chairman of the West India Merchants Committee.
Long had been summoned on a motion by Thomas Whately,[2]
but testified that the West Indies, or at least Antigua, faced
the threat of starvation and ruin because of the stop to American trade. It was either Long or one of the two preceding
witnesses who provided the evidence recapitulated by Conway
on 21 February, that the North American colonies had put
pressure on the West Indies by withholding the staves without
which the sugar islands could not make the hogsheads to
export their produce to Britain.[3] Long's role as an opposition
witness concerned not the Stamp Act, but the temporarily
irrelevant issue of whether Grenville's ministry had been
responsible for stopping Spanish bullion ships from entering
British colonial ports.[4] Grenville, in fact, was unable to produce any merchant or manufacturing witnesses to balance the
weight of testimony about the economic depression and the
importance of American trade. As the last witness of the day the
opposition therefore fell back on a retired American merchant,

[1] For the evidence of this day see B.M. Add. MSS. 33030, fos. 182–203; Harris
Diary, 17 Feb. 1766; and Newdegate MSS. B 2545/15. For statements by G.
Onslow that 17 and 18 Feb. were reserved for opposition witnesses see B.M. Add.
MSS. 32974, fo. 9; and *Chatham Papers*, ii. 381–2.

[2] *Commons Journals*, xxx. 546.

[3] *Ryder Diary*, p. 303.   [4] Below, p. 254.

Richard Oswald,[1] who was soon obliged to admit that he had not been to the colonies for twelve years. The purpose of his testimony was to show that the colonies were well able to pay the proposed stamp duties of £60,000, and he gave a detailed description of colonial prosperity: 'No people in the world live more comfortably than the people in America. They are the happiest farmers. The climate is good, and hitherto the taxes have been easy. I thought it happy the tenants of this country dont know it. It would soon depopulate England . . . The provisions are under half the value of England.'

That the opposition tactic was to arouse prejudice against America was confirmed by the proceedings on the following day, 18 February, when three more of Grenville's witnesses were heard.[2] Robert Hale, Customs Controller at Boston, described the riots there. Georgia agent William Knox gave evidence on the opposition to the Stamp Act in South Carolina; he was the only one of the ten agents summoned by Nugent to come before the Committee, presumably because the others all favoured repeal. Richard Maitland, a West India merchant, gave a very detailed account of the illicit trade of America, to the embarrassment of the ministry. Similar testimony was given by M.P. Sir Charles Hardy, who had been governor of New York from 1755 to 1757. The final opposition move was to have read out the account both of the cost of civil government in the colonies and of the outstanding colonial war debts. These showed that the total cost of internal government in the eight North American colonies for which accounts of varying dates were produced amounted only to £41,200; that the colonies had already paid off £1,800,000 of their war debts; and that the undischarged debts were a mere £760,000.[3] The contrast with the vastly greater burdens of Britain in both respects must have been apparent to all members present. As the Committee ended, Conway gave notice to the House

---

[1] Richard Oswald (1705–84), later Shelburne's envoy in the peace negotiations of 1782.

[2] For their evidence see Newdegate MSS. B 2545/15, and Harris Diary, 18 Feb. 1766. Nugent had moved the attendance of Knox and Hale, Whately that of Maitland. *Commons Journals*, xxx. 513, 538, 546.

[3] For these accounts see C.O. 324/17/fos. 497–8. An Address for them had been moved in the House on 22 Jan., and the papers presented by Dyson for the Board of Trade on 31 Jan. *Commons Journals*, xxx. 484, 506.

that he would propose the motion for the repeal of the Stamp
Act on Friday, 21 February.[1]

While the House of Commons was examining witnesses,
there had been some last attempts to avert repeal by a change
of ministry. On 9 February Grenville received a message that
he understood to come from Lord Bute, and a meeting was
arranged between Bute, Grenville, and Bedford. A double
misunderstanding about the time meant that this did not take
place until 12 February. The encounter proved barren, for
Bute said that he had sent no message, and declared that since
he never saw the King he could not make any representations
to him: while Bedford announced that he would never be a
minister again.[2] Three days later, on 15 February, Lord Harcourt sounded Grenville about taking office, and the same day
Temple told his brother that he had heard through Lord
Denbigh that Bute thought that 'some great Lord' should see
the King personally about the political situation. Denbigh
himself was at first willing to do so, but by 16 February had
changed his mind, telling Temple that 'the King did not like
to be spoken to on these subjects'. The next day George III's
brother the Duke of York sent a message by Lord Gower to
ask Bedford if he would be willing to see the King, and
Bedford replied that he was.[3] The matter was now becoming
urgent, for it was known that the House of Commons would
debate the repeal on 21 February. York accordingly sent
George III a memorandum stating that Bedford had told him
that 'should His Majesty be inclined to pursue the *modification*
instead of *the total repeal of the Stamp Act* which his ministers
intend to propose to Parliament' the Duke would be happy
to attend him. The King refused to see Bedford. 'I cannot take
notice of it as I do not think it constitutional for the Crown
personally to interfere in measures which it has thought proper
to refer to the advice of Parliament.' Although York then hinted
that Bedford's approach was only nominally with reference to
the Stamp Act and could be considered in a wider context,
George III refused to succumb to the improper temptation
to betray his ministers.[4]

[1] *S.C.H.G.M.* 26 (1925), 90.
[2] *Grenville Papers*, iii. 360–3.   [3] *Grenville Papers*, iii. 367–70.
[4] *Corr. of George III*, i. 272–3. Namier, *Additions and Corrections*, pp. 52–5. *Grenville Papers*, iii. 370–2. *Bedford Papers*, iii. 326–9.

On 21 February M.P.s began reserving seats for the great debate on repeal before 8 a.m.: the practice was for a member to pin a ticket with his name to a chosen seat, which he could then claim at Prayers later in the day.[1] Well over 400 members were to be present, and the Palace of Westminster was crowded with would-be spectators. Many of the merchants who had played an active part in the repeal campaign now added the moral pressure of their physical presence. About a hundred dined in the King's Arms Tavern in Palace Yard and then went together to fill the precincts of the House,[2] perhaps too late to find a place in the gallery: for James West reported to Newcastle at 7.30 p.m. that 'the lobby and the stairs were crowded with merchants'.[3] The lobby was separated from the chamber of the House only by the thickness of the doors, and consciousness of the noise and hubbub there must have pervaded the atmosphere of the debate.

The Parliamentary day began with obstruction by George Grenville.[4] He urged that a precipitate decision would be improper, claiming that news had come that day that some southern colonies in America had submitted to the Stamp Act. Pitt, who had arrived on crutches,[5] intervened to oppose any postponement; and Conway denied that any such reports had arrived at government offices. He also pointed out that resolutions of the Committee were not final, since they could be rejected on report to the House. Defeated on this point, Grenville next moved that some of the papers before the Committee should be read out again; but this proposal was rejected as unfair and unnecessary. Conway then began the debate at 4.35 p.m., apparently provoked by Grenville's

---

[1] *London Chronicle*, 25 Feb. 1766.

[2] *Lloyd's Evening Post*, 24 Feb. 1766.

[3] B.M. Add. MSS. 32974, fo. 46.

[4] For the debates of 21 Feb. 1766 see *Ryder Diary*, pp. 302–10; Harris Diary, 21 Feb. 1766; notes by Sir Roger Newdigate, Newdegate MSS. B 2546/4; H. Walpole, *Memoirs*, ii. 210–2; and the following letters: (a) J. West to Newcastle (three letters), B.M. Add. MSS. 32974, fos. 45–9; (b) G. Onslow to Newcastle, B.M. Add. MSS. 32974, fo. 51; (c) Revd. R. Palmer to Revd. R. Cust, *Cust Records*, iii. 96–7; (d) W. Baker to W. Talbot, *W.M.Q.* 26 (1969), 260–2; (e) C. Garth to S. Carolina, *S.C.H.G.M.* 26 (1925), 90; (f) Conway to George III, *Corr. of George III*, i. 273–4; (g) W. Rouet to Baron Mure, *Caldwell Papers*, ii (2), 73–4. All quotations, unless otherwise indicated, are from the *Ryder Diary*. For another account see Gipson, *P.M.H.B.* 86 (1962), 35–9.

[5] This was not theatrical. See *Chatham Papers*, ii. 391.

behaviour into making a better speech than usual. His main purpose was to recapitulate and emphasize the evidence given to the Committee on the decline of trade with America and the consequent economic effects in Britain, the debts owed by colonists to British merchants, and the adverse consequences for the West Indies. He reaffirmed Parliament's right of taxation, but it was a right that ought never to be exercised. A tax revenue of £60,000 was not an object worth the sacrifice of British trade to America, and still less so would be the revenue from a tax on cards and dice. This was the suggestion being canvassed by advocates of modification of the Stamp Act,[1] a policy attacked by Conway as giving up the substance and keeping the shadow, a shadow that would frighten the Americans like children. Conway then dealt with other arguments against repeal. The evidence of colonial resistance, he said, was not a reason for continuing a tax that was wrong. He disposed of the delicate military question by asserting that Britain could subdue any rebellion in America; but at the same time he reminded members that there were only 5,000 soldiers there to face a militia of 150,000 men, and warned that such a civil conflict would invite a war with France and Spain, citing the Bourbon Family Compact. Conway concluded a speech of under an hour by moving the resolution for a bill to repeal the Stamp Act.

Grey Cooper seconded Conway in an elegant speech full of classical quotations, a performance thought to be too flowery and artificial by some observers. He repeated Conway's warning about the danger of French intervention; but some of his other remarks caused the indignant James Harris to make this note in his diary. 'I never heard ever since I have sat in Parliament two speeches, where America was so completely set above Britain, and commerce above the constitution, and the British legislature.' The opposition reply was begun by Charles Jenkinson, who argued that repeal would only encourage the colonists to resist other Parliamentary legislation. Whether this was the right time to tax America depended on the relative ability of Britain and the colonies to pay, and on that question there could be no doubt. 'The present time the properest to tax the colonies, when they were grown able to

---

[1] Above, p. 213.

bear it and yet not strong enough to resist it.' Jenkinson ended by proposing an amendment to substitute the words 'explain and amend' for 'repeal', and a long debate followed involving eleven more speakers, that was, according to William Baker, 'very dull and tedious, a mere repetition of what had been so often canvassed before': but it was the occasion when Edmund Burke established his claim to be a Parliamentary speaker of the first rank, and when Pitt made a remarkable speech that was to be quoted against him a year later.

Charles Yorke spoke nearly an hour to argue that repeal was the least objectionable policy. He admitted having approved the Stamp Act at first, and then as having favoured only modification of it; but he was now convinced that complete repeal was the most prudent measure, citing Sir Robert Walpole's withdrawal of his Excise Bill in 1733 as an example of political wisdom. An unsuccessful attempt at enforcement would mean the end of Britain's authority in America. Yorke sought to balance his speech by urging the rigorous application of the trade laws and the use of force if the colonies did not accept this olive branch, but his performance earned this comment from Chaplain Palmer.

Upon the whole he was judged to acquit himself with little honour to himself or his cause. Sir Fletcher Norton seemed sensible of it, and therefore rose immediately on Mr. Yorke's sitting down. But luckily for them both Mr. Burke, a young member and secretary to Lord Rockingham getting up at the same instant, Mr. Fuller, the Chairman, probably foreseeing some mischief named Mr. Burke. I must tell you that this gentleman is one of the best speakers in the House of Commons at present, and promises great things. His knowledge of affairs is both deep and clear, his language copious and flowing, his classical allusions, with which he loves to ornament his speeches very pertinent, and his elocution ready, except that he sometimes or rather generally speaks too fast. His principal argument for the repeal of the act was a new one, at least I dont remember it to have been insisted on in the House in that light in which he placed it, which was, without entering on the *right* of taxation, to show from constant *usage*, that internal taxation was never once thought of since the first emigration of the Americans from this country, and that England never thought of any other power over them or interest in them, but that of regulating their commerce to the advantage of their mother country.

Burke's speech was the highlight of the debate. William Baker noted that he was 'the only man who could keep up the attention of the House on a subject already threadbare': and James Harris, although thinking Burke pro-American and 'saucy', captured this amusing image. 'Last year we were all asleep, now were awake, and like people just roused, a little disordered and in confusion.' Pitt, who rose much later, after 11 o'clock, complimented Burke on his performance; but in his speech of over an hour echoed Yorke in seeing the problem as a choice of evils and in voicing a determination to coerce America if the colonies were not now quiet. He said he would then 'give his vote for employing the last ship and the last man in this country to force them to perfect obedience . . . Hopes to be heard in America, and neither courts popularity there nor here.' Pitt then went out of his way to say that there could be no blame for the Stamp Act; he applauded the intention, but the method was erroneous. It was unfair to both tax America and control her trade and industry. Harris thought Pitt's speech excellent and moderate. 'Though some (I find) disliked it, it appeared to me to be as elegant as any of his speeches, and at the same time, more orderly, more reasonable in its length, and with far more semblance of regard to England than the speeches of Conway and the people in government.'

Grenville took an hour to answer him, making the point that the success of the colonists in paying off so much of their debts showed that they were well able to pay all his taxes; otherwise Grenville, according to Palmer, 'seeing, I suppose, the sense of the House did little more than struggle for some amendments at least in his act'. Opposition speakers throughout the debate either urged the case for American taxation only in general terms, or specifically suggested modification as the alternative to repeal. No speakers urged enforcement of the original Stamp Act. This shift of ground was thought to have caused some embarrassment on the government side of the House. Ill health may have been the reason why Charles Townshend did not speak for repeal, but the silence of William Dowdeswell was believed to be significant, Harris noting this rumour about the Chancellor of the Exchequer: 'some say he was in his private sentiments rather for a modification, than a repeal'.

Grenville's speech, which began after midnight, is not well reported, and later speakers received a noisy reception. The absent Horace Walpole understood that the debate was 'much abridged by the impatience of the Committee, worn out by so many successive discussions of the same subject. Many speakers had not been attended to; others forced to sit down without being heard. Something of this was imputed to the partiality of Rose Fuller, the Chairman.' The Committee divided at 1.45 a.m., voting to retain the word 'repeal' by 275 votes to 167.[1] Harris noted that 'as soon as it was declared, a rabble of Americans in the lobby shouted'. William Baker was more in sympathy with this reaction. 'No one who was not present can have an idea of the exultations in the crowded lobby on the declaration of the majority. The members of the ministry, as they came out of the House were deified with applause, the others were hardly secure from violence.' More dramatic detail was later given by Horace Walpole.

As Mr. Conway went away they huzzaed him thrice, stopped him to thank and compliment him, and made a lane for his passage. When Mr. Pitt appeared, the whole crowd pulled off their hats, huzzaed, and many followed his chair home with shouts and benedictions. The scene changed on the sight of Grenville. The crowd pressed on him with scorn and hisses. He, swelling with rage and mortification, seized the nearest man to him by the collar. Providentially the fellow had more humour than spleen—'Well, if I may not hiss', said he, 'at least I may laugh.'—and laughed in his face. The jest caught—had the fellow been surly and resisted, a tragedy had probably ensued.

The rejoicing in the lobby foreshadowed the wider popular reaction as the news became known. London newspapers reported that on

[1] James West had reported to Newcastle from the debate at 7.30 p.m. 'It is said they will not divide. I think we should, and if a list of those that are against the question be handed about, it will effectually do the business of the opposition in the City and in the manufacturing towns.' The minority list, which was printed that year ostensibly in Paris, was therefore probably compiled by the administration as a 'black-list'. Certainly minority lists survive in the papers of both Newcastle and Rockingham. For the location of Commons voting lists on repeal see Namier and Brooke, *The House of Commons 1754–1790*, i. 526. In his diary Harris named twenty-two members in the minority, including Lord Barrington and Lord George Sackville, and then added 'and all Lord Bute's people, George Grenville's, and the Duke of Bedford's'.

Saturday last there was an universal joy to be seen in the countenances of every lover of trade in the City, on the hopes of the Stamp Act being repealed, that the Merchant as well as the Mechanic may once more hope to be able to pay their just debts, and the many Factors be enabled to employ the poor, who have been too considerable a time destitute of the common necessaries of life. The bells in most churches rang from morning until night.[1]

The good news was at once sent to the provinces. Over 3,000 letters were posted by London merchants on that Saturday, and the immediate orders to Sheffield, Birmingham, Leeds and other manufacturing towns were estimated to be worth £40,000.[2] In London between 24 and 27 February over thirty ships were ordered to be made ready to sail for America.[3] Within a week, a similar reception of the news was being reported from other parts of the country.[4]

Letters from Bristol and Liverpool mention, that there were great rejoicings in those places, on receiving the news relative to the Stamp Act. Letters from Birmingham say, that as soon as the news relating to the Stamp Act arrived there on Sunday, the bells were directly set a ringing, other demonstrations of joy shown in the different parts of the town, and some hundreds of journeymen artificers, who had been unemployed, were immediately engaged again for the different manufacturers . . . The news relating to the American Stamp Act, which arrived in Leeds early on Monday morning last, was so agreeable to the merchants in that town, that the bells were immediately set a ringing, and continued to do so all day, and the evening concluded with bonfires, etc.

The popular assumption that the issue had now been decided was not shared by the administration. Ministers knew they needed the King's continuing support, and anticipated difficulty in ensuring the passage of the repeal through the House of Lords: but the large majority in the Commons was seen as a weapon to secure these objectives. Newcastle wrote to Rockingham on the morning after the debate, 'I conclude that we may depend upon *all*, who voted for us; and a majority

---

[1] This item appeared on 25 Feb. in the *London Chronicle* and in the *London Evening Post*.

[2] *St. James' Chronicle*, 25 Feb. 1766. *London Evening Post*, 25 Feb. 1766.

[3] *London Evening Post*, 27 Feb. 1766.

[4] *Lloyd's Evening Post*, 28 Feb. 1766. For other details of popular reactions see Clark, *British Opinion*, pp. 44–5.

of 108, in so full a House, is not to be thrown away; and, if we agree amongst ourselves, which, I hope, we shall, is sufficient to keep both Court and Parliament right.'[1]

Rockingham himself had been in the Commons, and afterwards went home to a celebratory supper that lasted until 5 a.m.[2] Then, before going to bed, he wrote to tell the King the result of the debate. 'Lord Rockingham can not nor ought not to disguise from his Majesty the pleasure he felt upon this event as he flatters himself—that it is a confirmation that the opinion he had humbly submitted to his Majesty was well founded in point of public opinion.' He asked George III for an audience that day, and the King appointed 3 p.m.[3] After the meeting Rockingham sent this report to Newcastle.[4]

His Majesty seemed to think the majority very great. I told him I expected it to have been even larger. We had 12 Members shut out and two miscounted. I remarked to His Majesty how strong the torrent of opinion in favour of the repeal was and is—when notwithstanding the checks of seeing so many persons in his Majesty's service voting against it and notwithstanding the great combinations there were in the House of Commons against it and ultimately the knowledge that had lately been given of his Majesty's own sentiments being for modification. Yet nevertheless 275 were for the total repeal and 167 only for modification. I also told him of the immoderate joy in the lobby and of what sort of persons it was composed—and then ended with lamenting that his Majesty had not adhered to the repeal.[5]

Rockingham's jubilation was amply justified. Despite the desertion of many of the customary 'court party', 290 M.P.s had been prepared to support repeal on 21 February.[6] The campaign to win over independent opinion in the House had

[1] B.M. Add. MSS. 32974, fo. 63.
[2] B.M. Add. MSS. 32974, fo. 65.
[3] *Corr. of George III*, i. 275.
[4] B.M. Add. MSS. 32974, fos. 67–8.
[5] Horace Walpole's account does scant justice to Rockingham's tact. 'Lord Rockingham with childish arrogance and indiscretion vaunted in the palace itself that he had carried the repeal against the King, Queen, Princess-Dowager, Duke of York, Lord Bute, the Tories, the Scotch, and the Opposition (and it was true he had).' *Memoirs*, ii. 211.
[6] This total includes the teller and takes account of the incidents mentioned by Rockingham.

been a great success. Palmer observed that 'as many voted for the repeal who are in the Opposition as who are with the Ministry':[1] and Richard Jackson confessed to Governor Fitch of Connecticut that the majority for repeal was 'greatly beyond the expectation I had formed three weeks ago, and I had reasonably good grounds to judge upon'.[2] But the ministry knew better than to relax its efforts for the report of the American resolutions on 24 February. Onslow told Newcastle the day before that 'care is taken for tomorrow, which I think will be a warmer day than any we have had. The huzzas of the people have exasperated them to the last degree, as well as the most extraordinary and honourable majority, against *King, Court, Favourite, Tories, Scotch*, and late Administration'.[3]

Public business in the Commons on 24 February began with opposition complaints about the events of the previous Friday both in the Committee and afterwards in the lobby.[4] Henry Shiffner, one victim of the noise during the debate, ironically proposed a vote of thanks to Chairman Rose Fuller for his impartiality. Onslow took the suggestion seriously, provoking the accusation that the Chairman should have prevented disturbances in the lobby. The House was told of insults offered to opposition members, and Grenville, according to Horace Walpole, declared that 'both England and America were now governed by the mob'. Members were also informed of another kind of pressure, banker George Prescott saying that an American merchant had recalled all his ready cash deposited with him, some £170, because he had voted against repeal. Lack of evidence prevented the House from taking action about the disorder in the lobby, but not until 5 o'clock did Fuller report to the House the resolutions of the American Committee.

---

[1] *Cust Records*, iii. 98.

[2] *Fitch Papers*, ii. 390–1. For some analysis of the voting on repeal see Langford, *Rockingham Administration*, pp. 169–73.

[3] B.M. Add. MSS. 32974, fo. 71.

[4] For the proceedings of 24 Feb. in the Commons see *Commons Journals*, xxx. 601–3; *Ryder Diary*, pp. 310–15; Harris Diary, 24 Feb. 1766; notes by Sir Roger Newdigate, Newdegate MSS. B 2546/3; H. Walpole, *Memoirs*, ii. 212–14; and the following letters: (a) G. Onslow (two letters) to Newcastle, B.M. Add. MSS. 32974, fos. 77–9; (b) Revd. R. Palmer to Revd. R. Cust, *Cust Records*, iii. 97–8; (c) W. Baker to W. Talbot, *W.M.Q.* 26 (1969), 262–4; (d) Conway to George III, *Corr. of George III*, i. 276; (e) G. Onslow to W. Pitt, *Chatham Papers*, ii. 394–5. All quotations are from the *Ryder Diary*, unless otherwise stated.

Lord Strange at once proposed the postponement of the first, declaratory, resolution, since the assertion was inconsistent with repeal: but this move was opposed even by Grenville, who argued for the preservation of some remnants of Parliament's authority. Dyson suggested that there should be further resolutions to condemn the colonial Congress and trade boycotts, only for Conway to score a popular point by denouncing 'the dictator of order' as being himself disorderly, such resolutions being the business of a Committee. John Huske, according to Harris, 'talked very obscurely about two internal taxes to be laid immediately' after the repeal. Fourteen members spoke in a discussion of over two hours before the original resolution was voted without a division.

The next five resolutions were accepted without discussion, but the seventh and final one, on repeal, led to a debate of four hours after James Oswald moved to recommit it. He argued that America was well able to pay the tax, since a labourer's average daily wage was 4*s.* 6*d.*, but he was willing to agree that the tax should not be used for the army until the debts of the individual colonies had been paid. Barré was the first to reply, reminding the House that he had always opposed the Stamp Act: but he then echoed the absent Pitt in saying that there was merit in the idea of seeking new sources of revenue, and in declaring that any other colonial claims must be resisted, even by the sword. Chaplain Palmer noted that Barré 'though not of great depth of thought in essential points is one of the most persuasive speakers in the House'. Hans Stanley argued for modification rather than repeal. The administration policy got the worst of both worlds, he said; assertion of the right of taxation would alienate the colonies, while repeal was a confession of weakness. Richard Hussey attacked the principle of the Stamp Act, and no colonial behaviour could justify it retrospectively. He declared that Britain's authority should be asserted by punishment of the rioters, not by retention of the Stamp Act. 'If money is wanted from America, why not do it now by requisition? . . . If they refuse this, then assert your right in fact. Pass an Act of Parliament. Tax them by Parliament, and they will have no reason, no just reason at least, to complain.' The only later speech of note was that from William Dowdeswell. The Chancellor of the Exchequer ended speculation about his personal opinion by advocating repeal on the ground that the colonies had their trade regulated by Britain and so were 'not in a taxable condition'. By now the subject of repeal was a dead duck in the Commons, and several reporters contented themselves with little more than a list of speakers. The attendance at the division fell from the 445 in the previous debate to 378, Oswald's motion being defeated by 240 votes to 133. The administration's majority, however, dropped by only one vote, from 108 to 107, and that some opposition members had already conceded defeat is shown by Horace Walpole's story that 'Grenville's friends, seeing the inutility of their struggles, laboured to persuade him to contest the matter no further; but it was too much to give up his favourite bill and his favourite occupation, talking, both at once'.

The division did not end debating for the day. When a motion was made to bring in a bill for repeal and for a Select Committee to draft it, William Blackstone proposed that this Committee should be instructed to restrict repeal to those colonies whose assemblies expunged any resolutions contrary to the right of Parliament. Rose Fuller objected on the ground that the questions of parliamentary right and of compensation should be embodied in separate legislation. Charles Yorke agreed, and said that in any case the Declaratory Act would be a virtual expunging of contrary resolutions. Grenville supported Blackstone's motion without enthusiasm. Burke argued that a repeal clogged with such a condition would delay the restoration of trade, and asserted that the resolutions could not be effaced from men's minds. Lord North made an ironical comparison between Parliament's supine behaviour and the spirit of the colonial assemblies. After eleven members had spoken Blackstone's motion was rejected without a division. The House then resolved that bills should be introduced to incorporate the first resolution concerning Parliament's right and the last one about repeal.

The Declaratory Bill and the Repeal Bill passed through the Commons with little discussion and no voting until the third reading stage. Both were introduced and received a first reading when the House next met, on 26 February. There was a debate of two hours in a poorly attended House, Onslow sending this report to Newcastle. 'Not much talking and wrangling which has only ended in G. Grenville's promising long debate on the second reading tomorrow; for which full care is taken.'[1] Precautions were unnecessary: again there was little debate in a thin House.[2] The following day, Friday 28 February, saw the Committee stage of both bills. Wedderburn proposed giving some teeth to the Declaratory Bill by a clause making it illegal to dispute Parliament's right in books or pamphlets. The suggestion, opposed by the administration, was attacked as worthy of Henry VIII or Charles II by Rose Fuller, whereupon Wedderburn said that it was copied from the Act of Settlement of 1701! The amendment was countered by precedents of laws that had been merely declaratory, such as the Petition of Right, and dropped after being criticized by Dyson.[3] The preamble of the Repeal Bill was altered at the suggestion of Conway, who remarked that 'the American opposition had been indecent and intemperate, a great deal, for so warm an advocate', thought James Harris.[4] Grenville raised the question of officials who might ignorantly enforce the Stamp Act after the official date of its repeal, 1 May, and Onslow answered that they would be covered by an act of indemnity. After an assurance had also been given that repeal would not involve abolition of the Vice-Admiralty Courts, the Committee completed the bill in time for a third successive early adjournment of the House. The two bills were reported without discussion on Monday 3 March, and their third reading and passage fixed for the next day.[5] The opposition had been reserving their fire for this stage of the Repeal Bill, and Pitt, it transpired, had been doing the same for the Declaratory Bill.

On 4 March Pitt began the debate on the passage of the Declaratory Bill with an hour-long speech, declaring his total

---

[1] B.M. Add. MSS. 32974, fo. 91. *Commons Journals*, xxx, 609. N. Ryder did not record the debate. *Ryder Diary*, p. 315.

[2] *Commons Journals*, xxx. 612. N. Ryder again did not record the debate, *Ryder Diary*, p. 315; but James Harris named four speakers. Harris Diary, 27 Feb. 1766.

[3] For the debates on 28 Feb. see *Commons Journals*, xxx. 615–16; Harris Diary, 28 Feb. 1766; *Ryder Diary*, p. 316; H. Walpole, *Memoirs*, ii. 214–15. Diarists Harris and Ryder both give Wedderburn's proposal as being made in the Committee: but the same motion appears in the *Commons Journals*, xxx. 620–1, as being made on the report on 3 Mar.

[4] Conway told Newcastle the next day, 'we have made the preamble to the Bill of Rights as full as possible, and we have made that of the repeal as general and as short; which circumstance we hope will save your Lordships some trouble'. B.M. Add. MSS. 32974, fo. 113.

[5] *Commons Journals*, xxx. 620–1; Harris Diary, 3 Mar. 1764.

opposition to the measure.[1] He cited the case of Ireland to show that the right of taxation could be distinguished from other aspects of sovereignty, and much of the subsequent discussion centred on the accuracy of this analogy. George Hay and Richard Rigby agreed that the bill was of no value if the repeal was passed, and there suddenly appeared the prospect that the administration might face a division on the bill against both Pitt's friends and those of Grenville and Bedford. Pitt himself frustrated this manoeuvre by moving to leave out the words 'in all cases whatever': for Grenville announced that he could not support this amendment. Dowdeswell said that the bill was essential, for otherwise the colonists would think that Parliament had surrendered the right of taxation: but at the same time he argued that total repeal had 'more dignity and more sense' than amendment. After twelve members had made twenty speeches Pitt's amendment was rejected without a vote and the Declaratory Bill passed the Commons soon after 7 p.m.

There followed the final stages of the Repeal Bill, which met with 'no attention in the House', according to James Harris: but nine members were to speak in the debate on its passage. Among those who opposed the bill was George Prescott, who reminded the House that bounties and other economic benefits given to the colonies far outweighed the £50,000 that had been anticipated from the stamp duties. Pitt, in his second long speech of the day, announced that he was more proud of being one of the majority for repeal than of having been the instrument of victory in the last war, and warned that enforcement of the Stamp Act would mean civil war, 'to dip the royal ermine in the blood of his British subjects in America'—a memorable phrase captured by three reporters. Grenville began by mentioning the noisy reluctance of the House to hear any argument, but said that he felt obliged to answer Pitt. He regretted to see such an anticlimax to the wartime triumphs, and again defended

---

[1] For the debates on 4 Mar. see *Commons Journals*, xxx. 626–7; *Ryder Diary*, pp. 316–20; Harris Diary, 4 Mar. 1766; notes by Sir Roger Newdigate, Newdegate MSS. B 2546/2; H. Walpole, *Memoirs*, ii. 215–8; and the following letters: (a) J. West (two letters) to Newcastle, B.M. Add. MSS. 32974, fos. 135–7; (b) G. Onslow to Newcastle, B.M. Add. MSS. 32974, fos. 139–42; (c) Conway to George III, *Corr. of George III*, i. 277; (d) W. G. Hamilton to J. Calcraft, *Chatham Papers*, ii. 377–9. (*sub* 11 Feb.); (e) W. Rouet to Baron Mure, *Caldwell Papers*, ii (2), 77–9.

the policy of the Stamp Act. He had had good reason to think the colonists would pay the duties, and leading Americans had accepted the office of Stamp-Distributor. When the House divided at 11 o'clock, the motion to pass the bill was carried by 250 votes to 122.

There remained the hurdle of the House of Lords. Supporters of the Repeal Bill had always been apprehensive about its prospects there. On 23 February, when writing in a state of euphoria produced by the triumphant majority for repeal in the Commons, George Onslow made this comment to Newcastle.[1]

I own I tremble for our fate in your House . . . Good God! If the King had but stuck to the repeal. Of all the mischiefs that fool Lord Bute has done him, this is the greatest. The general illumination of last night in the City, would have been in his honour, and he would have been what he has not been yet since he came to his throne. If the Lords reject the bill God knows what will be the consequence —*our* majority consists now of men not to be wrought upon.

Ministerial concern after the two Lords defeats early in February had been increased by the King's public declaration of his personal opinion, as Newcastle confided to the Archbishop of Canterbury on 15 February.

We hope, that the House of Lords will not venture to reject it afterwards, the consequence may be so alarming; which consequence will be strongly supported by the testimony of the first merchants in the City of London. Some fear, that the declaration for *modifications* may make some impression in the Lords; and particularly upon some on the Bench [of Bishops].[2]

The undesirability of a clash between the two Houses was to be an important argument in securing the assent of the House of Lords to repeal. After the great Commons majority for repeal on 21 February, Rockingham wrote in high spirits to Newcastle.

I have hopes that if it passes through the House of Commons in the style it has begun that His Majesty may be inclined to adopt the opinion that the House of Lords should not disagree with the Commons and I think if this can be done—it will be right for His Majesty to begin early to talk that idea to *all* Lords who frequent his Closet.[3]

[1] B.M. Add. MSS. 32974, fo. 71.   [2] Ibid., fos. 5–7.   [3] Ibid., fo. 68.

This general point was to be argued repeatedly in debate by government spokesmen in the Lords: but little was made of the subsidiary arguments that the Lords could not amend financial legislation and that defeat of repeal would be tantamount to taxation by the Lords alone.[1]

Rockingham hoped not merely for the King's general support but also for his personal pressure on the Lord Chancellor. This tactic was successful, as Newcastle told Archbishop Secker on 28 February.[2]

My Lord Rockingham, who now acts as the sole minister, . . . [was] yesterday, when he came out of the King's Closet, extremely pleased, and in high spirits. He told me, he hopes, the King would at last be for the repeal; for that he told him, the Chancellor was again wavering; his Majesty was to see the Chancellor again, on Sunday; and wished that my Lord Rockingham would see the Chancellor again, on Saturday evening, to prepare him. This, Lord Rockingham thought, was a good sign; and so it was.

Newcastle himself was more inclined to adopt traditional methods, as he told Rockingham on 23 February. 'Care should be taken to secure everybody, that can be had . . . I would propose as an old Parliament man, that your Lordship should soon have a meeting of very few Lords, chiefly speakers, as was always the way formerly, to consider of the method of proceeding.' The Duke assumed that, as in the Commons, the administration would attempt to substantiate the economic arguments that were the ostensible ground for repeal by the examination of witnesses.[3] He attached considerable importance to the presentation of this oral evidence to the Lords. His papers contain a list, dated 1 March, of questions that he proposed to have put to Trecothick;[4] and Trecothick himself was apparently expecting to be summoned as late as 3 March.[5] The plan was never adopted: but Newcastle regretted the decision even after such an interrogation of witnesses by the Lords was shown to

---

[1] Langford, *Rockingham Administration*, pp. 191–2, lays considerable stress on these other constitutional points, and contemporaries were certainly aware of them. B.M. Add. MSS. 32974, fos. 87, 153; 33001, fos. 102–3.

[2] B.M. Add. MSS. 32974, fo. 107.

[3] B.M. Add. MSS. 32974, fo. 69.

[4] B.M. Add. MSS. 33001, fos. 123–7.

[5] B.M. Add. MSS. 32974, fo. 133.

have been unnecessary.[1] There can be little doubt that Rockingham adopted the better strategy. In the Lords there was no
large body of independent opinion to be won over, such as
existed in the Commons. The political change that enabled
the ministry to carry repeal there was merely the conversion of
a small group of peers headed by Northington;[2] and although
much was said in debate of the economic situation, royal influence and the desire to avoid a clash with the Commons were
the significant factors in their decision.

The two bills were taken up to the House of Lords by a
crowd of 150 M.P.s on 5 March, the day after they had passed
the Commons.[3] A further attempt to influence the House
was made the same day, by the reading of petitions from the
London merchants trading to America and the Bristol Merchant Venturers. Both bills received a first reading, after a short
debate on the Repeal Bill, and the second reading stages were
fixed for 7 March.[4]

One hundred and thirty-six peers attended the House that
day, when petitions from Glasgow merchants and from
Virginia agent Edward Montagu were read. After the Declaratory Bill received a formal second reading, a debate took place
on the motion to commit the bill, and lasted sufficiently long
to cause a postponement of the Repeal Bill until Tuesday,
11 March, the Committee stage on the Declaratory Bill being
fixed for the day before.[5] This Committee on 10 March began

[1] He made this note on 16 Mar. 'The cause of the total stagnation the Stamp
Act. The *remedy* the *repeal*. This fact proved by the papers and by evidence. Sorry
they were not heard.' B.M. Add. MSS. 33001, fo. 163.

[2] Langford, *Rockingham Administration*, pp. 193–4, demonstrates this by a
comparison of the Lords division lists for 4 Feb. and 11 Mar. B.M. Add. MSS.
33035, fos. 276–7, 385–7. For Newcastle's lists of peers at this time see B.M. Add.
MSS. 33001, fos. 96–103, 113–15, 128–30, 147–54.

[3] *Chatham Papers*, ii. 403. The number reported in the press was over 200. 'An
instance of such a number going up with a single bill, has not been known in the
memory of man.' *London Evening Post*, 6 Mar. 1766.

[4] *Lords Journals*, xxxi. 291–2. For a copy of the London petition, dated 12 Feb.,
see B.M. Add. MSS. 32973, fo. 421. For the Bristol petition, dated 3 Mar., see
Minchinton, *Politics and the Port of Bristol*, pp. 104–5. The brief debate is mentioned
in a letter from W. G. Hamilton to J. Calcraft, *Chatham Papers*, ii. 379 (*sub* 12 Feb.).
For speeches allegedly made by Shelburne and Mansfield see Cobbett, *Parl.
Hist.* xvi. 165–6, 172–7.

[5] *Lords Journals*, xxxi. 295–7. The debate is mentioned in two letters: (a) W. G.
Hamilton to J. Calcraft, *Chatham Papers*, ii. 382–3 (*sub* 15 Feb.), (b) Hardwicke to
C. Yorke, *Rockingham Memoirs*, i. 313–14.

with an alteration of the preamble, proposed by Dartmouth on the ground that the resolutions of the American assemblies were open to differences of interpretation.[1] Marchmont then answered criticisms made by Mansfield in the previous debate; but, after defending the absence of an enacting clause, said that he regarded the bill as only a preliminary step. Mansfield replied that there ought to be provisions for dealing with any denial of Parliamentary authority, but did not carry out his plan, announced on 7 March,[2] to suggest some such alterations in the bill. Lord Pomfret did later propose an additional clause, that would require all governors, judges and J.P.s to take an oath acknowledging Parliament's supremacy, but withdrew it when he found only four peers willing to support him.

On the next day, 11 March, there took place one of the most important debates of the century in the House of Lords.[3] 136 peers attended, and the House was cleared of all strangers, even M.P.s. The Declaratory Bill was reported from Committee. The London petition was read again, on a motion from Newcastle, and after a formal second reading of the Repeal Bill a long debate ensued when Grafton moved to commit it. Coventry denounced the bill as based on 'imbecility and impotence'. Newcastle replied that Britain's trade was declining everywhere except to America. Sandwich sought to anticipate the argument that the Lords should agree with the Commons by declaring that the bill had 'forced its way through another House by means of that Democratic Interest which this House was constituted to restrain'. Suffolk later repeated the point when he said that the Lords constituted 'the hereditary Council of this kingdom, not subject to the caprice of interested

---

[1] For this day see *Lords Journals*, xxxi. 300; a report by Hardwicke, B.M. Add. MSS. 35972, fos. 76–81, printed, *A.H.R.* 17 (1911–12), 577–9 (to line 28): and two letters: (a) Rockingham to George III, *Corr. of George III*, i. 278–9; (b) W. G. Hamilton to J. Calcraft, *Chatham Papers*, ii. 383–4 (*sub* 17 Feb.).

[2] B.M. Add. MSS. 32974, fo. 155.

[3] For this day see *Lords Journals*, xxxi. 300–5; a report by Hardwicke, B.M. Add. MSS. 35972, fos. 82–87, printed *A.H.R.* 17 (1911–12), 579 (from line 29)–86; and the following letters: (a) Grafton to George III, *Corr. of George III*, i. 280–1; (b) Rockingham to George III, *Corr. of George III*, i. 281–2; (c) W. G. Hamilton to J. Calcraft, *Chatham Papers*, ii. 384–5 (*sub* 19 Feb.); (d) E. Burke to C. O'Hara, *Burke Corr.* i. 244. All quotations are from Hardwicke. For a version of Camden's speech see Cobbett, *Parl. Hist.* xvi. 178–81; and for a summary of Coventry's speech see B.M. Add. MSS. 33001, fos. 155–6.

electors'. Sandwich asserted that the Stamp Act was not the
real point at issue. The aim of the Americans was 'to try their
ground whether by resistance they can get themselves loose
from other acts more disagreeable and detrimental to them'.
Grafton answered that the Stamp Act was defective, and therefore unsuitable for maintaining Parliament's authority. He
reminded the House that 100,000 'manufacturers' were
unemployed. Failure to repeal would mean an increase in the
poor rates, a loss of customs revenue, and forfeiture of colonial
debts owed to British merchants. America was already taxed,
by economic restrictions and by internal taxes in individual
colonies. Halifax retorted that Grafton had not pointed out
any specific defects in the Stamp Act, which would enforce
itself if the administration had spirit: only a few ships were
needed, not 10,000 men. The sole alteration he would approve
of was the removal of duties on ships' papers. Halifax also went
out of his way to answer the charge made in the Commons on
14 February and perhaps repeated earlier that day in the
Lords that when Secretary of State he had failed to obey a
Privy Council instruction of 19 December 1764 to lay American
papers before Parliament. It is not known what Halifax said
on this matter, and Richmond claimed that he had not justified himself; but the general opinion seems to have been that
he had satisfactorily disposed of the point.

Then came the much-anticipated statement by Lord
Chancellor Northington. He began by saying that the Declaratory Bill could be the foundation of firm measures, and that it
had always been his opinion that the colonial opposition to the
Stamp Act was equivalent to rebellion: but these remarks
proved to be a preliminary to arguments for repeal. He repeatedly reminded the House that only the Commons could vote
taxation, and declared that the motive behind repeal was the
economic state of Britain. Mansfield later replied that repeal
was giving up the right of Parliament, and would be followed
by further colonial demands for freedom of trade and manufacturing. 'The gloomy prospect of the colonies throwing off all
allegiance . . . turned all his arguments', Rockingham reported
to George III. Camden denied the opposition claim that the
colonies had challenged Parliament, saying that colonial
resistance arose solely from 'the rigour and hardship of the

Stamp Act'. Altogether eighteen speakers took part in what was for the Lords a very long debate, lasting until nearly midnight. Ten of them opposed the bill, the last being the Duke of Bedford, whose absence through gout on 5 March had given rise to unfounded speculation.[1] The motion was carried by only twelve votes, 73 against 61, but the addition of proxies raised the majority to one of 105 to 71. Among those for repeal was Grenville's former President of the Board of Trade, Lord Hillsborough: in 1768 he told the House that 'he thought the Stamp Act was inexpedient, had advised against it when first proposed, and voted for its repeal upon that principle, as he believed almost everybody else had done'.[2] The minority included not only the Grenville and Bedford groups but also a substantial segment of the customary 'Court Party' in the House: one of the King's brothers, the Duke of York; Lord Chief Justice Mansfield; Lord Bute and a number of Scottish peers; Steward of the King's Household Lord Talbot and other court officials, including seven Lords of the Bedchamber; seven bishops, one by proxy; and Charles Townshend's brother Lord Townshend, who was Lieutenant-General of Ordnance.[3] George III had evidently talked only to Northington and not, as ministers had hoped, to members of the royal household. Lord Lyttelton had already drawn up a formal Protest against the Repeal Bill, and there had been speculation whether Lord Bute would sign it.[4] He did not, but thirty-three peers did, including Bedford, Halifax, Sandwich, and Temple.

On 13 March the Lords completed the final stages of the Declaratory Bill and considered the Repeal Bill in Committee: Rockingham was able to tell the King at 5 o'clock that business had ended 'without any obstruction except a speech from Lord Temple of no great matter'.[5] Another major debate was widely anticipated on the third reading, on Monday 17 March, and 115 peers attended that day: but only a brief debate took

---

[1] *Chatham Papers*, ii. 379.

[2] The quotation is from a letter of Connecticut agent W. S. Johnson. *Trumbull Papers*, p. 306.

[3] Debrett, *Parl. Reg.* iv. 374–5, prints a list of the minority, probably from a contemporary 'black list'.

[4] *Chatham Papers*, ii. 379.

[5] *Corr. of George III*, i. 282. See also the *Lords Journals*, xxxi. 307, and a letter from W. G. Hamilton to J. Calcraft, *Chatham Papers*, ii. 386 (*sub* 20 Feb.).

place on the final motion to pass the bill. Lyttelton, Bute, and
Gower opposed it, and Newcastle made a speech in support.[1]
Bute was thought to have spoken well, and, according to James
Harris, 'declared that he would never come into place again,
and denied his influence'. There was no division, but an additional Protest, supplementing the former one, was subsequently
signed by twenty-eight peers.[2] On the next day, 18 March,
George III went in state to the House of Lords to give the royal
assent to both bills amid scenes of public jubilation, the King
being cheered on his return from Westminster.[3]

Such reactions in Britain were extremely gratifying to the
ministers and other supporters of repeal: but they wanted to
avoid a similar reception of the news in America, since that
would substantiate the opposition assertion that the colonists
would regard the decision as a triumph for them over Parliament. Numerous messages were therefore sent to express the
hope that the news of repeal would be greeted only with quiet
satisfaction and answered by expressions of gratitude and loyalty.
On 28 February a letter from the London merchants trading
to America, with twenty-nine signatures, gave news of the
second reading of the Repeal Bill: but said that the measure
had been made more difficult by the colonial 'violence in words
and action', and warned that if 'it is talked of as a victory,
if it is said the Parliament have yielded up the right, then
indeed your enemies here will have a complete triumph'.[4]
A further letter on 18 March, bearing the names of fifty-five
individuals or trading houses, reported the passage of repeal,
but made this comment: 'We cannot but acquaint you that
had the Americans endeavoured to acquiesce with the law,
and dutifully represented the hardships as they arose, your
relief would have been more speedy, and we should have

[1] Newcastle's papers contain a memorandum, dated 13 Mar., and headed
'some points omitted in the last debate'. B.M. Add. MSS. 33001, fos. 159–60.

[2] *Lords Journals*, xxxi. 308–13. Harris Diary, 17 Mar. 1766. *Corr. of George III*, i.
284. Cobbett, *Parl. Hist.* xvi. 188–93.

[3] *London Evening Post*, 18 Mar. 1766. For details of rejoicing see Clark, *British
Opinion*, pp. 45–8.

[4] *London Merchants on the Stamp Act Repeal*, pp. 215–17. This was a circular letter
to prominent American merchants. For a copy printed in the *Virginia Gazette*
on 16 May see Morgan, *Prologue to Revolution*, pp. 157–8. For similar letters from
individuals see *Fitch Papers*, ii. 388–91; *Franklin Papers*, xiii. 178–9, 242–3; *Grenville
Papers*, iii. 237–8.

avoided many difficulties as well as not a few *unanswerable*
mortifying reproaches on your account.'[1]

Ministerial concern about American behaviour was reflected
in the circular letters sent to the colonial governors by Secretary of State Conway. His letter of 1 March merely announcing
the introduction of the Repeal Bill was evidently intended to
allay discontent:[2] and when on 31 March Conway enclosed
copies of the Declaratory Act and Repeal Act, he emphasised
'the moderation, the forbearance, the unexampled lenity, and
tenderness of Parliament towards the colonies, which are so
signally displayed in those acts'; expected a 'return of cheerful
obedience' and 'sentiments of respectful gratitude'; and added
a warning against 'the least coldness, or dissatisfaction on any
ground whatever of former heat'.[3]

The Parliamentary debates had shown the variety of motives
that led M.P.s and peers to support repeal. Pitt and his followers had challenged Parliament's right to tax America: but
for all except this small minority the formal assertion of
Parliament's sovereignty over the colonies was an essential
preliminary to repeal, and there had even been hints of the
future practical application of the Declaratory Act. Another
factor that must have weighed heavily in the scale for many
was the military situation. That the colonies would not be able
to resist British might was an assumption frequently voiced in
debate: but the attention of both Houses was drawn to the cost
of any such military operation, the size of the colonial militia,
and the probability of foreign intervention in any fighting.
For the great majority of M.P.s, however, fears about the
economic and social repercussions in Britain of the colonial
situation was the decisive factor: Horace Walpole was scarcely
exaggerating when he wrote, 'it was the clamour of trade,
of the merchants, and of the manufacturing towns that had
borne down all opposition. A general insurrection was apprehended as the immediate consequence of upholding the bill.'[4]
There had been hunger riots in 1765 and some minor disturbances occurred in western counties during January and Feb-

---

[1] *London Merchants on the Stamp Act Repeal*, pp. 217–20. The letter refers to the
previous one of 28 Feb. This copy was addressed to John Hancock of Boston.
[2] *Fitch Papers*, ii. 391–2.   [3] *Fitch Papers*, ii. 397–9.
[4] H. Walpole, *Memoirs*, ii. 211–12.

ruary. By then Parliament had already been taking action. Petitions about the high price of corn from London, Sheffield, Norwich, and the Scottish burghs were considered on 20 January by a Commons Committee, which recommended the next day that 'for a limited time' there should be a prohibition on the export of grain and permission to import American corn duty-free. Legislation enacting these proposals for a period of six months from 26 February was drafted by a Committee including both administration and opposition spokesmen and passed the Commons without a vote by 7 February, receiving the royal assent on 19 February. This prompt action was a clear indication of the fear at Westminster that violence might erupt if areas of industrial unemployment suffered food shortages; it was followed by lower prices and a virtual absence of further disorders during the period of the embargo.[1]

The parliamentary decision was a confirmation of the policy decided upon by the administration: but the method successfully adopted by ministers to secure the support of independent members for repeal should not be confused with their own motives. These were complex, varied, and even confused. Newcastle, for instance, told Archbishop Secker that repeal was undertaken for two reasons, to restore peace in America, and to recover for Britain the lost colonial trade, without which economic distress would produce 'as great riots . . . in the great manufacturing towns here'.[2] Ministers certainly knew that conciliation was the only possible short-term solution to the colonial problem. Rockingham observed to Charles Yorke on 25 January 1766 that if repeal was not carried 'I wish no man so great a curse, as to desire him to be the person to take administration and be obliged to enforce the act'.[3] The surviving papers in official and private files show that Rockingham and his colleagues had full and accurate information about events in America, and that by mid-December they faced a deliberate challenge to Britain's authority without any immediate prospect of remedying the situation. Conway,

---

[1] *Commons Journals*, xxx. 455, 459, 465, 467, 473, 491, 495, 500–21, 593. Shelton, *English Hunger and Industrial Disorders*, pp. 24–9.

[2] B.M. Add. MSS. 32974, fos. 5–7.

[3] B.M. Add. MSS. 35430, fos. 37–8.

I

writing to General Gage on 15 December, referred to 'what you say of the difficulty, or rather impossibility of drawing any considerable number of men together, and of the impracticability of attempting any thing by force in the present disposition of the people, without a respectable body of troops'.[1] Conway's speeches were to reflect his awareness of this problem and of the possible international consequences if direct military action met with resistance. He was a former soldier, and now the Secretary of State responsible for relations with France and Spain. How far other ministers believed their own public case of Britain's economic distress must remain a matter of surmise. It is clear that early in the crisis Rockingham had seen the value of this argument as the way to win support for a policy of conciliation. There would have been a volume of protest without government assistance, but Rockingham and several supporters connived in the agitation. He and other ministers thought the economic recession in Britain was an artificial creation of political pressure from American and British merchants alike, and they attempted to kill the two birds of British economic distress and American resistance with the one stone of repeal.

Repeal left several items of unfinished business. The administrative organization established to carry out the Stamp Act had to be dismantled, an Indemnity Act passed, and compensation secured for victims of the rioters. Such practical tasks as securing the scanty revenue raised, ensuring the safe return to Britain of any surviving stamped paper, and settling the accounts and claims of officials were not completed for many months.[2] They showed the total revenue from the Stamp Act to be a mere £3,292, with a nominal loss of £64,000 having been incurred in administrative costs and the value of missing consignments of stamped paper.[3] The actual costs apparently came to under £7,000: for the Treasury Office ordered payment of £4,974 to the Stamp Office on 17 September 1765, and of a further £1,889 on 4 April 1766.[4]

[1] *Gage Corr* ii. 30.
[2] For some Treasury Board decisions in 1766 see T. 29/37, pp. 414, 427; T. 29/39, pp. 127, 141, 172.
[3] Clark, *Rise of the British Treasury*, pp. 160–1.
[4] T.29/37, pp. 133–4, 405–8.

The Indemnity Bill was not passed until late in the session. It was originally based on the motion that Grenville had made in the American Committee on 5 February, reported as the sixth resolution on 24 February. The bill therefore contained a clause to require the previous payment of the relevant duties. Objection was made to this provision as involving only a partial and conditional repeal of the Stamp Act, and the Committee stage was postponed nine times from 9 April until 16 May.[1] On that day the clause was struck out in Committee, so that the bill gave complete indemnification without any restriction. Whately told Grenville on 24 May that the bill, 'though formed upon your motion, is now amended to the very reverse of your idea'.[2] The bill finally received its third reading and passage on 30 May, when its title was altered to omit any mention of payment.[3]

Compensation to the victims of the Stamp Act riots was a matter both Houses of Parliament had decided to refer to the colonial assemblies. Secretary of State Conway ignored the substitution of the word 'require' in the resolution of the Lords, and in his circular letter of 31 March asked the colonial governors to recommend to their assemblies that full and ample compensation should be made. He enclosed a copy of the relevant Commons resolution, the compromise one substituted by Grenville on 5 February with Pitt's support.[4] The response was varied, and never satisfactory. The Assembly of Rhode Island proved evasive, voting Thomas Moffatt £150 but never paying the money.[5] In New York the Assembly promptly voted £1,755 to Major Thomas James,[6] and further compensation to other sufferers: but refused to pay Lieutenant-Governor Colden the £195 he claimed.[7] Colden's application was again rejected later in the year, with the additional sting, he told

---

[1] Almon, *Debates*, vii. 151–2; *Commons Journals*, xxx. 602, 670, 672–3, 692, 712, 724, 750, 780–1, 797, 808, 819, 825.

[2] *Grenville Papers*, iii. 239.

[3] *Commons Journals*, xxx. 828, 830, 838–9.

[4] *Fitch Papers*, ii. 399.

[5] *Gentleman's Magazine*, 57 (1787), 278; *Grenville Papers*, iv. 170.

[6] *Annual Register*, 9 (1766), 159. Colden thought the ministry had told agent Robert Charles to urge the Assembly to give compensation to James, as a return for his evidence before the Commons. James also received £400 while in Britain. *Grenville Papers*, iv. 387.

[7] T.1/446, fo. 176.

Shelburne, of 'the reason being annexed, that I had brought my losses upon myself by my misconduct'.[1] In Massachusetts Governor Bernard submitted Conway's letter to the Assembly on 3 June: but, on a majority decision, this refused to take any action. Such intractable behaviour was embarrassing for friends of the colonies in Britain. The colony's agent De Berdt informed the Assembly's Speaker on 6 August that he had received a letter from Lord Dartmouth deploring this attitude and pointing out that New York had complied with the request. De Berdt himself hoped the report was untrue, after the battle at Westminster over the word 'recommend'.[2] He wrote again on 19 September to say that the new Chatham administration was equally insistent on compensation, Secretary of State Shelburne having 'desired you would finish the affair of the damages sustained because it gave occasion to yours and the enemies of the administration to upbraid them for the gentle measures they adopted'.[3] De Berdt's first letter was published in the *Boston Gazette* on 10 November, and this pressure doubtless contributed to the Assembly's decision to pass a bill in December granting compensation to Hutchinson and other victims: but it also pardoned all offenders in the Boston riots. This provision caused Bernard to sign the bill only with reluctance, and he did so in order to ensure that the compensation would be paid.[4] Fear of Parliamentary action had been the spur, and there can be little doubt that this would have occurred: Pitt himself had declared in the Commons Committee on 5 February that he would support an act to enforce compensation if the colonial assemblies refused to vote payment, and he was now head of the ministry as Lord Chatham.[5] Even as it was the indemnity provision aroused great indignation in Britain and posed a thorny problem for the Chatham administration in 1767.

[1] T.1/446, fo. 177. Colden's letter, dated 26 Dec. 1766, arrived 18 Feb. 1767. *Commons Journals*, xxxi. 232.

[2] *De Berdt Letters*, p. 322.

[3] *De Berdt Letters*, pp. 325–6.

[4] For this episode see Gipson, *British Empire*, xi. 18–25.

[5] The unanimity of British opinion on this point is shown by similar statements made privately by men like Rose Fuller, Richard Jackson, and Lord Rockingham. Gipson, *British Empire*, xi. 16–17.

13

The Rockingham Ministry
and the Empire

THE colonial policy of the Rockingham administration was
not limited to the repeal of the Stamp Act. The measures
considered by members of the administration included the
repeal of the Currency Act and the substitution of an alternative
scheme for colonial money; changes of policy for the interior
of North America and the government of Canada; and a
number of trade proposals that involved a reduction of the
molasses duty and a significant alteration in the imperial
system of trade regulation. Most of these wide-ranging ideas
failed to come to fruition, as the life of the ministry was cut
short. Only changes in the trade laws were to be enacted into
legislation before the end of the session, but they were of sufficient importance as to form a major achievement of the Rockingham administration. This policy was to be denounced by
Grenville as a breach of 'the old colonial system';[1] but it was
rather a sophisticated variant, being based on the principle of
devising trade laws that would benefit the different parts of
the empire.

The political background of this trade policy was markedly
different from that of the Stamp Act Crisis. The battles were
fought between vested interests, not between administration
and opposition; but ministers did seek to act as mediators and
negotiators, while Grenville usually opposed whatever he
thought they favoured. Nor did the subjects arouse much
public controversy. The Parliamentary attendance was poor,
and there were no permanent political alignments over the
complex issues involved. The attitudes of individual M.P.s
were unpredictable, as some followed their own prejudices or
constituency pressures. A number who had opposed repeal of
the Stamp Act were to support one or more of the measures
now suggested or backed by the Rockingham ministry, among
them Robert Nugent and Lord Strange, M.P.s respectively

[1] H. Walpole, *Memoirs*, ii. 224.

for Bristol and Lancashire: but opposition came from the hitherto favourable West India interest, and sometimes from William Pitt.

Ever since its formation the Rockingham ministry had been receiving abundant evidence of a trade recession in America, and had come under increasing pressure both from the colonies and from British merchants and manufacturers to remedy the situation. Public attention had centred on the Stamp Act, but evidence of colonial economic distress was widespread; and before the question of repeal superseded all other considerations the Rockingham administration had taken one step to meet complaints. This concerned the supply of foreign bullion into British colonies.

From about 1751 Spanish ships had begun to visit the British islands in the West Indies, bringing bullion to exchange for slaves and manufactures. This trade was a technical breach of the Navigation Acts,[1] and was threatened and interrupted by the measures taken by the Grenville ministry to enforce all existing and new trade regulations. British officials, notably Governor Thomas Lyttelton of Jamaica, acting on a circular letter from Secretary of State Egremont, stopped Spanish bullion ships entering British colonial ports.[2] In April 1764 Beeston Long, Chairman of the West India Merchants Committee, led a deputation of protest to the Grenville administration. Egremont's successor, Halifax, disclaimed any knowledge of the order, and Grenville himself held a conference with the merchants at the Treasury the next month, when he allowed them to draw up this new order for him to sign. 'I am to inform you that Spanish vessels coming for assistance or refreshment are to have the usual etc provided they do not bring or carry any foreign merchandise.' The bullion trade had been resumed under this specious excuse, and Grenville had not been asked for any further action.[3]

---

[1] The 1660 Act had excepted bullion, but this proviso was omitted from the 1696 Act.

[2] Harris Diary, 17 Feb. 1766. Harris was told this privately by Lord Adam Gordon, who had commanded a ship in West Indian waters.

[3] B.M. Add. MSS. 33030, fos. 190–2. This source is Long's evidence to the American Committee of the House of Commons on 17 Feb. 1766. The Treasury Board issued the appropriate orders on 6 June 1764. For more background detail see Armytage, *Free Port System*, pp. 22–6.

Spanish bullion ships, however, were still being seized, so Governor George Johnstone of West Florida reported to John Pownall later in the year:[1] and by the autumn of 1765 the general opinion was that Grenville had made a blunder; here is a comment of Lord Holland on 29 October:

They say his absurd orders and oaths that he got given to the captains of the ships of war, have actually prevented two millions of dollars from coming into our hands; which the Dutch and French have got. What could possess him, not compelled by law, treaty, nor even applied to by the Spaniards. He has made our vessels act as their Guardes de Costas, and do what we went to war in 1740 to prevent them from doing.[2]

The Rockingham administration received many complaints on the subject, alleging that there had been a fall in the supply of foreign bullion entering the British colonies, much of which had hitherto been remitted to Britain, and a consequent cancellation of many orders for British goods. Petitions on this subject were sent to the Treasury from Bristol, Manchester, Liverpool, Lancaster, Halifax, Leicester, and Derby. In October three papers on the subject written by Dowdeswell were circulated among members of the cabinet.[3] Rockingham sent them to Northington on 22 October, expressing complete approval of the suggestion therein that there should be no hindrance to the bullion trade: 'the admission of bullion and taking away British manufactures was a most profitable trade for this country'.[4] Northington agreed with Dowdeswell's opinion that the Navigation Acts 'never intended to exclude bullion',[5] and so did Newcastle.[6] This consensus of opinion foreshadowed the decision of the Treasury Board, which considered the complaints; obtained the opinion of the Attorney and Solicitor Generals that the import of bullion in foreign vessels would be legal; and prepared a minute that was formally signed on 15 November.[7] This described the situation,

---

[1] *H.M.C. Dartmouth*, ii. 12–13.
[2] B.M. Add. MSS. 51387, fos. 168–9. [3] B.M. Add. MSS. 32971, fos. 14–43.
[4] Northington MSS. [5] Wentworth Woodhouse MSS. R.1–513.
[6] B.M. Add. MSS. 32971, fos. 13–14, 46–68.
[7] This was the procedure suggested by Rockingham to Northington. Dowdeswell had envisaged an application from the Treasury Board to the Privy Council. Northington MSS., ibid. For the background to the Treasury minute of 15 Nov.

and then instructed customs officials, naval officers and others 'not to seize or molest foreign vessels bringing bullion into the plantations in like manner as hath been heretofore used and allowed, and which in its consequences tend so manifestly to the advantage of the trade both of the colonies and of these kingdoms'.[1] Newcastle at once saw that political capital could be made out of the minute. 'It is as strong an article of impeachment against George Grenville as can be found', he wrote to Rockingham.[2] The Marquess heard from his wife in Bath that Pitt approved the step, and asked her to assure the great man that this news was 'to me as strong confirmation of the minute's being right and proper as any of the letters of the thanks with which some of the great manufacturing and trading towns have honoured us at the Board of Treasury on this occasion'.[3]

These comments were misleading. The action merely rendered more positive and overt Grenville's decision of eighteen months earlier.[4] Only the bullion trade remained legal, and commerce with foreign colonies needed more help than official connivance at clandestine methods. Hence a demand for freer trade generally was added to the existing pressure for a reduction in the molasses duty; it included the novel demand for a 'free port' in the British West Indies, which would be permitted to trade with foreign colonies. The administration left the 'North Americans and West Indians' to settle the details while ministers concerned themselves with the Parliamentary battle over the Stamp Act.[5] An initial agreement was concluded on 10 March, at a meeting of 'the Committee of the West Indian and North American Merchants at the King's Arms Tavern'. The most important decision was a major concession by the West India interest, the reduction to 1*d.* of 'the duty on foreign molasses imported into North America'. It was also agreed that foreign sugar could be consumed in North America on

---

1765 see Armytage, *Free Port System*, pp. 22–31; Watson, Ph.D. Thesis, pp. 307–22; Langford, *Rockingham Administration*, pp. 112–15.

[1] B.M. Add. MSS. 32971, fos. 394–5.

[2] B.M. Add. MSS. 32971, fo. 422.

[3] Wentworth Woodhouse MSS. R.156–6.

[4] Grenville correctly denied that he had given orders to stop the bullion trade. See his letter of 3 Nov. 1765 to Lord Botetourt, Grenville Letter-Books, vol. 2; and his Commons speech of 14 Jan. 1766.

[5] *Burke Corr.* i. 240.

payment of a duty of 5*s*. a cwt, but that all sugar imported into Britain from there was to be deemed foreign. The interests of American distillers were safeguarded by the continued prohibition on the import of foreign rum.[1] Two days later a joint deputation from the two Committees reported the agreement to Rockingham, who at once informed George III that 'there is the greatest prospect of an advantageous system of commerce being established for the mutual and general interest of this country, N. America and the West India Islands'.[2]

This agreement, and any other alterations of the trade laws, could only be implemented by Parliamentary legislation. The administration decided to adopt again the tactic of the examination of witnesses by the Commons Committee on American Papers. The Committee had not met since the great debate over repeal on 21 February, but had been kept in existence by repeated postponements. On 21 March three more witnesses were ordered to attend the Committee, and on 24 March the Committee was ordered to hear the London merchants on the petition they had submitted on 17 January, and also to consider the trade laws.[3] Three days later, on 27 March, the Committee met to examine the first witnesses.[4]

New York merchant William Kelly made a second appearance before the Committee, and underwent a lengthy examination, mainly on the molasses duty. For North America as a whole imports had been between 70,000 and 90,000 hogsheads of 100 gallons, only 3,000 of which came from the British islands: the foreign molasses were paid for entirely in goods and not with money, a point that must have reassured mercantilist opinion. Since the import price of molasses was 6*d*. a gallon, the 3*d*. duty was a 50 per cent *ad valorem* duty; and,

[1] There were other provisions to ameliorate conditions of colonial trade. Several copies of the agreement survive, among them B.M. Add. MSS. 33030, fos. 206–7; 38339, fos. 235–6; P.R.O. 30/8/97, fos. 47–8; T.1/452, fo. 211. It was printed in the *Gentleman's Magazine*, 36 (1766), 228–31.

[2] *Corr. of George III*, i. 282. Pitt told Rockingham that he hoped the agreement 'will be productive of the best consequences'. Wentworth Woodhouse MSS. R.1–586.

[3] *Commons Journals*, xxx. 627, 646, 663, 673, 681, 688, 697.

[4] *Commons Journals*, xxx. 702. Chairman Rose Fuller subsequently reported to the House that the Committee had heard the London merchants, and examined witnesses. Evidence survives of the examination of four witnesses in the *Ryder Diary*, pp. 320–9.

I*

by raising the price of rum, had caused a fall of 60 per cent in the number of New York ships employed in the African trade.[1] Despite Kelly's insistence that the 3*d.* duty was being enforced, at least in New York, he said that a 1*d.* duty would produce a larger net revenue: his explanation was that more would be imported, and that enforcement costs would be lower since there would be less motive for evasion. The rest of Kelly's testimony was intended to show how Britain's American trade would benefit from other economic changes. During the five years ending in 1763 New York had imported £3,000,000 worth of goods from Britain: but they had been paid for almost entirely from the profits of the African trade, the bullion obtained from the Spanish colonies, and the re-export to Europe of foreign colonial products. The lesson was obvious: the repeal of the Stamp Act had restored the will of the colonists to trade with Britain, but revision of Grenville's other measures was necessary to give them the means to do so.

Kelly's statements were confirmed and amplified by three other witnesses. Brook Watson, a British merchant concerned primarily with the American fishing industry, explained its dependence on the foreign molasses trade. The British islands could not consume more than a quarter of the fish sent from North America to the West Indies, nor supply more than one-twentieth of the molasses needed there. Watson forecast that unless the molasses duty was reduced to 1*d.*, the French would make their molasses into rum themselves and illegally exchange it for New England fish by using their islands off Canada. A duty of 1*d.* was also urged by the next witness, John Wentworth, soon to be governor of New Hampshire. He added that if the American colonies were allowed to import foreign sugar duty free for their own use or for re-export they would be able to buy more British manufactures. The Committee then heard the testimony of a man who had been concerned with the application of the molasses duty, Robert Hale, the Customs Collector at Boston. He reported that the 3*d.* duty had yielded £4,000 at that port in the first year; but there had been widespread evasion, and he thought that a 1*d.* duty would provide more revenue. The sugar duty had produced only

[1] There is a discrepancy between this statement and his evidence on 12 Feb. above, pp. 220–1.

£200 in the year, and Hale echoed Wentworth's view that the free admission of foreign sugar would make it possible for the American colonies to buy more from Britain. The Committee then adjourned for the Easter recess, having failed to 'get through half our evidence', according to Edmund Burke.[1]

Ministerial hopes of a prompt and uncontroversial solution to the problem of the trade laws soon faded as difficulty arose over the free-port plan. The lead in the campaign for a free port was apparently taken by the Society of Merchant Venturers in Bristol. On 15 March the Committee of the Society decided to press for the making of Dominica into a free port, and the Society drafted a petition to this effect on 2 April.[2] The petition was presented to the House of Commons on 7 April, and supported on that day by others from the merchants of Lancaster and Liverpool, and on 8 April by one from the merchants and manufacturers of Manchester. Cotton, grown at this time in the West Indies but not yet in North America, was specifically mentioned by all three Lancashire petitions when they asked for a free port or ports in the West Indies for the import of foreign colonial goods.[3]

These petitions were referred to the American Committee, which sat on 7 April to hear the London merchants and to examine witnesses in favour of the plan to make Dominica an open port.[4] Edmund Burke optimistically thought the question as good as over: this, he wrote,

concludes the enquiry previous to the resolutions, that are to be the foundations of the North American Trade Act. These resolutions will be proposed in the Committee for America, next Monday. I do not now look for much opposition; the spirit of the adverse faction begins to evaporate; even Mr. Grenville begins to slacken in his attendance.[5]

Since their defeat over repeal Grenville and his friends had raised the American question only twice in Parliament: on

---

[1] *Burke Corr.* i. 247.
[2] Minchinton, *Politics and the Port of Bristol*, pp. 105–6.
[3] *Commons Journals*, xxx. 704, 708.
[4] No record of the testimony has been found, and the names of the witnesses are not known. Diarist James Harris noted merely that 'several witnesses were examined touching the making a free port of Dominica in America'.
[5] *Burke Corr.* i. 248.

17 March Grenville had moved an Address for a Board of Trade report on colonial trade and manufacturing; and he or his allies must have been responsible for the motions on 27 March for two Addresses asking for similar reports from colonial governors and for evidence of any encouragement of manufacturing by colonial assemblies.[1] Burke was almost justified in dismissing the disheartened Parliamentary opposition as of little consequence, but he was looking for trouble in the wrong direction. The challenge to the new American proposals came from the West India interest, headed by William Beckford. The West Indian merchants were not prepared to accept the free-port plan without a fight, seeing it as a threat to their trade monopoly, and the support of Beckford's mentor William Pitt was to render this challenge temporarily formidable.

The administration knew of Pitt's hostility by 11 April, when Rockingham sent Burke to discuss the free-port plan with him. Burke was accompanied by Lancaster merchant Abraham Rawlinson, a leading advocate of the scheme;[2] and later reported to his friend Charles O'Hara that they went to talk Pitt

out of his peevish and perverse opposition to so salutory and unexceptionable a measure. But on this point, I found so great a man utterly unprovided with any better arms than a few rusty prejudices. So we returned as we went, after some hours' fruitless conference. But the truth is, he determined to be out of humour; and this was the first object he had to display it upon, for he had in a better temper approved of all the previous regulations.[3]

A few days later a deputation of London merchants headed by Barlow Trecothick failed to persuade Pitt to change his attitude.[4] Pitt had been offended by the administration's increasing independence. The ministers had ceased pressing him to join them in office, and had now presumed to formulate policies without consulting him. At the interview with Burke he not only expressed disapproval of the free-port plan but also made

---

[1] *Commons Journals*, xxx. 663, 702. Harris Diary, *sub* 18 Mar. 1766.
[2] Wentworth Woodhouse MSS., Burke Letters 1/54, 55.
[3] *Burke Corr.* i. 251–2.
[4] B.M. Add. MSS. 32974, fo. 389.

it clear that the administration could no longer rely on his support.[1]

Realization by the ministers that they could no longer count Pitt as a friend came at the time when some decision on the American trade proposals was imperative. British merchants and manufacturers were making various demands for freer trade, and on 3 April a meeting of the joint Committees of the West Indian and North American Merchants had come to a second agreement. They decided to ask the ministry for legislation to permit any British manufactures or American provisions imported into Jamaica or Pensacola in West Florida to be freely re-exported in any ships.[2] Ministers were also under pressure on other points. Sugar refiners were preparing to petition Parliament for cheaper imports of foreign sugar; and Abraham Rawlinson had already asked the administration for the duty-free import of foreign cotton. Dowdeswell thought the advantage of this last idea so self-evident that he instructed Treasury official Robert Yeates to draft a resolution on the subject.[3] Parliamentary opposition, however, threatened to breathe new life into a problem that the administration might well have thought solved: despite the agreement of the North American and West Indian merchants on 10 March, the West Indian planters opposed the reduction in the molasses duty. There was still deadlock on the free-port plan, moreover, and the West Indian interest generally resented the fact that Parliament had heard evidence only on one side. In a letter of 18 April to Pitt William Beckford enclosed a copy of evidence he had submitted to 'the managers of the Sugar Island interest', with this comment:[4]

The question is of more consequence than our wise ministers are aware of. I shall therefore move to postpone the consideration until the next session. I hope their justice and wisdom will induce them to consent to such an adjournment. The evidence on behalf of the North Americans has been gone through and heard with patience. The Sugar Colonies have certainly a right to be admitted to give their evidence before any resolution is agreed to that may specifically affect them.

[1] B.M. Add. MSS. 32974, fos. 417–24.
[2] Wentworth Woodhouse MSS. R.–60.
[3] Wentworth Woodhouse MSS. R1.599.   [4] P.R.O. 30/8/19, fos. 80–1.

Rockingham held a cabinet meeting on 12 April to consider the various American trade proposals. Newcastle did not attend,[1] and Conway was absent because of a prolonged illness that kept him out of politics for several weeks.[2] Lord Chancellor Northington, Lord Egmont, and the Duke of Grafton favoured postponement of the free-port plan, perhaps on the news of Pitt's hostility to it; and although Dowdeswell, attending at Rockingham's request, supported the scheme, the cabinet decision was that there should be merely an Address from the House of Commons asking the King for the opinion of the Board of Trade on the subject.[3] Rockingham's conclusion from the meeting was that only the reduction of the molasses duty and the plan for importing sugar into America could be proposed that session.[4] But Dowdeswell was determined to press the free-port scheme, and wrote to Rockingham on the subject two days later:

If we are to be well supported and can be prepared with a plan, it would be more manly to go through with it this session. If not prepared with a plan, by all means an address, and if that address is to convey an approbation of the principle and to leave little more to the Board of Trade than to form a plan for the execution, I should like it the better.

He had already drafted a resolution for the Address, which Cooper had shown to Charles Townshend.[5]

On 14 April the introduction of any colonial measure was postponed for a week because Dowdeswell was ill, a circumstance that led James Harris to record the political situation in his diary:

---

[1] B.M. Add. MSS. 32974, fo. 350.

[2] B.M. Add. MSS. 32974, fos. 447–8. *Burke Corr.* i. 248–50.

[3] *Burke Corr.* i. 251.

[4] B.M. Add. MSS. 32974, fos. 348–9, 370–1.

[5] Wentworth Woodhouse MSS. R.1–599. In 1771 Dowdeswell told the Commons that he had overcome other opposition within the administration to the free-port scheme. Here is Horace Walpole's version of his anecdote. 'When Lord Rockingham had meditated the plan of a free port, Elliot, Dyson, and the King's friends declared against it. Still the Ministers had persisted, and Cooper, Secretary of the Treasury, was ordered to move it, but came in a fright, and said the friends would oppose it. Dowdeswell said he had snatched the bill from Cooper, and had added, he would be damned if they dared. He had moved it; they had not opened their lips for or against it, but had voted for it, and so they always would if the Ministers had courage.' H. Walpole, *Memoirs*, iv. 209–10.

Today we were to have gone on the regulations of American trade, that is to say, to please the foreigners, and our own selfish merchants here break into that established mode of commerce, which has had the experience of a century to justify its ability and importance to this country. Happily for us, Pitt had quarrelled with his creatures the ministry, and the West Indians with the North Americans, so he came down (as had been previously given out) to oppose the measure. This however was postponed.

Pitt, having made the effort to attend, nevertheless took the opportunity to attack the administration. When a debate arose over the militia he chose to detect a ministerial intention of undermining on grounds of economy the institution that had been part of his war strategy, and made a sharp attack on this subject. Burke attributed the speech to the administration's refusal to give way to unreasonable demands of Pitt for what amounted to a dissolution of the ministry; and he reported to O'Hara that Pitt has 'abused administration in the grossest and most unprovoked manner'.[1]

By 18 April Dowdeswell had sufficiently recovered to present his Budget.[2] In his speech he made two references to America: while estimating the annual cost of the cutters to stop smuggling at £150,000, he remarked that the number of seizures had been small; and he later said that the known American revenue amounted only to £21,000. The controversial part of the Budget was an extension of the window taxes. Even Grenville concentrated his attack on the plan for taxing all windows, 'making the poor pay for the light of heaven'; but he could not resist the opportunity of mentioning American taxation, claiming that the repeal of the Stamp Act would cost £110,000 a year and the reduction of the molasses duty another £30,000. The opposition took the rare step of forcing a vote on the Budget, being defeated on the window tax by 162 votes to 112.

When the Budget resolutions were reported to the House on 21 April a second long debate on the window tax began. By the time the tax had been confirmed by 179 votes to 114, it was too late for the American Committee, which was put off until 24 April. Pitt, who had attended the House for the

---

[1] *Burke Corr.* i. 250. For the debate see also the Harris Diary, 14 Apr. 1766, and H. Walpole, *Memoirs*, ii. 224–7.

[2] For this debate see Harris Diary, 18 Apr. 1766, and *Burke Corr.* i. 250.

American business at Beckford's request, withdrew into a Committee room and went home after waiting there for four hours. The day ended with further pressure on the free port issue: a petition of London merchants asked for one or more free ports in America, to encourage trade to Africa and the West Indies by providing the stimulus of cheap raw materials; and Bristol M.P. Robert Nugent moved for the attendance of seven witnesses, obviously to give evidence on the same subject.[1]

On 24 April American business was side-tracked by a petition from 'the Sugar Refiners of London', complaining that the high price of British sugar and the prohibitive duty on foreign sugar made the export of refined sugar uncompetitive and asking for a reduction in the duty on foreign sugar. It was supported by a similar petition from 'the Manufacturers, Dealers and Consumers of Sugar' in Bristol; and a debate began over a motion that the petitions should be referred to the American Committee. This was opposed by Beckford and other West Indian spokesmen, but supported by banker George Prescott, Charles Townshend, and Robert Nugent. Grenville and Dowdeswell both opposed the motion, but Pitt's support ensured its approval without a vote. The Committee then met, under Chairman Fuller, and examined some witnesses on this subject.[2] It adjourned to the next day, but it was to be postponed by lengthy debates on other political topics until 30th April.[3] Edmund Burke suspected an ulterior motive behind the variety of subjects raised or discussed at this time by the opposition in Parliament; for the window tax, the militia, and issues arising from general warrants were all debated repeatedly during the second half of April. 'The enemy's plan seems to be to start object after object to keep off our doing any thing on the American affairs. And they have hitherto been but too successful.'[4]

Pitt's hostility posed the two further threats of loss of control of the Commons and the disintegration of the ministry itself. Neither materialized: the balance of opinion in the House was

[1] *Commons Journals*, xxx. 750–1. Harris Diary, 21 Apr. 1766. Newdegate MSS. B 2546/21.
[2] *Commons Journals*, xxx. 759–60. Harris Diary, *sub* 23 Apr. 1766. H. Walpole, *Memoirs*, iii. 224–5. *Bedford Papers*, iii. 333–4. B. M. Add. MSS. 32975, fo. 13.
[3] *Commons Journals*, xxx. 772, 780–1. Wentworth Woodhouse MSS. R.1–603.
[4] *Burke Corr.* i. 252.

against Pitt on the free-port scheme; and while his attitude precipitated the resignation of the Duke of Grafton, this event did not bring the administration down, Grafton's post as Northern Secretary of State being taken by Conway, who was replaced as Southern Secretary by the inexperienced Duke of Richmond.[1] There remained a general lack of public confidence in the prospects of the administration, reflected in the failure to fill several minor offices that were vacant; the most damaging refusal was that of the impecunious Lord North a second time to take a Vice-Treasurership of Ireland. The King, however, intended to wait at least until the Parliamentary recess before making any move, and the ministers themselves were never to decide on resignation. The administration therefore proceeded with the colonial business, strengthened in the Commons by Conway's return.

During the second half of April, as well as such major issues as the molasses duty and the free-port scheme, the Rockingham ministry also had under consideration a number of other proposals concerning colonial trade. John Huske had suggested that European countries should be allowed to export their wine directly to America, on payment of a duty of £7 a ton on wine from Spain, Portugal, and Italy, and double that duty on wine from France and elsewhere. He also had proposed duties of 3*d*. a gallon on olive oil, 2*s*. 6*d*. a cwt on dried fruit, and 2*s*. 6*d*. a hundred on lemons and oranges, all the articles to be sent directly from their country of origin in Europe to the British colonies. The administration rejected or postponed the plan of wine duties, but decided to adopt Huske's other suggestions, though Rockingham insisted on much lower rates of duty. The colonial agents were informed of the detailed proposals; appropriate Parliamentary resolutions were drafted, and even taken to the House of Commons by Dowdeswell: but the controversy over the free-ports plan led to the abandonment of this scheme to obtain a colonial revenue by port duties on goods sent to America from Europe in deliberate breach of the Navigation Acts.[2]

---

[1] Grafton told Rockingham and Conway of his intention to resign on 27 Apr., George III on 28 Apr., and Pitt on 29 Apr., but, waiting the appointment of a successor, did not formally resign until 14 May. B.M. Add. MSS. 47584, fos. 43, 46.

[2] See Huske's letter of 9 Apr. 1767 to C. Townshend, printed Namier and

By 25 April the ministry had also decided on alterations of the 1764 duties on coffee and foreign textiles imported into America. Resolutions on these subjects were among fifteen moved by Dowdeswell in the Committee of Ways and Means on 30 April, the most important being the reduction of the duty on foreign molasses to 1*d.* a gallon. The proceeds of all the duties were to be used for 'defraying the necessary expenses of defending, protecting, and securing the said colonies and plantations'. Dowdeswell ended with the motion to address the King to take the opinion of the Board of Trade on the plan for a free port.[1] Beckford at once attacked the proposals as being beneficial to North America and the French West Indies at the expense of Britain and her own islands.[2] The reduction in the molasses duty would enable American distillers to compete with those in Britain, and would assist the French planters to sell their sugar cheaper because they could dispose of the by-product molasses. Such competition would harm both the older British islands and the plantations being established in the newly acquired islands. Beckford also criticized the idea of a free port, and ended by moving for the Chairman to leave the Chair, a procedural device to kill all the resolutions by putting an end to the Committee. Charles Townshend defended the 1*d.* molasses duty, but spoke mainly about the plan for a free port: according to James West he declared that this would be 'improper to the highest degree unless Great Britain was sure that every article of import and export were in her favour, which in fact is directly otherwise and therefore left the whole in the same uncertainty as he found it'; but James Harris on the other side of the House thought that Townshend 'defended the regulations, and the free-port in particular,

---

Brooke, *Charles Townshend*, p. 187. For the date of these schemes see Chaffin, *W.M.Q.* 27 (1970), 95.

[1] For a copy of the fifteen resolutions, dated 25 Apr., see B.M. Add. MSS. 33001, fos. 193–7. Resolutions 4 and 7–15 were reported to the House on 9 May as the Committee's resolutions 3–11 and 13. *Commons Journals*, xxx. 811. The others, concerning sugar and the free port, were to be altered in Committee on 8 May: see below, pp. 272–3.

[2] For this debate see Harris Diary, 30 Apr. 1766, and the following letters: (a) J. Harris to Hardwicke, B.M. Add. MSS. 35607, fos. 255–6; (b) J. West to Newcastle, B.M. Add. MSS. 32975, fo. 58; (c) G. Onslow to Newcastle, B.M. Add. MSS. 32975, fo. 56; (d) Conway to George III, *Corr. of George III*, i. 232–3.

in framing which I should imagine he had a principal hand'. Grenville then seconded Beckford's motion, attacking particularly the reduction in the molasses duty. 1*d*. a gallon was what the Americans usually paid for cheating, to secure the connivance of customs officials; and the lower duty was another instance of the Rockingham ministry taking off a colonial tax after only an *ex parte* examination of witnesses. Grenville also criticized the free-port scheme, as opening the way for widespread smuggling; and ended by attacking, as West noted, 'the overbearing delegation of administration to a Club of North American Merchants at the Kings Arms Tavern, who he hoped would never be suffered to give law to Great Britain'.

William Pitt again made the decision for the Committee. He suggested that the matter should be postponed until Monday, 5 May, so that Beckford could produce witnesses to challenge the North American evidence that had been heard: this was the aim Beckford himself had mentioned to Pitt in his letter of 18 April, and Pitt's speech may have been a debating tactic concerted between them. Pitt favoured a reduction of the molasses duty,[1] but he opposed the idea of a free port and thought it absurd to refer the matter to the Board of Trade. Beckford accepted Pitt's suggestion of a postponement; Dowdeswell concurred in it; and after Lord Strange and Robert Nugent had both declared for a free port, the Committee adjourned at 8 o'clock, Onslow reporting to Newcastle that 'it has been agreed on all sides to put off the matter till Monday, to hear evidence from the West India *Planters*'. On 2 May eighteen witnesses were ordered to attend the American Committee, and one more on 5 May.[2]

The hearing of Beckford's witnesses began on 5 May. Onslow told Newcastle at 9 o'clock, 'we are now in the American evidence. Got into it at last. God knows when we shall get out of it.' James West thought the examination would last two or three days: 'the ministry seemed united again and the lawyers attend well on their side'. Only one witness was heard the first day, an Alexander Hume of whose evidence no

---

[1] Diarist Harris summarized Pitt as saying 'he was for the reduction only to raise it': this could be taken to mean that Pitt had adopted the idea of a lower duty to produce more revenue.

[2] *Commons Journals*, xxx. 790, 797. Two witnesses had already been ordered in April. *Ibid.* 739, 778.

record has been found.[1] The next day, soon after the Committee met, Bedfordite Alexander Forrester moved to leave the Chair. He was seconded by William Burt, who owned estates in Nevis and St. Kitts. After a debate in which Grenville again attacked the Merchants' Committee the motion was defeated by 68 votes to 28, and Onslow told Newcastle that 'we shall finish this American thing very well'. Only one witness was examined, Jamaica merchant Thomas Collett. Beckford's questions elicited confirmation of what he had said himself in the House on 30 April. Collett emphasized the poverty of most sugar planters, whose debts to Britain amounted to £6,000,000. The French West Indies already sold more sugar more cheaply than the British islands, and the proposed low duty on their molasses would threaten the market of the British sugar plantations. Collett also forecast that a free port at Dominica would prove an even more pernicious centre of smuggling than the notorious Isle of Man.[2]

On 7 May, for the third day in succession, only one witness was examined by the Committee, Richard Maitland, and no M.P. apparently took note of what he said. James West reported to Newcastle at 7.30 p.m. that 'every person seems uneasy that some end is not put to an examination which is threatened to be prolonged, which can give no information and which is very ill attended': and Onslow later wrote to the Duke from the Committee: 'The same poor miserable evidence is still upon his legs, and giving answers to a thousand nonsensical questions, to about twenty of us which is the utmost of our number.'[3] Farce or filibuster, Beckford's presentation of the West Indian case to Parliament proved a hollow victory. While his witnesses were paraded before the sparsely attended American Committee, the real decision had been taken outside the House.

The administration had been attempting to persuade the West India Committee to yield the major points in dispute by the offer of alternative concessions. Circumstances made this solution both imperative and possible. By the end of April

---

[1] The only information on this day's Committee is in the brief letters from West and Onslow to Newcastle. B.M. Add. MSS. 32975, fos. 79–81.

[2] For the Committee see Harris Diary, *sub* 5 May 1766; and the letters from Onslow and West to Newcastle. B.M. Add. MSS. 32975, fos. 85–7.

[3] B.M. Add. MSS. 32975, fos. 97–8.

ministers were under pressure from merchants anxious about the delay of American business to move a question directly for a free port;[1] and it was generally anticipated that whatever the inclination of the Treasury Bench Robert Nugent would insist on bringing the subject before the Commons.[2] But if Parliamentary discussion of the free-port plan could not be avoided, the main Parliamentary obstacle to its implementation had been removed: after the debate of 30 April Pitt had left London for Bath on grounds of ill health.[3] Grafton's confidant Lord Villiers linked the final ministerial decision with this circumstance. 'Upon the strength of Mr. Pitt's being out of town administration alters the design of an Address only to the King to direct the Board of Trade to consider of the plan for a free port, and move at once to establish a free port.'[4]

It must soon have become evident that Beckford's tactics were not going to avert either the lower molasses duty or the free port. He therefore concurred in the strategy of the Fuller brothers, Rose and Stephen,[5] of salvaging the best possible terms for the West India interest: indeed, Lord Villiers noted of the final agreement that 'the American regulations were amicably settled with Beckford and the others'.[6] They succeeded so well that a West Indian celebration dinner was held afterwards, on 19 June.[7] Little information has survived on the negotiations, except that on 30 April Stephen Fuller sent Dowdeswell information on the rum and brandy trade that could be confirmed by Thomas Collett, Richard Maitland, and Beeston Long.[8] Nothing else is known of the discussions that preceded the final decision by the West India Committee on 8 May of terms for presentation to the North American Committee. This agreement superseded the two earlier ones of 10 March and 3 April.[9]

[1] Wentworth Woodhouse MSS. R.1–603.
[2] *Chatham Papers*, ii. 418.
[3] *Chatham Papers*, ii. 414–16.
[4] B.M. Add. MSS. 47584, fos. 45–6.
[5] B.M. Add. MSS. 32975, fo. 114.
[6] B.M. Add. MSS. 47584, fo. 45.
[7] B.M. Add. MSS. 32975, fos. 400, 416, 430.
[8] B.M. Add. MSS. 32975, fos. 62–5.
[9] For draft and final copies of the agreement see B.M. Add. MSS. 33030, fos. 243, 245; and for explanatory notes see ibid., fos. 247–8. The agreement and some notes are printed by Sutherland, *E.H.R.* 47 (1932), 71–2.

The West India interest had given way on most, although
not all, of the chief matters in contention. After a vain attempt
to postpone the Dominica free port the point was conceded.
The Free Ports Act was to allow the import into Dominica
of sugar and other hitherto prohibited colonial products, but
any sent to Britain were to be deemed foreign and taxed as
such unless certified as grown on the island. A second concession
that would adversely affect the British West Indies was the
removal of any duty on foreign cotton imported into Britain.
On this subject there had been several opinions. A compromise
solution suggested by Charles Townshend on 6 May was for a
bounty on cotton imports from British colonies to give them a
competitive edge if free import of foreign cotton was to be
permitted: Conway approved this plan, but it was not adopted.[1]
Pitt also favoured the idea of encouraging cotton production
in the British colonies, to avoid dependence on France.[2] He
was to be critical of the Rockinghamite decision, and in October
made it the excuse for not offering Edmund Burke a post in
his ministry.

As to his notions and maxims of trade, they can never be mine.
Nothing can be more unsound and more repugnant to every true
principle of manufacture and commerce, than rendering so noble a
branch as the cottons, dependent for the first material upon the
produce of French and Danish islands, instead of British.[3]

The third important concession was that already agreed on
10 March, the reduction of the colonial import duty on foreign
molasses from 3*d*. to a 1*d*. a gallon: but this was accompanied
by a remarkable new decision that had not been publicly
discussed, that molasses from the British islands should pay the
same duty. Rose Fuller's explanation to Newcastle on 10 May
linked this with the cancellation of a duty on sugar that would
cost the revenue only £1,700 and that fell on inter-island trade
in a manner that was unfair and inconvenient. He calculated
that the new duty would yield over £4,000 a year on molasses
exported from Jamaica to North America; but a greater
advantage to Britain would be the certainty that the duty on

[1] B.M. Add. MSS. 32975, fos. 97, 102.
[2] *Chatham Papers*, ii. 420.
[3] *Grafton Autobiography*, p. 108.

foreign molasses would now be paid, since fraud would no longer be possible; and the duty would 'accustom the North American colonies to obedience'. Fuller thought that whereas the 3d. duty on foreign molasses had raised only about £10,000 a year the new 1d. duty would bring in over £40,000.[1] There is no evidence as to the origin of this proposal, not even whether it came from the ministry or the West India interest: but the idea of taxing all molasses imports at the same rate was not new. John Temple, when criticizing the 3d duty on foreign molasses to Whately on 10 September 1764, had made this suggestion. 'I could wish Parliament had left only 2d per gallon on molasses imported into the colonies, and that duty to have been general on the produce of British as well as foreign molasses: it certainly would have raised something handsome, and the duty, I believe, would have been punctually paid.'[2] The colonial molasses duty, originally imposed to regulate trade, was now unequivocably a tax The preamble to the ensuing legislation shows that the administration knew what it was doing;[3] and Dowdeswell's appreciation of the significance of the step is underlined by his later fear that the colonial opposition to Charles Townshend's 1767 duties would jeopardize the revenue being produced by the molasses duty.[4] This revenue was substantial: in the five years from 1768 to 1772 the 1d. molasses duty yielded over £80,000.[5] The Rockingham ministry alone devised an effective means of taxing the American colonies during the Revolutionary period—a reversal of tradition by fact.

The West Indian interest made substantial gains in return for these concessions. The sugar trade was to enjoy continued protection of the British market; for, despite the petitions of the British sugar refiners, the existing high duty on foreign sugar entering Britain was to be maintained. Moreover, the duty on British sugar entering North America would be removed, while that on foreign sugar was continued; and there was added the important stipulation that all sugar exported

---

[1] B.M. Add. MSS. 32975, fos. 147–50. Langford, *Rockingham Administration*, p. 202, inexplicably states that such a 1d. duty already existed.

[2] *Bowdoin–Temple Papers*, p. 25.

[3] Barrow, *Trade and Empire*, p. 214.

[4] Dowdeswell MSS., W. Dowdeswell to Rockingham, 14 Aug. 1768.

[5] Dickerson, *Navigation Acts and the American Revolution*, pp. 184–6.

from North America to Britain should be deemed foreign. This removed the fear that foreign sugar would be smuggled through the new Dominica free port, and closed an existing loop-hole: for American re-exports to Britain of what purported to be sugar from the British islands exceeded the imports from those islands.[1] The sugar planters were also given two concessions concerning rum, which accounted for one-third of the produce of the sugar plantations. The period of time before excise had to be paid on bonded rum was extended from six months to a year, thereby reducing the pressure on owners to sell at a loss in times of bad markets: and the agreement promised either a reduction in the duty on rum or an increase in the duty on rum's competitor, brandy.[2] Finally, the West India interest obtained what might appear a paradoxical concession, the creation of a second free port in Jamaica. This was to be quite different from the one in Dominica, and was to achieve two aims long cherished by the Rockingham administration, by legalizing the Spanish trade in smuggled bullion and permitting the export of British manufactures.[3] No imports were allowed of foreign manufactures, and the same prohibition on such West Indian products as sugar, molasses, tobacco, and coffee safeguarded the interests of British planters.[4]

The agreement of 8 May was made before the American Committee of the House of Commons met that day. The Committee therefore decided to end the examination of witnesses after hearing Charles Townshend's friend John Bindley on the distilling of molasses. Dowdeswell then proposed a series of resolutions to correspond with the agreement. They were all carried by 9.30 p.m. without any division and after a short debate in which Charles Townshend distinguished himself by an attack on Grenville.[5] Rockingham commented to Newcastle on 'the very pleasing appearance in the House

[1] B.M. Add. MSS. 33030, fo. 247.

[2] Both concessions were secured. The duty on rum was reduced by 6*d.* a gallon, and that on foreign brandy increased by 1*s. Commons Journals*, xxx. 823.

[3] *Corr. of George III*, i. 306–7.

[4] For the differences between the two free ports see Armytage, *Free Port System*, pp. 42–3.

[5] For the proceedings of the Committee on 8 May see the following letters: (a) Rockingham to George III, *Corr. of George III*, i. 306–7; (b) J. West (two letters) to Newcastle, B.M. Add. MSS. 32975, fos. 110, 112; (c) G. Onslow to Newcastle, B.M. Add. MSS. 32975, fo. 114.

of Commons on the American and West India regulations and particularly on the general approbation with which the resolution on the free port was received'.[1]

The Committee resolutions of 30 April and 8 May were reported to the House on 9 May, when the appropriate legislation was ordered after the free-port proposal had been opposed by two Grenvillites, Simon Luttrell and James Harris, 'from the impossibility of supporting those restrictions, which its advocates allowed necessary, by revenue officers. They would be corrupted and intimidated. The place itself (Dominica) so situate, as smugglers might escape the strictest diligence. Stay, and see how America has received your late favours.'[2] During later business that day Grenville attacked ministers for 'the wicked principle of aiming to undo all done by their predecessors; have yet done nothing, except the miserable window-tax'. Conway replied by citing 'the American regulation and free-port, as something done'.[3]

The American Duties Bill and Free Ports Bill were passed by the Commons between 15 and 30 May, and the agreement of the Lords was reported on 6 June, when the bills received the royal assent.[4] There had been rumours of opposition to the Free Ports Bill;[5] and on 19 May Burke wrote to Abraham Rawlinson, now back in Lancaster, apparently warning him that he and other merchants might be required as witnesses.[6] The administration certainly feared trouble in the Lords. Newcastle was arranging proxies as early as 15 May,[7] and on 1 June Rockingham asked the Duke to attend the Lords Committee on the Free Ports Bill next day, 'lest anything should arise'.[8] No evidence has survived of any debate or division in either House, and opposition criticism seems to have been confined to private correspondence. Whately sent Grenville a copy of the Free Ports Bill on 23 May, with this comment:

[1] B.M. Add. MSS. 32975, fo. 116.
[2] Harris Diary, 9 May 1766. The safeguards did prove unworkable. Armytage, *Free Port System*, pp. 42–3. For the resolutions see *Commons Journals*, xxx. 811.
[3] Harris Diary, 9 May 1766.
[4] *Commons Journals*, xxx. 825–6, 832–5, 837–9, 843–4.
[5] *Burke Corr.* i. 255.
[6] Wentworth Woodhouse MSS.: Burke Papers, 1/55.
[7] B.M. Add. MSS. 32975, fos. 189–90.
[8] B.M. Add. MSS. 32975, fo. 325.

I am not master of the subject, and therefore cannot point out the imperfections of the scheme, but at first view I think everyone must be disappointed to see so great a liberty guarded by so few restrictions, and no additional provisions made against the new dangers to which this license will expose the commerce of the colonies.[1]

By the next day a detailed objection had occurred to Whately. 'There is no provision to prevent the importation of French manufactures, provided they be the produce of the West Indies.' He was afraid that the French would 'establish other fictitious manufactures in their islands, and under that colour supply our colonies with whatever they please'.[2] Robert Nugent thought the American Duties Act had been badly drafted. One accidental effect, he told Grenville on 17 June after reading the final act, would be to stop any trade between America and Ireland.[3] 'There are other curious particulars, too many for a letter, which will occur to you upon reading the act. N.B. I had no share in the consultations upon this act. It is the genuine production of the maiden and spotless Treasury. But I must not laugh; it hurts my bowels.'[4]

Although the Parliamentary opposition failed to challenge this legislation, one further debate on America was initiated by Rigby, who on 3 June moved for an Address asking the King to suspend the prorogation of Parliament until he had 'positive assurances' from the American governors 'that the people are returned to a due sense of their duty and obedience to the laws'.[5] He was seconded by Lord Frederick Campbell and, so he told the Duke of Bedford next day, was 'well supported by most of the ablest people left in town: such as Nugent, Lord North and Dr. Hay, Thurlow and Wedderburn . . . I do assure you I never saw a set of gentlemen receive so thorough a dressing in my life as the ministers did yesterday, nor a set of men defend themselves, their colleagues, or their measures

---

[1] *Grenville Papers*, iii. 234.

[2] *Grenville Papers*, iii. 240.

[3] The act used the words 'Great Britain'. Before it came into force on 1 Jan. 1767, Parliament passed an appropriate amending act, in Dec. 1766. *Commons Journal*, xxxi. 11, 15, 18, 20–2, 27, 46. For American concern see *Franklin Papers*, xiii. 419–21, 486.

[4] *Grenville Papers*, iii. 249.

[5] *Commons Journals*, xxx. 841. For the debate see two letters, Rigby to Bedford, *Bedford Papers*, ii. 336–8; and Conway to George III, *Corr. of George III*, i. 353.

worse than they did'. Rigby did not think it 'proper' to divide the House, but this exposure of the ministry's Parliamentary incompetence was another nail hammered into the coffin of the Rockingham administration.

Copies of the Indemnity Act, Duties Act, and Free Ports Act were enclosed in a circular letter of 13 June from thirty 'Merchants of London trading to America' to merchants in American ports. The letter explained that opposition had meant that the legislation was imperfect and might need amendment, and said that the colonial import of wines, fruit, and oil direct from Spain and Portugal had been postponed for further consideration: but it was made clear that the new legislation did not imply any breach in the old system of economic regulation. The merchants' letter expressed the hope that the colonies would prevent foreign states sharing in their trade, and warned that the prohibition on the export of colonial bar iron to foreign countries would not be removed, as requested by Pennsylvania, because it was thought beneficial to the British iron industry. The merchants suggested that the colonies should avoid any such applications that threatened to prejudice British manufacturing interests, either by supplying rivals with raw materials or by encouraging similar manufactures in the colonies.[1] 'In a word, the system of Great Britain is to promote a mutual interest by supplying the colonies with her manufactures, by encouraging them to raise, and receiving from them all raw materials, and by granting the largest extension to every branch of their trade not interfering with her own.'

These measures completed the colonial legislation of the administration; but any over-all assessment of the Rockinghamite attitude to America must include consideration of other policies intended and contemplated even though action was rendered impossible by the fall of the ministry. These concerned colonial currency, and the twin territorial questions of the Mississippi Valley and Canada.

Alteration to or repeal of the Currency Act was intermittently contemplated by the administration throughout the session. Benjamin Franklin apparently mentioned his scheme for a

---

[1] *London Merchants on the Stamp Act Repeal*, pp. 220–3.

general paper currency for the colonies[1] when he saw Rockingham and Dartmouth in November 1765, and the next month Franklin and Thomas Pownall had a discussion with Rockingham on the subject. Franklin was later to claim, in October 1766, that the prospect of an alternative colonial revenue from this source was one factor in the decision of the Rockingham administration to repeal the Stamp Act:[2] but there is no contemporary evidence to show that this argument influenced ministerial thinking.

The subject of colonial currency had then been pushed into the background by the repeal controversy and the question of colonial trade. During the hearing of evidence by the American Committee of the House of Commons in February 1766, however, Franklin and other witnesses mentioned the scarcity of colonial money in general and the adverse effect of the Currency Act in particular; and soon the first formal complaint came from America. A petition for repeal from the Pennsylvania Assembly was presented to the House of Commons on 20 March, being referred to the American Committee.[3] Although on 24 March information on colonial currency issues since 1749 was also referred to the Committee,[4] the subject obviously never came under consideration. Early in April, however, at the request of John Huske, Franklin drafted a bill to repeal the Currency Act and substitute his own scheme.[5] This bill embodied an important change from the one he and Pownall had submitted to Grenville and discussed with Rockingham in the previous year. It did not offer the British government the revenue from the interest arising from the bills of credit, and so was not open to the objection that it was a disguised method of Parliamentary taxation.[6] On 14 May in the House of Commons Huske moved for leave to introduce this bill, 'with the *seeming* approbation of the ministers', he told Charles Townshend the next year. The motion was opposed by Dyson of the Board of Trade and by Robert Nugent. It was defeated by the evasive device of the previous question,

---

[1] Above, p. 78 n 4.
[2] Ernst, *W.M.Q.* 25 (1968), 184–5; *Franklin Papers*, xiii. 449.
[3] *Commons Journals*, xxx. 676; *Franklin Papers*, xiii. 236.
[4] *Commons Journals*, xxx. 688.
[5] *Franklin Papers*, xiii. 238.
[6] For what appears to be the outline of the bill see *Franklin Papers*, xiii. 204–7.

on the tacit understanding that the subject was only being postponed until the next session.[1] Franklin had expected this outcome, for on 12 April he had warned the Pennsylvania Committee of Correspondence that he doubted 'whether if a bill be brought in, it will be completed this session; the ministry being inclined to consider the affair of paper money more extensively, and therefore to leave it to another year':[2] and in his report to Pennsylvania on 10 June he was confident that the bill would be carried if the Rockingham ministry survived.[3] This was a widespread assumption, for the circular letter of 13 June from the 'Merchants of London trading to America' stated that the currency regulations had been postponed to obtain colonial opinions on the subject.

Confirmation of ministerial goodwill on the currency question was provided by the prompt action taken by the administration to alleviate the monetary situation in New York. On 12 May the Board of Trade read a letter of 28 March from Sir Henry Moore, Governor of New York, on the currency problem in that colony. Two days later the Board considered the question and heard the colony's agent Robert Charles. It thereupon proposed a representation to the Crown suggesting that Moore's instructions be altered accordingly.[4] The Privy Council referred the matter to its Committee for Plantation Affairs, which on 13 June reported a recommendation that Moore should be allowed to consent to an act allowing £260,000 in bills of credit for a period of five years. The Privy Council confirmed a Board of Trade instruction to Moore on the point on 11 July, just before the fall of the ministry.[5]

The govenment of the new territorial acquisitions in North America posed a question to which the Proclamation of 1763 had provided no over-all or permanent solution; and an intended change of policy has sometimes been attributed to the Rockingham ministry, the abandonment to the Indians of the Mississippi Valley. This is because on 10 May 1766 Secretary at War Lord Barrington produced a report suggesting the

[1] *Commons Journals*, xxx. 822. Huske to Townshend, 9 Apr. 1767, printed, Namier and Brooke, *Charles Townshend*, pp. 187–8.
[2] *Franklin Papers*, xiii. 238.
[3] *Franklin Papers*, xiii. 297.
[4] *J.C.T.P. 1764–7*, pp. 279–81.
[5] *Acts P.C. Col.* iv. 754–5.

concentration of army units in East Florida and in Nova Scotia. Only a few soldiers should be left to garrison a handful of forts in the interior, he said, arguing that the existing policy of scattering fifteen battalions over half a continent was expensive and difficult to operate, demoralizing for the soldiers concerned, and quite inadequate to secure the triple objectives of defence against foreign attack, holding down the Indians, and protecting the fur trade. Since Britain now had no competition in this trade, it could be conducted at places appointed on the frontier settlements. Barrington clearly had the Stamp Act Crisis in mind, for he asked whether it was 'proper that this nation should be at so much charge for that purpose, when the Americans contribute nothing', and then made this observation on the future role of the army.[1]

Although the conduct of New England, New York and other provinces, and the temper of their inhabitants give an equitable pretence to keep troops among them, and afford strong reason to apprehend they may be wanted there; yet I see objections to a measure which might unnecessarily provoke. I am persuaded a good corps of troops always in readiness within a few days' sail of those colonies would produce the same effect on their minds as if they were actually on the spot; and probably the insolence of their conduct last year proceeded from a knowledge that it was impossible to assemble such a force as might constrain them to duty and obedience.

The aim of withdrawal of troops from the interior of the American continent, and a consequent reduction in army costs, has been linked with the repeal of the Stamp Act, as being implied by the apparent decision to abandon a colonial revenue.[2] This interpretation is neat and logical, but incorrect. The Rockingham ministry had made no such decision on American taxation, and the policy was that of Barrington alone. As early as October he had questioned the need of maintaining the army posts west of the Proclamation Line;[3] and stated in his report that he had worked out the alternative

---

[1] *Corr. of George III*, i. 432–41. For the background of and comments on Barrington's plan see Marshall, *J.A.S.* 5 (1971), 1–5, 9–11.

[2] Ritcheson, *British Politics and the American Revolution*, pp. 63–4.

[3] Shy, *Towards Lexington*, p. 224.

deployment of the army in America after consultation with
Gage and other officers there.[1] There was no Rockinghamite
policy on the west, for the ministry lacked the time to evolve
one, or even to consider Lord Barrington's report. That task
fell to the next administration.

If the Rockingham ministry devised no policy for the
Mississippi Valley, it was a decision on the related problem of
Canada that precipitated the administration's fall. Ironically,
the crucial part of its Canadian policy was based on a Board
of Trade report already drafted under the Grenville administration. Lord Hillsborough's Board had devoted considerable
attention to the problem of a suitable legal system for Canada,
where an ordinance of 17 September 1764 had established civil
courts.[2] Governor Murray had recommended to the Board that
the French Canadians should be admitted on juries and allowed
judges and lawyers who understood their language; but he
was regarded as unduly pro-Canadian by the small group of
British traders now settled in the colony. They submitted a
petition asking for his removal, a request supported by a
petition from prominent London merchants.[3] The Rockingham
ministry, always sensitive to mercantile pressure, was to
concede that demand in 1766; but on the question of the
French Catholic population of Canada proved as enlightened
as its predecessor. Hillsborough's Board had refused to be
swayed by racial or religious prejudice, and on 7 June 1765
asked Attorney-General Norton and Solicitor-General De Grey
for a report on the legal status of the Catholic inhabitants of
Canada. The opinion of those law officers, submitted on 10
June, was that 'His Majesty's Roman Catholic subjects residing
in the countries ceded to His Majesty in America, by the
definitive Treaty of Paris, are not subject, in those colonies,
to the incapacities, disabilities and penalties, to which Roman
Catholics in this kingdom are subject by the laws thereof'.[4]
This was the last stage in the completion on 12 June of a draft
report on Canadian laws.[5]

---

[1] For Gage's advice see *Gage Corr.* ii. 318–24.

[2] Shortt and Doughty, *Canadian Documents*, pp. 205–10. For further details on
Canadian problems at this time see Marshall, 'Quebec', pp. 50–5.

[3] Shortt and Doughty, *Canadian Documents*, pp. 231–6.

[4] Shortt and Doughty, *Canadian Documents*, p. 236.

[5] *J.C.T.P. 1764–7*, pp. 171, 180–3.

It was this report of Hillsborough's Board that, after consideration and amendment, formed the basis of the report officially signed by Dartmouth's Board on 24 September.[1] Among its recommendations were the adoption of French law in property cases; permission to Catholics to practise law; and the appointment of judges who understood French.[2] The Privy Council referred the matter to the law officers of the Crown in November, but there was a long delay before Attorney-General Charles Yorke drew up his report.[3] This opinion, dated 14 April 1766, confirmed and extended the proposals. It recommended that all criminal law should remain English, but that all property cases should be decided according to the existing French law in the colony: and criticized the absence of French language, lawyers, and jurors in the courts.[4] This report was considered by the Privy Council on 13 May, and forwarded to the Board of Trade for implementation. Yorke and the Board's Secretary John Pownall together drew up detailed instructions for the Governor of Quebec.[5]

The instructions were completed by 24 June and the cabinet met to consider the subject three days later. The other ministers must have anticipated opposition from Northington; for in the previous month he had objected to Yorke's report on the assumption that it was the basis of proposed legislation. 'Should it pass into a law, it would be the most oppressive to the subject that ever was enacted', he wrote to Rockingham on 22 May.[6] Dartmouth had therefore waited upon the Lord Chancellor with all the relevant papers; but Northington had not been won over to support of the proposals. The administration's intention to by-pass Parliament by incorporating the policy in royal instructions to the Governor of Quebec afforded him another ground for objection, and he began the cabinet dis-

---

[1] *J.C.T.P. 1764–7*, pp. 194, 197, 200, 202–3, 205.
[2] Shortt and Doughty, *Canadian Documents*, pp. 237–46.
[3] For his rough draft see B.M. Add. MSS. 35914, fos. 130–40.
[4] For copies of the report see B.M. Add. MSS. 33030, fos. 226–34; and Shortt and Doughty, *Canadian Documents*, pp. 251–7.
[5] Humphreys and Scott, *Can. H.R.* 14 (1933), 42–6: they print the text of the instructions, *ibid.*, pp. 54–61.
[6] *Rockingham Memoirs*, i. 343–4. Northington took a particular interest in Canada, and had in his possession a fifty-page legal memorandum dated 1 Mar. 1766 and headed 'Considerations on the Present State of the Province of Quebec'. B.M. Add. MSS. 35915, fos. 20–46.

cussion by raising the constitutional point as to whether it was legal for the Crown to act in this way. 'It was necessary to bring matters of such weight before Parliament.' Dartmouth replied that the proposed procedure was the practice for all colonies, and the Governor of Quebec had been given such powers by a commission sealed by Lord Chancellor Northington himself! When the detailed instructions were read out Northington made further objections. He doubted whether the Crown could appoint Roman Catholics as magistrates and judges, and declared that the old Canadian laws should have remained in force until altered by Parliament. The Lord Chancellor then disclaimed responsibility for actions of the Grenville ministry of which he had been a member, denouncing the 1763 Proclamation as 'very silly' for promising all new subjects the benefits of English law. He ended by announcing his refusal both to give any opinion on the subject or to attend the cabinet again.[1]

The ministry nevertheless decided to implement the policy while taking account of some of Northington's objections. On 2 July Rockingham saw Charles Yorke privately before a cabinet meeting on the subject; and there was another discussion on 4 July attended by Yorke and Solicitor-General De Grey.[2] The King now intervened: in an account of the political situation sent to Bute on 12 July George III confided that he had already decided to call on Pitt to form a new administration at the first opportunity, having ascertained through Camden that he would now do so. The occasion was provided by Northington's open breach with his cabinet colleagues. On 6 July, by prearrangement, Northington formally advised the King, as his Lord Chancellor, that the administration was too weak to continue.[3] George III then told Rockingham that both Northington and Egmont were of this opinion, and reminded him that the ministers themselves had sought vainly to strengthen the administration. The next day the King sent for Pitt, who returned to London and saw George III on 12 July.[4] The King informed Rockingham

[1] *Rockingham Memoirs*, i. 351–5. This is Richmond's account of the meeting.
[2] *Rockingham Memoirs*, i. 357.
[3] *Bute Letters*, pp. 250–4.
[4] *Corr. of George III*, i. 367–8; *Rockingham Memoirs*, i. 358; *Chatham Papers*, ii. 434–8.

K

of his action on 9 July: and the Marquess, determined to end his ministry on a note of success, told George III

that, by the last accounts from America, the repeal of the Stamp Act had had all the good effect, that could be proposed; had been received with the utmost duty, and gratitude, and that everything was quiet in America and no one mark left of disobedience, or discontent. The King replied he was perfectly satisfied with him.[1]

Despite George III's earlier reluctance to agree to repeal of the Stamp Act, royal disapproval of the Rockingham administration's American policy formed no part of the reason for its fall. It was only in retrospect that George III came to regret the repeal of the Stamp Act.[2]

[1] This is Newcastle's account two days later. Bateson, *Narrative*, p. 79.

[2] On 21 June 1779 the King surveyed his reign at a cabinet meeting summoned for that purpose. 'There was no one action of his life that he could blame himself for, but his changing his ministers in 1765, and consenting to the repeal of the Stamp Act. The ministers he then brought in did not, he said, intend to repeal the act until Lords Chatham and Camden made their declarations and they adopted that fatal measure. Could he have foreseeen the consequences, he certainly would not have passed the act, but it was to the repeal he imputed all the subsequent misfortunes.' This is the account Lord George Germain told William Knox. *H.M.C. Knox*, p. 260.

14

The Chatham Ministry
and America in 1766

G EORGE III had summoned Pitt to form a ministry in
accordance with the constitutional principles he had
proclaimed in a notable oration to the House of Commons
on 24 April.[1] Contemporaries did not know its historic importance, and the speech was badly reported; but something of its
flavour is conveyed in notes made by diarist James Harris.

The government was a free limited monarchy. Wishes for such a
ministry as the King himself should choose, the people approve,
and who should be eminent above others for their ability and in-
tegrity. That the people would grow weary of our divisions . . .
disclaimed all connections of personal bands (I never heard him
succeed better nor with more eloquence).[2]

Pitt's professed purpose was therefore to construct an administration of the best men in disregard of their political allegiance;
and his ministry has often been depicted as a famous experiment in non-party government: but in fact Pitt was to build
a ministry from a coalition of his own followers with the rump
of the Rockingham administration remaining after he had
removed such ministers as Newcastle and Rockingham
himself.[3]

After Pitt had seen the King on 12 July, George III went
through the formal routine of offering the Treasury to Lord
Temple and accepting his anticipated refusal on 17 July. Two
days later Pitt had a conference with Grafton to explain his
plans: in retrospect the chief American interest centres on the
appointment of Charles Townshend. Grafton's friend Lord
Villiers noted in his diary for that day that Pitt 'insists on the

---

[1] *Corr. of George III*, i. 368.
[2] Harris Diary, *sub* 23 Apr. 1766.
[3] The formation of the new ministry is described in Brooke, *Chatham Administration*, pp. 6–19. Additional detail has been obtained from the journal of Grafton's
confidant, Lord Villiers. B.M. Add. MSS. 47584, fos. 49–55. All relevant quotations are from this source, unless otherwise stated.

Duke's being First Lord of the Treasury, and desires him to send to *C. Townshend* to be his *Chancellor of the Exchequer*.[1] The initiative for this fateful choice of Townshend therefore came from Pitt himself and not from Grafton, as the Duke stated in his later memoirs.[2] Townshend was reluctant to exchange his role as Paymaster-General, worth £7,000, for a post involving much drudgery and a salary of only £2,500: and Pitt's handling of the situation both suggests that if he had remained in good health he could have controlled the wayward Townshend and also explains Grafton's mistake of memory: here is the account by Lord Villiers:[3]

July 24 . . . Charles Townshend makes a great difficulty to exchange the Pay Office for Chancellor of the Exchequer, almost to a refusal, and behaves in the most irresolute manner, afraid to refuse Mr. Pitt entirely, who holds a very high language to him, and miserable to think of giving up his old place; but Mr. Pitt had made it a rule that no man should be offered a place twice. Charles therefore goes to him the next day at Hampstead, and before the Duke of Grafton in the most submissive manner begs and entreats that he may be allowed to accept the offer. Mr. Pitt at first treats the thing as over, that other arrangements are formed, but at last consents that the Duke of Grafton and himself shall talk it over again, and in private agrees with the Duke that Charles upon this earnest entreaty may have it, the Duke of Grafton himself being desirous of it.

Grafton afterwards told Pitt that he was willing to retain Dowdeswell at the Exchequer, 'as I plainly perceive that it is for the general good, and very likely for my own private ease of mind'. George III warned Pitt that Townshend had told him 'that Lord Rockingham being quiet would much depend on Mr. Dowdeswell's remaining Chancellor of the Exchequer'. This only spurred Pitt to advise Dowdeswell's immediate dismissal; and he must bear almost sole responsibility for Townshend's appointment.[4]

At their meeting on 19 July Pitt also told Grafton of his plans to replace Richmond by Shelburne as Secretary of State

[1] B.M. Add. MSS. 47584, fo. 50.
[2] *Grafton Autobiography*, p. 92. This was written some forty years later, whereas the journal of Lord Villiers was contemporary.
[3] B.M. Add. MSS. 47584, fo. 51.
[4] *Chatham Papers*, ii. 459–66. *Corr. of George III*, i. 379–81.

for the South,[1] to retain Conway as the other Secretary, and to make Lord Camden Chancellor, with Northington moving to become Lord President of the Council. He must also have made clear to Grafton his intention to take not only the non-executive post of Lord Privy Seal but also a peerage; for he discussed the question of the lead in the Commons. 'Mr. Pitt strong in giving the preference to *Mr. Conway* over Mr. Charles Townshend, as Leaders of the House of Commons and men of weight, saying there were only two fit for that, *Mr. Conway* in one line, *G. Grenville* in the other.'[2] Pitt explained to Grafton that his aim was to keep 'all those who had an inclination to stay', such as Attorney-General Charles Yorke and First Lord of the Admiralty Lord Egmont: and that, although Dowdeswell was to be replaced at the Exchequer by Townshend, he was 'to have a good place'. Despite the dismissal of Rockingham there seemed a good chance that most of his colleagues would stay on in the new administration. After early hesitation Conway agreed to continue as Secretary of State and Leader of the House; and when Lord Villiers visited Newcastle's house on 20 July he found 'a large company composed almost entirely of the present late Ministers. The Duke of Newcastle talks to most of them in private expecting them not to be ready to join this new plan, but he finds them almost all without a doubt to support it.'

This mood was not to last, as Pitt's complete disregard for the susceptibilities of the former ministers became all too obvious. Lord Villiers noted the omen on 25 July: 'Lord Rockingham's party begin to be more angry complaining of disregard and want of attention in Mr. Pitt, from his not communicating with Lord Rockingham, and seem to threaten resignation.' When Pitt called at Rockingham's house on 27 July the Marquess refused to see him. Charles Yorke resigned the next day, incensed by Camden's forthcoming appointment as Lord Chancellor, which was a breach of the King's promise

---

[1] Shelburne appointed as his American Assistant Under-Secretary of State his own private secretary Maurice Morgann, a man unsympathetic to colonial claims. Wickwire, *British Subministers and Colonial America*, pp. 93-7.

[2] B.M. Add. MSS. 47584, fo. 51. But the great Irish Parliamentarian Henry Flood, after hearing the debate of 25 Nov. 1766 in which nearly all the leading members of the Commons took part, noted that there was 'no one person near Townshend. He is the orator; the rest are speakers'. *Chatham Papers*, iii. 144n.

to him the previous year. Pitt was not the man to be deterred by such setbacks. He had, indeed, temporarily abandoned his intention of taking a peerage, until he saw 'how the House of Commons goes on': but when his aim became public knowledge he realized that any postponement 'would look as if he mistrusted General Conway in the House of Commons', and told George III so on 28 July. Rockingham, Newcastle, Winchelsea, Richmond, and Dowdeswell were formally dismissed on 29 July, and the next day Pitt became Lord Privy Seal and Earl of Chatham, while Grafton, Townshend, and Camden accepted office. Dartmouth marred the occasion by resigning as President of the Board of Trade, and Dowdeswell later refused to accept either this post or half the Pay Office. By 3 August Lord Villiers thought that Pitt's attempted takeover of the previous ministry had been largely a failure. 'It seems to be the plan of those in the late administration who disapproved of this change, to remain in their places unless turned out, but not to accept others or to give any assurances of support.' The main Rockingham group adopted this passive role; and a further blow to the new administration came with the resignation on 13 August of Lord Egmont, who objected to Chatham's dictatorial behaviour in cabinet and was critical of his proposed foreign policy. Lord Villiers echoed Grafton's opinion in his diary note for that day. 'Upon this resignation at the Admiralty Board, and the backwardness in other parts of administration to give their cordial support, it becomes necessary for the ministry to call in a new set of men, not as a party, but also to enlarge the foundation. What this set should be is under consideration.' It could only be the Bedford group. Grafton obtained Chatham's approval for an approach to Bedford through his son Lord Tavistock, but the negotiation was abortive. Bedford declined to act as political broker, pointedly reminding Grafton of their difference on American policy. 'It cant be unknown to you how much the measures pursued in the last session of Parliament by the late, as well as the present, administration were opposed in the totality by myself and my friends.'[1] The only offer made was that of the Admiralty to Lord Gower, who refused to be 'the only man of his party to take so responsible a part'. The Admiralty was

---

[1] *Bedford Papers*, iii. 343–4.

finally given to an admiral, Rockinghamite Sir Charles Saunders, promoted from a junior place at the Board; and the cabinet was completed by the new Commander-in-Chief of the army, Pittite Lord Granby. It did not include Chancellor of the Exchequer Townshend, though he was to make good his claim to a place in the autumn; nor the new President of the Board of Trade, Lord Hillsborough, whose return to that office marked an important and deliberate change in the form of colonial administration.[1]

Pitt's previous experience as Secretary of State for the South had made him aware of the unsatisfactory administrative situation concerning the colonies, with information and policy-making being divided among several departments. Two courses of action were possible. One was the creation of a third Secretary of State, for the colonies; such an office would give its holder a seat in the cabinet, direct access to the sovereign, and the means to acquire comprehensive information about the colonies. During the formation of his ministry Pitt at first contemplated becoming Secretary for such an American Department himself:[2] but he soon changed his mind, and, refusing to allow anyone else to take such a post, was to adopt the alternative policy of the reduction of the Board of Trade to the inferior status it held before 1752: it would lose the right to make representations to the Privy Council and so in practice formulate a great deal of colonial policy.

Other politicians had also long seen the need for some change. Hillsborough, when President of the Board of Trade in the Grenville administration, was intending to insist on some alteration of status just before the dismissal of that ministry.[3] He may well have been thinking then of a more important role for the Board, because in September 1765 he urged his successor Dartmouth to insist on the same powers concerning trade and the colonies as the First Lords of the Treasury and Admiralty enjoyed in their respective departments.[4] During the ministerial crisis of May 1766 the elevation of either

[1] For a fuller account of what follows see Basye, *Board of Trade*, pp. 149–59.
[2] For a draft plan in his writing of a ministry incorporating this idea, printed and dated by C. R. Ritcheson as being in mid-July 1766, see *A.H.R.* 57 (1951–2), 376–83.
[3] *Grenville Papers*, iii. 294.
[4] *H.M.C. Dartmouth*, iii. 179.

Charles Townshend or Dartmouth to a third Secretaryship
of State had been widely and frequently canvassed. Dartmouth
himself wanted 'dignity and credit, as well as effectual authority'.[1] In the end no alteration of status was made. Dartmouth was dissatisfied,[2] and on the change of ministry refused
to remain in the same situation. Grafton warned Pitt on 15
July that Rockingham had told him 'that if Lord Dartmouth is
not made a third Secretary of State, he will retire'.[3] Pitt,
having already decided not to make such a change, therefore
unsuccessfully offered the Presidency of the Board of Trade to
James Grenville even before Dartmouth resigned on 30 July
after Pitt's formal refusal to make him Secretary of State for
America.[4] Lord Villers noted in his diary that 'Mr. Pitt's plan
is to lower that Board'.[5] He intended to reduce it to 'a mere
board of report upon reference to it for advice and information'.[6]
Shelburne, as Secretary of State for the South, would therefore
control colonial administration and patronage. After Dowdeswell had refused the office, Hillsborough accepted his former
post despite its now inferior status, explaining his apparently
inexplicable decision to Grenville on 6 August.

I turned it in my mind: not whether I should come to the Board as
it was constituted when you was minister, for I knew I could not
carry on the business in that manner; nor whether I should propose,
what is certainly most desirable for the public, that it should be
made an independent department on an extensive plan, for I knew
the disposition of some too well, to suppose that could be complied
with, by parting with any power or patronage; but whether I could
not contract the plan so that I might do the business in an easy
manner to myself, and free from that very unpleasant, and in some
manner, unbecoming attendance upon others, which is the consequence of unexplained connections of departments in business,
and always disagreeable to that which is considered the inferior
position.

[1] *H.M.C. Dartmouth*, iii. 182.
[2] B.M. Add. MSS. 32976, fo. 13.
[3] *Chatham Papers*, ii. 463.
[4] *Chatham Papers*, ii. 467. Massachusetts agent De Berdt informed William Smith
of New York on 5 Aug., 'Lord D. insists on such a scheme for America as will be
greatly to their advantage but Mr. Pitt objects to it, and he has the modelling
of the new ministry'. *De Berdt Letters*, p. 324.
[5] B.M. Add. MSS. 47584, fo. 53.
[6] Fitzmaurice, *Shelburne*, i. 284–5.

Hillsborough may have taken the initiative in suggesting this change as the solution to the problem of the Board of Trade, for he told Grenville so:

I resolved to accept, provided the Board should be altered from a Board of Representation to a Board of Report upon Reference only; that the order to the governors in America to correspond with the Board of Trade *only*, should be rescinded, and that every executive business that has by degrees crept into the Board should revert to the proper offices, particularly all Treasury business, and that I should not be of the Cabinet (which was also offered to me).[1]

This change was formally effected on 8 August. The Privy Council then directed the Board to instruct colonial governors in future to communicate with the Secretary of State; the Board itself was to receive duplicates of this correspondence, except in secret matters. The appropriate instructions were approved by the Council on 10 September, and by 23 October William Sharpe, as Clerk of the Council, had devised procedures to meet the new situation.[2]

The change was not a success. Hillsborough resigned in December, to become a Joint Postmaster-General, and was succeeded by Robert Nugent, created an Irish peer as Lord Clare the next month. Hillsborough had found the new arrangement even more unsatisfactory than the old one: on 14 December Lord Barrington told the British envoy in Berlin, Sir Andrew Mitchell, 'our friend Lord Hillsborough has left an office he did not like. It had the appearance and confinement of business without the reality or usefulness of it. He is laid up in lavender at the Post Office till he shall be wanted elsewhere.'[3] Hillsborough was not to wait long for congenial employment. In the ministerial reshuffle consequent on the accession of the Bedfords to the ministry in December 1767 the office of Secretary of State for the South was divided into two. Hillsborough became the first Secretary of State for America in January 1768.[4]

---

[1] *Grenville Papers*, iii. 293–4. Lord Villiers confirms that the inferior status of the Board was 'quite by Ld. Hillsborough's choice, nay he even wished it lower'. B.M. Add. MSS. 47584, fo. 54.

[2] *Acts P.C. Col.* v. 3–4; vi. 437–8.   [3] *Chatham Papers*, iii. 139.

[4] Brooke, *Chatham Administration*, pp. 327–32. Basye, *Board of Trade*, pp. 160–9. Lyttelton told Temple that Chatham was 'very angry at the creation of that new office, which he had always opposed'. *Grenville Papers*, iv. 250.

K*

The new administration in 1766 was confronted by the hostility of George Grenville. The Bedford party was in opposition, but open to offers. If the weight of the Rockingham party was also thrown into the opposition scale, the ministry might well fail to obtain majorities in the two Houses of Parliament, where it was even weaker than its predecessor. Nor, despite Rockinghamite suspicions, would it enjoy support from Lord Bute: as he finally withdrew from politics some of his followers merged into the court party, but others went various ways. By the end of the year the danger of a formidable Parliamentary opposition had materialized. Another ministerial negotiation with the Bedford group in October proved abortive. The next month the dismissal of Rockinghamite Lord Edgcumbe from his post as Treasurer of the Household in a minor reshuffle led to an open break with the main Rockingham party. Seven of their number still in office resigned, including Sir Charles Saunders from the Admiralty; and November also saw the faction voting in Parliamentary opposition. Grenville and Rockingham were soon to be joined by Bedford, after Chatham in a third negotiation had again failed to offer enough to win over his group: the Admiralty, the only vacant cabinet post, was not even tendered to Gower again, but instead bestowed on another admiral, Sir Edward Hawke. By the end of the year the Grenville, Rockingham, and Bedford parties were all in opposition.[1]

How far these factions would act together remained a matter of doubt. Newcastle noted on 18 December that Rockingham's decision was to go into 'general opposition . . . upon such points only, as were wrong in themselves and not inconsistent with our former behaviour, in the last opposition'. Rockingham himself had already made it clear to Lord Lyttelton that the American question precluded a working alliance with Grenville, since 'our whole conduct had been to show the impropriety of Mr. Grenville's measures; and, that the last administration had acted upon a direct contrary principle: and had endeavoured to overturn all that he had done, and had succeeded in it; and, by that, had given great satisfaction, and obtained the approbation of the nation'.[2] The opposition factions

[1] For the above see Brooke, *Chatham Administration*, pp. 20–67.
[2] B.M. Add. MSS. 32978, fos. 398–403.

nevertheless found co-operation less difficult than might have been expected, for America was not the main political issue. The foremost problem of the time was the crisis in the affairs of the East India Company. The state of the national finances, indeed, linked this subject with the American question. India represented an alternative source of revenue, and Chatham did not lack those who advised him to plunder the Company: already in October 1766 William Beckford warned him that 'unless you can procure a revenue of a million per annum without new taxations and oppressions on the people, there can be no salvation arise to Israel. We must look to the East and not to the West.'[1] For much of the Parliamentary session what seemed a Chathamite attack on the Company's property and chartered rights roused the three opposition groups to united hostility, and political self-interest widened this co-operation to other fields.

On America, however, an opposition alliance proved more difficult to construct than the faction leaders might have anticipated from the events of the Stamp Act Crisis, and especially the debates on the Declaratory Act. There was not the expected clear line of battle between an opposition that championed Britain's full sovereignty over the colonies and a ministry that qualified and failed to assert it: for although the politicians who had opposed the Declaratory Act were now in office, they fully accepted all the implications of that measure. The Chatham administration was to witness a sustained attempt to assert the supremacy of Crown and Parliament over the colonies, and a renewed attempt at American taxation. These policies were not inconsistent with Pitt's speeches on America during the previous session. He had then repeatedly declared that he would support sterner measures if conciliation failed to produce submission and quiet in the colonies; and just such a situation of unrest and defiance still prevailed in parts of America during his ministry. Similarly Pitt had condemned only 'internal' taxation by Parliament: and the tax measures devised by Townshend were in accordance with Pitt's doctrine as well as what was thought to be the American attitude.

Pitt's qualifications to his advocacy of conciliation had passed almost unnoticed during the excitement over the battle for

[1] P.R.O. 30/8/19, fo. 91.

repeal, though not by Grenville; and friends of America did not expect the change of administration to produce any alteration of policy. A typical reaction was that of Benjamin Franklin. 'We have the satisfaction to find, that, none of those whom we looked upon as adversaries of America in the late struggles, are come to power; and that tho' some of our friends are gone out, other friends are come in or promoted, as Mr. Pitt, Lord Shelburne, Lord Camden, etc.'[1] More cautious was the comment by Massachusetts agent De Berdt. 'We have lost several good friends by the change', he warned his Assembly Speaker Thomas Cushing on 2 September, when he evidently regarded Charles Townshend as one of the friends remaining.[2]

That a change of American policy from the conciliation of the previous year took place under the new ministry is a development frequently overlooked by historians dazzled by Chatham's reputation as a 'friend' of America, and therefore inclined to regard Townshend's policies as untypical of the administration's attitude to the colonies. Detailed investigation makes this traditional interpretation untenable. The Chatham cabinet was to be unanimous about the need to coerce New York into submission to the Mutiny Act, the chief issue of colonial policy during the first year of the ministry; while Townshend's taxation of the colonies was a measure endorsed by most of his cabinet colleagues, and not the solitary action of a headstrong individual.[3]

Chatham expressed his determination to assert Britain's authority over America soon after he came to power, and before news arrived of further colonial challenges to it. The occasion was the negotiation with the Bedford party during the autumn. When Lord Northington sounded the Duke on 19 October about joining the administration, he mentioned that 'to act with vigour to support the superiority of Great Britain over the colonies' formed part of Chatham's policy; and Bedford recorded that Chatham himself told him on 24 October 'that measures for the proper subordination of America must be taken'.[4] These remarks to Bedford were more than mere verbal assurances to win over a potential ally. They portended

---

[1] *Franklin Papers*, xiii. 384.   [2] *De Berdt Letters*, p. 325.
[3] For a revisionist approach see Chaffin, *W.M.Q.* 27 (1970), 90–121.
[4] *Bedford Journal*, pp. 591–2.

a change of attitude. Edmund Burke later recalled that by November

I was satisfied that a return to the principles of the Stamp Act was intended, the language of all those who adhered to Lord Chatham was totally changed. Lord Chatham indeed told Lord Rockingham that he could not resist the arguments which the King urged drawn from the Declaratory Act. Lord R. answered that he who made that act had been able to resist those arguments.[1]

This might appear hindsight by a man who disliked Chatham: but Burke at the time noticed the omen that the M.P. chosen by the ministry to move the Address on 11 November, Augustus Hervey, took the opportunity to 'abuse the repeal of the Stamp Act' even though there was no mention of America in the King's Speech.[2]

Already the Chatham administration had inherited from the Rockingham ministry what was to prove its foremost problem, the resistance in New York to the Mutiny Act.[3] On 5 February 1766 Conway received from General Gage a letter describing the first evasion by that colony's Assembly of his request for provisions, and this reminder arrived on 18 March. 'You have been informed, Sir, that the Assembly of this province would make no provision, to defray the expense of quartering His Majesty's troops, in conformity to the Mutiny Act for America.'[4] The Rockingham ministry took no action, perhaps because Governor Moore had adjourned the colony's Assembly until June. In May Gage again asked New York for supplies, informing Conway of his intention and commenting on the deficiencies of the Mutiny Act itself: the penalty of £5 on magistrates for not quartering troops was quite inadequate, and the whole measure depended 'too much upon the temper and whim of an Assembly'.[5] This time the Assembly yielded some ground, as Governor Moore reported in a letter of 20 June.

Tho' they did not choose to show that obedience which was due to an Act of Parliament, they were afraid of the consequences of refusing to comply with it. They have now ordered a bill for providing barracks, firewood, candles, bedding and utensils, but the

---

[1] *Burke Corr.* i. 280n.   [2] *Burke Corr.* i. 279–80. *Commons Journals*, xxxi. 3–5.
[3] For a detailed account see Gipson, *British Empire*, xi. 45–54.
[4] *Gage Corr.* i. 76–8, 84–5. See *ibid.* ii. 328–30, for Gage's report to Barrington.
[5] *Gage Corr.* i. 89.

articles of salt, vinegar and cyder or beer are omitted, because not provided in Europe for troops in barracks. I hope I shall be excused for passing this bill, as the General is satisfied nothing more can be expected at present, and the example of this province in making the provision required will have a greater influence on other colonies than any other motive whatsoever.

Moore enclosed the resolutions passed by the Assembly the previous day. These declared that the total number of troops for which provision might have to be made was unknown; that each soldier cost 3*d.* a day; and that the colony would pay a proportionate share of the total American expense. Accordingly, supplies for two battalions and one company of artillery were voted for one year. New York undoubtedly had a practical grievance, being the main port for military arrivals and departures: but the Assembly's refusal to carry out the full provisions of the Mutiny Act was a defiance of Parliament to which Moore drew attention in his letter. 'I state mere facts, that you may see the deference here paid to Acts of Parliament, and what may be our expectations upon future occasions. My opinion is that every Act of Parliament when not backed by a sufficient power to enforce it, will meet with the same fate.'[1]

This letter arrived on 25 July,[2] in time for Shelburne to read it when on taking up his appointment as Secretary of State he examined the state of current business in his department. He concluded from the news, despite Moore's comments, that the defiance of New York was a small and passing cloud on the colonial horizon. Here is his report to Chatham of outstanding colonial problems.[3]

The instructions to the Governor of Quebec have never yet been made out. Some doubts about the part that regards religion, and some about the mode of civil government remain . . . At New York they have made difficulties about quarters, but it appears to me by the letters that its only the remains of the storm, and wants a little good humour and firmness to finish.

---

[1] T. 1/446, fos. 175–6.
[2] *Commons Journals*, xxxi. 232.
[3] P.R.O. 30/8/56, fos. 60–1. This letter has later been docketed '20 Sept', and that date has been generally accepted: but internal evidence shows that it was certainly written between 30 July (Chatham's peerage) and 13 Aug. (Egmont's resignation), and probably on 3 Aug.

The cabinet on 5 August decided that Shelburne should write to Governor Moore,

acquainting him, that as it is the indispensable duty of His Majesty's subjects in America to obey the acts of the legislature of Great Britain, His Majesty expects and requires all due obedience to the same. And it cannot be doubted that the province of New York after the lenity of Great Britain so recently extended to North America will not fail duly to carry into execution the Act of Parliament passed last sessions for quartering His Majesty's troops.[1]

Shelburne wrote the letter on 9 August, incorporating this last sentence with the additional phrase, 'in the full extent and meaning of the act without reference to the usage in other parts of His Majesty's dominions'.[2]

For the remainder of the year the administration heard nothing of further American defiance, and devoted some attention to long-term colonial problems. In a confidential letter to General Gage on 11 December, Shelburne told the Commander-in-Chief what the ministry had under consideration.[3]

1st. A proper system for the management of the Indians, and for carrying on the commerce with them, on the most advantageous footing.

2nd. The most eligible manner of disposing of the troops; as well for convenience as for offence and defence.

3rd. A reduction of the contingent expenses of the establishment in North America and the raising an American Fund to defray American expenses in part or in the whole.

The Secretary of State, after asking Gage for advice and information on these matters, expanded on them. He was critical of the existing system of two Indian Superintendents, doubting 'whether any method of managing Indians can be found preferable to that of leaving the trade of each province to the particular care of that province, under some general rules and restrictions to which all the provinces must be subject

---

[1] Cabinet minute. P.R.O. 30/8/97, fo. 79.

[2] T. 1/446, fo. 176.

[3] Shelburne MSS., vol. 53, pp. 357–69; printed, from the original, in *Gage Corr.* ii. 47–51.

in general'. He was particularly severe on the management of the southern Indians by Superintendent John Stuart, as being apparently based on a strategy of fomenting wars and quarrels between Indian nations. On future plans Shelburne threw out a hint of new inland colonies: several suggestions had been made for a settlement in the Illinois country, he said, but any decision on such matters must form part of a general policy for America. The second matter of the disposition of the army was the one that concerned Gage directly. Shelburne told him that Lord Barrington had drawn up a plan, which the cabinet would consider: but it was probable that Gage's views would play a major part in any decision. As an interim measure Shelburne asked that as many soldiers as possible should be placed in the new colonies, to reduce the burden on the others.

The third subject of 'an American Fund' Shelburne deemed 'of the greatest consequence'. The Chatham ministry's quest for an American revenue had begun almost at once, and from the same motive as that of the two previous administrations, the heavy burden of maintaining an army in the colonies. The actual cost of the American army was over £400,000 a year, about double the original estimate which had first given rise to colonial taxation.[1] In October Shelburne told Benjamin Franklin of the ministry's concern at the high level of colonial expenditure, 'the Treasury being alarmed and astonished at the growing charges there, and the heavy accounts and drafts continually brought in from thence', particularly the costs being incurred by the army and the Indian Superintendents.[2] The Treasury Board's search for a new and less provocative method of raising money for this purpose commenced on 23 September with a request to the Auditor of Plantations for 'a state of the quit-rents of the several provinces in North America with an account of the monies actually received thereupon'.[3] Quit-rents were paid annually for certain lands granted for settlement in North America, and the Treasury obviously hoped for an income both from lands already granted and from new grants in areas as yet unsettled. Within a month official expectations of a substantial revenue from this source

---

[1] Shy, *Towards Lexington*, pp. 240–1.
[2] *Franklin Papers*, xiii. 447.
[3] T. 29/38, p. 126.

were widely known, for Whately informed Grenville of the project on 20 October.[1]

> A wild project is talked of for paying off the Civil List debt, and providing an American revenue, both together. It is only supposing that the quit-rents in the colonies, if properly collected, will be sufficient to support the military establishment there, and then the Crown may sell them to the public for four or five hundred thousand pounds. As extravagant as this may seem to you, the Auditor of the Plantations is directed to make out accounts and calculations which lead to such a proposition.

A week after instigating the inquiry into quit-rents the Treasury Board took another step concerning colonial finance, the purpose of which is less clear. On 30 September the Board's Secretary Charles Lowndes sent circular letters to all colonial governors requesting accounts of each colony's income and expenditure, including details of every salary and local tax.[2] This might have been a precursor to Charles Townshend's final scheme of paying the costs of civil government in America from taxation levied by Parliament; but there is no other evidence that Townshend had this idea in mind at the time. The aim may have been to devise new taxes that would not conflict with existing ones;[3] for the inquiry would reveal the internal tax burdens on the colonies, the weight of which had been an argument against Parliamentary taxation. Certainly wrong, however, was the optimistic assumption of Governor Bernard that the intention was to increase the quite inadequate salaries paid to governors and other officials![4]

The continued interest of the Chatham administration in colonial finance was shown by a circular letter sent on 11 December by Secretary of State Shelburne to 'all the Governors on the continent of America'. It asked for 'an exact estimate of the annual charge of maintaining and supporting the entire establishment of his Majesty's colony of——, distinguishing the different funds and the different services to which those funds are appropriated'. This request duplicated the Treasury circular of 30 September; but Shelburne also asked for 'a full and clear account of the manner of imposing quit-rents

[1] *Grenville Papers*, iii. 334–5.   [2] T. 28/1, fo. 56.
[3] Chaffin, *W.M.Q.* 27 (1970), 92, makes this assumption.
[4] *Barrington–Bernard Corr.*, pp. 122–3.

and of levying them as also the mode of granting lands in your colony'.[1] The intention behind this last inquiry was explained by Shelburne in his letter to Gage the same day.[2]

The forming an American Fund, to support the exigencies of government in the same manner as is done in Ireland, is what is so highly reasonable that it must take place sooner or later. The most obvious manner of laying the foundation for such a fund, seems to be by taking proper care of the quit-rents, and by turning the grants of land to real benefit, and which might tend to increase rather than diminish the power of government in so distant a country.

The 'American Fund' envisaged was intended to finance only the cost of the army in America, and not that of the civil government there.[3] Shelburne, indeed, then discussed possible economies in military expenditure, and asked Gage for information on the subject. That Chatham's ministry, like those of Grenville and Rockingham, was also thinking of the revenue from customs duties is suggested by Shelburne's final comment on finance: 'The suppression of smuggling in North America and the Islands, has a very natural reference to this article, as it in a most essential manner regards the well-being of commerce in general, and the finances of this country in particular.'

Little was to be achieved towards the solution of these problems in 1767. This was partly because deadlock developed between Charles Townshend's plans for financial economies and Shelburne's schemes for development of the west: but also because these interrelated problems of Indian relations, army locations, and military costs did not have a high priority with either administration or Parliament. The whole question of America was the subject in 1767 of only a few cabinet meetings and Parliamentary debates: and most of this attention was concerned not with the solution of the long-term problems outlined by Shelburne to Gage but with further colonial defiance of Britain. The public debate on this was conducted

[1] C.O. 5/112, fo. 1.

[2] Shelburne MSS., vol. 53, pp. 363–6.

[3] Chaffin, *W.M.Q.* 27 (1970), 97, makes the contrary assumption. But Shelburne's later references to 'an American Fund' can also only be read in such a military context: and not until May 1767 did Townshend obtain cabinet consent to his plan of financing colonial civil lists from colonial taxation. Below, pp. 354–5.

in an atmosphere of consensus that afforded a remarkable contrast to the bitter arguments of the Stamp Act Crisis. Little controversy now arose, because of the lack of any sustained defence of American opinion and behaviour. Even men like Chatham, Shelburne, and Beckford were to be annoyed and dismayed by the fresh news from the colonies: indeed, the new colonial challenge to the authority of Britain centred on military defence and trade regulation, matters regarded by Chatham as cornerstones of imperial policy and dear to his heart. Decisions and debates on America were concerned with the nature, extent, and timing of punitive and coercive measures, not with the principle of the assertion of British authority. The administration was as intent on that as the opposition.

Chatham himself was to play little part in the formulation of policy. Until his return to London in March 1767 he remained at Bath for reasons of ill health, and both before and afterwards proved increasingly unwilling to offer guidance on the American problems reported to him by Grafton and Shelburne. The decision of policy fell into other hands; but it would be a mistake to regard this circumstance as an exoneration of Chatham from responsibility for the American measures of his administration. Horace Walpole suspected that that was his aim: indeed, Walpole believed that Chatham, anxious to preserve his reputation as a 'friend' of America, not only wished to avoid personal involvement in measures that would prove unpopular in the colonies but might even have instigated Beckford into attacking them.[1] Another unflattering contemporary interpretation was that Chatham simply wanted to avoid taking difficult decisions. Lord Harcourt forecast as early as September 1766 that Chatham would take refuge in 'bad health' from this motive.[2] Certainly Chatham was guilty of the sin of omission, failing to give sufficient guidance: his cabinet colleagues would never have dared to act contrary to what was believed to be his opinion, and followed obsequiously any hints he threw out. What policies Chatham himself would have pursued must remain a matter of speculation: his comments and papers suggest coercion of New York, but accompanied by a new Declaratory Act; and there is no evidence at all of his contemporary views on Townshend's taxation.

[1] H. Walpole, *Memoirs*, iii. 26.   [2] *Jenkinson Papers*, pp. 433–4.

Iɴ January 1767 the first discouraging news came from America, a singularly ill-timed petition signed by 240 New York merchants. This lengthy document complained of the restrictions imposed on colonial trade by the Duties Acts of 1764 and 1766, and asked for a great many concessions: they included complete freedom to export lumber and provisions; the replacement of the 5s. a cwt duty on foreign sugar by a more moderate duty; permission to export sugar directly to foreign countries without the need to land it first in Britain; and abolition of the clause in the 1766 Duties Act designating all sugar exported from North America as foreign and therefore subject to duty. The petition contained many other complaints and suggestions about matters ranging from the Vice-Admiralty Courts to the unsatisfactory operation of the Free Ports system. The over-all impression it conveyed was of an attack on the traditional mercantilist system of imperial trade.[1]

The petition had been instigated by the same William Kelly who had given evidence before the House of Commons in 1766. He claimed to have the approval of Charles Townshend for providing the administration with information in this way, and sent a private copy of the petition to the Chancellor of the Exchequer.[2] The official copy, addressed to the House of Commons, was presented to Governor Moore on 28 November 1766, and forwarded by him on 10 December to the Board of Trade.[3] The Board considered the petition on 29 January, deciding to send it to Secretary of State Shelburne.[4] He in turn reported the matter to the absent Chatham in a letter of 1 February which described discussions he had had about the petition with

---

[1] For copies of the petition see P.R.O. 30/8/97, fos. 87–90; C.O. 5/1137, fos. 8–10; *Commons Journals*, xxxi. 158–60; and Almon, *Debates*, vii. 315–22.

[2] Gipson, *British Empire*, xi. 55n. For evidence suggesting that Kelly had met Townshend when in Britain the previous year see Charles Townshend Letters, pp. 149–51, 175.

[3] P.R.O. 30/8/97, fos. 95–6.   [4] *J.C.T.P. 1764–7*, pp. 360–1.

London merchants trading to America. He had told them 'that it was well known some of those who opposed the Stamp Act opposed it upon very extensive principles, with regard to American trade, upon a supposition that the advantages of it must finally centre with the mother country'. This was a reminder of Chatham's own ground for attacking the principle of direct taxation of the colonies, ground now itself challenged by the petition. Shelburne said he had left the merchants

to judge how very imprudent the present moment was chosen, when, on the one hand, they saw how far the prejudices about the Stamp Act still prevailed, and on the other, an assembly imprudent enough to hesitate about obeying an act of parliament in its full extent, after the tenderness which had been shown America; not to mention their manner of sending it over. The merchants and the Americans here seem sensible of its being the height of imprudence, and are sorry.

Shelburne's chief concern, however, was not the dismay of the colonists' friends but the advantage afforded by the petition to their critics. 'It has occasioned a number of reports and is likely, in the talk of the town, to undergo the imputation of rebellion, and will probably be mentioned as such by Mr. Grenville in the House of Commons without seeing it.'[1] Chatham's reply from Bath two days later was vague and unhelpful, but reflected his changing attitude to the colonies.[2]

America affords a gloomy prospect. A spirit of infatuation has taken possession of New York: their disobedience to the Mutiny Act will *justly* create a great ferment here, open a fair field to the arraigners of America, and leave no room to any to say a word in their defence. I foresee confusion will ensue. The petition of the merchants of New York is highly improper; in point of time, most absurd; in the extent of their pretensions, most excessive; and in the reasoning, most grossly fallacious and offensive. What demon of discord blows the coals in that devoted province I know not; but they are doing the work of their worst enemies themselves. The torrent of indignation in Parliament will, I apprehend, become irresistible, and they will draw upon their heads national resentment by their ingratitude, and ruin, I fear, upon the whole state, by the consequences. But I will not run before the event, as it is possible your Lordship may receive an account more favourable.

[1] *Chatham Papers*, iii. 186–7.   [2] *Chatham Papers*, iii. 188–9.

This faint hope was killed on 4 February, when news came from America not only that both New York and New Jersey had defied the Mutiny Act but also that the Massachusetts Assembly had incorporated an indemnity into their compensation act.[1] In New York Governor Moore had forwarded Shelburne's letter of 9 August to the Assembly on 17 November in a message anticipating that 'no difficulties can possibly arise, or the least objection be made to the provision for the troops as required by the Act of Parliament'.[2] He must have known that this was mere form. When Moore wrote on 19 December to report the Assembly's refusal to vote any military supplies at all he told Shelburne that 'it never was a question whether they comply or not, but that the whole of their deliberations related only to the form in which their refusal should appear. . . . The House were unanimous in this opinion.'[3] He enclosed a copy of the Address of 15 December in which the Assembly declined to make any contribution: this pointed out that by providing for two battalions and one company the colony had undertaken 'a burden much greater than any of the neighbouring governments'.[4]

Together with this not unexpected news from New York had come an account from Governor Franklin of New Jersey of defiance of the Mutiny Act in his colony. In a letter of 18 December he reported to Shelburne that the Assembly there had not complied with the act but had merely voted 'firewood, bedding, blankets and such other necessaries as have been heretofore usually furnished'. He had accepted this measure, without complaint from the army; but drew attention to the Assembly's declaration that 'they looked upon the Act of Parliament for quartering soldiers in America, to be virtually as much an act for laying taxes on the inhabitants as the Stamp Act, and that it was more partial, as the troops were kept in a few of the colonies whereby others were exempted from contributing anything towards the expense'.[5]

Meanwhile, apparently before the arrival of this further American news, Shelburne had raised the question of the

---

[1] On this last point see above, p. 252.
[2] P.R.O. 30/8/97, fos. 85–6.   [3] Ibid., fo. 103.
[4] Ibid., fos. 104–5. For another copy see T.1/446, fos. 176–7.
[5] P.R.O. 30/8/97, fo. 97.

New York merchants' petition at a cabinet meeting on 4 February, and he sent this report to Chatham in a letter of 6 February. 'No decided opinion was come to, on account of your Lordship's absence; but it seemed the opinion of every lord present, that it deserved no notice except Mr. Grenville moved for it.' Shelburne also enclosed copies of the American papers that had arrived on 4 February, and made this commentary on the colonial situation:[1]

The merchants here unanimously disavow the New York petition, and say that a Mr. Kelly has been the demon who has kindled this fire and who is the sole author of it. Their letters, however, confirm Sir Henry Moore's account of the disposition of the people in regard to the Mutiny Act, and explain it to be owing to their jealousy of being some time or other taxed internally by the Parliament of Great Britain. The same reasoning has prevailed, your Lordship sees, in New Jersey.

Shelburne realized that the administration could not overlook the usurpation by the Massachusetts Assembly of the royal prerogative of pardon any more than the defiance of the Mutiny Act elsewhere; and he told Chatham that Grenville intended to raise the matter in the House of Commons. An official report from Governor Bernard came on 9 February. Bernard was uneasy at having passed the bill, saying he had done so in accordance with instructions from Conway and Shelburne; and he warned that there was in Massachusetts a determined effort to reduce the governor 'to the standard of a Rhode Island governor'.[2]

Shelburne made no suggestion to Chatham on 6 February about Massachusetts, but he had considered the problems arising from the Mutiny Act, and offered this tentative advice to Chatham:

As to that which regards the existence of government, after a great deal of painful consideration on so disagreeable a subject, I have nothing to submit to your Lordship, except what I took the liberty to say to the King this morning; namely that I had hoped both he and Parliament would distinguish between *New York* and *America*.[3]

Chatham's reply next day was again one of despair.

[1] *Chatham Papers*, iii. 191–3.   [2] P.R.O. 30/8/97, fos. 92–3.
[3] *Chatham Papers*, iii. 192.

The advices from America offer unpleasing views. New York has drunk the deepest of the baneful cup of infatuation, but none seem to be quite sober and in full possession of reason. It is a literal truth to say that the Stamp Act, of most unhappy memory, has frightened those irritable and unbrageous people quite out of their senses.[1] I foresee that, determined not to listen to their real friends, a little more frenzy and a little more time will put them into the hands of their enemies.

This time, however, Chatham did offer advice, on the simplest of the colonial problems. 'As to the New York Petition, I am clearly of opinion that it ought to be laid before the House, and not to be smothered in the hands of the King's servants; from the latter of which (were it to happen) much advantage would be taken against government.'[2] Although quite contrary to the unanimous opinion of the cabinet on 4 February as reported by Shelburne, this suggestion was promptly adopted as official policy. On 13 February Shelburne returned the petition to the Board of Trade with an instruction that it should be laid before the House of Commons. The Board considered the matter on 16 February, and its President Lord Clare presented the petition to the Commons the same day.[3]

The administration plan was to read the petition, to show that the House was willing to hear colonial complaints, and then to take no further action by letting it lie on the Table; and Lord Clare accordingly proposed this course of action. There was no chance of opposition support for the petition, since it complained of the legislation of the Grenville and Rockingham ministries alike; and the general expectation was rather that a motion would be made for its rejection. Rockingham and Dowdeswell had discussed the matter with Charles Townshend and Conway on 15 February, and had agreed to support the ministerial plan.[4] Burke therefore spoke for the motion in the debate. Even Grenville and his friends did not move the rejection of the petition, choosing instead to express the hope that administration would soon lay more American papers before the House. Conway admitted that other American business might come before Parliament, and Wedderburn

[1] Shelburne had blamed the Declaratory Act. *Chatham Papers*, iii. 191–2.
[2] *Chatham Papers*, iii. 193–4.   [3] *J.C.T.P. 1764–7*, p. 366.
[4] B.M. Add. MSS. 32980, fos. 108–9.

seized on this remark to urge that American policy should be decided in Parliament and not in cabinet.[1] The ministry disposed of the petition in this way, but its effect on political opinion was not to be easily expunged, as Charles Garth warned South Carolina. 'Administration much displeased and Opposition appealing thereto for a confirmation of the opinions expressed last year that nothing will give satisfaction to the colonists but an absolute repeal of all regulations and restrictions and in the end independence upon Great Britain.'[2]

On the same day Shelburne wrote again to Chatham, for there remained the problem of the Mutiny Act. It was 'the general opinion' of the cabinet that the American packet should not sail without some decision on New York, but the ministers did not know what to do. 'Though everybody is strongly for enforcing, nobody chooses to suggest the mode. I presumed to ask the King whether any occurred to his Majesty, but I could not find that any had, except that it should be enforced.' Shelburne foresaw two difficulties in any such action. One was the danger of establishing a precedent 'which may hereafter be turned to purposes of oppression, and to promote measures opposite to those general public principles upon which the Stamp Act was repealed'. The other was the probable intervention of France and Spain if the colonists should resist by force. Yet political feeling in Britain made some action imperative.[3]

The public conviction goes so strongly to believing the dependence of the colonies at stake; and the opinion is so confirmed by their conduct since the repeal, which it must be expected will be both coloured and heightened by the acts of their enemies, that, be the danger what it will, government appears called upon for some measure of vigour, to support the authority of Parliament and the coercive power of this country.

Shelburne then put forward his own plan for Chatham's consideration before submitting it to the cabinet.[4] This involved

[1] For this debate see *Commons Journals*, xxxi. 158–60; *Ryder Diary*, p. 330; and two letters: (a) Conway to George III, *Corr. of George III*, i. 450; (b) C. Garth to South Carolina, *S.C.H.G.M.* 29 (1928), 216–17.
[2] For similar remarks see *H.M.C. Stopford-Sackville*, p. 26; and *Trumbull Papers*, pp. 215–16.   [3] *Chatham Papers*, iii. 206–11.
[4] P.R.O. 30/8/3, fos. 210–14. This part of the same letter was left out of the printed version, where it should appear at *Chatham Papers*, iii. 210. The omission was noted by Ritcheson, *British Politics and the American Revolution*, p. 89.

the replacement of Governor Moore by 'some one of a military character, who might at the same time be entrusted with the intentions of government, and discretionary to act with force and gentleness as circumstances might make necessary'.[1] The new governor, if the Assembly continued its resistance to the Mutiny Act, must then 'billet *on private houses as was the practice during the war*'. This Shelburne regarded as a moderate step, preferable to 'more violent measures', since the colonists could prevent its implementation by obedience. Objections might be made that it was a temporary expedient, 'deferring the evil day, which must come'; and that it concerned only one colony. This last point, Shelburne thought, could be countered by three arguments: that New York had no charter; that it had benefited especially from the army during the last war;[2] and that the colony had behaved with 'peculiar ingratitude since the repeal'.

Chatham disapproved of this proposal on the same ground as he had the cabinet's idea about the New York merchants' petition, that it was administrative action without reference to Parliament. The disobedience of the New York Assembly, he said in his reply the next day, was 'a matter so weighty' that it should not be decided by the cabinet.

The memorial transmitted by the governor of New York, relative to this event, ought in the proper manner, to be laid before Parliament, in order that his Majesty may be founded in, and strengthened by, the sense of his grand council, with regard to whatever steps shall be found necessary to be taken in the most unfortunate business.[3]

What Chatham himself had in mind can perhaps be deduced from the existence in his papers of draft copies of a proposed Declaratory Bill on the subject of the army in America, intended both to assert the authority of Crown and Parliament and to allay any fear of the colonists that the army might be used against them. This bill would have declared that 'the legal, constitutional and hitherto unquestioned prerogative of the

---

[1] He suggested either Colonel John Burgoyne, who had not yet served in America, or General Robert Monckton, who had.

[2] Gage made this point in a letter of 17 Jan. to Shelburne, *Gage Corr.* i. 118.

[3] *Chatham Papers*, iii. 215.

Crown', with Parliamentary consent, to send the army to any British possessions 'cannot be rendered dependent on the consent of a provincial assembly in the colonies, without a most dangerous innovation, and derogatory to the dignity of the Imperial Crown of Great Britain': but it would also have declared 'that no military force (however raised and kept, according to law) can be lawfully employed to violate and destroy the just rights of the people'.[1]

Chatham, however, was never to introduce any such measure, and took increasingly little interest in politics. When he returned to London in March he did not attend cabinet, and proved inaccessible even to his ministerial colleagues: Charles Townshend complained to Grenville that Chatham was 'in a morning, not up; at noon, taking the air; in the evening, reposing and not to be fatigued'.[2] His suggestion that the problem of New York was a matter for legislative and not executive action was his last positive intervention in American policy that year. It was promptly adopted by the cabinet, which read over the American papers at a meeting on 18 February. Shelburne reported to Chatham next day that the ministers had been undecided whether to lay before Parliament the letter from Governor Franklin of New Jersey. It would be prudent to confine any action to New York, he thought, and the technical excuse could be made that Franklin's letter contained only the observations and opinions of the Governor. Lord President Northington had therefore suggested that the matter should be left 'to Lord Shelburne's own discretion and his knowledge of Lord Chatham's future intentions as to the proceedings, which was what he desired to act conformedly to'.[3] It is not known whether Chatham made any reply to this further request for guidance. When on 17 March the American papers were laid before the House of Commons, they included the letter from Governor Franklin;[4] but there

[1] P.R.O. 30/8/74, fos. 167–75.   [2] *Grenville Papers*, iv. 220.
[3] P.R.O. 30/8/56, fos. 74–5. This letter is dated 'Thursday'. I have attributed it to 19 Feb. because it refers also to a cabinet discussion the previous evening of a royal message that was sent to the House of Commons on 19 Feb. *Commons Journals*, xxxi. 236–7. The date of 12 Feb. is ascribed to it by Norris, *Shelburne and Reform*, p. 39n.
[4] *Commons Journals*, xxxi. 231–2. Some papers on New York had already been presented to the Commons on 29 Jan., and others concerning New York and Massachusetts were to follow on 7 April. *Commons Journals*, xxxi. 85–6, 287.

had been no change in the policy of confining punitive action to New York. By that date the cabinet had already decided upon the measures to be adopted towards that colony, at a meeting on 12 March.

This time Shelburne's letter to Chatham reported a decision and did not ask for guidance. Four proposals were considered by the cabinet. Shelburne's own plan to empower the Governor of New York to billet soldiers on private houses was unanimously rejected 'as being a free quarter in point of principle, and hence highly exceptionable both here and there'. Conway then suggested that Parliament should raise the money directly by 'a local extraordinary port duty' on New York. This was rejected on three grounds: as inefficient, since it would give rise to smuggling; as an obstacle to trade; and as failing to 'bring about the principle which is wanted'. Conway still clung to his solution, and was to produce it again in the Commons. The third plan considered was Townshend's suggestion of an Address from the House of Commons to the King asking him not to assent to any New York legislation at all until the Mutiny Act was fully obeyed in that colony. Northington opposed the suggestion, both because it was confined to one colony and because it was so extreme a step that Parliamentary legislation was necessary. The cabinet discussion centred on this plan and, despite an objection by Shelburne, 'the opinion of the meeting inclined to prefer this, and in the shape of an act'. Little attention was paid to a fourth proposal, one to insert an appropriation clause directing the Governor of New York to give priority to 'the service of the province' in any revenue bills passed by the assembly. The cabinet policy was therefore an Act of Parliament to prohibit any further New York legislation until the colony complied with the Mutiny Act.[1] It was regarded as

---

[1] P.R.O. 30/8/56, fos. 86–90. The letter itself is headed '1767', but the date of '26 April' has later been added, and generally assumed to be correct. There are two other letters, however, that show that it describes the cabinet meeting of 12 Mar. On 13 Mar. Grafton informed Chatham that 'the American, or rather New York point is settled, and that it should be by act of parliament. Mr. Conway had his doubts, but would endeavour everything he could to bring his mind to it.' Grafton had intended to inform Chatham in person, but had been too ill to do so. Shelburne, in his letter of 13 Mar. to Chatham, merely said, 'I take it for granted he will inform you of what passed at the meeting last night particularly. The third proposition was in general agreed to by the King's servants, except by General Conway, who declared he could not give a decisive opinion until he had

a firm decision at this meeting on 12 March by Grafton, but not by Townshend himself. The Duke had agreed to the plan beforehand, and afterwards defended it as 'a temperate, but dignified proceeding, and purposely avoiding all harsh and positive penalties'.[1]

Shelburne's opposition to this measure and his criticism of the others suggested had not stemmed from any desire on his part for leniency. In the same letter he privately suggested to Chatham another and more severe plan. This involved the passage of a new act that would recite the Declaratory Act, grant pardon for all past offences against it, but enact that from three months after the new act reached the colonies it would be

High Treason to refuse to obey or execute any laws or statutes made by the King with the advice of Parliament . . . and misprision of treason for any person or persons in these colonies either by writing, preaching, or speaking to express publish or affirm that the King etc hath not power and authority to make laws etc to bind their American subjects. All offenders to be tried either *within the colonies or sent over to Great Britain* to be tried here. This is to be supported by the military power.

This was the suggestion of a man who had himself opposed the Declaratory Act a year earlier! It went further than the attempt then of the Grenvillite opposition to put teeth into that measure, or later proposals of Hillsborough and North to deal with more significant colonial resistance. Shelburne had not even dared to suggest it to the cabinet. His change of heart on America was confirmed by his concluding comment on 'the unreasonableness of the conduct of the colonists even on their own principles, since the repeal of the Stamp Act was enough to show them that it was the decided opinion of Parliament not to lay an internal tax in point of policy'.

Two months were to pass before this policy decision was translated into Parliamentary action. It was a period dominated

---

further time to consider of it.' *Chatham Papers*, iii. 231–3. These letters could refer only to the meeting described in Shelburne's unpublished letter, which was presumably written when he learnt that Grafton had not seen Chatham.

[1] Grafton MSS., no. 453. *Grafton Autobiography*, p. 126.

by ministerial discord and opposition pressure. The administration was weakened by Chatham's absence and by internal dissension caused by personal antipathies and disagreements over policies for India and America. At the very same time it faced a sustained opposition attack sparked off by a famous and fortuitous defeat of the ministry on the land tax in the House of Commons on 27 February by 206 votes to 188. This gave rise to opposition hopes of forcing the resignation of the ministry by Parliamentary pressure. They were unfounded. Dowdeswell's motion to reduce the tax from 4s. to 3s. had been popular with independent members who would otherwise support government, Lord Chesterfield commenting that 'it is plain that all the landed gentlemen bribed themselves with this shilling in the pound':[1] and George III made clear to his ministers his intention of disregarding the event.[2] Nevertheless, after their successful *ad hoc* co-operation on this point, opposition leaders began negotiations for a permanent alliance, and Newcastle resorted to his customary Parliamentary calculations. His list of 2 March named 547 M.P.s and comprised the following analysis of the House of Commons: 232 administration supporters; 91 independents; 103 supporters of Rockingham; 54 supporters of Bedford and Grenville; and 69 members rated doubtful or absent.[3] This analysis was optimistic, and misleadingly precise;[4] but it seemed to promise a reasonable chance of opposition success. Events were to show that in fact the administration faced a greater danger of defeat over America in the House of Lords.

The opposition negotiations of March and early April aimed at an alliance to overthrow the Chatham ministry and form a new administration in its stead.[5] They failed because neither Rockingham nor Grenville would concede the Treasury to the other.[6] The Rockingham party would have preferred

---

[1] *Chesterfield Letters*, vi. 2799.

[2] *Chatham Papers*, iii. 224. *Corr. of George III*, i. 455.

[3] B.M. Add. MSS. 33001, fos. 357–63.

[4] For a comparison of this list with one made earlier in the session by or for Rockingham see Brooke, *Chatham Administration*, pp. 241–3. Although the over-all totals are similar, the two lists differ considerably, even in the composition of the Rockingham group.

[5] On this see Brooke, *Chatham Administration*, pp. 121–6.

[6] The two men apparently never even met at this time. On 2 Apr. Grenville arrived at Mansfield's house when Rockingham was there. He left before Mansfield

to bring the ministry down by the defection of Conway and Charles Townshend, and did not discuss detailed proposals with the other opposition groups until that hope faded. Rockingham's demands were then pitched too high, and Grenville's counter-suggestion of 'a middle way' would have left him in effective control of the Commons in the proposed new administration.[1] A formal alliance of the opposition groups was prevented by disagreement over places and power, not by any clash on America. It was only after deadlock was apparent that Rockingham told Newcastle that he intended to insist on acceptance of his administration's American policy. A memorandum by Newcastle on 31 March noted that Rockingham's terms were not 'merely to have a majority of friends in the cabinet' but also comprised the following points of policy.[2]

To give the whole care of the West Indies, and North America, to my Lord Dartmouth, with the Seals as Third Secretary of State.

To insist, that Mr. Grenville should have nothing to do with North America.

That the measures, which were taken by his Lordship in the Treasury, with regard to the trade and commerce in America, and the laying taxes there, should be maintained and pursued.

Even so America alone would not have prevented an opposition alliance. On the next day Newcastle saw Bedfordite Rigby, who argued 'that Mr. Grenville would never think of renewing any of those measures which had been set aside and overruled in my Lord Rockingham's administration, particularly with regard to North America'.[3] And on 4 April Newcastle reported to Rockingham a conversation with Lord Mansfield the previous day which gave ground for hopes of an opposition alliance on policies.[4]

---

could call him in, and did not return until Rockingham had gone. B.M. Add. MSS. 32981, fo. 31.

[1] *Grenville Papers*, iv. 220.

[2] B.M. Add. MSS. 32980, fo. 450.

[3] B.M. Add. MSS. 32981. fos. 1–3.

[4] B.M. Add. MSS. 32981, fo. 34. For Newcastle's notes on the conversation see ibid, fos. 28–9. Mansfield had seen Grenville on 1 Apr. *Grenville Papers*, iv. 221.

In the East India affairs, I think, Mr. Grenville and Mr. Dowdeswell are agreed; and by what my Lord Mansfield tells me, I hope, we shall not differ about North America. Mr. Grenville assured him, that nothing would be attempted or proposed . . . that could, in any degree, be contrary to, or inconsistent with the part we have taken relating to North America, or that we can have any objection to, on that account.

Over a month earlier the opposition leaders had given notice of their intention to bring before Parliament the question of colonial subordination to Britain even if, as they wrongly suspected, the administration intended to avoid doing so. In the House of Lords on 25 February the Duke of Bedford announced that the following week he would move for American papers unless the ministry gave an assurance that they would be laid before the House: for he meant to raise the issue of colonial non-compliance with acts of Parliament. The Duke of Grafton at once rose to declare that the administration already intended to produce them, and suggested consideration of the subject in a fortnight's time. Bedford thereupon said that he would not make any motion for the time being, and the matter ended after a brief debate.[1] Contemporaries noted the new ministerial posture: Lord George Sackville told General Irwin on 2 March, 'It is believed Lord Chatham has changed his ideas on America, and means to act with vigour. The Chancellor held very stout language upon that head the other day in the House of Lords.'[2] Bedford meanwhile kept up the pressure. On 5 March he went to the House of Lords 'to inquire about the papers the Duke of Grafton had promised should be laid before the House, relating to America'. Since Grafton was absent he spoke to Camden, who promised to write to Grafton; and Shelburne afterwards told Bedford that he understood the papers were promised for a week's time.[3] Shelburne duly laid copies of many American papers before the House on 12 March.[4]

Bedford's initiative had taken the other opposition leaders

---

[1] *Lords Journals*, xxxi. 496; *Bedford Journal*, p. 599; *Chatham Papers*, iii. 225.

[2] *H.M.C. Stopford-Sackville*, p. 26.

[3] *Bedford Journal*, p. 599.

[4] *Lords Journals*, xxxi. 516–17. Others were submitted on 3 and 6 Apr., and 11 May. *Ibid.*, pp. 553, 558, 594.

by surprise. Lord Suffolk told Grenville that it had been 'without any previous concert'. He thought the move timely, and suggested that they should consider 'how to regulate our conduct so as to take with us our former opponents, without departing a jot from our principle', urging that there ought to be 'more co-operation than has existed between us of late'.[1] If Suffolk hoped for an opposition alliance on America, Newcastle feared that the subject would prevent such co-operation just when the administration defeat on the land tax seemed to promise Parliamentary success. He was apprehensive of a motion on the colonies that the Rockingham group would be unable to support, and he asked Rockingham both to sound Mansfield and Hardwicke on the subject and to 'enquire of Trecothick, or some of our American friends, what the fact is, that is complained of: how far they have refused to comply with the resolutions of the House of Lords, or the directions of Parliament'.[2]

The situation was further complicated by a hunting accident to Bedford's heir Lord Tavistock on 9 March, when he sustained injuries from which he died on 22 March: for Bedford withdrew from the political scene for a month. On 20 March Grafton and Camden discussed the question of the American papers privately in the House of Lords with Bedford's lieutenants Sandwich and Gower, Rigby being summoned from the Commons to join them. Grafton afterwards moved that the House should take the American papers into consideration on 30 March, declaring that he did so because Bedford was absent and adding that the matter would be postponed if Bedford was unable to attend then. Rockingham was puzzled by this step. 'I don't know particularly what the administration mean to do, or whether they mean anything', he commented to Newcastle, who in reply expressed annoyance about circumstances conveying 'the appearance of a concert, for which, I daresay, there was no foundation'. He urged Rockingham to 'speak to Rigby upon it, and show him, what hurt these appearances must do, just at this time' when the opposition leaders were feeling their way to an alliance.[3]

[1] *Grenville Papers*, iv. 4–5.
[2] B.M. Add. MSS. 32980, fos. 187–8.
[3] *Lords Journals*, xxxi. 531; B.M. Add. MSS. 32980, fos. 350–1, 358–9.

L

Lord Tavistock's death two days later meant that Bedford was not present on 30 March, when consideration of the American papers was adjourned after a debate which was short but significant in its reflection of political attitudes.[1] Camden took the opportunity to criticize the disobedience of the colonies and to announce that his opinion was now based on the Declaratory Act. He was reminded that he and his friends had encouraged colonial resistance by their earlier behaviour, and courtier Lord Talbot tartly commented that 'new converts were always the most zealous'.[2] Altogether the ministry had an uncomfortable time, as Lord Rockingham reported to his wife: 'the five Lords, who were against this country's having the right over N. America last year were well dressed. *Our opponents* of last year were *mighty civil* to *us*'.[3] Connecticut agent William Johnson observed with concern the hostility shown towards the colonies because of their alleged ingratitude and disobedience, and noted that some peers believed that a desire for independence explained the behaviour of New York and Massachusetts. Several suggestions for dealing with the colonial situation were canvassed during the debate, including some for strong measures, but no motion was made because Grafton assured the House that the ministry had a plan ready.[4]

By now it must have been widely realized in the political world that this policy would be some means of enforcing British authority in America. Chatham was known to be particularly incensed about the resistance to the Mutiny Act, and early in April Bedford was boasting that he would have his support for strong measures.[5] Nor was it any secret that Conway found himself alone in the cabinet as an advocate of moderation. Charles Townshend told Grenville that on American policy Conway was 'below low-water mark',[6] and Newcastle reported to Rockingham on 4 April that

---

[1] *Lords Journals*, xxxi. 546. H. Walpole, *Memoirs*, ii. 318–19, is misleading.

[2] *H.M.C. Stopford-Sackville*, p. 27.

[3] Wentworth Woodhouse MSS. R.156–8.

[4] *Trumbull Papers*, p. 224; Grafton MSS., no. 453. Since the cabinet decision on New York had been taken on 12 Mar., Chaffin is mistaken in his contention that by this announcement Grafton publicly committed the administration to a policy. *W.M.Q.* 27 (1970), 104.

[5] B.M. Add. MSS. 32981, fos. 65–6.

[6] *Grenville Papers*, iv. 222.

there is an open difference between these two, upon the American affairs. Charles Townshend is loudly with my Lord Chatham. Conway is strongly against him, and says he will not depart from his opinion. I understand the difference is, Lord Chatham and Charles Townshend are for stronger measures against the Americans than Conway will come into.

Newcastle saw in this situation an opportunity to detach Conway from the administration.[1] But Rockingham would give no lead, as Newcastle reported in despair to Mansfield on 8 April. 'He will not say one word of America and so we must shift for ourselves.' Newcastle had heard that Bedford was angry at the failure of the negotiations for an opposition alliance. 'He says, had that succeeded, he would have done nothing upon the American affairs, that could be disagreeable to us: but that being over, he will push his own opinion, as far as he can.'[2]

Newcastle had in mind the forthcoming Lords debate on 10 April. Lord Temple had summoned the House for that day, and public notice had been given that a motion 'of the greatest consequence' would be made although the subject of it was kept secret.[3] The lead was to be taken by Bedford, whose respectable and responsible character would give any proposal more weight than one moved by the violent and erratic Temple. According to Edmund Burke, Bedford was persuaded by his friends 'to plunge into politics as a diversion from the grief occasioned by his late great loss'. Newcastle's fears were not realized. The motion made by Bedford was one both in subject and manner that the Rockingham party could have supported without sacrificing their consistency on America, and he afterwards told Newcastle that it had been intended to be 'moderate and inoffensive' to such prospective allies.[4]

The subject was the Massachusetts Compensation and Indemnity Act. Chatham's insistence on Parliamentary consideration of American problems did not extend to this one, and the administration intended to dispose of it by executive action. The matter was in the hands of the Board of Trade, which had received official intimation of it on 10 March,

[1] B.M. Add. MSS. 32981, fos. 34–5.   [2] B.M. Add. MSS. 32981, fos 65–6.
[3] H. Walpole, *Letters*, vii. 102. *Burke Corr.* i. 306.
[4] B.M. Add. MSS. 32981, fos. 156–60; *Burke Corr.* i. 306.

and two days later had referred the subject to the consideration of the Attorney- and Solicitor-Generals.[1] No further move had been made a month later, and Bedford therefore took the tactical opportunity of embarrassing the ministry by an Address asking the King to consider in Privy Council the validity of the part of the Massachusetts Act that constituted a pardon: and, if it was judged void, to order measures to be taken to restrain the colony and assert the exclusive royal right of pardon.[2]

Bedford may have drafted the motion to win the support of the Rockingham group, but he had kept the subject secret from them, for fear of a leak to administration through their friendship with Conway. Rockingham was offended by this behaviour, and his indignation was increased by an impolitic attack by Halifax on Conway, one that Sandwich had vainly spent two hours to dissuade him from making.[3] The subject of the debate aroused little controversy, for, as Newcastle observed, 'every lord in the House agreed, that the act was illegal; but the administration thought, the motion carried with it a reflection upon them, as if they had been negligent of their duty'.[4] Grafton therefore moved the previous question, after Northington, as Lord President of the Council, had told the House that the Board of Trade had not yet reported on the subject. Rockingham intimated to his friends that he meant to support administration. Newcastle spent the debate trying privately to persuade him to change his mind; and, when he realized that Rockingham was adamant, ostentatiously left the House with a dozen of his friends to avoid a public split in the party. His own inclination, he told Mansfield the next day, would have been to speak and vote for Bedford's motion. Apart from the obvious tactical advantage of an opposition

---

[1] *J.C.T.P. 1764–7*, pp. 373, 375.

[2] For the debate see *Lords Journals*, xxxi. 566; *Bedford Journal*, p. 601. H. Walpole, *Memoirs*, ii. 322–3; *Franklin Papers*, xiv. 108–9; *Grenville Papers*, iv. 222–3; and the following letters: (a) Grafton to George III, *Corr. of George III*, i. 468; (b) George III to Grafton, Grafton MSS., no. 494 (misdated as 10 March by the King): for the draft (correctly dated) see *Corr. of George III*, i. 468–9; (c) Rockingham to Lady Rockingham, Wentworth Woodhouse MSS. R.156–13; (d) E. Burke to C. O'Hara, *Burke Corr.* i. 306–7; (e) H. Walpole to Sir H. Mann, H. Walpole, *Letters*, vii. 102–3; (f) Newcastle to Princess Amelia, B.M. Add. MSS. 32981, fos. 125–6; (g) Newcastle to Mansfield, B.M. Add. MSS. 32981, fos. 127–8; (h) W. S. Johnson to W. Pitkin, *Trumbull Papers*, pp. 224–6.

[3] B.M. Add. MSS. 32981, fos. 156–60.   [4] Ibid., fos. 125–6.

alliance, he thought 'the arguments made use of against the question, were most trifling, for an administration to wait for the opinion of a Board of Trade, upon such an illegal act as this'.[1] Seventeen peers took part in the debate: Mansfield supported Bedford's motion, and Camden spoke for spirited though prudent action against the colonies. One American observer, probably Franklin, was disturbed 'to find much resentment against the colonies in the disputants. The word *rebellion* was frequently used.'[2] Another, William Johnson, reflecting on this and the previous Lords debate, sent this warning back to Connecticut:[3]

I was chagrined upon both these occasions to observe so much warmth against the colonies, but am satisfied it is in some degree owing to the spirit of party, and that, when they declaim against the Americans, they mean to attack the administration as the supposed friends of the colonies (from the part they took in the repeal of the Stamp Act) at least as much as they do the colonies themselves. Very unhappy, however, it is for us, that maltreating us should subserve the purposes of opposition, and that we should become the object of party, since, if it produces no other ill effect (which is much to be feared), yet at least it certainly tends to alienate affection and instil principles most pernicious to both countries.

The administration triumphed by 63 votes to 36 when the House divided at the end of the debate. Rockingham and five friends, including Dartmouth and Richmond, voted with the ministry, but at least two others with the opposition. It was widely realized that a united opposition would have pushed the administration very hard. Newcastle calculated that the minority would have been increased by fourteen peers who, like him, had deliberately left before the division, and by the six voting with the ministry, resulting in a probable administration majority of one:[4] and he lamented to Sir William Baker the loss of an opportunity that might never come again.[5]

It would have showed my Lord Bute, and my Lord Chatham (and that is *my* point) that, with the Duke of Bedford etc, we were masters of the House of Lords. It would be showing a spirit, upon a point,

---

[1] Ibid., fos. 127–8.
[2] *Franklin Papers*, xiv. 108.   [3] *Trumbull Papers*, p. 226.
[4] For his lists see B.M. Add. MSS. 32981, fos. 109–14.   [5] Ibid., fos. 137–8.

that concerned no other colony, but this; and was entirely separate from all other considerations and disputes, relating to North America; and by taking this early step we might be enabled perhaps the better to resist other violent measures that may be proposed in the course of this affair. It would have been paying a very innocent compliment to the Duke of Bedford: and might have been a means of union, and concert, during the remainder of this session.

Grenville intended to make the same motion in the Commons on 13 April,[1] but was forestalled by prompt administrative action. The Attorney- and Solicitor-Generals submitted their report on the Massachusetts Act to the Board of Trade on 10 April, stating that the colony did not have the power to enact a pardon without previous royal consent. The Board considered the report at its next meeting, on 13 April; and, acting with unwonted haste, at once prepared and signed a representation to the Privy Council.[2] The Council met the same day and referred the subject to its Committee on Plantation Affairs.[3] When James West heard the news he commented to Newcastle, 'so there is an end of that motion';[4] and the subject of the Massachusetts indemnity was not raised in the Commons that day.

Three days later Parliament adjourned for the Easter recess. When it reassembled on 28 April the House of Commons became the forum for American business, as the administration began to implement its policy for New York; but not before William Beckford made a last-minute attempt to avert it by this letter to Chatham on 29 April.[5]

The American papers are to be taken into consideration on the morrow, and I hear the quartering act is to be enforced . . . Recall your troops from the old provinces in America, where they are not wanted, and the cause of anger, hatred and malice is removed. I am confident the Americans will in their own assemblies, make any reasonable provision that shall be required. The quartering act has so much of the appearance of arbitrary military power, that I did foretell in the House, it would not be submitted to with patience.

---

[1] Ibid.

[2] *J.C.T.P. 1764–7*, pp. 380–1. For a copy of this representation see B.M. Add. MSS. 32982, fos. 64–5.

[3] B.M. Add. MSS. 32982, fos. 66–7. *Acts P.C. Col.* vi. 447–8.

[4] B.M. Add. MSS. 32981, fos. 141–2.   [5] *Chatham Papers*, iii. 251–2.

The appeal was doomed to failure, if only because Chatham no longer dictated policy: but the administration had in Conway a Leader of the House who disagreed with the measure agreed upon, refused to be responsible for it in the Commons, and made his attitude clear during the Committee on American Papers when it resumed on 30 April.[1] Rigby asked what the administration meant to do that day. If after the disgraceful procrastination of all public business only the reading out of the papers was intended, he and many who had already read them would go home. Conway announced that he had nothing to propose but would hear what was said in debate and then 'form his opinion', a statement extremely proper for an ordinary member of the House but an extraordinary one for the cabinet minister who was its Leader. Grenville said he would not ask what the government plan was but only when it would be proposed. Charles Townshend declared that his mind was made up, and after this hint the Committee decided to read the papers that day and discuss policy on 5 May. Townshend was the obvious ministerial choice to take the lead in place of Conway, especially as the plan was essentially the one he had suggested in the cabinet of 12 March; and his papers contain the draft resolutions on New York with alterations in his own hand.[2]

The professed ignorance of Rigby and Grenville about administration policy may have been genuine, but the Rockingham party knew the plan, though not its restriction to New York. Richmond had already told Rockingham that the ministry was going to 'propose a bill to direct all the governors in North America not to give their assent to any bill from their respective assemblies, until the assembly has made provision for the due compliance on the quartering bill'. Charles Yorke thought 'the mode improper', and Rockingham assured him that Lord Mansfield 'treated it as a most absurd proposition from Government, but not the less likely to be their plan'. Rockingham therefore had high hopes of a hostile Parliamentary reception for the policy, as he told Newcastle on 4 May.

---

[1] *Commons Journals*, xxxi. 333. For the debate see J. West's report to Newcastle. B.M. Add. MSS. 32936, fos. 321–2. This is misdated '3 April', and the debate has sometimes been attributed to that day.

[2] *H.M.C. Weston Underwood*, p. 405; Namier and Brooke, *Charles Townshend*, p. 177.

'I hear General Conway much dislikes it, but *this is a secret*. If so, and the different corps concur in thinking the mode improper, tomorrow may be a curious day. In the mean time I have wished our friends to attend.'[1]

Anticlimax came on 5 May. The previous evening Townshend had a fall in which he hurt his eye. He therefore sent for Lord North, and gave him his papers and copies of the resolutions so that he could move them instead. Before the Committee met, however, Rigby opposed this course of action, declaring that it was impossible to proceed without the minister best informed on the subject, and the House agreed to postpone the matter until 11 May.[2]

The next day the Bedford and Grenville factions proposed a surprise motion in both Houses.[3] It was to address the Crown for copies of all papers from the Board of Trade, Secretary of State, and Privy Council relating to the Massachusetts Indemnity Act. This time the Rockingham group was informed in advance, Lord Gower telling Rockingham 'in secret' on 3 May. Rockingham assured Gower that he approved of the plan, and told Newcastle that he assumed there was reason to believe that the administration had not declared the indemnity void.[4] The Committee of the Privy Council, in fact, had not then come to any decision, although it had met on 1 May and was due to sit again on 4 May.[5] Mansfield excused himself from the debate since it was the first day of the law term, but in a letter to Newcastle approved the motion as providing a potential basis of opposition unity on America.[6]

It is a topic for talk: if there be any doubt they should lay the matter before the House, before the Council decides; if no doubt why delay? You will do very right to support it, and it may let you in to say what you think proper upon the principle which produced the Declaratory Bill . . . if a handle were taken from it, to give an appearance that you might all agree upon the interesting point between England and America, it might have the greatest consequence.

---

[1] B.M. Add. MSS. 32981, fos. 287–8; 35430, fos. 73–4.

[2] For this episode see *Commons Journals*, xxxi. 341; *Ryder Diary*, p. 341; H. Walpole, *Memoirs*, iii. 15; and two letters: (a) E. Burke to C. O'Hara, *Burke Corr.* i. 311–12; (b) J. West to Newcastle, B.M. Add. MSS. 32981, fo. 305. Only Walpole thought Townshend's injury a pretence, but Burke doubted if he would thank Rigby for 'his kindness and candour'.   [3] H. Walpole, *Memoirs*, iii. 15.

[4] B.M. Add. MSS. 32981, fo. 288.   [5] Ibid., fos. 289–90.   [6] Ibid., fos. 297–8.

Mansfield's optimism was justified by the debate in the Lords. The motion, made by Gower, produced a long discussion in which sixteen peers took part.[1] It was supported by spokesmen from all three opposition groups, Richmond and Newcastle speaking on the same side in an American debate as Sandwich, Suffolk and Temple. The motion was defeated by only nine votes, 52 to 43, although proxies swelled this to a court majority of 71 against 49. Newcastle gleefully anticipated 'frequent days of business in the House of Lords', and a worried Grafton told the King that 'the whole of the opposition had brought their united strength which his Majesty will see is numerous'.

The administration fared better in the Commons. The motion there was proposed by Grenville, and supported by Rigby and Dowdeswell, the acknowledged spokesmen of the other two opposition parties: but after a debate involving eleven speakers the opposition did not divide the House against the defeat of the motion by the previous question.[2]

This was a favourable omen for the reception there of the ministry's American policy. On 11 May East India Company business caused a postponement of the American Committee for another two days. 'The House sitting so late and everybody eager to go to dinner the American business is put off till Wednesday', Newcastle was told by James West, who also reported this declaration by the Chancellor of the Exchequer. 'Mr. C. Townshend said that he was a true friend to America though both there and here he had been represented as an enemy, and begged he might not be forejudged till his actions appeared.'[3] Certainly his proposals on New York were to be arguably more moderate than the alternatives preferred by the opposition factions. Grenville was to suggest an Act of Parliament ordering the colonial treasury of New York to pay the army costs out of general taxation. Rockinghamite discussions culminated in a meeting of Dowdeswell, Sir George Savile, and Sir William Meredith at Rockingham's house, as the Marquess reported to Newcastle. 'The chief point will

---

[1] *Lords Journals*, xxxi. 588–9, and two letters: (a) Newcastle to Manchester, B.M. Add. MSS. 32981, fo. 313; (b) Grafton to George III, *Corr. of George III*, i. 470–1.

[2] *Commons Journals*, xxxi. 342; and Conway to George III, *Corr. of George III*, i. 471. [3] B.M. Add. MSS. 32981, fo. 359.

L*

be, to object to their proposed bill and Mr. Dowdeswell's idea will be thrown out for consideration.' This plan, which Charles Yorke also approved, was the same as Shelburne had suggested to Chatham in February and in the cabinet of 12 March, to execute the Mutiny Act by quartering troops in private houses.[1]

On 13 May the American Committee began at 5 o'clock.[2] For the first time that session admittance to the gallery of the House was restricted, agent Johnson reporting to Connecticut that 'although there had been an indulgence to strangers before that time, it was to our great surprise specially ordered upon this occasion that the agents of the colonies should be excluded, and neither they nor the American merchants were allowed to be present at the debates'. The motive was to prevent the colonies being misled by unofficial misrepresentations of government policy, so Garth assured South Carolina, and not any desire for secrecy. The debate opened with a long speech from Charles Townshend. He said that three points deserved attention: the Massachusetts Indemnity Act; the resistance to the Mutiny Act, especially in New York; and the resolutions of some colonial assemblies inconsistent with their dependency on Britain. He proposed to move resolutions only on the second subject. The Privy Council already had the first matter in hand, and 'a paper war' of resolutions with the assemblies would be undignified and futile. He then explained why coercive action would be confined to New York. Disobedience to the Mutiny Act was not universal in America. Pennsylvania and Connecticut had complied with the act; defiant resolutions in Massachusetts had not been followed by actual disobedience; New Jersey had not formally complied with the act, but had voted a satisfactory sum of money: but New York had been completely defiant.[3] Several assemblies contained factions determined

---

[1] B.M. Add. MSS. 32981, fos. 365–6.

[2] Seven reports have been found of this debate. *Ryder Diary*, pp. 342–7; H. Walpole, *Memoirs*, iii. 21–9; and the following letters: (a) J. West (three letters) to Newcastle, B.M. Add. MSS. 32981, fos. 375–80; (b) J. Harris to Hardwicke, B.M. Add. MSS. 35608, fos. 17–18; (c) T. Bradshaw to Grafton, *Grafton Autobiography*, pp. 176–8; (d) C. Garth to South Carolina, *S.C.H.G.M.* 29 (1928), 223–6; (e) W. S. Johnson to W. Pitkin, *Trumbull Papers*, pp. 230–2.

[3] For colonial reactions to the Mutiny Act see Shy, *Towards Lexington*, pp. 250–7. Townshend's summary was reasonably accurate, for news of Georgia's defiance had not yet arrived.

to win popularity by challenging Britain. He would therefore make an example of New York, in order to show Britain's determination to assert her sovereignty. The method would be a law to prevent the passage of any legislation in New York until the colony obeyed the Mutiny Act. After a digression about his taxation plans Townshend announced that he would propose three resolutions to the Committee: that the New York Assembly had refused to supply provisions in accordance with the 1765 Mutiny Act; that the Assembly had passed an act inconsistent with that measure; and that until the Assembly made provision to supply everything required by the 1765 act, the Governor, Council and Assembly should be restrained and prohibited from passing any legislation whatsoever.[1] Townshend admitted that this procedure was open to some objections, notably that it punished innocent and guilty alike: but this disadvantage, as well as others, also applied to such other schemes as a naval blockade of the colony, billeting on private houses, and a local tax on New York.

Dowdeswell rose first in reply. He criticized Townshend's plan as inadequate, for it would not execute the Mutiny Act. He therefore put forward the agreed Rockingham suggestion for an act to empower the quartering of soldiers in private houses. Beckford opposed Townshend's resolution as too severe, a move that Horace Walpole thought might be explained 'by concert with Lord Chatham, that while the ministers humbled the colonies, his lordship might still be supposed favourable to them'. Grenville then made a comprehensive attack on the administration, recalling Chatham's declaration on 21 February 1766 about the use of ships and soldiers in the event of further colonial resistance. James West reported him as 'very hot and furious': attacking Conway for 'his neglect, weakness and irresolution', and especially for deserting his post as Secretary of State for the South 'as soon as he saw the fire kindled'; and denouncing the reduction in status of the Board of Trade. 'The most useful middle board in the kingdom was annihilated and made an insignificant board of report.' Grenville thought that Parliament ought to compensate those victims of the Stamp Act riots who had been given nothing by their assemblies; and he threw out the suggestion that an

[1] For the resolutions see *Commons Journals*, xxxi. 364.

oath acknowledging the subordination of the colonies to Britain should be made compulsory for all public officials and members of assemblies. In his scathing denunciation of the ministry's handling of the colonial situation Grenville paid little attention to Townshend's resolutions, but he did suggest that an act to order payment of army costs from the New York treasury would be a preferable course of action.

Conway both defended himself against Grenville and criticised Townshend's resolution. He put forward the suggestion of a local tax on New York that he had proposed in cabinet on 12 March, and evidently portrayed this method as more lenient, for diarist Ryder made this note on his speech. 'He spoke much too strongly in favour of the North Americans and upon the whole it was the worst speech I have heard from him this session.' Townshend rose to answer Conway and to point out that the suggestions of Dowdeswell and Grenville were not in accordance with the Mutiny Act. Charles Yorke opposed Townshend's resolutions and took up Grenville's suggestion of a Test Act for America. James West noted that Yorke 'thought the measures could scarce be too strong'; that Sir George Savile spoke for 'strong measures', turning Townshend's argument about 'paper war' against his own resolutions; and that Lord John Cavendish was 'in the same way of thinking'. Earlier Edmund Burke had also opposed the ministerial plan, which he wrongly ascribed to Chatham and by which, he said, the House would be giving the New York Assembly a share in legislation. James Harris formed the impression that Dowdeswell thought the plan 'too much', but Grenville thought Dowdeswell's scheme preferable to Townshend's: and contemporary reports of this debate do not bear out Horace Walpole's later claim that 'Lord Rockingham's party contended still for moderate measures'.

There remained the tactical problem of framing a motion that would secure the support of all those who opposed Townshend's proposal. This was publicly discussed between Conway and Grenville for nearly an hour, before Grenville put forward an agreed amendment to Townshend's third resolution, proposing instead a bill to enforce the Mutiny Act. Such pro-Americans as Conway and Horace Walpole voted with Grenville, but Townshend's resolution obtained a majority of 180 votes against 98 when the Committee divided after a debate of eight hours. The opposition may have suffered from a mistake in the counting: for James Harris told Lord Hardwicke the next day that it was 'thought by many that the minority was wrong told, and that a row was omitted. They were certainly much fewer, than they appeared.' The margin of the administration's victory was a great shock to the united opposition, as James West reported to Newcastle. 'Our friends were a good deal surprised at the division . . . Sir W. Meredith and Mr. Aufrere told me they would come no more to Parliament this year and most people look upon the session as in a manner over and are going out of town.'

Agents Garth and Johnson warned their colonies that the debate had reflected almost universal agreement on the policy of compelling New York to submit to the Mutiny Act, and that the discussion had been about the best method of achieving this end. Garth portrayed the vote as a victory for moderation. 'The majority of the Committee seemed to be of opinion that the people of New York would hardly run the risk of a continuation, not to say a repetition of disobedience', and that, if this proved not to be the case, 'the measure proposed would be abundantly less severe than any of the others suggested'. Johnson was more pessimistic. He noted the general hardening of political opinion: 'that by repealing the Stamp Act they had already greatly weakened the authority of Parliament; that they must therefore repeal no more acts upon such pretences'. His analytical mind exaggerated the coherence and consistency of official policy. He believed the administration had deliberately chosen between New York and Massachusetts, in order to make an example of one colony as part of a sinister new tactic.

Sensible of the danger of involving all the colonies in one common controversy, the present policy seems to be to attack them singly as occasion may require, and by degree reduce them all to that state of subordination and humble obedience which they very injudiciously seem to think necessary to their safety and happiness.

In the debate of 13 May the opposition had not been near either temporary victory or permanent success. Even another bench of supporters would still have left them about fifty votes behind administration. The opposition coalition was in any case an artificial one that would have fallen apart on any attempt to draft the bill for which the different opposition factions had voted. Political self-interest could not override the basic split on America between the Rockingham faction and the Grenville and Bedford groups. This had been concealed in the debate on Townshend's proposals by the strong and ambiguous language of Rockinghamite spokesmen; but the true position was to become apparent, and the opposition disunity made manifest, when Townshend's resolutions were reported from the American Committee to the House of Commons on 15 May. Three separate debates ensued.[1] Charles Garth moved to recommit the first resolution, denying that there was clear evidence of New York's disobedience, since the governor had failed to carry out the procedure specified in the Mutiny Act. This technical point also worried some administration supporters. When Townshend had called a meeting of leading ministerial supporters in the Commons to explain his plan, Secretary at War Lord Barrington had made this very same objection. 'He was of opinion, that the conduct of the Assembly of New York did not amount to an actual disobedience of the Mutiny Act, although their disposition to disobey was too evident.' Barrington voted for Townshend's resolution on 13 May, but the next day, so Grafton was told by Treasury Secretary Thomas Bradshaw, 'sitting in the House, by Mr. Cooper (who was also present at the meeting at Mr. Townshend's) told him he continued of the same opinion. Sir W. Baker came up to them and said the same thing.'[2] After Garth's motion had been seconded by the Committee's Chairman Rose Fuller, Attorney General De Grey therefore rose to dispose of the point, and the debate moved from this technicality to grounds of general policy.

Dowdeswell supported Garth's motion as the way to 'more

---

[1] For the proceedings of this day see *Commons Journals*, xxxi. 363–5; *Ryder Diary*, p. 348; Harris Diary, 16 May 1767; H. Walpole, *Memoirs*, ii. 29–30; Almon, *Debates*, vii. 301–15, reprinted in Cobbett, *Parl. Hist.*, xvi. 331–41; and the following letters: (a) J. West (three letters) to Newcastle, B.M. Add. MSS. 32981, fos. 391–5; (b) Newcastle to Rockingham, B.M. Add. MSS. 32982, fos. 51–2; (c) J. Yorke to Hardwicke, B.M. Add. MSS. 35374, fos. 320–1; (d) T. Bradshaw to Grafton, *Grafton Autobiography*, pp. 179–81. (e) C. Garth to South Carolina, *S.C.H.G.M.* 29 (1928), 226–7; (f) W. S. Johnson to W. Pitkin, *Trumbull Papers*, pp. 232–4.

[2] *Grafton Autobiography*, pp. 180–1.

just and less offensive resolutions'. Grenville favoured recommitment for the opposite reason, 'if it was intended to come to more strong and vigorous resolutions, but not if it was intended to whittle these trifling ones still lower'. Thomas Pownall then made the first of many Parliamentary speeches on America. He reminded the House that he had helped the Grenville administration to draft the Mutiny Act, but it had not followed the precedent of his own legislation in Massachusetts by being self-enforcing. He challenged the administration case that only New York had defied the Mutiny Act, for the other assemblies had all deliberately made variations from it when voting the army supplies. He proposed that either the assemblies should be given discretion in the voting of military supplies or the Crown should make requests directly to each one without the interposition of Parliament.[1] There followed a three-sided debate: Conway, Burke, and Lord John Cavendish spoke for recommitment 'to weaken the resolutions', Master of the Rolls Sewell and George Hay in order to strengthen them, and administration speakers opposed the motion altogether. Agent Johnson noted that 'all who spoke . . . agreed (except Mr. Beckford whom nobody would mind) that it was become absolutely necessary to do something to assert and support the sovereignty of this country and the dignity of Parliament'. For a time many thought that the resolution might be recommitted, but the opposition was in disarray. The Rockingham party had now altered or clarified their position, and the difference between their advocacy of leniency and that of Grenville for more severity was now all too clear. Townshend took advantage of the situation, and successfully appealed to the opposition factions not to wreck his American policy by a temporary alliance. Garth's motion was then negatived without a division.

Grenville took up the attack, with an amendment asserting that several assemblies continued to deny Parliament's right of taxation. This was an attempt to widen the question and to prepare the ground for his proposed American Test Act. The

[1] This summary of Pownall's speech is based on the later printed version to be found in the collections compiled by Almon and Cobbett. There are several discrepancies between that later version and the note of the speech by West, who thought Pownall favoured Grenville's idea of an instruction to the New York colonial treasury.

facts were accepted as true, but administration opposed the motion for two reasons: it was contrary to their policy of restricting action to New York, and Grenville's proposed test would be a new cause of colonial union. The amendment was criticized by Sir William Meredith as well as Charles Townshend, and the Rockingham party voted with the administration to defeat it by 150 votes to 51.

Grenville nevertheless persisted in his line of action. After the House had agreed to all three of Townshend's resolutions, and ordered a bill based on the third one, he proposed a resolution that all colonial officials should subscribe to a declaration affirming the subordination of the colonies to Britain and the legislative monopoly of Parliament. This was not the formal oath he had earlier mentioned, but his tactical modification was of no avail. The administration countered this move to enforce the principles of the Declaratory Act with a direct negative; and the Rockingham party found a distinction between the act itself and this attempt to make colonists subscribe to it. 'I am fully convinced, that it would have flung that whole country into the utmost confusion, and would scarcely have been taken by any body', Newcastle wrote afterwards to Rockingham. Sir William Baker, who had favoured Grenville's idea, absented himself from the debate. Dowdeswell and Burke spoke against Grenville's motion, which was defeated by 141 votes to 42. Newcastle regretted this breach between the opposition groups: 'I am sorry it was persisted in', was his final comment to Rockingham. His criticism of the tactic made no allowance for the principles of the Grenville group, among whom James Harris thought the vote 'a very remarkable event . . . Adieu to the supremacy over the colonies and to the act of Parliament declaratory thereof, the authority whereof the representatives in America are not forced to avow.' All Grenville salvaged from the day's proceedings was an Address asking the Crown to confer some mark of favour on the colonial governors and officials who had supported British authority in the Stamp Act Crisis.

These opposition defeats and dissensions prevented any resistance to the New York Restraining Bill itself. Even Grenville gave up the struggle before the bill was introduced.[1]

[1] B.M. Add. MSS. 32982, fo. 55.

Nor was opposition revived when the administration case for confining action to one colony was undermined on 27 May by news that the Georgia Assembly had also refused to make any provision under the Mutiny Act.[1] Solicitor-General Willes presented the New York bill to the House that day. It received a second reading on 1 June; was considered in Committee on 11 June; was reported on 12 June, when Frederick Montagu told Newcastle that this had been done 'without any opposition';[2] and passed the Commons on 15 June. There is no evidence of any discussion of the measure in either House, though the Commons extended the scope of the bill to include all decisions by the Assembly, and the Lords inserted an amendment to exclude from this prohibition the election of an Assembly Speaker. The final bill received the royal assent on 2 July.[3]

This whole political exercise was soon found to have been superfluous. The New York Restraining Act was due to go into force on 1 October: but in June, six months after refusing to pay anything towards army costs, the New York Assembly voted £3,000 for military supplies: this was a sum sufficient to pay for everything stipulated in the Mutiny Act, but no reference was made to that measure.

Governor Moore reported to Shelburne in a letter of 11 June that the Assembly had complied with the Mutiny Act, an optimistic assessment or a white lie. Shelburne had received the news before he sent Moore a copy of the Restraining Act on 18 July, for he commented that 'the prudent conduct of the Assembly has already rendered the provisions contained in it unnecessary'. The Assembly's action ended the matter as far as the ministry was concerned: the indefatigable Grenville in the next Parliamentary session was to raise the question of whether the Assembly's action justified the non-implementation of the Restraining Act, but the point sparked off no political interest.[4]

[1] Conway laid the relevant papers before the Commons on 3 June. *Commons Journals*, xxxi. 397. For copies of them see B.M. Add. MSS. 32981, fos. 46–53. Benjamin Franklin mistakenly thought the Restraining Act applied to Georgia as well as New York. *Franklin Papers*, xiv. 184.

[2] B.M. Add. MSS. 32982, fo. 319.

[3] *Commons Journals*, xxxi. 387, 392, 395, 400, 402, 403, 404–5, 417–18; *Lords Journals*, xxxi. 634, 649, 651, 662–3.

[4] On this end to the episode see Varga, *New York History*, 37 (1956), 250–2; and Gipson, *British Empire*, xi. 63–7.

For some time it had been apparent that the opposition would press the administration harder on America in the Lords than in the Commons. Here the opposition leaders decided to attack first the handling by the Privy Council of the Massachusetts Indemnity and Compensation Act. The Plantations Committee of the Council came to a final decision on 9 May, when twenty-six members were present. They included Camden, Northington, Shelburne, Grafton, Conway, North, Townshend, and other office-holders, and also Speaker Cust and Lord Chief Justice Wilmot. The opinion of the Committee was that the act should be disallowed, since the Assembly had incorporated in it a power of pardon without previous royal consent; and that the Governor should be instructed to require the Assembly to pass a separate Act of Compensation if this was still necessary. The opinion was tendered without prejudice to consideration of the question whether the act had been null and void from the beginning. The Privy Council, attended by George III himself, received and approved this report on 13 May.[1]

The decision had not been unanimous. Sir John Wilmot had wanted to declare the part of the act relating to the indemnity null and void, and the part concerning compensation good. From such distinctions Lord Mansfield fashioned an opposition strategy that was to embarrass the administration sorely in the Lords. On 13 May he suggested to Newcastle three resolutions to put before that House: that the part relating to the indemnity was void; that the part concerning compensation was valid; and that the King in Council had the right, in considering acts of assemblies, to reject part of an act and accept the rest of it.[2] The next day, with the prior knowledge and approval of Mansfield, Newcastle, and Rockingham, Lord Gower took the preliminary step of moving an Address for all the relevant papers.[3] Shelburne presented the papers on 18 May, and the House decided to take them into consideration on 22 May.[4] The opposition alliance on this subject was not

---

[1] B.M. Add. MSS. 32982, fos. 68–70; *Acts. P.C Col.* v. 86–7.

[2] B.M. Add. MSS. 32981, fos. 382–3.

[3] B.M. Add. MSS. 32981, fos. 382, 385; *Lords Journals*, xxxi. 599.

[4] *Lords Journals*, xxxi. 604–5. On 14 May a similar Address was made in the Commons, and Treasurer of the Household John Shelley laid the papers before

factious; Rockingham himself was in private highly critical of the Massachusetts Assembly for having gone beyond 'the limits of their constitution' in usurping such a power of pardon.[1]

A second line of attack was to be on the ministry's failure to do anything about the government of Canada. This tactic had been under consideration in February, when Richmond was 'vehement' on the subject and Hardwicke optimistic about the prospect of a general opposition coalition on the point: and it had the added attraction of affording ground for a personal attack on Northington for his behaviour of the previous year.[2] By early May Richmond had received encouragement on the subject from Mansfield, Temple, Bedford, and Gower; and the Rockingham faction decided to support him after a meeting on 11 May. Newcastle, who had paid no attention to the subject when in office, was soon whipping up support and urging Rockingham 'to summon all our friends' for 20 May, the day Richmond meant to bring the matter before the Lords.[3]

Richmond's motion then was for copies of all papers relating to Canada since the Proclamation of 1763. Lord President Northington signified the administration's consent, and only a brief debate took place: but Grafton was rightly apprehensive in his report to the King. 'There was a very full House: and the Duke of Grafton believes the numbers very near.'[4] George III's reply made clear his determination to ignore any defeat in the Lords: he looked on 'success as certain though I know a few rugged paths must be gone through'.[5]

Battle was joined two days later, on 22 May, when the Lords went into Committee on the Massachusetts papers. Lord Gower moved that a formal question should be put to 'the Judges', already summoned to attend, on the nullity or validity of the indemnity part of the Massachusetts Act.

---

that House on 18 May: but no further action was taken there. *Commons Journals*, xxxi. 360, 369; *Acts. P.C. Col.* v. 87.

[1] *Grenville Papers*, iv. 12n.

[2] *Rockingham Memoirs*, ii. 37–40.

[3] B.M. Add. MSS. 32981, fos. 367, 369, 397; 32982, fos. 32, 48–52; 35430, fos. 75–6.

[4] For the debate see *Lords Journals*, xxxi. 610–1; *Bedford Journal*, pp. 601–2; and Grafton's report to George III, *Corr. of George III*, i. 474.

[5] *Corr. of George III*, i. 474–5.

Camden and Northington made such able speeches in reply that Grafton felt there was no need for him to speak, or so he told the King. The motion was supported by Mansfield, Newcastle, Richmond, Suffolk, Temple, and Bedford, and the united opposition was defeated by only six votes, 62 to 56. 'All Lord Bute's friends voted to a man with the Court, in direct contradiction to their opinions in the last session', noted Mrs. Grenville scornfully in her diary. Horace Walpole believed that 'the judges would not have given their opinions if asked', and thought the administration, possessing thirty proxy votes to only ten for the opposition, would have reversed any defeat on report to the House.[1]

Much contemporary interest centred on the behaviour of the King's brothers. On the previous day Lord Chancellor Camden had gone 'into the King's Closet, where he stayed near an hour, and was observed to come out pretty ruffled'. The ministers were less sanguine about the prospect of a defeat in the Lords than the King himself, and Camden had been to ask George III to persuade his brothers to attend the debate. The King swallowed the anger he felt at the request and agreed to act as a royal whip; for he wrote to one brother, the Duke of Gloucester, asking him to vote for the administration on 22 May and to pass on the request to his other brothers, the Dukes of Cumberland and York. Gloucester and Cumberland were to obey this command, but when York received the message he at once went to tell the King 'that he had a character and reputation to maintain in the House of Lords which he could not give up'. In the debate York supported Gower's motion, 'saying that the rambling minds of the Americans ought to be restrained'. He left the House before the vote, telling Grafton that 'the most respectful thing for him to do was to withdraw, since he must differ from the King's servants': but George III received him 'coldly' the next day, 'telling him that question had been meant to be the push of the session'.[2]

A second question that Gower intended to propose to the

---

[1] For the debate see *Lords Journals*, xxxi. 614; *Bedford Journal*, p. 602; Mrs. Grenville's diary, *Grenville Papers*, iv. 224–5; and two letters: (a) Grafton to George III, *Corr. of George III*, i. 475; (b) H. Walpole to Sir H. Mann, H. Walpole, *Letters*, vii. 110–13. For a list of the opposition minority, containing fifty-eight names, see B.M. Add. MSS. 32982, fos. 99–100.

[2] This account is based on Mrs. Grenville's diary, *Grenville Papers*, iv. 224–7.

judges had been postponed until the Committee resumed on 26 May.[1] Newcastle told Rockingham on 23 May that he thought there was a good chance of victory. 'If all of us take proper care, we shall beat them in the Committee on Tuesday, if the Court dont bring down greater numbers than they did yesterday.'[2] The political world saw the rare spectacle of frantic whipping for a Lords debate, George III heading the field with another request to the Duke of York.[3]

Gower's second question for the judges was whether the two parts of the Massachusetts Act, being unconnected, should be considered separate acts, so that the nullity of one would not affect the validity of the other.[4] Camden, Grafton, and Hillsborough were the chief speakers against his motion that this question should be put, which was defeated by three votes, 65 to 62. Gower followed it up by proposing a resolution that it was the Committee's opinion that the part of the Massachusetts Act relating to pardon had always been null and void.[5] After twelve peers had spoken, including Mansfield, Bedford, and Newcastle in favour and Grafton, Egmont, Camden, and Shelburne against it, a motion by Grafton to end the Committee was carried by the same majority of 65 to 62. Lord Botetourt then proposed a vote of approbation to the Privy Council for its decision, but Grafton promptly quashed the idea, realizing the danger of defeat on such a provocative motion. He knew that the ministry had escaped by a narrow margin; the opposition had brought ten new voters, but six of those in the minority on 22 May had failed to attend. Even so, as Grafton later confessed to Chatham, the majority had been secured 'by the votes of two of the King's brothers, and some lords brought down from their very beds'.[6]

---

[1] For the two questions see Cobbett, *Parl. Hist.* xvi. 360.

[2] B.M. Add. MSS. 32982, fos. 95–6.

[3] *Grenville Papers*, iv. 227. The Duke was to be absent. For opposition activity see B.M. Add. MSS. 32982, fos. 99–100, 134–6.

[4] For the Lords debates of 26 May see *Lords Journals*, xxxi. 618; *Bedford Journal*, pp. 602–3; a report in the Hardwicke Papers, printed in Cobbett, *Parl. Hist.* xvi. 360–1; and two letters: (a) Shelburne to Chatham, *Chatham Papers*, iii. 253–4; (b) Grafton to George III, *Corr. of George III*, i. 476. For a division list see B.M. Add. MSS. 33037, fos. 51–4. For comments, see Brooke, *Chatham Administration*, p. 147.

[5] He had sent a copy of the resolution to Rockingham that morning. B.M. Add. MSS. 32982, fos. 134–6.

[6] *Chatham Papers*, iii. 258.

The Duke was demoralized by the combination of opposition pressure on America and India and internal dissensions in the ministry; and at the end of May the whole administration was on the point of collapse.[1] Chatham was still absent, nursing his illness, when George III wrote to him on 30 May of the 'coldness' shown by Shelburne to Grafton, Northington and Camden; 'the avowed emnity' of Townshend; and Conway's inclination to resign. The King even suggested that he himself should visit Chatham, a royal condescension his minister declined. Grafton was fortified by George III's determination to prop up his administration, a marked contrast to his treatment of Rockingham a year earlier; and by a personal interview with Chatham in which he obtained permission to negotiate again with the Bedford group. He withstood the last attempt by the united opposition 'to storm the closet' by a Lords motion on America.

This took place on 2 June, and concerned Quebec. On 27 May Shelburne, in accordance with the Address of 20 May, laid the Quebec papers before the House, which decided that they should be read on 1 June and considered the next day, in Committee.[2] The initiative on 2 June was taken by Richmond, who moved a resolution declaring that Quebec needed further regulations 'relating to its civil government and religious establishment', and in his speech announced that he would afterwards propose a second resolution stating that nothing had been done in this respect since the previous June, an implied censure on the ministry. These resolutions he intended to follow by an Address asking the King to order appropriate action.[3] Lord Botetourt, Chairman of the Committee, put the question on both resolutions together, a procedure to which Bedford rightly made objection. The first one was then passed unanimously, but the second was countered by a motion from

[1] For this ministerial crisis see Brooke, *Chatham Administration*, pp. 148–53. It can be followed in *Chatham Papers*, iii. 254–68; *Corr. of George III*, i. 476–82; Namier, *Additions and Corrections*, pp. 75–7; and *Grafton Autobiography*, pp. 132–40.

[2] *Lords Journals*, xxxi. 620–1, 624–5, 628.

[3] For the motions see B.M. Add. MSS. 32982, fos. 225–6. For reports of the debates see *Bedford Journal*, p. 603; a report from the Hardwicke Papers, printed in Cobbett, *Parl. Hist.* xvi. 361; and Grafton's report to George III, *Corr. of George III*. i. 483. For a division list (two copies, with discrepancies) see B.M. Add. MSS. 33037, fos. 73–80.

Grafton to leave the Chair. The ministry won by 73 votes to 61; and when in the resumed House Richmond moved an address to the King on the basis of the first resolution Grafton killed the proposal by carrying an adjournment motion without a division. The size of the ministerial majority had been a disappointment to the opposition, whose continued unity had been shown by speeches from Bedford, Sandwich, Gower, and Newcastle. Hardwicke, who had spoken on the opposition side, made this note at the end of his report. 'It was not expected the majority would have been so large; but the Court had exerted themselves to draw their strength together'. Newcastle told the absent Mansfield two days later that 'the Court fetched up Lords who had scarce ever been in the House or had been absent many years'.[1]

The ministry had put up a united front on Quebec in Parliament, but behind this political battle the administration itself was divided on policy.[2] Shelburne had opposed the motions by Richmond, which had presumably been intended to secure the implementation of Charles Yorke's detailed instructions of the previous year, suspended on the fall of the Rockingham ministry: yet he was himself in favour of this course of action. The rumours in February of a Parliamentary attack on the subject had led Shelburne to consider the question of Canada, but Yorke's plan had been lost somewhere in the government offices. After an amusing episode in which Shelburne's Under-Secretaries put forward different theories as to the document's fate, it was found at the Board of Trade. Northington, an old opponent of the scheme, meanwhile, as Lord President of the Council, prevented any action by refusing to recognize a mere copy of the document. The delay meant that the Privy Council did not consider the plan until 29 May, a few days before the Lords' debate on the subject. Northington then repeated both the detailed objections he had made in the cabinet of 26 June 1766 and his general argument that Parliamentary legislation was a more correct form of procedure than prerogative action. The Privy Council evidently adopted Northington's views, for on 20 June Shelburne, despite his own earlier approval of Yorke's plan, wrote to ask the new governor

---

[1] B.M. Add. MSS. 32982, fos. 237–8.
[2] See Humphreys and Scott, *Can. H.R.* 14 (1933), 49–54.

of Quebec, Guy Carleton, for information that would provide a basis for legislation on the legal system of the colony.[1] The ministry devoted considerable attention to the subject later that summer. On 9 August Northington reminded Grafton that any plan for Quebec needed both 'the full sense of the King's servants' and 'the sanction of Parliament'.[2] Within three weeks any decision had been indefinitely postponed. On 28 August the Privy Council finally rejected Yorke's plan and decided to send out a messenger for information;[3] and nothing was to be done until the Quebec Act of 1774.

North America had presented the best chance of an opposition victory in the Lords, and the debate of 2 June marked the turning of the tide. Although the opposition did not give up the challenge on other topics, the American situation no longer provided the ground of political action in either House. The tax proposals of Charles Townshend, rightly seen in retrospect as the most important American decision of the session, were to pass the Commons that month with virtually no opposition.

[1] Shortt and Doughty, *Canadian Documents*, i. 281.
[2] *Grafton Autobiography*, pp. 170–1.
[3] *Acts. P.C. Col.* v. 94–6.

16   Charles Townshend and American Taxation in 1767[1]

CHARLES Townshend's taxation of the American colonies has been the subject of many myths. The old picture was of the Chancellor of the Exchequer spontaneously pledging himself in the House of Commons on 26 January 1767 to raise an American revenue in a manner that would not arouse further colonial resistance, a solution which proved to be the exploitation of what was thought in Britain to be the colonial distinction between internal and external taxation; and then proceeding to do so against the wishes of his colleagues in the Chatham ministry. The first significant challenge to this traditional account was made by Sir Lewis Namier. He argued that Townshend had in fact a consistent American policy and was carrying out in 1767 a scheme he had favoured as a junior member of the Boards of Trade and Admiralty over a decade earlier. In 1753 and 1754 he had made clear his belief in the need to free the administration of government in America from financial dependence on the colonial assemblies. In 1767 he intended to do this by paying the salaries of the governors, judges, and other officials from the receipts of the new duties he then proposed.[2]

This interpretation is misleading in so far as it attributes to Townshend a unique approach to the American problem. Many British observers of the colonial scene had long thought that the constitutional encroachments of the assemblies on the prerogative of the Crown were based on their power of the purse; and the Grenville ministry had considered, but refused to adopt, the solution Townshend sought to impose in 1767.[3] Nor did Townshend, when planning a colonial revenue as Chancellor of the Exchequer, always intend to use it to pay the

---

[1] Parts of this chapter are taken from my paper of the same title in the *E.H.R.* 83 (1968), 33–51. I am indebted to the editor for permission to reprint them. Further research has caused me to modify some interpretations and assumptions.

[2] Namier and Brooke, *Charles Townshend*, pp. 37, 40, 172–9.

[3] Above, pp. 35–6.

costs of civil government in America. His fertile mind played with other possibilities: when writing to Adam Smith in the autumn of 1766 about ways of increasing the income of the sinking-fund, Townshend ended with this remark, 'I would add to them a real American revenue'.[1] This may have been a fleeting notion; but there is abundant evidence that both before and for some time after his promise to the Commons on 26 January Townshend was envisaging that any American revenue would, as earlier, be applied towards defraying the costs of the army in America.

Townshend's announcement of a project of colonial taxation could not have been the complete shock to his cabinet colleagues portrayed by Grafton in his *Autobiography*.[2] Written nearly forty years later, that is an unsound source for two reasons, the fallibility of Grafton's memory and his concern to excuse the rest of the Chatham administration from any share of the responsibility for the decision to tax America in 1767. Townshend doubtless surprised and offended his colleagues by his unauthorized announcement on 26 January; but leading members of the administration had already accepted the idea of an American revenue before this public commitment to such a policy.[3] Grafton himself, moreover, regularly attended meetings of the Treasury Board and could not have been ignorant of the preliminary decisions and inquiries.[4] Afterwards, when the administration considered the implications of Townshend's public promise, the ministerial debate, both in cabinet and outside, concerned the method and the purpose of new colonial taxation, but not its principle. That was accepted even by such men as Grafton, Shelburne, and Camden. Townshend's ministerial colleagues were neither ignorant beforehand of or opposed afterwards to his policy of American taxation.[5]

The occasion of Townshend's announcement was the debate of 26 January in the Committee of Supply on the army.[6]

---

[1] Quoted by Scott, *Econ. Hist. Rev.* 6 (1935–6), 88.

[2] *Grafton Autobiography*, pp. 126–7.

[3] Above, pp. 296–8.   [4] T. 29/38.

[5] The traditional interpretation on the point was first challenged by Chaffin, *W.M.Q.* 27 (1970), 90–121.

[6] The sources for this debate are numerous but brief. Information can be found in the Newdigate Diary; H. Walpole, *Memoirs*, ii. 293–4; *Grafton Autobiography*, pp. 126–7; and the following letters: (a) G. Onslow to Newcastle, B.M. Add. MSS. 32979, fo. 343; (b) (J. Harris) to Hardwicke, B.M. Add. MSS. 35608, fos. 1–2;

Usually the passage of resolutions allotting various sums of money to the different parts of the military establishment was a formality; but a debate began after Lord Barrington, as Secretary for War, had moved the fourth resolution, for a sum of £405,607 for the maintenance of the army in the colonies.[1] Grenville at once moved an amendment. 'This I proposed should be all defrayed by America and the West Indies, after having reduced it near one half by striking off the unnecessary articles', he told Lord Buckinghamshire the next day.[2] Charles Garth sent to South Carolina what was evidently a summary of Grenville's speech. 'Administration was called upon to know if any steps or measures had been thought of or taken to relieve the people of Great Britain from a burthen which it was said the colonies only ought to bear, that the amount of this expense with contingencies was upwards of £400,000, near a shilling in the pound of land tax upon Great Britain.'

Grenville was seconded by Thomas Pitt, but only Lord George Sackville spoke in favour of his amendment. It was opposed by Beckford, Thomas Townshend, Lord Granby, Lord Barrington, Richard Jackson, and Charles Townshend, to whose speech contemporaries paid particular attention. James Harris noted that he 'opposed the motion but with great civility—much approved the general idea of taxing America—said even of the Stamp Act, that it was a *well chosen article* and that the notion of Internal Taxation and External was *perfect nonsense*'. This last point was noted by several observers and with especial delight by Grenville. 'Mr. Townshend in answer to this, though he refused to consent to it, yet held a very strong

---

(c) G. Grenville to Lord Buckinghamshire, Grenville Letter-Books, vol. 2, *sub* 27 Jan., printed in *H.M.C. Lothian*, pp. 274–5; (d) Conway to George III, *Corr. of George III*, i. 451; corrected by Namier, *Additions and Corrections*, p. 70; (e) C. Garth to South Carolina, *S.C.H.G.M.* 29 (1928), 132; (f) W. Beckford to Chatham, *Chatham Papers*, iii. 176–8; (g) Lord Charlemont to H. Flood, *Chatham Papers*, iii. 178n; (h) Shelburne to Chatham, *Chatham Papers*, iii. 182–8; (i) W. Rouet to Baron Mure, *Caldwell Papers*, ii (2), 100–1; (j) E. Sedgwick to E. Weston, *H.M.C. Weston Underwood*, pp. 402–3; (k) W. S. Johnson to W. Pitkin, *Trumbull Papers*, pp. 215–16; (l) anon (?B. Franklin) to ?, *Franklin Papers*, xiv. 21–2.

[1] *Commons Journals*, xxxi. 75. The total was unusually high. Shy, *Towards Lexington*, pp. 246–7. Shy, however, is mistaken in his statement that there were no extraordinaries later in the session. Below, p. 343.

[2] Since the debate was in Committee there is no record of the precise wording of Grenville's motion.

language that America ought to pay that expense, and disclaimed in very strong terms almost every word of Lord
Chatham's language on this subject, treating his Lordship's
distinction between Internal and External Taxes with the same
contempt as I did.'[1] Not one speaker in the debate defended
the position on American taxation that Chatham had adopted
in the previous session: but the day proved a disaster for Grenville. He obtained the assistance of neither of the other two
opposition groups. The supporters of the Duke of Bedford
walked out of the House. They might have been expected to
back Grenville on grounds of policy; but the debate apparently
coincided with Bedfordite hopes of a return to office and their
consequent unwillingness to jeopardize such a chance. The
behaviour of the Rockingham group was more predictable.
Disapproval of Grenville's motion would not lead them to
support the administration in speech or vote; and so Newcastle
was informed that 'all the Cavendishes, Dowdeswell, etc.'
left before the division. This description is that of their former
associate, George Onslow, who, like Conway, had chosen to
stay on in office under the new administration. At the end of
the debate, Grenville was left with only 'his own people' in a
minority of 35 against 106, and the money was then voted.
On the report of the resolution next day Grenville tried again,
and obtained only 19 votes, against 70, for this amendment,
which might well have been identical with the one he had
moved in the Committee.[2] 'That such forces as shall be kept
up and employed in and for the defence and service of any of
His Majesty's colonies in America, or the West Indies . . . be
maintained, and the expense thereof defrayed by a revenue
to be raised from the said colonies.'

It was only Charles Townshend's promise on American
taxation that gave significance to the debate of 26 January:
yet it was recorded in a mere six out of fourteen contemporary
reports of the debate.[3] Grenville himself either did not remember

---

[1] Contemporaries noted that Townshend, when denouncing this distinction,
deliberately addressed the galleries of the House where some colonial agents were
present. *Franklin Papers*, xiv. 22; *Trumbull Papers*, p. 216.

[2] *Commons Journals*, xxxi. 76.

[3] I discussed this point in *E.H.R.* 83 (1968), 37–8. Rouet, Sedgwick, and (?)
Franklin should be added to the list there of those who noted it. George Onslow
was not one of them, and D. H. Watson errs in deducing from his report of the

the pledge or did not think it worth mentioning in the account he sent to Lord Buckinghamshire; and it was Lord George Sackville, not Grenville, who in the debate attempted to obtain the fullest possible commitment of Townshend to his statement. The general absence of interest may have been due to Townshend's reputation for such personal irresponsibility that little reliance could be placed on his word: an alternative explanation might be the lack of news value if there was already current a belief that the administration intended to tax America.

Why did Charles Townshend make the promise? There was no question of tactical expediency on the day. The attendance was low and the administration had a comfortable majority among the members present. Not a single independent member rose to support Grenville, or, indeed, to speak at all. Undoubtedly the prospect of an American revenue would be popular in Parliament, but there is no evidence to support a theory of pressure from M.P.s in the debate. Some observers suspected that Townshend's promise had been made with an eye not on the Commons but on the Court; Edward Sedgwick made this comment to his former colleague Edward Weston on 3 February: 'These declarations, in the opinion of some, may cost the gentleman his place; while others on the contrary say that he stands higher in favour than ever with the most powerful supporter, and is destined to be Prime Minister very shortly.' [1]

The importance of Townshend's announcement, of course, was that as Chancellor of the Exchequer he was widely believed to be speaking on behalf of the ministry. It was in this sense that Charles Garth reported his speech to South Carolina.

The Chancellor of the Exchequer declaring that Administration had applied their attention to give relief to Great Britain from bearing the whole of the expence of securing, defending and protecting America and the West India Islands, and that he should

---

debate to Newcastle that the Rockingham party realized the significance of Townshend's pledge. *E.H.R.* 84 (1969), 561. The remark by Onslow that he quotes to support this opinion, 'You see the mischief and the intent of it', referred to Grenville's motion and not to Townshend's promise, which is not mentioned in the letter. Watson also apparently forgets that Onslow had broken with the Rockingham party by remaining in office under the Chatham ministry.

[1] *H.M.C. Weston Underwood*, pp. 402–3.

bring into the House this session some propositions that he hoped might tend in time to ease the people of England upon this head and yet not be heavy in any manner upon the people in the Colonies, but of which nature these propositions are he did not disclose.

The ministerial reaction to Townshend's promise is misrepresented in that much-quoted source, Grafton's *Autobiography*. Grafton there stated that on the next day the cabinet questioned Townshend about his pledge, on the ground that it was contrary to administration policy. But Townshend had spoken the truth. The ministry had been considering an American revenue to reduce the burden of the colonial army costs on Britain;[1] and Grafton has misled historians by his later and long-accepted statement that Townshend 'had ventured to depart on so essential a point from the profession of the whole ministry'.[2] It must be doubtful whether there was a cabinet meeting on 27 January at all: Shelburne would surely have mentioned it to Chatham in his letter of 1 February about Townshend's promise; and he did not do so. Shelburne's concern was not with the principle of colonial taxation, but with Townshend's promise that some American revenue would be raised that session; for he did not see how that would be possible with quit-rents, the method the administration had hitherto been contemplating.

Mr. Townshend . . . *pledged himself* to the House to find a revenue, if not *adequate* . . . yet nearly sufficient to answer the expense, when properly reduced. What he means, I do not conceive. I have always thought the quit rents may be so managed, without having too great a retrospect, as to produce a certain sum; and I have likewise had reason to think that such a new method of granting lands might be devised, under the direction of my Lord President, as might give infinite satisfaction to America, contribute to the ascertaining property, preventing future suits at law, and in great measure prevent the Indian disturbances, and besides all, *incidentally* produce a certain revenue, without its being the object; but I do not conceive either of them can possibly take place this year, there not being materials in any office here sufficient to form a final judgement of them. Many of them must come for that purpose from America.[3]

---

[1] Above, pp. 296–8.   [2] *Grafton Autobiography*, pp. 126–7.
[3] *Chatham Papers*, iii. 184–5.

Townshend did not tell M.P.s on 26 January what method of taxation he proposed to adopt: but the idea of a revenue from duties on goods imported into America was not new. Grenville's Duties Act of 1764 had established the practice with respect to goods from foreign colonies. The Rockingham administration had considered its extension to goods imported from Europe, and had abandoned any pretence at trade regulation by the molasses duty. And Shelburne, in his letter to Gage on 11 December 1766, assumed that customs duties would be a source of colonial revenue. Townshend himself had this method of taxation in mind; for in the very same letter of 1 February that informed Chatham of Townshend's promise Shelburne reported this rumour:[1]

I have heard, indeed, from general conversation, that Mr. Townshend has a plan for establishing a board of customs in America, and by a new regulation of the tea duty here, and some other alterations, to produce a revenue on imports there. I am myself in no respect able or sufficiently informed to form a judgement how far this may be likely to answer the end or no; but in many views it appears a matter that will require the deepest consideration at this time especially.

Shelburne's account makes it clear that the plans of Townshend for colonial import duties, so far from being concerted with the other ministers,[2] were not even known to the cabinet. Townshend had already been working on these revenue proposals for some weeks, but their detailed formulation extended over several months and was not to be completed until May. The method soon became public knowledge, for on 12 February agent Johnson was reporting to Connecticut a plan to put duties on 'tea and china ware':[3] and Townshend told M.P.s about it in the next Commons debate over American finance, on 18 February; diarist Ryder noted that he 'spoke of the distinction between internal and external taxes as not founded in reason but proper to be adopted in policy'.[4]

[1] *Chatham Papers*, iii. 185.
[2] Grafton has the misleading implication in his *Autobiography*, p. 127, that the cabinet thought of 'port duties' in order 'to render the business as little offensive as possible'.
[3] *Trumbull Papers*, p. 218.
[4] *Ryder Diary*, p. 331. Lord Barrington apparently told Shelburne of this announcement. *Chatham Papers*, iii. 233–5.

This occasion was the Committee of Supply on the army extraordinaries. A motion was made, presumably again by Lord Barrington, for a further sum of £315,917,[1] and a debate was begun by George Grenville, who now followed up his vague suggestion of economy on 26 January by constructive ideas.[2] He proposed the withdrawal of as many soldiers as possible from the interior of America, to reduce the enormous cost of maintaining such outposts; and suggested that the Indian expenses should be thrown on the colonies concerned. The administration saw that Grenville might steal the credit for proposals that the ministers already had under consideration; and Townshend rose to answer him. While agreeing on the desirability of withdrawing soldiers from the outposts, he turned the tables on Grenville by blaming the military arrangements framed during his ministry for the high level of current expenses. The Rockingham group took little part in the debate, and left the House shortly before the division because of attacks made on their American policy by Grenville. The administration then defeated Grenville's motion by 131 votes to 67, but contemporary observers reckoned that the division would have been very close if only Grenville could have curbed his tongue.[3]

At the next cabinet meeting on America, on 12 March, Townshend not only secured adoption of his policy for New York, but also threatened resignation if the cabinet refused to accept his financial plans for the colonies.[4] These now incorporated the ideas of withdrawing soldiers from the forts in the interior of the continent and obliging the colonies to bear the Indian costs themselves. The cost remaining after the reduction of expenses would be defrayed by an American port duty. Shelburne told Chatham that Townshend said 'that he had

---

[1] *Commons Journals*, xxxi. 171. For the accounts to be paid see *ibid.*, 124–38. They included over £167,000 of colonial expenses, nearly all from North America.

[2] For this debate see *Ryder Diary*, pp. 330–1; H. Walpole, *Memoirs*, ii. 296; and the following letters: (a) Conway to George III, *Corr. of George III*, i. 453; corrected by Namier, *Additions and Corrections*, p. 70; (b) George III to Conway, *Corr. of George III*, i. 450–1; corrected by Namier, *Additions and Corrections*, pp. 69–70; (c) J. Harris to Hardwicke, B.M. Add. MSS. 35608, fos. 3–4; (d) W. Rouet to Baron Mure, *Caldwell Papers*, ii (2), 106–7; (e) Lord Charlemont to H. Flood, *Chatham Papers*, iii. 210n.

[3] Since the debate was in Committee the precise wording of Grenville's motion is not known.

[4] Reports of this part of the meeting were sent to Chatham by Grafton and Shelburne. *Chatham Papers*, iii. 232–5.

promised this to the House, and upon the authority of what passed in the cabinet'. Townshend's claim that his announcement of a colonial revenue from customs duties in the Commons debate of 18 February had been based on a prior decision of the cabinet may well have been true: for Shelburne did not deny it.

Townshend's plans for military economy clashed with the policy for the interior of the American continent being devised in the office of Secretary of State Shelburne. The result was a long departmental memorandum dated 30 March 1767, and headed 'Reasons for not diminishing American expence this year': it is apparently a brief from which Shelburne could argue in cabinet.[1] The main point was that the information necessary for the formulation of a new policy was not yet available, as replies had not come to the inquiries sent to Gage, the colonial governors and the Indian superintendents. This argument was reinforced by the observations that no one had a plan ready; that constant changes of policy weakened the authority of government; and that one more year's delay would do little harm.

After putting the case for at least postponing any economies in more detail, Shelburne's brief dealt with finance. It accepted that 'a fund for American expenses may be reasonably enough expected in process of time . . . Its basis must be laid on proper regulations for the better management and receipt of the quit rents, and the future grants of lands . . . but chiefly on requisitions from the different provinces to be granted annually by their assemblies according to their respective abilities.' This change of emphasis from quit-rents back to the old and unsatisfactory method of requisitions may have been the result of two early replies to Shelburne's circulars of 11 December, which had both arrived on 25 March. Governor Franklin of New Jersey said that there were no quit-rents in his colony, while Governor Moore of New York reported an income of only £1,806.[2] Later reports were to be equally discouraging. There were no quit-rents in Massachusetts and Connecticut; those in Georgia and the two Carolinas were heavily in arrears; and in Maryland they were paid to the Proprietor.[3] An over-all

---

[1] Shelburne MSS., vol. 85, fos. 102–9.   [2] C.O. 5/112, fos. 51–2, 63.
[3] C.O. 5/112, fos. 47–8, 75–6, 82, 142, 144, 150, 156.

M

assessment of the situation was made by Gage in a letter received on 15 May.[1] He explained that the Proprietory and Charter colonies paid only a mere token to the Crown, and 'the unchartered provinces little more till within these few years'. This was because collection of the quit-rents had been 'long shamefully neglected', and there was no effective machinery to enforce payment. In New York, where he confirmed Moore's estimate of the nominal income as £3,000 local currency or £1,800 sterling, the arrears were about £20,000 currency and the income was already charged with the payment of £465 sterling for certain salaries. Gage said that he had not been able to find out 'what at an average the whole quit-rents of North America might amount to, if duly collected': but he did not think that 'any very great and considerable sum will accrue to the Crown therefrom for many years to come' from either old or new colonies. No advice could have been more explicit, but Shelburne took no notice: his plans for the west presented to the cabinet later that year assumed that quit-rents in new colonies would provide an immediate and growing revenue.[2]

From April 1767 the issue of a policy for the western lands became divorced from that of colonial revenue. There is a gap in the evidence, but subsequent events show that Shelburne must have succeeded in obtaining from the cabinet a rejection of Townshend's demand for military economy and an agreement to maintain the existing deployment of the American army until he was able to formulate proposals for new colonies and the management of the Indians.

With the abandonment of quit-rents as a potential source of colonial revenue Townshend concentrated his attention on the alternative means that had been in his mind for some time, import duties on goods entering colonial ports: and he proposed to use this money to carry out a scheme of long standing. Hitherto the official intention behind any American revenue had been the same as that of the Grenville and Rockingham administrations, to use it towards the maintenance of the military establishment in the colonies. This had been the assumption in the Commons debates of 26 January and 18

[1] *Gage Corr.* i. 130–2.
[2] For these plans see Sosin, *Whitehall and the Wilderness*, pp. 153–9.

February, and at the cabinet meeting of 12 March. Townshend now planned to use the anticipated revenue from customs duties for the payment of the costs of civil government in the colonies, the idea he had conceived as long ago as 1753 and had since advocated from time to time, most recently in the Commons debate of 7 February 1766. In 1767 he was to resurrect the plan and carry it out as Chancellor of the Exchequer. It was apparently revived before the abandonment of the hope of a revenue from quit-rents, for, in an undated letter to Grafton, Townshend asked whether he had 'any orders to communicate to him relative to the payment of American salaries out of the quit-rents, agreeably to what Lord Shelburne mentioned last week in cabinet and the Duke of Grafton yesterday . . . Mr. T. understood the Duke of Grafton that he would obtain this declaration today.'[1] Townshend's proposed use of the American revenue was soon public knowledge, for on 11 April Franklin reported to Pennsylvania 'that a project is on foot to render all the governors and magistrates in America independent of the annual support they receive of their several assemblies'.[2]

Contemporaries failed to perceive an important implication of this change. The great attraction of an American tax for the House of Commons had always been to relieve the burden on the British taxpayer. In the debate of 27 February on the land tax, Grenvillite George Hay used Townshend's earlier promise as an argument in favour of the lower rate of tax proposed by the opposition, Horace Walpole noting that 'he artfully took notice that Townshend had said he would propose some tax this year on America'.[3] The loss of government revenue of some £500,000 arising from this ministerial defeat was for long linked by historians with Townshend's plan for American taxation. It has now been realized that Townshend's pledge on the subject had been made a month earlier, and that his anticipated American revenue of about £40,000 was insignificant by comparison with the fall in the land tax: but not that Townshend's plan made the projected American revenue a

[1] Grafton MSS., no. 441. The letter is headed 'Sunday even.'; internal evidence points to a date between 29 Mar. and 10 May. Chaffin, *W.M.Q.* 27 (1970), 108, suggests 12 Apr. The letter seems to imply that royal approval was the final obstacle.

[2] *Franklin Papers*, xiv. 109.   [3] H. Walpole, *Memoirs*, ii. 299.

matter of no fiscal significance whatever. Since most colonial officials were already paid from American sources, Townshend's proposed use of the new revenue changed the mode of payment rather than the incidence of the burden from Britain to the colonies. It is true that Townshend, in his Budget Day speech on 15 April, did mention American taxation as a minor means of balancing the national account, as James Harris told Hardwicke. 'The ways and means fell short of the supplies about £33,000: this defect he pledged himself to make up by amelioration of our resources, and by an *American* tax.'[1] Either Townshend did not realize himself that his plan put his American taxation outside the scope of the British national budget, or he was deliberately misrepresenting the situation from political motives. Certainly the fact that Townshend's taxation scheme met the popular demand for a colonial tax without fulfilling the implicit purpose of transferring part of the British tax burden to America appears to have been overlooked at the time, and afterwards.

By April Townshend was busy formulating in detail his proposals for a colonial revenue from import duties, and he completed his first plan by early May. His ideas were numerous and varied. He revived the project of the Rockingham ministry for obtaining an income from this source: for it was evidently in response to an inquiry from Townshend that John Huske informed him on 9 April of the proposals he had made to that administration the previous year for duties on foreign wines, olive oil, dried fruit, and citrus fruit.[2] Townshend now incorporated them into his tax plans virtually without alteration. He anticipated a revenue of £7,000 from £7 a ton on foreign wine; £2,500 from 2s. 6d. a cwt on dried fruit; £3,000 from 4d. a hundred on oranges and lemons; £9,920 from £5 a ton on olive oil; and £1,000 from small duties on capers, olives, and corkwood. Townshend also had other duties in mind. His papers show that he hoped to obtain £5,000 a year from small duties on glass sent to America; £2,000 from a duty on 'red and white lead and painters' colours'; and £5,000 from a

---

[1] B.M. Add. MSS. 35608, fos. 14–15. Neither of the other two reports of the speech found, by Nathaniel Ryder and James West, mention American taxation. *Ryder Diary*, p. 340; B.M. Add. MSS. 32981, fo. 175.

[2] Namier and Brooke, *Charles Townshend*, p. 187.

9 per cent duty on paper. His idea to raise money from china exports to America was not an import duty but the cancellation of the export rebate in Britain, amounting to £8,000. Altogether he expected a total revenue of £43,420 from these measures.[1]

There were significant omissions from this list. There had long been rumours of Townshend's intention to impose a tea duty; but nothing could be decided on that subject until an agreement with the East India Company: and if Townshend had not yet adopted what was to be his most famous duty, he had already abandoned one that threatened to be controversial, a duty on salt. When John Huske heard about this idea on 9 April he at once warned Townshend that 'a more fatal imposition to both Great Britain and her colonies could not be devised'.[2] Townshend thereupon explained that he intended to levy a duty of 6*d.* a bushel on salt imports, to be offset by a proportionate bounty on fish and salt-meat exports. He asked Huske for his objections, and Huske called for help on Benjamin Franklin, who soon produced the arguments that the duty would be unpopular, productive of only a trifling net revenue, and obstructive to trade.[3] Colonial agents and London merchants conducted a vigorous and successful campaign against the salt duty, as agent Johnson reported to Governor Pitkin of Connecticut on 16 May. 'Mr. Jackson has been very assiduous upon this occasion, and we are again beholden to the merchants, with Mr. Trecothick at their head, for their kind interposition in our behalf.'[4] Townshend saved face by telling the House of Commons that he had abandoned the salt duty because of the difficulty of calculating the rebate to be allowed for salted fish and meat.[5] There is no evidence that the colonial agents asked Townshend to abandon any other duties, and he made clear to them his determination to carry out his taxation plan, as Johnson told Governor Pitkin.[6]

---

[1] *Ibid.*, pp. 189–91.   [2] *Ibid.*, p. 188.   [3] *Franklin Papers*, xiv. 119, 184.
[4] *Trumbull Papers*, p. 229.   [5] *S.C.H.G.M.* 29 (1928), 229.
[6] *Trumbull Papers*, p. 229. Johnson records Townshend as declaring that the aim of the taxes was the maintenance of the army, purporting to quote him as saying that 'an American army, and consequently an American revenue, are essentially necessary': yet Johnson was writing on 16 May, three days after Townshend had told M.P.s his intention of paying civil government costs from this revenue.

The Chancellor of the Exchequer (who is at present in great esti-
mation, is the principal manager in the House of Commons, and
bids fair to conduct the counsels of the nation) declared at one of
these meetings that although he did not in the least doubt the right
of Parliament to tax the colonies internally, and that he knew no
difference between internal and external taxes, (which, by the way,
is a doctrine very generally adopted here,) yet since the Americans
were pleased to make that distinction he was willing to indulge them,
and chose for that reason to confine himself to regulations of trade,
by which a sufficient revenue might be raised in America.

In addition to his import duties Townshend may already
have been considering an American revenue from a quite
different source, colonial currency. The movement for repeal
of the Currency Act had been building up since the Rockingham ministry had postponed any decision the previous year.[1]
New York had subsequently refused to accept the concession
made by that administration through dislike of the attached
conditions. In July 1766 Charles Garth advised South Carolina
to petition, since the lack of complaint, apart from the Pennsylvania petition, was being used as an argument against repeal;
and he had a favourable reception when he presented the
colony's petition to Shelburne in January 1767.[2] Soon afterwards, on 4 February, the Secretary of State received from
Governor Moore of New York the draft of a repeal bill originally sent to that colony by its agent Robert Charles.[3] The
support of the Committee of North American Merchants was
secured when a meeting on 28 January, attended by Garth
and Franklin, agreed on a policy of repeal, on condition that
colonial legal-tender money was not to be used for payment
of sterling debts; and at once appointed six of their number to
lobby the administration.[4] The optimism engendered by these
events was quenched by the mounting resentment against the
colonies caused by the news in February from New York and
Massachusetts. On 12 March Garth warned his colony that
'the ministry grown exceedingly cool upon, not to say shy of it
[repeal]; we are asked with what propriety can government
give countenance and support to an indulgence for America,

---

[1] On this subject see Ernst, *W.M.Q.* 25 (1968), 190–207.
[2] *S.C.H.G.M.* 29 (1928), 41, 129.   [3] *Franklin Papers*, xiv. 39–40.
[4] *S.C.H.G.M.* 29 (1928), 129–30.

when their requests to America are directly refused?' Since
the support of the administration was essential, the only hope
was for the British merchants to petition Parliament for repeal.[1]
Franklin, Garth, Montagu, Charles, Sherwood, and De Berdt
all attended meetings of merchants on the subject, and the
agents persuaded them to continue the campaign.[2] The first
fruit was the presentation to the ministry of a memorandum
from 'the Merchants of London trading to America . . . That
the most speedy and effectual relief to the colonies in respect
to the present distressed state of their commerce, for want of a
medium of trade', would be a repeal of the 1764 Currency Act:
and that such a repeal would not injure British merchants if it
contained a clause declaring that colonial money could not be
legal tender for sterling debts.[3] The Board of Trade, standing
by its 1764 report on colonial currency, opposed repeal: but
Franklin heard on 14 April that its President Lord Clare was
willing 'to allow the legal tender, provided the bills are issued
on land security, and the sum limited'.[4] Charles Townshend,
too, was believed to favour repeal. John Huske, in his letter of
9 April to Townshend, had urged the relevance of this policy
to the desire for a colonial revenue: 'be assured that no regulation or measure that is to raise money can be agreeable or
practicable in the continent colonies till you give them a
currency. Till then you are demanding brick without straw.'[5]
Some agents evidently pointed out to Townshend that there
were direct revenue possibilities involved in the issue of colonial
currency that bore interest:[6] but the Chancellor of the Exchequer had come to no decision on this subject when he chose to
announce his provisional schedule of import duties to the
American Committee of the House of Commons on 13 May
during his speech proposing the coercive resolutions on New
York.[7]

Townshend told the Committee what he had told the agents,
that he was adopting the method of import duties because of

---

[1] *S.C.H.G.M.* 29 (1928), 219–20. [2] *Franklin Papers*, xiv. 107–8.
[3] *Franklin Papers*, xiv. 164–5. This is a copy sent by B. Franklin to J. Galloway
on 20 May. I do not know the date nor to whom it was presented.
[4] *Franklin Papers*, xiv, 123–5.
[5] Namier and Brooke, *Charles Townshend*, pp. 187–8.
[6] *S.C.H.G.M.* 29 (1928), 228–9.
[7] For the sources for this debate see above, p. 322, n. 2.

the American distinction between internal and external taxes, even though he did not accept it. He then stated the duties he had already decided upon, estimating the total revenue to be under £40,000.[1] Townshend also announced for the first time the way he now meant to use this American revenue. Diarist Ryder noted only the general purpose, 'that the judges and magistrates who are now in many colonies dependent every year for their salary or at least part of it on the assembly ought to be made independent'; but two agents recorded more details. William Johnson believed that Townshend had said 'that the Governor and Chief Justice in the King's governments should be rendered more independent by giving the first £2000 and the latter £500 per annum, to be paid out of the American revenue'; and Charles Garth sent this report back to South Carolina.

The Chancellor of the Exchequer did likewise in the Committee open a plan for improving the system of government in the colonies in order that the authority of the executive power might carry with it in the several departments the weight and respect essentially necessary to answer the ends of its institution, and for that purpose after showing in what manner the civil officers of the Crown were provided for and the extent of such provision, he should propose that, out of the fund arising from the American duties now, or to be imposed, His Majesty should be enabled to establish salaries that might be better suited to support the dignity of the respective officers, and for which to be no longer dependent upon the pleasure of any assembly.[2]

In the ensuing debate only George Grenville commented on Townshend's tax proposals. He denounced them as quite inadequate, suggesting that pressure from within the administration had prevented more extensive measures; attacked the plan for duties on wine, fruit and oil as subversive of the Navigation Acts; and suggested as an additional source of revenue 'a general paper currency for the colonies, to be issued

---

[1] Lists of the dutiable goods were made by Charles Garth, William Johnson, Nathaniel Ryder, and James West. Johnson noted the glass as 'window-glass', Garth the dried fruit as 'raisons' and not only 'paper' but 'coloured papers for furniture', and both of them that the lead was that used in painting.

[2] H. Walpole, *Memoirs*, iii. 23, stated that this plan was to apply only 'to the offending provinces' and not to all the colonies. This qualification is not recorded by Garth, Johnson, or Ryder, or confirmed in any other source.

on loan and the interest remitted here and applied to the increase of the American revenue'.[1]

Townshend replied to Grenville's comments on taxation when he rose later in the debate to defend his proposals for New York. He denied that he had given up any taxes because of cabinet pressure on him. The salt duty had been dropped as impractical, and there would be a tea duty, but the details depended on an agreement with the East India Company. Townshend agreed with Grenville's idea of an income from colonial paper currency, and Garth understood him to promise what the colonies wanted: repeal of the Currency Act of 1764 and 'a permission to establish a loan office in the respective provinces with a power of issuing paper currency carrying an interest'. This money would be used for 'the King's service', but Garth believed that no decision had been taken as to whether Parliament or the colonial assemblies should appropriate it.[2] That was the important constitutional point for the colonies. Franklin therefore exerted himself to persuade the administration to adopt the procedure of 'a requisition from the Crown' to the assemblies for any money derived from such issues of colonial currency.[3] By the end of May he was confident that he had killed the idea of Parliamentary appropriation by his argument that no colony would make money on such a condition, and that the anticipated commercial benefits to Britain would therefore be lost; whereas the assemblies, on occasional requisitions from the Crown, would make voluntary appropriations of most of the money.[4]

Charles Townshend's tax proposals were not mentioned in the debate on the report of these resolutions on 15 May, and he took no further Parliamentary action on the matter that month. The Committee of Ways and Means did meet on 18 May, but apparently to consider postage rates in Britain. The next meeting was ordered for 20 May, but postponed successively to 22, 25, and 27 May, until the Committee eventually met on 1 June.[5] One reason for this delay, as Townshend had

---

[1] This is Johnson's summary of the suggestion: it was also noted by Ryder, Walpole, and West.

[2] *S.C.H.G.M.* 29 (1928), 228–9.

[3] *Franklin Papers*, xiv. 163–4.

[4] *Franklin Papers*, xiv. 180–1.

[5] *Commons Journals*, xxxi. 370, 381, 384, 388, 392.

M*

told M.P.s in his second speech on 13 May, was the negotiation with the East India Company. It was the Company's tea that would bear the duty he intended; and the Company's financial stability that would be further jeopardized by any contraction of business that might result. Townshend's plan to avert this catastrophe, as Garth already knew by mid-May, was to allow a rebate of the 25 per cent British import duty on any tea exported to America.[1] The negotiation was concluded by 20 May, when the Company submitted to the House of Commons a petition that included a request for such a rebate.[2] On 22 May, in a Committee of the Whole House on the state of the East India Company, Townshend proposed a resolution to this effect. Diarist Ryder noted that this motion 'was objected to by Mr. Grenville but agreed to at last without a division'.[3] The provision was included in the Indemnity Act granted to the Company that came into operation in July.[4]

There was another important reason for the postponement of the Townshend duties. This was the reluctance of the cabinet to approve Townshend's plan to use the new revenue for the salaries of governors, judges, and other officials in the colonies. Grafton's correspondence contains the following undated letter:

Mr. Townshend presents his compliments to the Duke of Grafton. He sincerely laments that the opportunity has not been taken of soliciting his Majesty's assent to the proposition of independent salaries for the civil officers of North America, especially as he had pledged himself to the House for some measure of this sort, and had the assurances of Lord Shelburne in the last cabinet for the whole extent of the establishment, and the Duke of Grafton on Saturday adopted the idea at least as far as New York. In this distress Mr. Townshend does not think he can with honour move the resolutions this day, and therefore hopes either to have the authority or that some means may be found of postponing the matter for a day or two till he can receive it. He feels his honour absolutely at stake. He did not suggest the matter to the King, because as the Duke of Grafton knows, he has *never* presumed to move in such high matters alone or originally.

---

[1] *S.C.H.G.M.* 29 (1928), 229.

[2] *Commons Journals*, xxxi. 377–8. For the background, without reference to the tea duty, see Sutherland, *East India Company*, pp. 169–74.

[3] *Ryder Diary*, p. 350.

[4] Labaree, *Boston Tea Party*, pp. 13, 20.

This letter must have been written at some time after the debate of 13 May, and presumably on one of the days for which an order made for a meeting of the Committee of Ways and Means was postponed.[1] By 1 June Townshend had apparently obtained the authority of King and cabinet for his idea, and proposed his American taxation plan that day.

The delay meant that attendance in the Commons on the introduction and passage of the Townshend duties was very thin. A division in the House immediately before the Committee of Ways and Means met on 1 June showed that only 90 members were then present.[2] Townshend's final proposals differed considerably from his suggestions of 13 May.[3] There was now the import duty on tea, but only 3*d*. a lb., the rate of 6*d*. Garth had expected 'being deemed too high'. Townshend anticipated a revenue of £20,000 a year from this tax.[4] He also told the Committee of the duties on glass, paper, and lead, and of the cancelled rebate on china exports: these measures would produce a further £20,000.[5] They were the only duties, for Townshend announced that he had dropped those on fruit, wine, and oil because of objections to them. These complaints had come not from the American agents, who favoured the idea as ending one restriction on colonial trade, but from 'the merchants trading to Portugal and Spain', who had protested strongly against a direct trade between those countries and America.[6] Agent Johnson believed that there was also a political

[1] Grafton MSS., no. 445: quoted in Namier and Brooke, *Charles Townshend*, pp. 177–8. The dates of 5 and 11 May have been attributed to this letter: Namier and Brooke, *Charles Townshend*, p. 177; Norris, *Shelburne and Reform*, pp. 49–50. But the reference to Townshend's statement in the Commons places it after 13 May, with 25 May as a probability: before the phrase 'on Saturday' the word 'yesterday' is deleted, an implication that the letter was written on a Monday; 25 May was the only Monday when the Committee was postponed.

[2] *Commons Journals*, xxxi. 392.

[3] Only Charles Garth recorded them. *S.C.H.G.M.* 29 (1928), 295-6.

[4] This calculation was wildly optimistic, anticipating a legal taxed trade of 1,600,000 lb. a year. Labaree, *Boston Tea Party*, p. 7, has estimated the average annual consumption for the years 1760 to 1766 at 1,200,000 lb., of which over three-quarters was smuggled.

[5] Garth misunderstood Townshend as expecting £9,000 instead of £5,000 from the duties on paper, and £3,000 instead of £2,000 from those on lead. An estimate in Townshend's papers incorporating the changes in goods shows no alteration in the estimated yield from the other duties. Scott, *Econ.H.R.* 6 (1935–6), 89. Garth's figures form the basis for the total of £45,000 that is sometimes stated to have been the estimated yield.   [6] *Franklin Papers*, xiv. 184.

motive behind the decision, a reluctance both to please 'the Americans' and to modify the Navigation Acts at a time when the colonies were disputing with Parliament.[1]

The total income Townshend anticipated from his proposals was a meagre £40,000. When he had completed his speech Grenville rose to the attack: here is the report sent by Benjamin Franklin to Joseph Galloway.

In the House, when the Chancellor of the Exchequer had gone through his proposed American revenue, viz. by duties on glass, china ware, paper pasteboard, painters colours, tea, etc Grenville stood up and undervalued them all as trifles, and, says he, I'll tell the honourable gentleman of a revenue that will produce something valuable in America: make paper money for the colonies; issue it upon loan there; take the interest and apply it as you think proper. Mr. Townshend, finding the House listened to this and seemed to like it, stood up again, and said, that was a proposition of his own, which he had intended to make with the rest, but it had slipped his memory, and the gentleman, who must have heard of it, now unfairly would take advantage of that slip, and make a merit to himself of a proposition that was anothers; and as a proof of this, assured the House that a bill was prepared for the purpose and would soon be laid before them.[2]

Townshend's acceptance of the idea of Parliamentary appropriation of the interest from colonial currency struck consternation into the agents and merchants lobbying for repeal of the Currency Act.[3] The London merchants had prepared a petition to Parliament on which repeal was to be based, and Charles Garth and Richard Jackson had agreed to present it. The petition was now kept back, to avoid giving Townshend any pretext for such a plan of taxation. Although

---

[1] *Trumbull Papers*, p. 236.

[2] *Franklin Papers*, xiv. 181. This exchange is commonly ascribed to the debate of 13 May. I prefer the date of 1 June, for the following reasons: (a) Franklin's list of dutiable articles, including tea, points to 1 June and not 13 May; (b) Garth's version of Townshend's reply on 13 May is quite different; (c) if Townshend had made such a declaration then, Franklin would have mentioned it in his letter of 20 May to Galloway. It is inconceivable that, with Garth present at the debate, Franklin would not have known of it a week later; (d) Garth and Franklin would not have gone ahead with their currency plans for the rest of May, and then dropped them in June, if Townshend's statement was made on 13 May and not 1 June.

[3] Garth thought that Townshend also said that such a revenue would be used towards the cost of the army in America. *S.C.H.G.M.* 29 (1928), 297.

other members of the administration disapproved of Townshend's statement, it effectively killed any hope of repeal while he remained in office.[1]

Grenville misunderstood Townshend's purpose, which was not simply or merely to obtain as large a revenue as possible from America. His aims were political rather than financial, the re-establishment of the practice of colonial taxation and the making of Parliamentary provision for the costs of civil government and the administration of justice in the colonies: both were clearly stated in the ensuing Revenue Act of 1767. The proposed use of the new revenue aroused concern among some colonial agents. William Johnson sent an alarmist letter to Governor Pitkin on 13 July, forecasting that the assemblies would never meet.[2] Charles Garth warned South Carolina that the Crown, which mean in practice the administration, was given full power to use the money from the duties 'to provide for the officers in administration of justice, and for the better support of the civil government when it shall be found necessary', and made this comment.[3]

It is the sort of discretion I could have wished not to have been lodged in the manner it is, as wherever exercised it must operate to render the assembly rather insignificant in that particular at least, and being unlimited as to time or place, the reasoning is alike applicable. Indeed the bill did not pass the Commons without an intimation of this kind to the House, but the measure was taken, and the friends of America are too few to have any chance[4] in a struggle with a Chancellor of the Exchequer.

Garth does not say, indeed, that there was any Parliamentary opposition to the bill: that none took place is virtually certain from the complete absence of any information either on debates or on divisions, which would have been recorded in the *Journals* of the House except for the Committee, and that lasted only one day. The American Revenue Bill had its introduction and first reading on 10 June, the second reading on 11 June, and its

---

[1] *Franklin Papers*, xiv. 181–2. *S.C.H.G.M.* 29 (1928), 296–7. By the end of the month Townshend was threatening that the next session he would propose his plan even without the excuse of a petition. *S.C.H.G.M.* 29 (1928), 300.

[2] *Trumbull Papers*, p. 239.

[3] *S.C.H.G.M.* 29 (1928), 299–300.

[4] The printed text has 'share'.

Committee stage on 15 June.[1] It was at this point that some opposition was threatened from the Rockingham group. On 12 June Frederick Montagu reported to Newcastle, 'I understand Dowdeswell and Sir W. Baker mean to attack the American duties on glass'.[2] No evidence has been found as to why this should have been thought an appropriate target of criticism, or whether any such challenge was made.[3] The report stage was on 16 June, when James West told Newcastle, 'there has nothing happened material in the House of Commons today . . . There were not above fifty members in the House at any one time.'[4] The third reading and passage took place on 18 June, and the bill received the royal assent on 26 June.[5]

This absence of opposition to the Townshend duties reflected the general assumption in Britain that the American colonies had made a distinction between internal and external taxes and had no objection to the latter. The Rockinghamite party when in office had accepted the principle of Parliament's right to tax America, and must have seen no reason to oppose the Townshend duties on the ground of impolicy: the colonies were thought not to object to this method of taxation, and the taxes themselves could not be considered an onerous burden. There is no record of any challenge to the Townshend duties from any Rockinghamite speaker in the debate of 13 May or later on the revenue bill. During the Stamp Act Crisis, too, Pitt and his followers had adopted what was thought to be the colonial view of a distinction between internal and external taxes, and this had become the official Chathamite line: Edmund Burke later recalled that 'Lord Camden and others resorted to the old distinction of internal and external taxes and contended that these were external'.[6] James Harris scornfully noted that in the debate of 13 May 'Barré asserted, as far as he dared, his doctrine of external and internal taxation'.[7] In so far as this statement referred to Townshend's plans

---

[1] *Commons Journals*, xxxi. 398, 401, 407.

[2] B.M. Add. MSS. 32982, fos. 317–18.

[3] Newcastle was confused by Montagu's rumour when he told James West on 13 June, 'I find some of Mr. Townshend's taxes were opposed yesterday in the House of Commons'; B.M. Add. MSS. 32982, fo. 327: for the American Revenue Bill had not been under consideration on 12 June.

[4] B.M. Add. MSS. 32982, fo. 346.　　　[5] *Commons Journals*, xxxi. 407–8, 412.

[6] *Burke Corr.*, i. 280n.　　　[7] B.M. Add. MSS. 35608, fo. 17.

it would seem to indicate Barré's support: but no specific comment on the suggested taxes can be found in the admittedly meagre reports of the speeches made then by either Barré or William Beckford. Indeed, Chatham's acceptance of the Declaratory Act implied an abandonment of the whole distinction, and this is what Thomas Whately told John Temple in America had taken place.[1]

The distinction between internal and external taxes frequently occurs, not now as a subject of debate, but as a matter of reproach to those who maintained last year that Parliament had not a right to lay the former as well as the latter . . . those who defended it then disclaim it now, by alleging that the Declaratory Act has put an end to the question, and determined the law.

The acceptance of Townshend's tax proposals was shared by men more obviously 'friends of America' than these Parliamentary factions. John Huske had encouraged Townshend to adopt this method of taxation as unobjectionable in his letter of 9 April. 'Permit me to remark to you that it is certain by a regulation of the trade of America for the reciprocal interest of both mother and children, you may have a sufficient revenue to pay all Great Britain's expense for the colonies and in a manner perfectly agreeable to both under your conduct.'[2] There is no evidence of any opposition to or even criticism of the Townshend duties by the colonial agents at the time of their enactment, a marked contrast to their attempts to prevent the Stamp Act. This passive acquiescence may have stemmed from pessimism, the realization of the futility of any resistance: but both Benjamin Franklin and William Johnson appear to have positively regretted the abandonment of the scheme for direct trade from Europe to America at the price of import duties for revenue on the commodities involved.[3]

Townshend, who knew the difficulties of enforcing trade laws in America, was determined to see that his duties came

---

[1] *Bowdoin–Temple Papers*, p. 83. This was on 2 May. Already on 25 Feb. Whately had told Temple that 'the tide is entirely turned here with respect to America, that the distinction between external and internal taxes is totally exploded, that every doubt upon the right is ridiculed and censured whenever it is mentioned'. *Ibid.*, p. 79.

[2] Namier and Brooke, *Charles Townshend*, p. 187.

[3] *Franklin Papers*, xiv. 184. *Trumbull Papers*, p. 236.

into effective operation. He adopted the remedy that had long been obvious to customs officials there, the creation of a superior authority on the spot. This was to be a separate Board of Customs Commissioners based in America.[1] Townshend began work on the scheme before the end of 1766, and on 1 February Shelburne told Chatham that he had heard of the plan 'from general conversation'.[2] Townshend told M.P.s of the project when he announced his American duties on 13 May: Charles Garth noted his claim that the new Board would not only oblige negligent or corrupt officials to do their duty but also give colonists a convenient and inexpensive way of making complaints about the working of the customs service.[3] By that date plans were well advanced. The British Customs Board thoroughly approved the idea, seeing an opportunity to protect customs officials from unfair prosecutions, and submitted proposals for a Board of seven members at Philadelphia. The Treasury decided on one of five Commissioners at Boston. Final details were not settled until after the passage in June of the Act of Parliament apparently thought necessary to convince the colonists of the legality of the new institution.[4] On 29 July the Treasury approved the revised plan for the American Customs Board, but having heard objections that day from Beeston Long and Richard Maitland on behalf of the West Indian merchants decided to confine the authority of the Board to North America. On 27 August Shelburne's office was formally notified of the appointment of the Board.[5]

Townshend's practical concern for enforcement of the customs laws was also shown by a provision in his Revenue Act to legalize the right of search by customs officers:[6] but the establishment of additional Vice-Admiralty Courts, authorized

---

[1] For more details on the creation of the Board see Barrow, *Trade and Empire*, pp. 218–24; Wickwire, *British Subministers and Colonial America*, pp. 124–30; and Chaffin, *W.M.Q.* 27 (1970), 109–11.

[2] *Chatham Papers*, iii. 185.

[3] *S.C.H.G.M.* 29 (1928), 228. By 19 Mar. Johnson had heard other arguments. 'It is said that such board will be more eligible to the people, as they will be less despotic than a single officer; and that the Crown will be better served by a number of gentlemen, who will be in effect checks upon each other, as well as add weight and dignity to the whole system relative to the customs.' *Trumbull Papers*, p. 220.

[4] *Commons Journals*, xxxi. 395–6, 399, 401, 403, 405, 412, 415.

[5] T. 29/38, fos. 443–4, 459–60.

[6] Wickwire, *British Subministers and Colonial America*, pp. 131–3; Clark, *Rise of the British Treasury*, pp. 174–5.

that year and implemented the next, was not part of his programme.[1] Townshend was absent from the cabinet meeting of 19 August that made this decision: and the alteration then envisaged, the substitution of three courts at Nova Scotia, Boston, and Charleston for the existing one at Halifax, was not to be the arrangement made after Townshend's death on 4 September.[2]

There remains the question of whether, if Townshend's policy had come into operation, it would have proved to be any solution to the British government's problem of ruling the American colonies. The idea was attractively simple, a plan to recover full control of the local executives from encroachments by the colonial assemblies by removal of the power of the purse which had proved so effective a weapon of Parliament against the Crown earlier in Britain. For this a large sum of money was not necessary. The total annual cost of financing the executive and judiciary in the thirteen colonies that were to break with Britain appears to have been little more than £40,000, the same as the estimated yield of the Townshend duties.[3] Townshend had done his sums right, if he had tried to balance the two totals.

How far would such a change have been relevant to the political situation in the colonies? Governor Bernard of Massachusetts was enthusiastic about the idea, declaring that 'a civil list is a measure most immediately wanting to the regulation of the American governments', and sending Shelburne a detailed account of how the assembly in his colony used its financial power as a political weapon.[4] But only five other governors were entirely dependent for their salaries on annual

---

[1] Chaffin, *W.M.Q.* 27 (1970), 111, corrects the error on this point of Ubbelohde, *Vice-Admiralty Courts and the American Revolution*, p. 130.

[2] Shelburne MSS., vol. 161, fos. 7–9.

[3] An exact computation is difficult, as there are omissions in and discrepancies between the three sources of information used: (a) the Board of Trade return submitted to the House of Commons on 29 Jan. 1766. C.O. 324/17, p. 497; (b) the answers of ten governors to Shelburne's inquiry of 11 Dec. 1766. C.O. 5/112; (c) the reply of the Board of Trade on 16 Apr. 1767 to a request by Shelburne on 9 Apr. for information on the salaries of governors and offices concerned in the administration of justice, C.O. 324/18, fos. 74–85. An approximate total from collation of this evidence is £41,000 for twelve colonies, there being no information on Delaware.

[4] C.O. 5/112, fos. 39–43.

votes by their assemblies, those in New Hampshire, New York, Connecticut, Rhode Island, and South Carolina. The Treasury already paid the civil list for Georgia, and £1,000 to the governor of North Carolina. Permanent funds virtually or entirely supported the governors and other officials in Virginia, New Jersey, Maryland, and to a lesser extent in Pennsylvania. Moreover, payment of salaries from Britain would be of little significance if the Crown did not appoint the officials. This was the case in the proprietory colonies, while in Connecticut and Rhode Island the governors were elective. Townshend's plan, even if fully implemented, would therefore have had a limited impact on the relationship of the colonies with Britain. Benjamin Franklin was so little alarmed that he never mentioned this proposed use of the taxation revenue in his correspondence. The hopes of Governor Bernard and the fears of agents Garth and Johnson were misleading as to the likely over-all consequences: and the partial application of Townshend's idea suggests that it would not have achieved its objective even in the colonies where it seemingly could be adopted with maximum effect. The fund derived from his duties was to be used to pay salaries to the Attorney-General of New York and the Chief Justice of Massachusetts from 1768: to the Governors of New York and Massachusetts from 1770: and to the Chief Justices of New York and New Jersey from 1772. From that year salaries were also paid to the Attorney-General, Solicitor-General, and five lower judges in Massachusetts, and the colony then had a civil list controlled by the Crown.[1] So far from enabling the British government to establish a firmer hold on events in that colony, the step proved counter-productive, and resentment at it contributed to the deterioration of the political situation there.[2]

Townshend's scheme was not the solution to Britain's problem of maintaining control of her American colonies. He had failed to appreciate the lesson of the Stamp Act Crisis. The matter was not simply one of constitutional forms.[3] Whether or not an assembly controlled the salary of its governor

[1] Dickerson, *New England Quarterly*, 31 (1958), 238–41.

[2] Gipson, *British Empire*, xii. 47, 139–44.

[3] Perhaps some tighter enforcement of trade and other laws might have come from judges paid by the Crown; but this would have been only a marginal factor in the general context of the colonial situation.

was not to be a significant factor in the path of a colony to revolution. Colonial governors and other officials were rendered powerless by violent opposition if they lacked the military and naval support necessary to enforce their legal authority. An empire based not on force but on the assumption of the consent of the governed was not suited for dealing with a situation where that consent was no longer forthcoming.

Conclusion: British Politicians
                and America in the 1760s

The clamour certainly rises against Mr. Grenville, but it is not less
difficult to correct than it has been in him injudicious to raise the
American clamour: the remedy may bring the discontent home,
and a distinction between British and American ministers grow to
take the place of Whig and Tory.[1]

This was the reflection of Charles Townshend on the reaction
in Britain near the end of 1765 to the colonial resistance to the
Stamp Act. It has often been an assumption by historians of
the American Revolution that some such distinction did develop
as a result of the Stamp Act Crisis, with the Rockingham and
Chatham groups being divided over the American question
from the Bedford and Grenville factions: and undue significance has been attached to the fact that by the accidents of
British politics in the later 1760s 'The Stamp Men' rather than
'the No Stamp Men'[2] were to be in power at the time of the
final American crisis during the North ministry. The super-
ficial truth of this analysis has concealed the deeper reality
of the almost universal consensus of opinion in Britain on the
question of Parliamentary supremacy over America which is
apparent in the attitudes of the various factions towards the
colonies during the middle 1760s.

The American measures of the Grenville ministry had seemed
at the time both necessary and reasonable to British political
opinion, and they had aroused little controversy at Westminster until the colonial objections erupted into violent and
determined resistance. The role then adopted by the Grenville
and Bedford groups was consistent and logical. The Stamp Act
had been imposed to assert Parliament's right to tax the colonies
as well as to raise a revenue: Grenville had already been aware
of the wider issue of sovereignty implied by the colonial objections to the proposed Stamp Act, for on 6 February 1765,

[1] Charles Townshend Letters, pp. 178–9.
[2] This was the phraseology of Lord Camden. B.M. Add. MSS. 32987, fo. 149.

when introducing the resolutions for stamp duties, he had told M.P.s that the American arguments against taxation applied to 'all laws in general'.[1] Freed from the responsibility of office afterwards, Grenville and his allies asserted the need to enforce the Stamp Act.[2] Their public pronouncements on the subject reflected opinions sincerely held in private, and were not merely intended to embarrass the Rockingham administration or motivated by unthinking defence of earlier measures. Bedford's papers contain a memorandum of 24 January 1766 setting out his views on the line to be adopted in Parliament. He thought that in America there existed an 'actual state of rebellion' which had to be quelled 'by gentle means if possible, if not by every means in our power'. The guiding principle in every debate should be to consider 'the submission of the Americans to the Stamp Act, as the palladium, which, if suffered to be removed, puts a final period to the British Empire in America'.[3] Bedford, however, was not anticipating such a disaster in the immediate future: it was 'in half a century' that he feared a constitutional challenge by the Americans if the colonial claims were not rebuffed.[4]

The arguments and assumptions of Bedford and Grenville during the Stamp Act Crisis represented the majority view of British political opinion. Practically every other British politician would have been proud to make the claim of Grenville in a letter of 17 July 1768 to Thomas Pownall.

I have done my duty by endeavouring to assert the sovereignty of King and Parliament of Great Britain over all the dominions belonging to the Crown, and to make all the subjects of the kingdom contribute to the public burdens for their own defence, according to their own abilities and situation.[5]

Grenville had not been unyielding and unconstructive in his attitude to the American question. In 1766 he expressed his willingness in principle to modify the Stamp Act even before expediency led him to adopt this line of action as the only

---

[1] *Ryder Diary*, p. 254; quoted more fully above, p. 89.
[2] Brooke, *King George III*, p. 126, suggests that if Grenville had still been minister the practical problems of enforcement might have led him to adopt concessions.
[3] Bedford Office MSS., H.M.C. No. 8, vol. 53, fo. 16.
[4] Ibid., fo. 20.
[5] *Grenville Papers*, iv. 317–18.

alternative to repeal: and once repeal was an accomplished fact Grenville never thought of re-enacting the Stamp Act or any similar measure of direct taxation. Moreover, within a year of perceiving the constitutional problem of imperial rule in 1765, he was advocating a solution to it: but, as he admitted in the same letter to Pownall, it was not one likely to find favour in either Britain or the colonies.[1]

As to the great question of our Parliament's granting to America a competent number of representatives to sit in our House of Commons, you are no stranger to the declarations I repeatedly made in the House, at the time when the repeal of the Stamp Act was agitated, 'that if such an application should be properly made by the Colonies to Parliament, in the same manner as those which were made from Chester and Durham, and probably from Wales, it would in my opinion be entitled to the most serious and favourable consideration'.

I continue still in the same sentiments, but I am much afraid that neither the people of Great Britain nor those of America are sufficiently apprized of the danger which threatens both from the present state of things, to adopt a measure to which both the one and the other seem indisposed.

Some of the colonies in their Address to the *Crown* against some late *Acts of Parliament*, have, if I mistake not, expressly disclaimed it, and I do not think it has been kindly received in Great Britain, when it has been thrown out in Parliament, or started in any pamphlet or printed paper.

The fullest conviction of its necessity, and the hearty concurrence both of the Government and of the people, are indispensably necessary to set so great a machine in motion, as that of uniting all the outlying parts of the British dominions in one system.

The idea of colonial representation at Westminster was also considered by Chatham, and is indeed one reason why he has usually been regarded as sympathetic to American grievances.[2] That whole assumption about Chatham's attitude stands in need of qualification. As 'the Great Commoner' he had been absent from the American debates during the Grenville ministry, and not until the Rockingham administration did he and his supporters attack Parliament's right to tax the

---

[1] *Grenville Papers*, iv. 317. I have not found any report of a speech by Grenville in 1766 advocating colonial representation at Westminster.

[2] Williams, *E.H.R.* 22 (1907), 756–8.

colonies. The position he then adopted, that Britain could instead exercise complete control over the colonial economy, was one that appeared to some Americans as dangerous as the right of taxation.[1] Nor could the behaviour of Chatham in office have enhanced his reputation as a friend of America. He and his followers had then accepted that the Declaratory Act established Parliament's right of taxing America: and even though this change of attitude may not have been public knowledge[2] the Chatham administration had acted firmly to enforce Britain's authority in recalcitrant colonies.

Like Pitt the Rockingham party had not formulated a distinctive attitude to America before the crisis they faced in office. Until then they had implicitly accepted the Grenville ministry's case for colonial taxation. The line of action they adopted in 1766 has often been understood as combining a formal assertion of the principle of American taxation with opposition to its expediency. That this interpretation is erroneous can be seen from their adaptation of the molasses duty in 1766 and passive acceptance of the Townshend duties in 1767. What the Rockingham group thought inadvisable was direct taxation of the colonies, but not an American revenue by other means. Their position was set out in a long letter from Dowdeswell to Rockingham on 14 August 1768, after news had come of colonial objections to the Townshend duties.[3]

Charles Townshend's duties are I believe not so heavy as to justify me in saying that they are grievous burdens on the colonies. The people there do not appear to make this stand against *these duties* on account of their purpose, but against the general principle of raising

---

[1] Connecticut agent Johnson, who had not been in Britain in 1766, wrote that Pitt had then proposed to prohibit the colonies, 'as we know he expressed it in his speech at the repeal of the Stamp Act, from manufacturing *even a horseshoe*'. *Trumbull Papers*, p. 366. Contemporary reports do not make it clear when Pitt said this, but Ryder summarized a statement by him on 21 Feb. 1766 that 'if we do not tax them we may prevent their manufactures'. *Ryder Diary*, p. 309. Grenville thought the idea 'unjust, as well as impracticable'. *H.M.C. Knox*, pp. 95–6.

[2] Chatham told Rockingham this privately. *Burke Corr.* i. 280n. W. S. Johnson in 1769 wrote that 'Chatham gives up the right of taxation'. *Trumbull Papers*, p. 366.

[3] Dowdeswell MSS.; partly printed by Brooke, *Chatham Administration*, pp. 369–73. Dowdeswell commented that the distinction between internal and external taxation had 'been found frivolous, as indeed, I always thought it. And your Lordship knows that'.

any revenue in America . . . One might argue for the repeal of Charles Townshend's duties, as injudiciously laid, being injurious to the manufactures of this country, and operating as bounties upon the like manufactures in America. But this would be avoiding the real question . . . A repeated opposition from that side of the water, upon a principle directed against all duties for revenue, must be met. It must either be admitted which is timidity, weakness, irresolution, and inconsistency: or it must be resisted and the arms of this country must be exerted against her colonies.

Dowdeswell therefore argued that repeal of the Townshend duties would be desirable only from a position of strength, to 'add good humour to submission' once British control had been restored. In accordance with this view he was to fail to support in debate a motion of 19 April 1769 for a Committee to consider Townshend's Revenue Act.[1] Nor did he or such other prominent Rockinghams as Edmund Burke and Lord John Cavendish speak in the debate of 5 March 1770 on Thomas Pownall's amendment to add the tea duty to the list of those to be repealed.[2] Towards the end of the letter Dowdeswell's remarks do indicate that a Rockingham ministry in the next decade might have been more conciliatory than the North ministry was to prove. He anticipated a general policy of concession and retreat to avoid the ultimate disaster of civil war; and his open advocacy of repeal of the tea duty on 19 April 1774 was therefore consistent with the views he enunciated in 1768.[3]

That lay in the future, and the guiding motive envisaged was expediency rather than sympathy with colonial demands. America was less a divisive factor among British politicians than has been commonly supposed. It is true that they blamed each other for making things worse. Grenville repeatedly claimed that colonial resistance had been encouraged by irresponsible speeches from Pitt and his friends and by the weak surrender of the Rockingham ministry over the Stamp Act. Dowdeswell, in his letter of 14 August 1768 to Rockingham, agreed in blaming Chatham, 'the folly of one Great Man, who held out food to the enthusiasm of that country, and raised a spirit there not to be laid by him when he became a minister'; but he also blamed Grenville and his friends, 'the

[1] B.M. Eg. MSS. 219, pp. 284–307.   [2] B.M. Eg. MSS. 221, pp. 1–94.
[3] B.M. Eg. MSS. 255, pp. 229–31 (shorthand).

obstinacy of others, who constantly holding a threatening
language . . . have kept the Americans on their guard and in
each day's debate tied still more strongly that bond which held
them all together'; and he threw the more immediate responsibility on Charles Townshend, 'the weakness of my successor,
who afraid to face his opponents, or desirous of agreeing with
them, or looking perhaps to future connections . . . [imposed]
a foolish tax upon our own manufactures without any other
object than that that tax might be collected in America'. The
political leaders might blame everyone but themselves for the
colonial crises: but they did not regard the American question
as an insuperable barrier to an alliance; and the negotiations
of July 1767 between Rockingham, Bedford, and Grenville
for a new or reconstructed ministry did not break down over
America.[1] All British politicians were agreed on the basic
issue of Parliamentary sovereignty, and their differences over
taxation were becoming marginal. Connecticut agent William
Johnson, after nearly three years' close observation, could find
little to choose between them in 1769.[2]

How these three seemingly opposite parties may agree upon the
subject of America, I have, I believe, before mentioned to you.
Mr. Grenville will give up the idea of direct taxation for the purpose
of revenue only, to unite with Lord Rockingham in maintaining the
right even to that, (though not expedient to be directly exercised at
present,) and effecting the same thing in a less odious manner by
commercial regulations, in which Lord Chatham will concur, though
he gives up the right of taxation; while he adds to the commercial
principle of the two former the dangerous idea of a right to restrain
us absolutely from every species of manufacture . . . At least, it is so
uncertain which set of men will be most beneficial for us, and so
doubtful what principles will be adopted by either of them, that
(merely as Americans) I think we need neither anxiously hope nor
fear a change, but may fairly stand by and let them squabble it out
as they can, while (as, if I recollect right, I have before suggested)
we embark deeply with neither, but attentively mind our own
business, get rid as we may of the burdens we are now under, and
prepare ourselves to meet the measures of either party which may
happen to possess power, or of all of them, whenever we find them
inconsistent with the true interest of the colonies.

[1] Brooke, *Chatham Administration*, pp. 204–9.
[2] *Trumbull Papers*, pp. 366–7.

The Stamp Act Crisis had shown that policy would be made by those political factions that were in office; and the lobby of colonial agents and British merchants had been far less significant in the determination of policy than historians of these pressure groups have assumed. Their role in the repeal of the Stamp Act had been ancillary to, and an excuse for, a decision taken by the administration. Thereafter the political importance of the colonial agents declined rapidly. Events in America and Britain came to render obsolete their function as intermediaries; and they increasingly lost that support of British merchants which alone gave them an effective voice in London. Already by 1767 colonial observers were noting with concern that, despite the help British merchants then gave to the agents on such matters as the salt duty and the currency question, their general sympathy with America was waning fast. This disenchantment with the colonies preceded the expansion of new markets elsewhere that is the customary explanation for their later lack of support for America.[1] There were two reasons for the change of attitude. The anticipated revival of American trade after the repeal of the Stamp Act had not materialized, for that measure had not been directly or indirectly the real cause of the economic depression in the colonies. The value of Britain's exports to the thirteen colonies had actually declined further, from £1,915,000 in 1765 to £1,737,000 in 1766:[2] and British traders and manufacturers felt natural resentment that they had not obtained the expected material reward for their efforts. 'The merchants, too, are grown very cool in their regard to us, partly because they have not received the remittances they expected since the repeal of the Stamp Act', agent Johnson reported to

[1] The growth in eastern trade, moreover, was virtually confined to imports. Marshall, *H.L.Q.* 27 (1963–4), 139–40.

[2] Jenkinson's papers contain this detailed calculation, based on the customs house returns. B.M. Add. 38338, fo. 303.

Exports to	1765	1766
New England	451,299	409,642
New York	382,349	330,829
Pennsylvania	363,368	327,314
Virginia and Maryland	383,224	372,548
Carolina	334,709	296,732
	1,914,949	1,737,065

Connecticut on 14 March 1767.[1] To this disappointment was added annoyance at the colonial lack of gratitude for the efforts of the merchants in the previous year. Johnson noted this mood, and Benjamin Franklin told Joseph Chew on 13 June that he had heard the same complaint.[2]

It was said that in the opposition they gave the Stamp Act and their endeavours to obtain the repeal, they had spent at their meetings and in expresses to all parts of this country to obtain petitions, and for a vessel to carry the joyful news of the repeal to North America, and in the entertainments given our friends both Houses etc near £1500. That for all this, except from the little colony of Rhode Island, they had not received so much as a *Thank Ye*. That on the contrary, the circular letters they had written, with the best intentions, to the merchants of the several colonies, containing their best and most friendly advice, were either answered with unkind reflections, or contemptuously left without answer.

The Stamp Act Crisis raised a new issue for consideration by British political opinion, the role of the settlement colonies in the imperial system of government: but, unlike most political problems, it produced a virtual unanimity of mind. The American challenge to Parliament's sovereignty outraged the contemporary British interpretation of the constitution. Repeal of the Stamp Act had come about only because the Rockingham administration could see no alternative practical policy: and Rockingham, when replying on 11 May 1767 to the vote of thanks from the Massachusetts Assembly, commented that 'I shall always consider, that this country, as the parent, ought to be tender and just, and that the colonies, as the children, ought to be dutiful'.[3] Only Pitt had gone some way towards meeting colonial objections by his qualification of Parliament's right of taxation. He had obtained little support for that view, and he had himself declared in favour of coercion if the colonies failed to accept the olive branch offered to them. The lesson of the Stamp Act Crisis was that there would be very few 'friends of America' in Britain in any future clash with the colonies.

---

[1] *Trumbull Papers*, p. 487.   [2] *Franklin Papers*, xiv. 183.
[3] *Grenville Papers*, iv. 13n.

Select Bibliography

PRIMARY SOURCES

A. MANUSCRIPTS

i. *In the British Museum*

Egerton MSS. 215–63, 3711. The Parliamentary Diary of Sir Henry Cavendish 1768–1774.

Stowe MSS. 264–5. Stamp Act Papers.

Add[itional] MSS. 6804–71. Sir Andrew Mitchell Papers.

Add. MSS. 11514. Essay by Henry McCulloh.

Add. MSS. 22358–9. Buckinghamshire Papers.

Add. MSS. 32679–3201. Newcastle Papers.

Add. MSS. 35349–6278. Hardwicke Papers.

Add. MSS. 38190–489. Liverpool Papers.

Add. MSS. 41346–1475. Samuel Martin Papers.

Add. MSS. 42083–8. Grenville Papers.

Add. MSS. 47584. Journal of Lord Villiers 1760–1766 (MS. copy made in 1821 by Lord Holland).

Add. MSS. 51318–2254. Holland House Papers.

ii. *In the Public Record Office*

Colonial Official Papers (cited as C.O.).

State Papers (cited as S.P.).

Treasury Papers (cited as T.).

Chatham Papers (cited as P.R.O. 30/8).

Egremont Papers (cited as P.R.O. 47/26).

iii. *In other repositories*

Dartmouth MSS. Staffordshire County Record Office. (By permission of the Earl of Dartmouth.)

Dowdeswell MSS. William L. Clements Library.

Fitzwilliam (Milton) MSS. Northamptonshire County Record Office. (By permission of Earl Fitzwilliam.)

Grafton MSS. Bury St. Edmunds and West Suffolk Record Office. (By permission of the Duke of Grafton.)

Letter-Books of George Grenville, 1763–1770, Stowe MSS., 7, vols. 1 and 2. Henry E. Huntingdon Library.

Newdegate MSS. The personal diary and other papers of Sir Roger

Newdigate. Warwickshire County Record Office. (By permission of Mr. Humphrey FitzRoy Newdegate. Diary cited as Newdigate Diary.)

Northington MSS. Northamptonshire County Record Office. (By permission of Lord Henley.)

Shelburne MSS. William L. Clements Library.

John Temple–Thomas Whately Letters, Stowe MSS. Henry E. Huntingdon Library.

Charles Townshend Letters. William L. Clements Library.

Wentworth Woodhouse MSS. Sheffield City Library. (By permission of Earl Fitzwilliam and his Trustees.)

iv. *In Private possession*

Bedford Office MSS. In the possession of the Duke of Bedford.

Malmesbury MSS. The Parliamentary diary and other papers of James Harris. In the possession of the Earl of Malmesbury. Diary cited as Harris Diary.

B. PRINTED SOURCES

i. *Official and Parliamentary Sources*

Acts of the Privy Council of England. Colonial Series (6 vols., 1908–12; cited as *Acts. P.C. Col.*).

Calendar of Home Office Papers . . . 1760 to 1775 (4 vols., 1878–99).

Journals of the Commissioners for Trade and Plantations 1704–1782 (15 vols., 1920–38; cited as *J.C.T.P.*).

Journals of the House of Commons (cited as *Commons Journals*).

Journals of the House of Lords (cited as *Lords Journals*).

ALMON, J., *The Debates and Proceedings of the British House of Commons from 1743 to 1774* (11 vols., 1766–75; cited as Almon, *Debates*).

COBBETT, W., *Parliamentary History of England from . . . 1066 to . . . 1803* (36 vols., 1806–20; cited as Cobbett, *Parl. Hist.*).

DEBRETT, J., *The History, Debates and Proceedings of Both Houses of Parliament . . . 1743 to . . . 1774* (7 vols., 1792; cited as Debrett, *Debates*).

ii. *Contemporary Correspondence and Memoirs*[1]

Historical Manuscripts Commission (cited as *H.M.C.*).

   9 Report, Part III (1884), pp. 1–150. *Stopford Sackville MSS.*
   10 Report, Part I (1885), pp. 199–452. *Weston Underwood MSS.*
   11 Report, Part IV (1887). *Townshend MSS.*
   Dartmouth MSS. (3 vols., 1887–96).
   Lothian MSS. (1905).
   Various MSS., VI (1906), pp. 81–296, 440–50. *Knox MSS.*

[1] Periodicals also contain such source material printed as 'documents' or 'notes'.

English Historical Documents. IX. *American Colonial Documents to 1776* (ed. M. Jensen, 1955; cited as Jensen, *American Colonial Documents*).

Prologue to Revolution. Sources and Documents on the Stamp Act Crisis, 1764–1766 (ed. E. S. Morgan, Chapel Hill, U.S.A., 1959; cited as Morgan, *Prologue to Revolution*).

The Barrington–Bernard Correspondence and Illustrative Matter 1760–1770 (ed. E. Channing and A. C. Coolidge, Cambridge, U.S.A., 1912).

Correspondence of John, fourth Duke of Bedford, selected from the originals at Woburn Abbey, with an introduction by Lord John Russell (3 vols., 1842–6; cited as *Bedford Papers*).

'Private Journal of John, Fourth Duke of Bedford . . . 19 October 1766 . . . to . . . 28 December 1770', *Sir Henry Cavendish's Debates of the House of Commons during the Thirteenth Parliament of Great Britain* (ed. J. Wright, 2 vols., 1841–3), I. 591–631 (cited as *Bedford Journal*).

The Bowdoin and Temple Papers. Collections of Massachusetts Historical Society, 6th series, 9 (1897). Cited as *Bowdoin–Temple Papers*.

The Correspondence of Edmund Burke, vol. i (ed. T. W. Copeland, Cambridge, 1958; cited as *Burke Corr.*).

Letters from George III to Lord Bute 1756–1766 (ed. R. Sedgwick, 1939; cited as *Bute Letters*).

Politics and the Port of Bristol in the Eighteenth Century. The Petitions of the Society of Merchant Venturers 1698–1803 (ed. W. E. Minchinton, Bristol Record Society, 1963).

Selections from the Family Papers preserved at Caldwell (ed. W. Mure, 2 vols., Glasgow, 1854).

Documents Relating to the Constitutional History of Canada 1759–91 (ed. A. Shortt and A. G. Doughty, 2nd ed., Ottawa, 1918; cited as Shortt and Doughty, *Canadian Documents*).

Correspondence of William Pitt, earl of Chatham (ed. W. S. Taylor and J. H. Pringle, 4 vols., 1838–40; cited as *Chatham Papers*).

The Letters of Philip Dormer Stanhope, 4th Earl of Chesterfield (ed. B. Dobrée, 6 vols., 1932).

Records of the Cust Family, vol. 3 (ed. Lionel Cust, 1927; cited as *Cust Records*).

'Letters of Dennys De Berdt, 1757–1770', *Transactions of the Colonial Society of Massachusetts*, 13 (1910–11), 293–461 (cited as *De Berdt Letters*).

The Political Journal of George Budd Dodington (ed. J. Carswell and L. A. Dralle, Oxford, 1965).

The Fitch Papers. Correspondence and Documents During Thomas Fitch's Governorship of the Colony of Connecticut 1754–1766, Volume II, 1759–1766, Connecticut Historical Society Collections, 18 (1920) (cited as *Fitch Papers*).

The Papers of Benjamin Franklin, vols. 10–14 (ed. L. W. Labaree, 1966–70).

The Correspondence of General Thomas Gage with the Secretaries of State, and with the War Office and the Treasury 1763–1775 (ed. C. E. Carter, 2 vols., New Haven, U.S.A., 1931–3; cited as *Gage Corr.*).

The Correspondence of King George the Third from 1760 to December 1783 (ed. Sir John Fortescue, 6 vols., 1927–8; cited as *Corr. of George III*).

Additions and Corrections to Sir John Fortescue's Edition of the Correspondence of King George the Third (Vol. I) (By L. B. Namier, Manchester, 1937; cited as Namier, *Additions and Corrections*).

Autobiography and Political Correspondence of Augustus Henry, Third Duke of Grafton (ed. Sir William R. Anson, 1896).

The Grenville Papers: being the correspondence of Richard Grenville, Earl Temple, K.G., and the Right Honourable George Grenville, their friends and contemporaries (ed. W. J. Smith, 4 vols., 1852–3; cited as *Grenville Papers*).

Additional Grenville Papers, 1763–1765 (ed. J. Tomlinson, Manchester, 1962).

The Diary and Letters of his Excellency Thomas Hutchinson, Esq. (ed. P. O. Hutchinson, 2 vols., 1883–6).

'A Selection from the Correspondence and Miscellaneous Papers of Jared Ingersoll', ed. F. B. Dexter. *Papers of New Haven Colony Historical Society*, 9 (1918), 201–472 (cited as *Ingersoll Papers*).

The Jenkinson Papers 1760–1766 (ed. N. S. Jucker, 1949).

'London Merchants on the Stamp Act Repeal', *Proceedings of the Massachusetts Historical Society*, 55 (1921–2), 215–23 (cited as *London Merchants on the Stamp Act Repeal*).

A Narrative of the Changes in the Ministry 1765–1767 told by the Duke of Newcastle in a series of letters to John White, M.P. (ed. M. Bateson, Camden Second Series, Royal Historical Society, 1898; cited as Bateson, *Narrative*).

The Commerce of Rhode Island 1726–1800, vol. i, *1726–1774*, Collections of Massachusetts Historical Society, 7th series, 9 (1914) (cited as *Commerce of Rhode Island*).

Memoirs of the Marquis of Rockingham and his Contemporaries (ed. George Thomas, Earl of Albemarle, 2 vols., 1852).

'The Parliamentary Diaries of Nathaniel Ryder 1764–1767' (ed. P. D. G. Thomas, *Camden Miscellany XXIII*, pp. 229–351, Camden Fourth Series, vol. vii, Royal Historical Society, 1969; cited as *Ryder Diary*).

The Fourth Earl of Sandwich: Diplomatic Correspondence 1763–1765 (ed. F. Spencer, Manchester, 1961).

'Stamp Act Papers', *Maryland Historical Magazine*, 6 (1911), 282–305.

'Letters of William Samuel Johnson to the Governors of Connecticut', *Trumbull Papers. Collections of Massachusetts Historical Society*, 5th series, 9 (1855), 211–490. Cited as *Trumbull Papers*.

The Letters of Horace Walpole, Fourth Earl of Orford (ed. Mrs. Paget Toynbee, 16 vols., Oxford. 1905. Cited as H. Walpole, *Letters*).

Horace Walpole. Memoirs of the Region of King George the Third (ed. G. F. Russell Barker, 4 vols., 1894; cited as H. Walpole, *Memoirs*).

iii. *Periodical and Pamphlets*

(a) *Periodicals*

Annual Register
Gentleman's Magazine
Lloyd's Evening Post
London Chronicle
London Evening Post
North Briton
St. James' Chronicle

(b) *Pamphlets*

The Celebrated Speech of a Celebrated Commoner (1766).
Political Debates (Paris [*sic*], 1766).
The Speech of Mr. P . . . and several others, in a certain august Assembly on a late important Debate (1766).

SECONDARY WORKS

A. BOOKS

ADOLPHUS, J., *The History of England from the accession of King George the third, to the conclusion of peace in the year 1783* (2nd. ed. 3 vols., 1805).

ARMYTAGE, F., *The Free Port System in the British West Indies. A Study in Commercial Policy 1766–1822* (1953).

BAILYN, B., *The Ideological Origins of the American Revolution* (Cambridge, U.S.A., 1967).

BARGAR, B. D., *Lord Dartmouth and the American Revolution* (Columbia, U.S.A., 1965).

BARROW, T. C., *Trade and Empire. The British Customs Service in Colonial America 1660–1775* (Cambridge, U.S.A., 1967).

BASYE, A. H., *The Lords Commissioners of Trade and Plantations, Commonly Known as the Board of Trade, 1748–82* (New Haven, 1925).

BROOKE, J., *The Chatham Administration, 1766–1768* (1956).

—, *King George III* (1972).

BROWN, P., *The Chathamites* (1967).

CHRISTIE, I. R., *Crisis of Empire. Great Britain and the American Colonies 1754–1783* (1966).

—, *Myth and Reality in late Eighteenth Century British Politics and other Papers* (1970).

CLARK, D. M., *British Opinion and the American Revolution* (2nd ed., New York, 1966).

—, *The Rise of the British Treasury. Colonial Administration in the Eighteenth Century* (New Haven, 1960).

CURREY, C. B., *Road to Revolution. Benjamin Franklin in England 1765–1775* (New York, 1968).

DICKERSON, O. M., *The Navigation Acts and the American Revolution* (New York, 1951).

ELLIOT, G. F. S., *The Border Elliots and the Family of Minto* (Edinburgh, 1897).

FITZMAURICE, LORD, *Life of William Earl of Shelburne, afterwards First Marquess of Lansdowne* (2 vols., 1912).

GIPSON, L. H., *Jared Ingersoll. A Study of American Loyalism in Relatoin to British Colonial Government* (New Haven, 1920).

—, *The British Empire before the American Revolution*, vols. X–XII (New York, 1961–5).

GREENE, J. P., *The Quest for Power: the Lower House of Assembly in the Southern Royal Colonies 1689–1776* (Chapel Hill, 1963).

GUTTRIDGE, G. H., *English Whiggism and the American Revolution* (Berkeley, U.S.A., 1942).

N

KAMMEN, M. G., *A Rope of Sand. The Colonial Agents, British Politics and the American Revolution* (Ithaca, 1968).

KNOLLENBERG, B., *Origin of the American Revolution* (New York, 1961).

LABAREE, B. W., *The Boston Tea Party* (New York, 1964).

LANGFORD, P., *The First Rockingham Administration 1765–1766* (1973).

MORGAN, E. S. and H. M., *The Stamp Act Crisis* (Chapel Hill, 1953).

NAMIER, SIR LEWIS, *The Structure of Politics at the Accession of King George III* (2nd ed., 1957).

—, *England in the Age of the American Revolution* (2nd ed., 1961).

—, and BROOKE, JOHN, eds., *The House of Commons 1754–1790. The History of Parliament* (3 vols., 1964).

—, and —, *Charles Townshend* (1964).

NORRIS, J., *Shelburne and Reform* (1963).

OLSON, A. G., *The Radical Duke. Career and Correspondence of Charles Lennox third Duke of Richmond* (1961).

PARES, R., *Yankees and Creoles* (1956).

PENSON, L. M., *The Colonial Agents of the British West Indies* (1924).

RITCHESON, C. R., *British Politics and the American Revolution* (Norman, U.S.A., 1954).

SAINTY, J. C., *Treasury Officials 1660–1870* (1972).

SHELTON, W. J., *English Hunger and Industrial Disorders. A Study of social conflict during the first decade of George III's reign* (1973).

SHY, J., *Towards Lexington. The Role of the British Army in the Coming of the American Revolution* (Princeton, 1965).

SOSIN, J. M., *Whitehall and the Wilderness. The Middle West in British Colonial Policy 1760–1775* (Lincoln, U.S.A., 1961).

—, *Agents and Merchants. British Colonial Policy and the Origins of the American Revolution 1763–1775* (Lincoln, U.S.A., 1965).

SUTHERLAND, L. S., *The East India Company in Eighteenth Century Politics* (Oxford, 1952).

THOMAS, P. D. G., *The House of Commons in the Eighteenth Century* (Oxford, 1971).

TURNER, E. R., *The Privy Council of England in the Seventeenth and Eighteenth Centuries 1603–1784* (2 vols., 1927–8).

—, *The Cabinet Council of England in the Seventeenth and Eighteenth Centuries* (2 vols., 1930–2).

UBBELOHDE, C., *The Vice-Admiralty Courts and the American Revolution* (Chapel Hill, 1960).

WILLIAMS, B., *The Life of William Pitt Earl of Chatham* (2 vols., 1913–14).

WINSTANLEY, D. A., *Personal and Party Government 1760–1766* (Cambridge, 1910).

WINSTANLEY, D. A., *Lord Chatham and the Whig Opposition* (Cambridge, 1912).

—, *The University of Cambridge in the Eighteenth Century* (Cambridge, 1922).

WICKWIRE, F. B., *British Subministers and Colonial America 1763–1783* (Princeton, 1966).

WIGGIN, L. M., *The Faction of Cousins: A Political Account of the Grenvilles, 1733–1763* (New Haven, 1958).

B. PERIODICALS[1]

BARNWELL, J. W., ed., 'The Correspondence of Charles Garth', *South Carolina Historical and Genealogical Magazine*, 26 (1925), 67–92; 28 (1927), 79–93; 29 (1928), 41–8, 115–32, 212–30, 295–305. This source cited as *S.C.H.G.M.*

BARROW, T. C., 'A Project for Imperial Reform: Hints Respecting the Settlement for our American Provinces, 1763', *W[illiam and] M[ary] Q[uarterly]*, 24 (1967), 108–26.

CANNON, J., 'Henry McCulloch and Henry McCulloh', *W.M.Q.* 15 (1958), 71–3.

CHAFFIN, R. C., 'The Townshend Acts of 1767', *W.M.Q.* 27 (1970), 90–121.

CHRISTIE, I. R., 'The Cabinet During the Grenville Ministry', *E[nglish] H[istorical] R[eview]*, 73 (1958), 86–92.

—, 'Was there a "New Toryism" in the Earlier Part of George III's Reign?', *J[ournal of] B[ritish] S[tudies]*, 5 (1965–6), 60–76.

CRANE, V. W., 'Hints Relative to the Division and Government of the conquered and newly acquired countries in America', *M[ississippi] V[alley] H[istorical] R[eview]*, 8 (1921–2), 367–73.

DICKERSON, O. M., 'Use made of the Revenue from the Tax upon Tea', *New England Quarterly*, 31 (1958), 232–43.

ENGLEMAN, F. L., 'Cadwallader Colden and the New York Stamp Act Riots', *W.M.Q.* 10 (1953), 560–78.

ERNST, J. A., 'Genesis of the Currency Act of 1764: Virginia Paper Money and the Protection of British Investments', *W.M.Q.* 22 (1965), 33–74.

—, 'The Currency Act Repeal Movement: a Study of Imperial Politics and Revolutionary Crisis 1764–1767', *W.M.Q.* 25 (1968), 177–211.

EVANS, E. G., 'Planter Indebtedness and the Coming of the Revolution in Virginia', *W.M.Q.* 19 (1962), 511–33.

---

[1] Articles and notes are usually cited by author, periodical and date, as Morgan, *W.M.Q.* 7 (1950). All references to the *William and Mary Quarterly* are to the Third Series.

N*

GIPSON, L. H., 'The Great Debate in the Committee of the Whole House of Commons on the Stamp Act, 1766, as Reported by Nathaniel Ryder', P[ennsylvania] M[agazine of] H[istory and] B[iography], 86 (1962), 10–41.

GREENE, J. P., ' "A Dress of Horror": Henry McCulloh's Objections to the Stamp Act', H[untingdon] L[ibrary] Q[uarterly], 26 (1962–3), 253–62.

—, and JELLISON, R. M., 'The Currency Act of 1764 in Imperial-Colonial Relations, 1764–1776', W.M.Q. 18 (1961), 485–518.

HUGHES, E., 'The English Stamp Duties, 1664–1764', E.H.R. 56 (1941), 234–64.

HULL, C. H., and TEMPERLEY, H. W. V., 'Debates on the Declaratory Act and the Repeal of the Stamp Act, 1766', A[merican] H[istorical] R[eview], 17 (1911–12), 563–86.

HUMPHREYS, R. A., 'Lord Shelburne and the Proclamation of 1763', E.H.R. 49 (1934), 241–64.

—, 'Lord Shelburne and British Colonial Policy 1766–1768', E.H.R. 50 (1935), 257–77.

—, and SCOTT, S. M., 'Lord Northington and the Laws of Canada', Can[adian] H[istorical] R[eview], 14 (1933), 42–61.

IMLACH, G. M., 'Earl Temple and the Ministry of 1765', E.H.R. 30 (1915), 317–21.

JARRETT, D., 'The Regency Crisis of 1765', E.H.R. 85 (1970), 282–315.

JOHNSON, A. S., 'The Passage of the Sugar Act', W.M.Q. 16 (1959), 507–14.

—, 'British Politics and the Repeal of the Stamp Act', South Atlantic Quarterly, 62 (1963), 169–88.

KIMBALL, D. A., and QUINN, M., eds., 'William Allen–Benjamin Chew Correspondence, 1763–1764,' P.M.H.B. 90 (1966), 202–226.

LAPRADE, W. T., 'The Stamp Act in British Politics', A.H.R. 35 (1930), 735–57.

MACALPINE, I., and HUNTER, R., 'A Clinical Reassessment of the "Insanity" of George III and some of its Historical Implications', B[ulletin of the] I[nstitute of] H[istorical] R[esearch], 40 (1967), 166–85.

MAHONEY, T. H. B., 'Edmund Burke and the American Revolution: the Repeal of the Stamp Act', Burke Newsletter, 7 (1966–7), 503–21.

MARSHALL, P., 'The British Empire and the American Revolution', H.L.Q. 27 (1963–4), 135–45.

—, 'Colonial Protest and Imperial Retrenchment: Indian Policy 1764–1768', J[ournal of] A[merican] S[tudies], 5 (1971), 1–17.

—, 'The Incorporation of Quebec in the British Empire, 1763–1774', Of Mother Country and Plantations: Proceedings of the Twenty-

Seventh Conference in Early American History (eds. V. B. Platt and D. C. Skaggs, Bowling Green, U.S.A., 1971. Cited as Marshall, 'Quebec').

MINCHINTON, W. E., 'The Stamp Act Crisis: Bristol and Virginia', *V[irginia] M[agazine of] H[istory and] B[iography]*, 73 (1965), 145–55.

MORGAN, E. S., 'Colonial Ideas of Parliamentary Power 1764–66', *W.M.Q.* 5 (1948), 311–41.

—, 'The Postponement of the Stamp Act', *W.M.Q.* 7 (1950), 353–92.

NAMIER, L. B., 'Charles Garth and his Connections', *E.H.R.* 54 (1939), 443–70, 632–52.

NORRIS, J. M., 'Samuel Garbett and the Early Development of Industrial Lobbying in Great Britain', *Econ[omic] Hist[ory] Rev[iew]* 2nd series, 10 (1957–8), 450–60.

PENSON, L. M., 'The London West Indian Interest in the Eighteenth Century', *E.H.R.* 36 (1921), 373–92.

RITCHESON, C. R., 'The Elder Pitt and an American Department', *A.H.R.* 57 (1951–2), 376–83.

—, 'The Preparation of the Stamp Act', *W.M.Q.* 10 (1953), 543–59.

SCOTT, W. R., 'Adam Smith at Downing Street 1766–7', *Econ. Hist. Rev.*, 1st Series, 6 (1935–6), 79–89.

SHERIDAN, R. B., 'The Molasses Act and the Market Strategy of the British Sugar Planters', *Journal of Economic History*, 17 (1957), 62–83.

SOSIN, J. M., 'A Postscript to the Stamp Act. George Grenville's Revenue Measures. A Drain on Colonial Specie?', *A.H.R.* 63 (1954–5), 918–23.

—, 'Imperial Regulation of Colonial Paper Money', *P.M.H.B.* 88 (1964), 174–98.

SUTHERLAND, L. S., 'Edmund Burke and the First Rockingham Ministry', *E.H.R.* 47 (1932), 46–72.

THOMAS, P. D. G., 'Charles Townshend and American Taxation in 1767', *E.H.R.* 83 (1968), 33–51.

TYLER, J. E., 'John Roberts, M.P., and the first Rockingham Administration', *E.H.R.* 67 (1952), 547–60.

—, ed., 'Colonel George Mercer's Papers', *V.M.H.B.* 60 (1952), 405–20.

VARGA, N., 'The New York Restraining Act: Its Passage and Some Effects', *New York History*, 37 (1956), 233–58.

WATSON, D. H., 'William Baker's Account of the Debate on the Repeal of the Stamp Act', *W.M.Q.* 26 (1969), 259–65.

WATSON, D. H., 'The Rockingham Whigs and the Townshend Duties', *E.H.R.* 84 (1969), 561–5.

WICKWIRE, F. B., 'John Pownall and British Colonial Policy', *W.M.Q.* 20 (1963), 543–54.

WILLIAMS, B., 'Chatham and the Representation of the Colonies in the Imperial Parliament', *E.H.R.* 22 (1907), 756–8.

C. UNPUBLISHED UNIVERSITY THESES

HARDY, A., The Duke of Newcastle and his Friends in Opposition 1762–1765 (M.A. Manchester, 1956).

LANGFORD, P., The First Rockingham Administration 1765–1766 (D. Phil. Oxford, 1971).

SMITH, B. R., The Committee of the Whole House to consider the American Papers (January and February 1766) (M.A. Sheffield, 1956).

TOMLINSON, J. R. G., The Grenville Papers 1763–1765 (M.A. Manchester, 1956).

WATSON, D. H., Barlow Trecothick and Other Associates of Lord Rockingham During the Stamp Act Crisis 1765–1766 (M.A. Sheffield, 1957).

—, The Duke of Newcastle, the Marquis of Rockingham, and Mercantile Interests in London and the Provinces 1761–1768 (Ph.D. Sheffield, 1968).

Index

Abercromby, James (1707–75), 30, 63
Admiralty, 22, 27, 46–7, 67, 125
Albemarle, Lord, *see* Keppel, George
Allen, William (1704–80), 24, 63,
American Board of Customs, 343, 360
American Duties Act (1764), 32, 77,
  90, 99, 108, 111, 266, 300, 343;
  background of, 44–50; passage of,
  55–61
American Duties Act (1766), 253,
  273, 274, 275, 300, 343
American Revenue Act (1767): details
  of, 348–9, 351–3, 355; enacted,
  357–8, 359, 360
American Trade Act (1765): back-
  ground of, 108–11; passage of,
  111–12
American trade, value of, 217–18,
  221–2, 230
Amyand, George (1720–66), 57
Annapolis, 139
Annual Register, the, 1
Antigua, 225
army in America, 37–8, 38–9, 101–2,
  295, 296; costs, 54, 296, 338, 339,
  344, 346–7, 349 n.; *see also* Mutiny
  Act (American).
Aufrère, George (1715–1801), 163, 325

Bacon, Anthony (*c.* 1717–86), 57,
  64–5, 66
Baker, Sir William (1705–70), 31, 53,
  54, 57, 57–8, 58, 59, 61, 65, 66, 67,
  74, 85, 98, 103, 104, 108, 158, 161,
  162, 163, 190, 317, 326, 328, 358
Baker, William (1743–1824), 231,
  232, 233
Balfour, James (*d.* 1775), 219, 220
Barclay, David, 30
Barré, Isaac (1726–1802), 31, 88,
  91–2, 92, 92–3, 93, 95, 126, 128,
  189, 198, 199, 202, 237, 358, 359
Barrington, William Wildman, 2nd
  Viscount Barrington (1717–93), 20,
  35, 85, 225, 277–9, 289, 326, 339,
  343 n, 344
Bath, 154, 167, 168, 256, 269, 299, 301

Beckford, William (1709–70), 32, 51,
  52–3, 55, 57, 58, 61, 74, 75, 88, 91,
  93, 98 and n, 101, 103, 104, 109,
  128, 156 and n, 158, 159, 167, 172,
  175, 179, 197, 260, 261, 264, 266,
  267, 268, 269, 291, 299, 318, 323,
  327, 339, 359
Bedford, Duke of, *see* Russell, John
Belfast, 111
Bentinck, William Henry, 3rd Duke
  of Portland (1738–1809), 121, 200
Berkeley, Norborne, 4th Baron Botetourt (*d.* 1770), 179, 194, 333, 334
Bernard, Francis (1712–79), 35, 80,
  134, 135, 137 and n., 150, 152, 252,
  297, 303, 361, 362
Bessborough, Lord, *see* Ponsonby,
  William
Bindley, John, 272
Birmingham, 110, 147, 147–8, 187,
  218, 234
Blaekstone, William (1723–80), 197
  and n., 238
Blair, William, 81
Board of Trade, 22, 24–6, 27, 29, 30,
  34, 40, 41, 42, 43, 44, 45, 62, 63,
  63–4, 65, 66, 66–8, 69, 87, 88, 97,
  110, 113, 125, 131, 133, 134, 135,
  150, 152, 158, 159, 260, 262, 277,
  279–80, 287–9, 300, 304, 315–6,
  316, 317, 318, 320, 323, 335, 351;
  President of, 22, 23, 24, 25, 39, 43,
  69, 122, 125, 286, 287–9; Secretary
  of, 26, 42, 72, *and see* Pownall, John
Bollan, William, 160
Boston, 97, 132, 133, 134, 138 n., 162,
  218, 227, 258, 360, 361
Boston Gazette, the, 252
Botetourt, Lord, *see* Berkeley, Norborne
Bradford (Yorks.), 221
Bradford (Wilts.), 187
Bradshaw, Thomas (1733–74), 326
Brettell, John, 26, 81
Bristol, 63, 65, 92, 136, 146, 147, 148,
  149, 187, 208, 216, 218, 222, 234,
  254, 255, 264; *see also* Society of
  Merchant Venturers

Bristol, Lord, *see* Hervey, George William

Buckinghamshire, Lord, *see* Hobart, John

Budget Day: (1764), 53–5, 56, 68, 72–75; (1765), 113; (1766), 263; (1767), 348

bullion trade, with Spanish colonies, 226, 254–6, 272

Bunney, Joseph, 221

Burgoyne, John (1723–92), 306 n.

Burke, Edmund (1729–97), 1, 126, 150 n., 160, 163 n., 177, 188, 189, 198, 202, 207, 213, 231, 232, 238, 259, 260, 263, 264, 270, 273, 293, 304, 315, 320 n., 324, 327, 328, 358, 368

Burke, Richard, 213

Burke, William (1729–98), 126

Burlington, 144

Burrell, Peter (1723–75), 9

Burt, William (d. 1781), 268

Bute, Lord, *see* Stuart, John

Byng, George, 4th Viscount Torrington (1740–1812), 196 n.

cabinet, 23, 25, 42, 43, 113, 116–17, 129, 133, 136, 155, 161, 170, 255, 262, 280–1, 287, 289, 295, 303, 304, 305, 307–9, 338, 342, 343, 344–5, 346–7, 354, 355

Calcraft, John (1726–72), 105

Calder, Sir James, 70, 71

Cambridge University, election at, 53, 56, 86

Camden, Lord, *see* Pratt, Charles

Campbell, Lord Frederick (1729–1816), 198, 274

Canada, *see* Quebec

Canterbury, Archbishop of, *see* Secker, Thomas

Carleton, Guy (1724–1808), 336

Carr, James, 226

Cavendish, Lord John (1732–96), 38, 125, 126, 190, 324, 327, 340, 368

Cavendish, William, 4th Duke of Devonshire (1720–64), 5, 10–1, 22, 52, 60, 85

Chatham, Lady, *see* Pitt, Hester

Chatham, Lord, *see* Pitt, William

Chesterfield, Lord, *see* Stanhope, Philip Dormer

Clare, Lord, *see* Nugent, Robert

Colville, Alexander, 7th Baron Colville (1717–70), 135, 138, 198

Conway, Henry Seymour (1717–95), 20, 94, 98 n., 120, 123, 123–4, 124, 133, 135, 137, 138 and n., 140, 141, 142, 144, 146, 151, 152, 154, 158, 159, 161, 162, 163, 165, 168, 169, 172, 173, 177, 178, 180, 182, 183, 184 and n., 186–7, 187, 188, 189 and n., 190, 191, 193, 196–7, 198, 199, 201, 203, 204, 208, 209, 213 n., 217, 225, 227–8, 229, 229–30, 233, 237, 239, 248, 249–50, 250, 251, 252, 262, 265 and n., 270, 273, 285, 286, 293, 303, 304, 308 and n., 311, 314, 315, 316, 319, 320, 323, 324, 327, 329 n., 330, 334, 340

Cooke, George (c. 1705–68), 156, 167, 171, 172, 175, 179, 189, 190

Cooper, Anthony Ashley, 4th Earl of Shaftesbury (1711–71), 174

Cooper, Grey (c. 1726–1801), 126, 202, 222 n., 230, 262 and n., 326

Cork, 111

Cornwallis, Charles, 2nd Earl Cornwallis (1738–1805), 196 n.

Coventry, 110, 187

Coventry, George William, 6th Earl of Coventry (1722–1809), 244

Charles, Robert, 29, 49, 64, 277, 350, 351

Charleston, 97, 361

Chew, Joseph, 138 n., 371

Chippenham, 187

cider tax, 5–6, 16–17, 18–19, 51, 90, 123, 129

Colden, Cadawallader(1688–1776),139, 141, 150, 192 n., 251 and n., 251–2

Collett, Thomas, 268, 269

colonial agents, 28–31, 61, 64, 65, 65–6, 67, 75–6, 77–9, 100, 105, 106, 142–4, 216–7, 265, 349, 351, 355, 359, 370; *see also* under individual colonies

colonial government costs, 227, 297, 337, 361; payment of, 35–6, 337, 347–8, 352, 357, 361–2

Committee of London American Merchants, 30, 31, 105, 106 n., 146, 148, 219, 243, 256, 257, 261, 267, 268, 269, 350, 351

Committee of West India Merchants, 226, 254, 256, 257, 261, 268–9, 269

Connecticut, 77, 80 n., 95, 100, 171, 236, 317, 322, 343, 345, 349, 362; agents, 29, 314, 343, 369, 371

Corn riots, 248–9

Cotton trade, 259, 261, 270

Crafton, Robert, 221

Cruger, Henry (1739–1827), 149, 208, 212, 216, 218–9, 221

Cruwys, Thomas Augustus, 70 and n., 71, 72 and n., 81, 82, 82–3

Cumberland, Prince Henry, Duke of (1745–90), 332, 333

Cumberland, Prince William, Duke of (1721–65), 116, 117, 118, 119, 120, 121, 122, 123, 128 n., 129, 136, 139, 140, 141

Currency Act (1764), 112, 253, 275, 276, 350, 351, 353, 356–7; background, 62–4; passage, 64–5

currency, colonial, 62, 63, 69–70, 71, 78 n., 83, 276–7, 350, 351, 352–3, 353, 356

Cushing, Thomas, 292

Cust, Sir John (1718–70), Mr. Speaker, 22, 178, 203, 330

Cust, Peregrine (1723–85), 59, 65

Customs Board, 26, 27, 44, 45–6, 47–8, 48, 67, 135, 152, 360; Secretary, 26, 50; Solicitor, 50

Cuthbert, W. 81

Dartmouth, Lord, *see* Legge, William

Dashwood, Sir Francis (1708–81), 5, 6

Dawson, Obadiah, 221

De Berdt, Dennis, 30 n., 162, 164, 184 and n., 189 and n., 190, 252, 288 n., 292, 350

debts, American trade, 218–19, 221, 222, 230, 245

Declaratory Act (1766), 293, 304 n., 309, 328, 359, 367; background of, 162, 180, 181–4; passage of, 238–40, 243–6

De Grey, William (1719–81), 94, 178, 203, 255, 279, 281, 316, 318, 326

Delaware, 80 n.; agent, 30

Denbigh, Lord, *see* Feilding, Basil

Derby, 255

Devonshire, Duke of, *see* Cavendish, William

Dickinson, John (1732–1808), 174 n.

Dodington, George Bubb (?1691–1762), 4

Dominica, 259, 268, 270, 272, 273

Dowdeswell, William (1721–75), 18, 94, 113–14, 123, 125, 154, 161, 161–2, 162, 163, 170, 172, 178, 180, 187, 190, 197, 198, 232, 237–8, 240, 255 and n., 262 and n., 263, 264, 265, 266, 267, 269, 271, 272, 284, 285, 286, 288, 304, 310, 312, 321, 322, 323, 324, 326–7, 328, 340, 358, 367–8, 368

Dyson, Jeremiah (?1722–76), 94, 95–6, 159, 170, 189, 193, 201, 202, 227 n., 237, 239, 262 n., 276

East Florida, 42, 218, 278

East India Company, 89, 291, 310, 312, 321, 334, 349, 353, 354

Edgcumbe, George, 3rd Baron Edgcumbe (1720–95), 290

Egmont, Lord, *see* Perceval, John

Egremont, Lord, *see* Wyndham, Charles

Elam, Emanuel (1732–96), 221

Eliot, Edward (1727–1804), 25

Elliot, Sir Gilbert (1722–77), 94, 122, 155 n., 156, 170 n., 193, 202, 203, 204, 262 n.

Ellis, Henry (1721–1806), 23, 24, 41–2, 42

Ellis, Welbore (1713–1802), 38, 101, 102, 103, 104, 106 and n., 108, 189

Farrar, Benjamin, 221

Fauquieur, Francis (?1704–68), 62, 80, 133, 135, 152

Feilding, Basil, 6th Earl of Denbigh (1719–1800), 228

Fermor, George, 2nd Earl of Pomfret (1722–85), 244

Fetherstonehaugh, Sir Matthew (?1714–74), 140

Finch, Daniel, 8th Earl of Winchelsea (1689–1769), 124, 158, 159, 286

Fitch, Thomas (c. 1700–74), 93, 171, 236

Fitzmaurice, Thomas (1742–93), 128

Fitzmaurice, William, 2nd Earl of Shelburne (1737–1805), 6, 8, 9, 12, 13, 14, 25, 31, 42, 105, 106 and n., 125, 158, 167 and n., 195, 196 n., 252, 284, 288, 292, 294, 295, 295–6, 296, 297–8, 298 and n., 299, 300, 300–1, 302, 302–3, 303,

Fitzmaurice, William,—*cont.*
305–6, 307, 308, 309, 312, 322,
329, 330, 333, 334, 335, 338, 342,
343 and n., 344–5, 345, 346, 347,
350, 354, 360
Fitzroy, Augustus Henry, 3rd Duke
of Grafton (1735–1811), 5, 11, 20,
119, 120, 123 and n., 124, 126,
140, 146, 152, 157, 158, 159, 161,
168, 169, 176, 179, 180, 195, 199,
200, 212 n., 244, 245, 262, 265 and
n., 269, 283, 284, 285, 286, 288,
299, 308 n., 309, 312, 313, 314,
316, 321, 326, 330, 331, 332, 333,
334, 335, 336, 338, 342, 347, 354
Flood, Henry (1732–91), 285 n.
Forrester, Alexander (?1711–87), 268
Fox, Henry, 1st Baron Holland (1705–
74), 1, 2, 3, 4, 6, 7, 7–8, 8, 9, 10,
20, 39, 118, 155, 189, 255
Fox, Joseph, 213
Franklin, Benjamin (1706–90), 26,
29, 33, 37, 59 n., 70, 78 and n.,
96, 100, 106, 107, 109, 111, 138 n.,
142–4, 172, 213 and n., 216, 223–5,
275–6, 276, 277, 292, 296, 317,
329 n., 347, 349, 350, 351, 353,
356, 359, 362, 371
Franklin, William (1731–1813), 143,
152, 302, 307
free ports (West Indies), 256, 259,
260, 261, 262, 264, 265, 266, 267,
268, 269, 270, 272, 273, 300;
Free Ports Act (1766), 270, 273,
275
French and Indian War, *see* Seven
Years War
Frome, 187
Fuller, Rose (?1708–77), 32, 55, 56–7,
57, 60, 92, 93, 94, 96, 104, 159,
217, 226, 231, 233, 236, 238, 239,
252 n., 257 n., 264, 269, 270–1,
326
Fuller, Stephen, 217, 226, 269
fur trade, 67, 77, 101, 110

Gage, Thomas, General (1721–87),
101, 102, 104, 112, 135, 138 and n.,
139, 141–2, 151, 152, 198, 250,
279, 293, 295–6, 296, 298, 306 n.,
343, 345, 346
Garbett, Samuel, 147, 148
Garth, Charles (*c.* 1734–84), 29, 30,

64, 65, 67, 75, 76–7, 77, 78 and n.,
92, 95, 96, 96–7, 104, 105, 106,
170, 174, 187, 188, 196, 199 n.,
209, 213, 305, 322, 325, 326, 327,
339, 341–2, 350, 350–1, 351, 352,
353, 354, 355 and n., 356 and n.,
357, 360, 362
Garth, John (1701–64), 30
Gascoyne, Bamber (1725–91), 171
Gazetteer, the, 143
general warrants, 15, 16, 18–20, 85,
129, 264
George III, King (1738–1820), 1, 2, 3,
4, 5, 6, 7, 8, 9, 10, 11, 12, 13 and n.,
14, 15, 17, 19, 21, 22, 25, 39, 43,
98, 102–3, 115, 116, 117, 118, 119
and n., 120, 121, 121–2, 122, 123,
128–9, 130, 140, 155, 157, 158,
159, 161, 164, 164–5, 165, 165–6,
166, 168, 169, 170, 175, 176, 176–7,
177, 180, 186, 190, 193, 194, 196 n.,
199, 200, 201, 205, 205–6, 208,
209, 209–10, 210 and n., 211, 212,
228, 234, 235, 236, 241, 242, 245,
246, 248, 257, 265 and n., 281,
281–2, 282, 283, 284, 285–6, 286,
303, 305, 310, 321, 330, 331, 332,
333, 334, 347 n., 354, 355
Georgia, 23, 24, 80, 322 n., 329 and n.,
345, 362; agent, 29, 64, 188, 227
Glasgow, 63, 110,187, 216, 218, 243
Glassford, John, 216, 222
Gloucester, Prince William, Duke of
(1743–1805), 205, 212, 332, 333
Glover, Richard (?1712–85), 55, 59,
105, 106 n., 108
Lord Adam Gordon (?1726–1801),
254 n.
Gore, Thomas (?1694–1777), 103
governors, colonial, 25, 45, 63, 66, 80,
131, 141, 152, 251, 260, 289, 297,
328, 361–3
Gower, Lord, *see* Leveson-Gower,
Granville
Grafton, Duke of, *see* Fitzroy, Augustus
Henry
Granby, Lord, *see* Manners, John
Grantham, Lord, *see* Robinson,
Thomas
Grenville, Mrs. Elizabeth, 36, 209 n.,
332
Grenville, George (1712–70), 1, 2, 3,
6, 7, 7–8, 8, 8–9, 9, 10, 11, 12, 13

Grenville, George,—*cont.*
  and n., 14, 15, 16, 17, 18, 19, 20,
  24 and n., 30, 31, 36, 37, 39, 40,
  45, 48, 49, 52, 53–4, 55, 56, 57,
  58, 59, 60, 61, 68, 70, 71, 72–4,
  74, 75, 75–7, 78 and n., 79, 82,
  86–7, 87, 89–91, 92, 94, 96, 97,
  98, 99, 100, 102, 103, 104, 105–6,
  106, 107, 108, 109, 111, 112, 113,
  115, 116, 117, 119, 122, 124, 127,
  129, 129–30, 130, 136, 154, 155,
  156, 157, 158, 159, 160, 164, 165,
  171, 172, 173–4, 175, 176, 178,
  185, 186, 190, 193, 197, 198, 202,
  203, 204, 205, 206, 207–8, 208,
  209, 212, 217, 219, 224, 225, 226,
  228, 229, 232, 233, 236, 237, 238,
  239, 240, 240–1, 251, 253, 254,
  255, 256 and n., 259, 260, 263,
  264, 267, 268, 272, 273, 274, 276,
  285, 288, 289, 290, 292, 297, 301,
  303, 304, 307, 310 and n., 311
  and n., 312, 313, 314, 318, 319,
  321, 323–4, 324, 327, 328, 329,
  339, 339–40, 340, 341, 344, 352–3,
  354, 356, 357, 364, 364–5, 365,
  365–6, 368, 369
Grenville, James (1715–83), 126, 288
Grenville Temple, Richard, 2nd Earl
  Temple (1711–79), 2, 13, 118
  and n., 120, 155, 157, 167, 169,
  175, 176, 179, 180, 199, 205, 209,
  228, 246, 283, 289 n., 315, 321,
  331, 332

Hale, Robert, 227, 258–9
Haliday, William, 222
Halifax, Lord, *see* Montagu Dunk,
  George
Halifax (Nova Scotia), 47, 97, 361
Halifax (Yorkshire), 221, 255
Hall, David, 96
Hamilton, Robert, 222
Hanbury, Capel, 209, 219, 220
Hancock, John (1737–93), 248 n.
Harcourt, Simon, 1st Earl of Harcourt
  (1714–77), 186, 201, 228, 299
Hardwicke, Lord, *see* Yorke, Philip
  (two entries)
Hardy, Sir Charles (*c.* 1714–80), 227
Harris, James (1709–80), 9, 16, 17,
  18–19, 51, 52, 55, 57, 58, 60, 65,
  73, 86, 94, 104, 108, 119, 124,

  159, 165, 171–2, 172, 175, 178,
  185, 204, 216, 223, 224–5, 230,
  232, 233, 237, 239, 240, 262–3,
  266–7, 273, 283, 324, 325, 328,
  339, 348, 358
Harrogate, 11
Harvey, Eliab (1716–69), 189
Hat Act (1732), 110
Hawke, Sir Edward (1710–81), 290
Hay, George (1715–78), 240, 274,
  327, 347
Hellawell, Benjamin, 109
hemp and flax, bounty on colonial
  exports, 67
Henley, Robert, 1st Earl of Northington (*c.* 1708–72), 120, 122,
  124, 129, 139–40, 157, 161, 164,
  177, 179, 180, 184, 194, 196,
  199, 200, 205, 242, 243, 245, 246,
  255 and n., 262, 280 and n., 280–1,
  281, 285, 292, 307, 308, 316, 330,
  331, 332, 334, 335, 336
Henry, Patrick (1736–99), 132
Hervey, Augustus (1724–79), 293
Hervey, George William, 2nd Earl of
  Bristol (1721–75), 10
Hewitt, James (1712–89), 179, 197
Hill, Wills, 1st Earl of Hillsborough
  (1718–93), 14, 43, 63, 64, 161 n.,
  246, 279, 280, 287, 288, 289 and n.,
  309, 333
Hillsborough, Lord, *see* Hill, Wills
Hobart, John, 2nd Earl of Bucking-
  hamshire (1723–93), 20, 127, 149,
  157, 339, 341
Holland, Lord, *see* Fox, Henry
Hood, Zachariah, 139, 144
Hose, John, 222
House of Lords, 6, 60–1, 97, 98,
  117–18, 156–8, 179–80, 191, 194,
  195–6, 199–200, 204–5, 211, 234,
  241–7, 273, 312–14, 315–17, 329–
  36
Howard, George (1718–96), 208, 225
Howard, Henry, 12th Earl of Suffolk
  (1739–79), 157, 179, 180, 185 n.,
  199, 244–5, 313, 321, 332
Howard, Martin, 135, 192
Howe, Richard, 4th Viscount Howe
  (1726–99), 189
Hudson's Bay Company, 67–8
Hughes, John, 144
Hume, Alexander, 267–8.

Hume-Campbell, Hugh, 3rd Earl of Marchmont (1708–94), 195 n., 199, 244

Hunter, Thomas (*c.* 1716–69), 17, 94, 124

Huske, John (1724–73), 31, 51, 54–5, 57, 59, 60, 61, 74, 75, 104, 108, 172, 177, 189, 223, 237, 265, 276, 348, 349, 351, 359

Hussey, Richard (?1715–70), 181, 197, 237

Hutchinson, Thomas (1711–80), 135, 252

Indemnity Act (1766), 250, 251, 275

Indian problems, 34, 42–3

Indian Superintendents, 295–6, 296

indigo duties, 50, 57

Ingersoll, Jared, 29, 78, 81, 91, 93, 93–4, 98–9, 100, 106

Ireland, 225, 240

iron trade, colonial, 110, 111, 275

Irwin, James, 226

Irwin, General Sir John (*d.* 1788), 312

Jackson, Richard (?1721–87), 29, 30–1, 57, 59 n., 63, 78, 92, 93, 95, 98, 111, 128, 140, 170–1, 236, 252 n., 339, 349, 356

Jamaica, 94, 217, 226, 254, 261, 270, 272

James, Thomas, 150–1, 192 and n., 251 and n.

Jenkinson, Charles (1729–1808), 13 n., 17, 22 n., 39, 47, 48 n., 50, 54, 57, 67, 70, 79, 81, 94, 99, 106, 106–7, 107, 109, 110, 111, 125, 128, 155, 177, 189, 207, 230–1, 370 n.,

Jenyns, Soame (1704–87), 25, 66, 98

Johnston, Augustus, 135

Johnstone, George (1730–87), 255

Johnson, William Samuel, 314, 317, 322, 325, 327, 343, 349, 350, 352, 355–6, 357, 359, 360 n., 362, 369, 370–1, 371

Kelly, William (*d.* 1774), 220–1, 257–8, 300 and n., 303

Kempe, John Tabor, 72 n., 80 and n., 82

Keppel, Augustus (1725–86), 125, 126

Keppel, George, 3rd Earl of Albemarle (1724–72), 120, 193, 200

Knox, William (1732–1810), 29, 34, 64, 77, 188, 227

Lancashire, 254, 259

Lancaster, 187, 218, 255, 259, 260, 273

land tax, 310, 339, 347

Leeds, 146 n., 147, 149, 187, 218, 221, 234

Legge, Henry (1708–64), 5, 10, 13, 38, 53, 56, 85, 125

Leicester, 187, 221, 255

Legge, William, 2nd Earl of Dartmouth (1731–1801), 125, 136 n., 143, 148, 157, 161 n., 162, 163, 179, 181, 189 n., 199, 243, 252, 280, 281, 286, 287, 288 and n., 311, 317

Lennox, Charles, 3rd Duke of Richmond (1735–1806), 245, 265, 284, 286, 317, 319, 321, 331, 332, 334, 335

Leveson-Gower, Granville, 2nd Earl Gower (1721–1803), 6. 8, 149, 154, 157, 179, 228, 247, 286, 290, 313, 320, 321, 330, 331, 332, 333, 335

Lincoln, John (Green) Bishop of (*d.* 1779), 137

linen duty, 55, 56, 59

Liverpool, 57, 63, 65, 92, 147, 148, 187, 218, 222, 234, 255, 259

Lloyd's Evening Post, 142

London, 63, 89, 110, 142, 147, 187, 188 n., 218, 219, 221, 222, 222–3, 234, 243, 247, 249, 257, 259, 260, 300; *see also* Committee of London American Merchants

London Chronicle, the, 142

Long, Beeston, 226, 254, 269, 360

Lowndes, Charles (?1699–1783), 126, 297

lumber trade, colonial, 110, 111, 300

Luttrell, Simon (1713–87), 273

Lyttelton, George, 1st Baron Lyttelton (1709–73), 129, 157, 179, 180, 186, 195–6, 199, 246, 247, 289 n., 290

Lyttelton, Thomas, 254

Macclesfield, 187–8

McCulloh, Henry (*d.* 1779), 36, 69, 69–70, 70, 71, 71–2, 72, 81, 83, 84, 160–1

McEvers, James, 136
Maitland, Richard, 227, 268, 269, 360
Manchester, Duke of, *see* Montagu, George
Manchester, 147, 187, 188, 218, 222, 255, 259
Manners, John, Marquess of Granby (1721–70), 209, 287, 339
Mansfield, Lord, *see* Murray, William
Marchmont, Lord, *see* Hume-Campbell, Hugh
Maryland, 57, 80, 139, 141, 144, 199 n., 219, 345, 362
Massachusetts, 27, 35, 61 and n., 63, 73, 77, 80, 87, 106, 133–4, 139, 150, 160, 189, 190, 218, 224, 252, 278, 314, 322, 325, 345, 350, 361, 362, 370 n., 371; agents, 27, 36, 48–9, 61, 73, 161, 164, 288 n.
Massachusetts Indemnity and Compensation Act, 252, 302, 303, 315–17, 318, 320–1, 322, 330–1, 331–3
Masterman, George, 222 and n.
Mauduit, Israel, 29, 61, 73, 75 n.
Mauduit, Jasper, 29, 36, 48–9, 61, 73, 75
Melksham, 187
Mellish, Joseph, 126
Mercer, George, 100, 192, 216, 220
Meredith, Sir William (?1725–90), 19, 57, 65, 66, 92, 94, 95, 125, 148, 202, 217, 321, 325, 328
Meserve, George, 100
Mildred, Daniel (1731–88), 219
militia, 263, 264
Minehead, 187
Mitchell, Sir Andrew, 289
Moffatt, Thomas, 136, 192, 251
Molasses Act (1733), 32, 39, 40, 44–5, 90, 94
molasses duty, 39, 40, 44–5, 47–9, 54, 57–8, 109, 220–1, 253, 256, 257–8, 261, 262, 263, 266, 267, 268, 269, 270–1, 343
Molyneux, Thomas (?1724–76), 207
Monckton, Robert (1726–82), 306 n.
Montagu Dunk, George, 2nd Earl of Halifax (1716–71), 3, 6–7, 7, 8, 9, 11, 12, 14, 15, 16, 23, 24, 25, 36, 41, 43, 69, 79–80, 82, 87, 97, 101, 102, 103, 117, 125, 154, 157,

161 n., 180, 225, 245, 246, 254, 316
Montagu, Edward, 29, 63, 73, 75, 95, 104, 105, 188, 243, 351
Montagu, Frederick (1733–1800), 329, 358 and n.
Montagu, George, 4th Duke of Manchester (1737–88), 157
Montagu, John, 4th Earl of Sandwich (1718–92), 9, 14, 119, 154, 157, 179, 180, 199, 200, 209, 244, 245, 246, 313, 316, 321, 335
Moore, Sir Henry (1713–69), 277, 293, 293–4, 294, 295, 300, 302, 303, 306, 329, 345, 350
Morgann, Maurice, 285 n.
Morin, Peter, 24
Morris, Thomas, 221
Murray, James (?1725–94), 279
Murray, William, 1st Baron Mansfield (1705–93), 12, 41, 87, 157, 176, 179, 196, 199, 203, 205, 244, 245, 246, 310 n., 311 and n., 312, 313, 315, 316, 317, 319, 320, 321, 330, 331, 332, 333, 335
Mutiny Act, American (1765), background of, 101–2, 104–8; passage of, 102–4, 108; colonial resistance to, 292, 293–4, 301, 302, 303, 329,; British opinion on, 305–9, 314, 318, 321–9.

Newcastle, Duke of, *see* Pelham-Holles, Thomas
Newdigate, Sir Roger (1719–1806), 223
New Hampshire, 80; agents, 31, 49, 100, 141, 152, 160, 258, 362
New Jersey, 80, 141, 152, 302, 303, 307, 322, 345, 362; agent, 29, 64
Newport (Rhode Island), 135
New York, 63, 77, 80, 82, 87, 88, 95 n., 102, 136, 139, 151, 192, 218, 228, 251–2, 277, 278, 292, 293–4, 299, 300, 302, 303, 304, 305–6, 306–7, 314, 321–9, 344, 345, 346, 350, 351, 362, 370 n.; agents, 29, 30, 49, 64; *see also* New York City, New York Restraining Act, petition of New York merchants
New York City, 134, 150–1, 151, 155, 219, 220, 257, 258
New York Restraining Act, passage of, 328–9

North, Frederick, Lord North (1732–92), 6, 18, 92, 94, 98, 125, 141, 159, 238, 265, 274, 309, 320, 330

North Briton, the, 15, 16, 17–18, 18, 19, 51

North Carolina, 62, 65, 77, 80 n., 345, 362; agent, 64

Northington, Lord, *see* Henley, Robert

Northumberland, Lord, *see* Percy, Hugh Smithson

Norton, Sir Fletcher (1716–89), 15, 20, 94, 155, 156, 190, 198, 207, 208, 231, 279

Norwich, 146 n., 147, 249

Nottingham, 187, 221

Nova Scotia, 47, 63, 80 n., 278, 361

Nugent, Robert, 1st Viscount Clare (1709–88), 65, 92, 93, 98, 127, 171, 177, 197, 203, 208, 217, 224, 225, 253–4, 264, 267, 269, 274, 276, 289, 304, 351

O'Hara, Charles (*d.* 1775), 163 n., 188, 260, 263

Oliver, Andrew (1706–74), 135

Onslow, George (1731–1814), 5, 59–60, 85, 93, 96, 104, 125, 151, 154, 159, 167, 169, 178–9, 189, 191, 192, 193, 208, 225, 236, 238, 239, 241, 267, 268, 340 and n.

Oswald, James (1715–69), 6, 7, 8, 34, 122, 159, 193, 237, 238

Oswald, Richard (1705–84), 227 and n.

Otis, James, (1725–83), 196

Palmer, Rev. W., Speaker's Chaplain, 197, 198, 207, 231, 232, 236, 238

Parker, James, 144 and n.

Paterson, John (?1705–89), 96

Peace of Paris (1763), 3, 4, 12, 13, 15, 279

Pelham, Henry (*c.* 1696–1754), 1

Pelham, Thomas (1728–1805), 125

Pelham-Holles, Thomas, 4th Duke of Newcastle (1693–1768), 1, 2, 3, 4, 5, 10, 11, 12, 13, 16, 25, 31, 32, 38, 52, 53, 54, 55, 56, 57, 59, 60, 61, 74, 85, 86, 93, 96, 104, 105, 113, 119, 120, 121, 123, 124, 125, 129, 136 and n., 137, 140, 140–1, 141, 144, 150, 151, 154, 154–5, 155, 157, 159, 161, 162, 163, 164, 167, 168 and n., 168–9, 169, 170,
176, 178, 179, 181, 182, 191, 193, 193–4, 194, 195, 196, 199, 200, 202, 203, 209, 211, 217, 229, 234–5, 235, 236, 238, 241, 242, 244, 247, 249, 255, 256, 262, 267, 268, 270, 272, 273, 283, 285, 286, 290, 310, 311, 313, 314–15, 315, 316, 316–17, 317–18, 318, 320, 321, 325, 328, 329, 330, 331, 332, 333, 335, 340, 358

Pennsylvania, 24, 63, 77, 80, 111, 141, 174, 213, 218, 224, 275, 276, 277, 322, 347, 350, 362, 370 n., agents, 26, 29, 63, 111

Perceval, John, 2nd Earl of Egmont (1711–70), 120, 122, 124, 125, 161, 162, 163, 165, 177, 179, 181, 262, 281, 285, 286, 333

Percy, Hugh Smithson, 1st Duke of Northumberland (1714–86), 118

petition of New York merchants, 300, 300–1, 303, 304–5, 306

Philadelphia, 59, 97, 109, 144, 151, 219, 360

Pitkin, William (1694–1769), 349, 357

Pitt, Hester, Countess of Chatham (1720–1803), 154 n., 199, 203

Pitt, Thomas (1737–93), 9, 125, 127, 197, 198, 339

Pitt, William, 1st Earl of Chatham (1708–78), 1, 2, 3, 4, 6, 10, 12, 13, 14, 16, 19, 32, 38, 38–9, 52, 53,, 56, 58, 59, 85, 105, 118 and n., 119, 120, 121, 122, 125, 126, 127, 128, 129, 140, 141, 154 and n., 157, 164, 166–7, 167, 168, 169, 171, 172 and n., 173, 174 and n., 175, 176, 177, 179, 180, 183, 185, 186, 189–90, 190 and n., 191, 192, 193, 198, 199, 201–2, 202, 203, 204, 207 and n., 229 and n., 231, 232, 233, 237, 239, 239–40, 240, 248, 252, 254, 256, 257 n., 260, 261, 263, 263–4, 264, 265, 267 and n., 269, 270, 281, 283, 283–4, 284, 284–5, 285, 286, 287, 288 and n., 289 n., 290, 291–2, 292, 293, 299, 300, 301, 303, 303–4, 305, 306–7, 307, 308 and n., 310, 312, 314, 315, 317, 318, 319, 322, 323, 324, 333, 334, 340, 342, 343, 344, 358, 360, 366–7, 368, 369, 371

Pomfret, Lord, *see* Fermor, George

Ponsonby, William, 2nd Earl of Bessborough (*c.* 1704–93), 193, 200

Pontiac Rising, 42

Portland, Duke of, *see* Bentinck, William Henry

Post Office, colonial, 37, 90, 93

Poulett, Vere, 3rd Earl of Poulett (1710–88), 195, 196 n.

Powlett, Lord Harry (1720–94), 51, 52

Pownall, John (1720–95), 26 and n., 42, 43, 72, 150, 255, 280

Pownall, Thomas (1722–1805), 27, 78 n., 106, 106–7, 107, 143 n., 276, 327, 365, 366, 368

Pratt, Charles, 1st Baron Camden (1713–94), 16, 122, 122–3, 126, 157, 175, 185, 196 and n., 199, 245–6, 281, 285, 286, 292, 312, 313, 314, 317, 330, 332, 333, 334, 338, 358, 364 n.

Prescott, George, (*c.* 1711–90), 236, 240, 264

Princess Dowager of Wales (*d.* 1772), 116, 117, 118

Prior, Matthew (1664–1721), 173

Privy Council, 21–3, 24, 25, 27, 43, 45, 46, 47, 64, 65, 68, 87, 88, 97, 134, 135, 137, 150, 152, 255 n., 277, 280, 287, 289, 316, 318, 320, 330, 335–6; Council Committee for Plantation Affairs, 22, 64, 68, 87, 97, 134, 137, 277, 318, 320, 330

Proclamation of 1763, 27, 41, 51, 112, 113, 277, 281, 331; background of, 41–3

Prussia, 3, 129

Public Advertiser, the, 143

Quebec, 42, 48, 80 n., 218, 253, 258, 275, 279–81, 294, 331, 334–6

Queen Charlotte (*d.* 1818), 116, 117

quit-rents, colonial, 296, 296–7, 297–8, 298, 342, 345–6, 347

Rawlinson, Abraham, 260, 261, 273

Reeve, William, 216, 222

Regency Act, (1765), 105, 116–18

Regency Bill Crisis (1765), 116–18

requisitions (colonial), 33, 143, 198, 223, 345, 353

Rhode Island, 77, 80, 88, 94, 135, 139, 141, 192, 251, 303, 362, 371; agent, 29, 49

Rice, George (?1724–79), 25, 51, 65, 66

Richmond, Duke of, *see* Lennox, Charles

Rigby, Richard (1722–88), 38, 158, 177, 202, 240, 274, 274–5, 311, 313, 319, 320, 321

Roberts, John (*c.* 1711–72), 137

Robinson, John, 135

Robinson, Thomas, 1st Baron Grantham (1695–1770), 181, 193

Rockingham, Lady, *see* Watson-Wentworth, Mary

Rockingham, Lord, *see* Watson-Wentworth, Charles

rum trade, colonial, 50, 51, 54

Russell, Francis, Marquess of Tavistock (1739–67), 286, 313, 314

Russell, John, 4th Duke of Bedford (1710–71), 1, 3, 9–10, 10, 12, 14, 38, 154 and n., 155, 156, 157, 158, 179, 196, 199, 200, 209, 228, 240, 246, 274, 286, 290, 292, 310, 312, 313, 314, 315, 316, 317, 331, 332, 333, 334, 335, 340, 365, 369

Ryder, Nathaniel (1735–1803), 73, 74, 93, 324, 343, 352, 354

Sackville, Lord George (1716–85), 122, 124, 127, 141, 156, 173, 176, 193, 203, 205, 208, 312, 339, 341

salt trade, colonial, 66–7; salt duty, proposed, 349

Sandwich, Lord, *see* Montagu, John

Sargent, John (1715–91), 30 and n.

Saunders, Sir Charles (*c.* 1713–75), 125, 126, 287, 290

Savile, Sir George (1726–84), 178, 321, 324

Scotland, 118; army in, 103, 104; election in, 193; Scottish burghs, 249

Secker, Thomas, Archbishop of Canterbury (1693–1768); 183, 195 n., 241, 242, 249

Secretary of State for America, 287–9, 311

Secretary of State for South, 1, 22, 23, 23–4, 27, 36, 43, 77, 113, 131, 284–5, 320

Sedgwick, Edward, 24, 26, 36, 87, 88, 102, 125–6, 341

Seven Years War, 1, 33

Sewell, Sir Thomas (c. 1710–84), 203, 327

Seymour, Henry (1729–1807), 171, 206

Shaftesbury, Lord, see Cooper, Anthony Ashley

Sharpe, William, 289

Sheffield, 110, 218, 234, 249

Shelburne, Lord, see Fitzmaurice, William

Shelley, Sir John (?1730–83), 330 n.

Sherwood, Joseph, 29, 49, 351

Shiffner, Henry (1721–95), 236

Smith, Adam (1723–90), 338

Smith, John, 162

Smith, William (1728–93), 288 n.

Society of Merchant Venturers (Bristol), 145–6, 148, 188 n., 222, 243, 259

South Carolina, 50, 63, 65, 77, 80 n., 95, 96, 105, 187, 188–9, 209, 227, 305, 322, 339, 341, 345, 350, 352, 357, 362, 370 n., agent, 29, 64, *and see* Garth, Charles

Speaker, the, see Cust, Sir John

Spry, William, 47

Stamp Act (1765), preparation of, 69–84; passage of, 85, 89–98; colonial resistance to, 77, 129, 131–6, 139, 150–1, 192, 214–15, 218, 223–4, 227, 237, 251–2; repeal of, 164, 171–5, 180, 181–4, 233–4, 238–47; hearing of witnesses on, 215–28; cost of, 250; revenue from, 250. *See also* Indemnity Act

Stamp Act Congress, 141, 143; petition of, 189–90

Stamp Distributors (American), 71, 100, 132, 135, 136, 139, 141, 144

Stamp Office, 26, 70, 99–100, 135, 152; Secretary, 26; Solicitor, 70

Stanhope, Lovell, 16, 126 n.

Stanhope, Philip Dormer, 4th Earl of Chesterfield (1694–1773), 24, 124, 127, 128, 154, 310

Stanley, Hans (1721–80), 171, 197, 206, 238

Stanley, James Smith, Lord Strange (1717–71), 193, 204, 209–10, 237, 253–4, 267

Strange, Lord, *see* Stanley, James Smith

Stuart, John (?1700–79), 296

Stuart, John, 3rd Earl of Bute (1713–1792), 1, 2, 3, 4, 5, 6, 7, 8, 9, 10, 11, 12, 13 and n., 14, 15, 17, 24, 25, 34, 39, 62, 115, 116, 117, 119 and n., 120, 121, 128, 129, 155, 157, 159, 164, 165, 166, 174, 180, 186, 193, 194, 199, 200 n., 202, 204, 205 and n., 208, 209, 228, 236, 241, 246, 247, 281, 290, 317, 332

Stuart Mackenzie, James (?1719–1800), 118, 120, 121, 174–5

Suffolk, Lord, see Howard, Henry

Sugar Act (1764), see American Duties Act (1764)

sugar trade, 49, 55, 57, 256–7, 258–9, 261, 262, 264, 270, 271–2, 300

Talbot, William, 1st Earl Talbot (1710–82), 246, 314

Taunton, 187

Tavistock, Lord, see Russell, Francis

tea duty, American (1767), 343, 349, 353, 354, 355, 368

Temple, John (1732–98), 49, 81, 86, 92, 108, 271, 359

Temple, Lord, see Grenville Temple, Richard

Thomlinson, John (ob. 1767), 31

Thomlinson, John (1731–67), 31, 49

Thurlow, Edward (1731–1806), 274

Torrington, Lord, see Byng, George

Townshend, Charles (1725–67), 5, 6, 7, 8, 9, 13, 19, 25, 36, 39, 40, 48, 51, 52, 53, 54, 56, 58–9, 59–60, 60, 61, 65, 66, 85, 88, 92, 93, 101, 104, 113, 118, 120–1, 122, 123, 124, 128, 132 n., 141, 155 n., 156, 169, 177, 178, 180, 206–7, 208, 217, 224, 232, 246, 262, 264, 266–7, 270, 271, 272, 276, 283–4, 285 and n., 286, 287, 288, 292, 297, 298 and n., 300, 304, 307, 308, 309, 311, 314, 315, 319, 320 and n., 321, 322–3, 324, 326, 327, 328, 330, 334, 336, 337, 337–8, 338, 339, 339–40, 340 and n., 341–2, 342, 343, 344, 344–5, 346, 347, 348, 349 and n., 350, 351, 351–2, 353, 353–4, 354, 355, 356, 357

Townshend, Charles,—*cont.*
and n., 358–9, 359–60, 361, 362, 367, 369
Townshend duties, *see* American Revenue Act (1767)
Townshend, George, 4th Viscount Townshend (1724–1807), 246
Townshend, Thomas (1733–1800), 5, 58, 85, 92, 98, 104, 108, 125, 168, 171, 189, 339
Thynne, Thomas, 3rd Viscount Weymouth (1734–96), 118, 154, 179, 204–5
trade laws, 44–50, 59, 98, 111, 129, 220, 253, 257, 265
Treasury, the, 22, 26, 27, 29, 30, 36, 44, 46, 47, 48, 49, 67, 72, 81, 84, 86–7, 97, 110, 113, 124–5, 152, 158, 159, 255 and n., 256, 296, 297, 338, 360
Trecothick, Barlow (?1718–75), 31, 106 n., 108, 136, 144, 145, 146, 146–7, 148, 148–9, 149, 150 and n., 154, 163, 164, 187, 209, 217–19, 242, 260, 313, 349
Turner, Sir John (1712–80), 124
Tyton, John, 50
Vice-Admiralty Courts, 46–7, 97–8, 162, 239, 300, 360–1
Villiers, George Bussey, Viscount Villiers (1735–1805), 125, 171, 269, 283–4, 284, 285, 286, 288, 289 n.
Virginia, 62, 63, 66, 77, 80, 100, 132–3, 134, 141, 152, 192, 219, 220, 222, 362, 370 n.; Resolves, 132–3, 134, 139, 219; agents, 29, 30, 63, 64, 73, 95, 104, 188, 243

Walpole, Horace (1717–97), 51, 53, 95, 157, 159, 160, 174, 193, 209, 233, 236, 238, 248, 299, 320 n., 323, 324, 332, 347
Walpole, Thomas (1727–1803), 126
Walsall, 110
Ward, Samuel (1725–76), 135
Watson, Brook (1735–1807), 258
Watson-Wentworth, Charles, 2nd Marquess of Rockingham (1730–82), 5, 11, 12, 13, 38, 60, 83, 85, 113, 119, 120, 121, 122, 123, 124, 125, 126, 128, 136 and n., 140, 141, 143 n., 144, 145, 149–50, 150, 154, 155, 157, 160, 161, 162, 163,

163–4, 164, 165, 168, 169, 170, 173, 175–6, 176, 178, 179–80, 180, 181, 182, 182–3, 183, 184, 189, 191, 193, 194, 195, 200, 202, 204, 205, 205–6, 209, 210, 211, 222 n., 231, 234, 235, 241, 245, 246, 249, 250, 252 n., 255 and n., 256, 257 and n., 260, 262 and n., 265 and n., 272–3, 273, 276, 280, 281, 282, 283, 284, 285, 286, 288, 290, 293, 304, 310 and n., 311, 313, 314, 315, 316, 317, 319–20, 320, 321, 321–2, 324, 328, 330, 331, 333, 334, 367, 368, 369, 371
Watson-Wentworth, Mary, Marchioness of Rockingham (*d.* 1804), 150 n., 181, 256, 314
Webb, Philip Carteret (?1700–70), 16
Wedderburn, Alexander (1733–1805), 156, 159, 197, 239, 274, 304–5
Wentworth, Benning (1696–1770), 80, 152
Wentworth, John (1737–1820), 160, 258, 259
West, James (1703–72), 56, 59, 125, 172, 175, 204, 209, 217, 229, 266, 267, 268, 318, 321, 323, 324, 325, 358
western lands question, 34, 277–9, 344, 345, 346; *see also* Proclamation of 1763
West Florida, 42, 218, 255, 261
West India interest, 31–2, 49, 56–7, 254, 260, 261, 263, 264, 267, 268, 270–2; *see also* Committee of West India Merchants
West Indies, 144, 220, 226, 230, 254, 258, 259, 263, 264, 268, 270–2; *see also* bullion trade, free ports, Committee of West India Merchants, West India interest
Weston, Edward (1703–70), 24 and n., 26, 87, 88, 126, 341
Weymouth, Lord, *see* Thynne, Thomas
whale fishing, 67
Whately, Thomas (*c.* 1728–72), 48 n., 49 and n., 55, 59, 71, 72, 80–2, 84 and n., 86, 94, 97, 99, 108, 124, 136, 156, 226, 251, 271, 297, 359
White, John (1699–1769), 155, 161, 168
Whitehaven, 218
Whitney, 188

Wilkes, John (1725–97), 15, 16, 17, 18, 19, 51
Willenhall, 110
Willes, Edward (1723–87), 316, 318, 329
Wilmot, Sir John, 330
Winchelsea, Lord, *see* Finch, Daniel
window tax, 263, 264
Wolverhampton, 110, 187
Wood, William, 26, 50
Wyndham, Charles, 2nd Earl of Egremont (1710–63), 3, 6, 7, 8, 9, 11, 12, 14, 16, 23, 24, 36, 40–1, 41, 42, 45, 254

Yeates, Robert, 50, 261
York, Prince Edward, Duke of (1739–67), 116, 117, 143 n., 199, 205, 212, 228, 246, 332, 333 and n.
Yorke, Charles (1722–70), 5, 10, 11, 15, 20, 43, 53, 56, 58, 60, 85, 95, 97, 122, 123, 161, 162, 164, 165, 169–70, 170, 173, 177–8, 180, 182, 183, 184, 190 n., 197, 202, 203, 207, 208, 231, 232, 238, 249, 255, 280, 281, 285, 319, 322, 324, 335, 336
Yorke, Sir Philip, 1st Earl of Hardwicke (1690–1764), 2, 5, 10, 12, 13, 15, 38, 53
Yorke, Philip, 2nd Earl of Hardwicke (1720–90), 53, 122, 157, 161, 165, 183, 184, 190 n., 313, 325, 331, 335, 348